The Dominie Books of
A.S. NEILL

The Dominie Books of
A.S. NEILL

A DOMINIE's LOG

A DOMINIE IN DOUBT

A DOMINIE DISMISSED

With an Introduction by Harold H. Hart

Hart Publishing Company, Inc.
New York City

HART PUBLISHING COMPANY, INC., NEW YORK, N. Y. 10012

ISBN NO. 0-8055-1141-5 (Paperback 0-8055-0202-5)

MANUFACTURED IN THE UNITED STATES OF AMERICA

Contents

Introduction

In 1960, when I suggested to Neill that two or three of his previous books might be combined into one volume, under the title SUMMERHILL, he replied: "Why would any American publisher be foolish enough to publish any of my books? None of them has sold in America, and why would you want to take on another failure?" The sincerity and forthrightness of this reply marked the measure of the man. And for a while it seemed that Neill's estimate of his appeal here in the United States was correct, for when SUMMERHILL: *A Radical Approach to Child Rearing* was first published, this company didn't have a single advance order for the book.

Little did Neill envision that in the course of time SUMMERHILL would sell far over a million copies. Today, Neill's seminal work is published in translation in German, French, Italian, Dutch, Spanish, Portuguese, Swedish, Danish, Norwegian, Finnish, Hebrew, Greek, Croatian, and Japanese.

Neill has had and still has a worldwide influence. His principles are still matters of intense discussion in any conclave of educators, and are taken up in virtually all current books on education. Schools all over the world have adopted many of his basic tenets; and in other institutions of learning where Neill's principles have not been adopted outright, the man still has made a tremendous impact, which is manifested in a more relaxed attitude toward the bare accumulation of knowledge, and a deeper concern for the feelings of the student and for the development of his character.

In essence, Neill's great contribution was that he held children more important than so-called learning. He emphasized that no school, no parent, had a right to exert pressure on the child; allowing a child to grow in strength and understanding and achievement—*in accordance with his own natural pace*—was of paramount importance. This meant permitting a child to attend or not to attend classes as he wished. It meant that parents and teachers must renounce *persuading* a child to achieve scholastic standards. Needless to say, Neill's concepts were revolutionary. In his school, a child was permitted freedom of language, freedom to choose what clothing he wore, freedom to do what he wanted, such freedom being inhibited by one—and only one—restriction: that no act trespass on the rights of others. That single restriction called for the discipline all too often lacking in the so-called progressive school. Neill summed up his credo in the phrase "freedom without license."

Despite the calumnies of its detractors, Summerhill School did not enthrone permissiveness. A teacher would not allow a boy or girl to wantonly interrupt a lesson to which others were listening. Nor would an adult suffer a child to trespass on his privacy or appropriate his property.

On the other hand, in Summerhill, no adult would have the effrontery to tell a child just how he should dispose of his time. In Neill's precincts, if a child preferred to play rather than listen to a concert, that choice would be respected.

In such an atmosphere there was little need to rebel against parent or teacher. The child got to know just what he could do and what he couldn't do. He learned that adjustments were necessary, that he could not make brattish demands to the detriment of others. In consequence, objective observers noted, Summerhill children grew up to be exceptionally outgoing and well mannered. Since goals were set by them and not for them, the children of Summerhill were not obliged as adults to fit into a societal pattern; they did not grow up to be so many Babbitts. Neill stressed imagination in learning, and his children grew up to have ideas of their own.

It has been amply demonstrated that the children of Summerhill achieved scholastically at least as much as children reared in conventional schools. Yet by far the greater achievement is that Neill's children grew up to be more integrated, happier human beings.

The world in which we live is indeed a sorrowful one: a world in which there are wars and constant threats of war, a world of apartheid and of anti-Semitism, a world of crime and repression. Human beings hate their neighbors, quarrel with their spouses, browbeat their children, bully their employees, and beat a steady path to the offices of psychiatrists. Our accepted methods of rearing children have done nothing more than yield generations on generations of unhappy people. Our world knows great trouble, for each one of us is in his own way a troubled human being. Each one of us carries on his back a legacy of hate bequeathed to him by his parents which he, in turn, must discharge upon those around him—most frequently those dearest to him.

Each parent fervently hopes that he will bring up his child to be a happier human being than he is; yet each one of us passes onto his child the aggressions born of excessive restriction and the need to punish. Each one of us acts toward his child as a tin god, a tyrant who knows precisely what the child should do at each and every moment, knows what his child should like, when his child should play, what his child should study.

Erich Fromm has written that Neill's ideas are the most optimistic of our day because they offer new hope for the world. Henry Miller has declared, "Summerhill is a tiny ray of light in a world of darkness. Its aim is to create happy, contented people, not cultural misfits dedicated to war, insanity, and canned knowledge."

One of the root troubles in our educational system is that parents believe that the most important thing is to get the child to learn—and, of course, to learn *early*.

"To what end?" asks Neill. "The important thing," says Neill, "is to rear a happy child." The paramount matter is the integrity of the child's psyche. Knowledge *is* important, but *secondary*.

In one of his lectures, Erich Fromm summed up this

viewpoint by asking: "What is more important—the maximum productivity of man, or the maximum development of man?" Fromm and Neill hold that optimum productivity can only be reached if there is maximum development. A happy child will become a better student—"better" in that he will be more receptive to learning. Yet this, too, does not go to the essence. Neill plainly asserts: "I would rather see a child become a happy plumber than a neurotic professor."

The child must be given complete opportunity to live out his play period. As Neill says, the child has "a right to play and play and play and play." In due time, when his natural curiosity takes hold, the child will become less interested in play and give himself over to study. The student may emerge months—or even years—later, but there is every confidence that the student will emerge. And when the desire to study does indeed take hold, the child will be able to expand his energies and study in the optimum manner—not fritter away his energies in neurotic defenses.

Where did Neill develop these radical theories? Our first records of his thinking are to be found in his earliest book, which he titled *A Dominie's Log.* This work appeared in 1915 when Neill was thirty-two. He had gone through a university training, and had taken up teaching in a little Scottish village. The community was, to put it mildly, benighted, and the parents were dedicated strictly to a teaching of the three R's. They expected that a good dominie would certainly whack the kids around, and enforce strict discipline. They held with the dictum of Genesis that "Man is evil from his youth." It was the province of the teacher to force his charges to absorb learning, by any manner he chose. After a while in this stifling atmosphere, Neill knew exactly where he was going. He abjured physical punishment, downgraded learning by rote, scorned the teaching of meaningless facts, and settled down to try to get his pupils to think.

In his second book, *A Dominie in Doubt*, he tells of his frustrations, of the scorn heaped upon him by his fellow teachers and his supervisors, and the uncomprehending parents of his *bairns*, as he called them. But he was fast developing a very firm notion that the traditional manner of teaching in the schools was quite wrong, that the attitudes were baleful, and that the children were being betrayed. We have more than glimmerings here of the eventual path he would take. One finds these two books laden with charm and redolent with compassion.

In *A Dominie Dismissed*, we learn that the inevitable has happened. The parents of his community have been unable to fathom this strange young man who refuses to pummel their children, or to abide by a set curriculum. Neill is fired, and for a while becomes a farmhand, cleaning out the muck of the stables. But this experience only serves to fortify his resolve. He is convinced that the world is wrong, and that there is a better way in education.

It was from these rude beginnings that the great educationist came forth to give the world a concept that now goes by the name of "Summerhill." Perhaps the epitome of Summerhill can be best stated in Neill's dictum that "Only love can save the world." In this sense, Neill can be regarded as one of the world's great religious leaders, though I am sure he would turn on me with enormous disapprobation if he heard himself characterized in this fashion. But Neill exuded love. He loved his pupils, and he surrounded them with an embrace of love. He wanted them to enjoy life always, but especially when they were young.

These three books, too, exude love. They are warm, sincere, ingenuous, and the reading of them is, in a way, a religious experience.

HAROLD H. HART

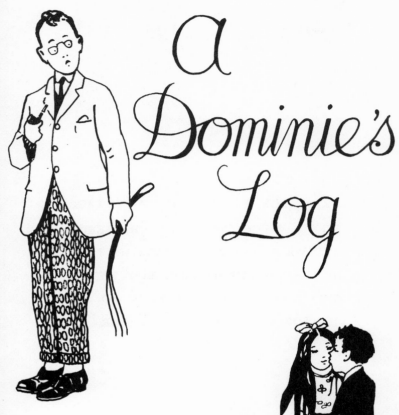

A Dominie's Log

By

A.S.NEILL

AS A BOY I ATTENDED A VILLAGE SCHOOL WHERE THE BAIRNS CHATTERED AND WERE HAPPY. I TRACE MY LOVE OF FREEDOM TO MY FREE LIFE THERE, AND I DEDICATE THIS BOOK TO MY FORMER DOMINIE, MY FATHER.

A DOMINIE'S LOG

I.

"NO reflections or opinions of a general character are to be entered in the log-book."—Thus the Scotch Code.

I have resolved to keep a private log of my own. In the regulation volume I shall write down all the futile never-to-be-seen piffle about Mary Brown's being laid up with the measles, and about my anxiety lest it should spread. (Incidentally, my anxiety is real; I do not want the school to be closed; I want a summer holiday undocked of any days.) In my private log I shall write down my thoughts on education. I think they will be mostly original; there has been no real authority on education, and I do not know of any book from which I can crib.

To-night after my bairns had gone away, I sat down on a desk and thought What does it all mean? What am I trying to do? These boys are going out to the fields to plough;

these girls are going to farms as servants. If I live long enough the new generation will be bringing notes of the plese-excuss-james-as-I-was-washing type....and the parents who will write them went out at that door five minutes ago. I can teach them to read, and they will read serials in the drivelling weeklies ; I can teach them to write, and they will write pathetic notes to me by and bye ; I can teach them to count, and they will never count more than the miserable sum they receive as a weekly wage. The "Three R's" spell futility.

But what of the rest ? Can I teach them drawing ? I cannot. I can help a boy with a natural talent to improve his work, but of what avail is it ? In their future homes they will hang up the same old prints—vile things given away with a pound of tea. I can teach them to sing, but what will they sing ?....the *Tipperary* of their day.

My work is hopeless, for education should aim at bringing up a new generation that will be better than the old. The present system is to produce the same kind of man as we see to-day. And how hopeless he is. When first I saw Houndsditch, I said aloud : "We have had education for generations....and yet we have this." Yes, my work is hopeless. What is the use of the Three R's, of Woodwork, of Drawing, of Geography, if Houndsditch is to remain? What is the use of anything?

* * *

I smile as I re-read the words I wrote yesterday, for to-day I feel that hope has not left me. But I am not any more hopeful about the three R's and the others. I am hopeful because I have found a solution. I shall henceforth try to make my bairns realise. Yes, realise is the word. Realise what? To tell the truth, I have some difficulty in saying. I think I want to make them realise what life means. Yes, I want to give them, or rather help them to find an attitude. Most of the stuff I teach them will be forgotten in a year or two, but an attitude remains with one throughout life. I want these boys and girls to acquire the habit of looking honestly at life.

Ah! I wonder if I look honestly at life myself! Am I not a very one-sided man? Am I not a Socialist, a doubter, a heretic? Am I not biassed when I judge men like the

Cecils and the Harmsworths ? I admit it. I am a partisan, and yet I try to look at life honestly. I try....and that is the main point. I do not think that I have any of the current superstitions about morality and religion and art. I try to forget names ; I try to get at essentials, at truth. The fathers of my bairns are, I think, interested in names. I wonder how many of them have sat down saying : "I must examine myself, so that I may find out what manner of man I am." I hold that self-knowledge must come before all things. When one has stripped off all the conventions, and superstitions, and hypocrisies, then one is educated.

* * *

These bairns of mine will never know how to find truth ; they will merely read the newspapers when they grow up. They will wave their hats to the King, but kingship will be but a word to them ; they will shout when a lawyer from the south wins the local seat, but they will not understand the meaning of economics ; they will dust their old silk hats and march to the sacrament, but they will not realise what religion means.

I find that I am becoming pessimistic again, and I did feel hopeful when I began to write. I *should* feel hopeful, for I am resolved to find another meaning in education. What was it?....Ah, yes, I am to help them to find an attitude.

* * *

I have been thinking about discipline overnight. I have seen a headmaster who insisted on what he called perfect discipline. His bairns sat still all day. A movement foreshadowed the strap. Every child jumped up at the word of command. He had a very quiet life.

I must confess that I am an atrociously bad disciplinarian. To-day Violet Brown began to sing *Tipperary* to herself when I was marking the registers. I looked up and said: "Why the happiness this morning, Violet?" and she blushed and grinned. I am a poor disciplinarian.

I find that normally I am very, very slack; I don't mind if they talk or not. Indeed, if the hum of conversation stops, I feel that something has happened and I invariably look towards the door to see whether an Inspector has arrived.

I find that I am almost a good disciplinarian when my liver is bad; I demand silence then....but I fear I do not get it, and I generally laugh. The only discipline I ask for usually is the discipline that interest draws. If a boy whets his pencil while I am describing the events that led to the Great Rebellion, I sidetrack him on the topic of rabbits....and I generally make him sit up. I know that I am teaching badly if the class is loafing, and I am honest enough in my saner moments not to blame the bairns.

I do not like strict discipline, for I do believe that a child should have as much freedom as possible. I want a bairn to be human, and I try to be human myself. I walk to school each morning with my briar between my lips, and if the fill is not smoked, I stand and watch the boys play. I would kiss my wife in my classroom, but....I do not have a wife. A wee lassie stopped me on the way to school this morning, and she pushed a very sticky sweetie into my hand. I took my pipe from my mouth and ate the sweetie—and I asked for another; she was highly delighted.

Discipline, to me, means a pose on the part of the teacher. It makes him very remote; it lends him dignity. Dignity is a thing I abominate. I suppose the bishop is dignified because he wants to show that there is a real difference between his salaried self and the underpaid curate. Why should I be dignified before my bairns? Will they scorn me if I slide with them? (There was a dandy slide on the road to-day. I gave them half-an-hour's extra play this morning, and I slid all the time. My assistants are adepts at the game.)

But discipline is necessary; there are men known as Inspectors. And Johnny must be flogged if he does not attend to the lesson. He must know the rivers of Russia. After all, why should he? I don't know them, and I don't miss the knowledge. I couldn't tell you the capital of New Zealand....is it Wellington? or Auckland? I don't know; all I know is that I could find out if I wanted to.

I do not blame Inspectors. Some of them are men with what I would call a vision. I had the Chief Inspector of the district in the other day, and I enjoyed his visit. He has a fine taste in poetry, and a sense of humour.

The Scotch Education Department is iniquitous because it is a department; a department cannot have a sense of humour. And it is humour that makes a man decent and kind and human.

If the Scotch Education Department were to die suddenly I should suddenly become a worse disciplinarian than I am now. If Willie did not like Woodwork, I should say to him: "All right, Willie. Go and do what you do like, but take my advice and do some work; you will enjoy your football all the better for it."

I believe in discipline, but it is self-discipline that I believe in. I think I can say that I never learned anything by being forced to learn it, but I may be wrong. I was forced to learn the Shorter Catechism, and to-day I hate the sight of it. I read the other day in Barrie's *Sentimental Tommy* that its meaning comes to one long afterwards and at a time when one is most in need of it. I confess that the time has not come for me; it will never come, for I don't remember two lines of the Catechism.

It is a fallacy that the nastiest medicines are the most efficacious; Epsom Salts are not more beneficial than Syrup of Figs.

A thought!....If I believe in self-discipline, why not persuade Willie that Woodwork is good for him as a self-discipline? Because it isn't my job. If Willie dislikes chisels he will always dislike them. What I might do is this: tell him to persevere with his chisels so that he might cut himself badly. Then he might discover that his true vocation is bandaging, and straightway go in for medicine.

Would Willie run away and play at horses if I told him to do what he liked best? I do not think so. He likes school, and I think he likes me. I think he would try to please me if he could.

* * *

When I speak kindly to a bairn I sometimes ask myself what I mean (for I try to find out my motives). Do I want the child to think kindly of me? Do I try to be popular? Am I after the delightful joy of being loved? Am I merely being humanly brotherly and kind?

I have tried to analyse my motives, and I

really think that there is little of each motive. I want to be loved; I want the bairn to think kindly of me. But in the main I think that my chief desire is to make the bairn happy. No man, no woman, has the right to make the skies cloudy for a bairn; it is the sin against the Holy Ghost.

I once had an experience in teaching. A boy was dour and unlovable and rebellious and disobedient. I tried all ways—I regret to say I tried the tawse. I was inexperienced at the time yet I hit upon the right way. One day I found he had a decided talent for drawing. I brought down some of my pen-and-ink sketches and showed him them. I gave him pictures to copy, and his interest in art grew. I won him over by interesting myself in him. He discovered that I was only human after all.

Only human! ....when our scholars discover that we are only human, then they like us, and then they listen to us.

I see the fingers of my tawse hanging out of my desk. They seem to be two accusing fingers. My ideals are all right, but....I whacked Tom Wilkie to-night. At three o'clock he bled Dave Tosh's nose, and because

Dave was the smaller, I whacked Tom. Yet I did not feel angry; I regret to say that I whacked Tom because I could see that Dave expected me to do it, and I hate to disappoint a bairn. If Dave had been his size, I know that I should have ignored their battle.

* * *

I have not used the strap all this week, and if my liver keeps well, I hope to abolish it altogether.

To-day I have been thinking about punishment. What is the idea of punishment? A few months ago a poor devil of an engine-driver ran his express into a goods, and half-a-dozen people were killed. He got nine months. Why? Is his punishment meant to act as a deterrent? Will another driver say to himself: "By Jove, I'll better not wreck my train or I'll get nine months." Nine months is not punishment, but the life-long thought: "I did it," is hell.

I am trying to think why I punished Lizzie Smith for talking last Friday. Bad habit, I expect. Yet it acted as a deterrent; it showed that I was in earnest about what I was saying—I was reading the war news from the *Scotsman*.

I am sorry that I punished her; it was weakness on my part, weakness and irritation. If she had no interest in the war, why should she pretend that she had? But no, I cannot have this. I must inculcate the idea of a community; the bairn must be told that others have rights. I often want to rise up and contradict the minister in kirk, but I don't; the people have rights; they do not come out to listen to me. If I offend against the community, the community will punish me with ostracism or bitterness. We have all a right to live our own lives, but in living them we must live in harmony with the community. Lizzie must be told that all the others like the war news, and that in talking she is annoying them. Yes, I must remember to emphasise continually the idea of a corporate life.

* * *

I see that it is only the weak man who requires a strap. Lord Kitchener could rule my school without a strap, but I am not Kitchener. Moreover, I am glad I'm not. I do not want to be what is called a strong man. John Gourlay, in *The House with the Green Shutters* was strong enough to rule every school in Scotland with Sir John Struthers superadded ; yet I do not want to be Gourlay. His son would have been a better teacher, for he was more human. Possibly Kitchener is very human ; I do not know.

11.

I HEARD a blackie this morning as I went to school, and when I came near to the playground I heard the girls singing. And I realised that Lenten was come with love to Town.

The game was a jingaring, and Violet Brown was in the centre.

The wind and the wind and the wind blows high,
The rain comes pattering from the sky.
Violet Brown says she 'll die
For the lad with the rolling eye.
She is handsome, she is pretty,
She is the girl of the golden city;
She is counted one, two, three,
Oh! I wonder who he 'll be.
Willie Craig says he loves her......

My own early experiences told me that Willie wasn't far off. Yes, there he was at the same old game. When Vi entered the ring Willie began to hammer Geordie Steel with his bonnet. But I could see Violet watch him with a corner of her eye, and I am quite sure that she was aware that the exertion of hammering Geordie did not account for Willie's burning cheeks.

Then Katie Farmer entered the ring.... and Tom Dixon at once became the hammerer of Geordie.

Poor wee Geordie! I know that he loves Katie himself, and I know that between blows he is listening for the fatal "Tom Dixon says he loves her."

I re-arranged seats this morning, and Willie is now sitting behind his Vi, but Tom Dixon is not behind Katie. Poor despised Geordie is there, but I shall shift him to-morrow if he does not make the most of his chances.

* * *

This morning Geordie passed a note over to Katie, then he sat all in a tremble. I saw Katie read it....and I saw her blush. I blew my nose violently, for I knew what was written on that sacred sheet; at least I thought I knew...."Dear Katie, will you be my lass? I will have you if you will have me—Geordie."

At minutes I listened for the name when Katie went into the ring. It was "Tom Dixon" again. I blew my whistle and stopped the game.

At dinner-time I looked out at the window, and rejoiced to see poor Geordie hammering

Tom Dixon. I opened the window and listened. Katie was in the ring again, and I almost shouted "Hurrah!" when I heard the words, "Geordie Steel says he loves her." But I placed Tom Dixon behind Katie in the afternoon; I felt that I had treated poor Tom with injustice.

To-night I tried to tackle Form 9b, but I could not concentrate. But it wasn't Violet and Katie that I was thinking of; I was thinking of the Violets and Katies I wrote "noties" to many years ago. I fear I am a bit of a sentimentalist, yet....why the devil shouldn't I be?

* * *

I have discovered a girl with a sense of humour. I asked my Qualifying Class to draw a graph of the attendance at a village kirk. "And you must explain away any rise or fall," I said.

Margaret Steel had a huge drop one Sunday, and her explanation was "Special Collection for Missions." Next Sunday the congregation was abnormally large; Margaret wrote "Change of Minister."

Few bairns have a sense of humour; their's is a sense of fun. Make a noise like a duck and they will scream, but tell them your best joke and they will be bored to tears.

I try hard to cultivate their sense of humour and their imagination. In their composition I give them many autobiographies.. ....a tile hat, a penny, an old boot, a nose, a tooth. To-day I asked them to describe in the first person a snail's journey to the end of the road. Margaret Steel talked of her hundred mile crawl, and she noted the tall forests on each side of the road. "The grass would be trees to a snail," she explained.

Poor Margaret! When she is fourteen she will go out to the fields, and in three years she will be an ignorant country bumpkin. Our education system is futile because it does not go far enough. The State should see to it that each child has the best of chances. Margaret should be sent to a Secondary School and to a University free of charge. Her food and clothes and books and train fares should be free by right. The lassie has brains....and that is argument enough.

Our rulers do realize to a slight extent the responsibility of the community to the child. It sends a doctor round to look at Margaret's teeth; it may feed her at school if she is starving; it compels her to go to school till she is fourteen. At the age of fourteen she is free to go to the devil—the factory or the herding.

But suppose she did go to a Secondary School. What then? Possibly she would become a Junior Student or a University Student. She would learn much, but would she think? I found that thinking was not encouraged at the university.

* * *

To-day I asked Senior I. to write up "A hen in the Kirk," and one or two attempts showed imagination.

Is it possible that I am overdoing the imagination business? Shall I produce men and women with more imagination than intellect? No, I do not think there is danger. The nation suffers from lack of imagination; few of us can imagine a better state of society, a fuller life.

Who are the men with great imagination? ....Shelley, Blake, Browning, Nietzsche, Ibsen, Tolstoy. These men were not content with life as it was; they had ideals, and ideals are creatures of the imagination.

I once saw a book by, I think, Arnold Forster; a book that was meant to teach children the meaning of citizenship. If I remember aright it dealt with parliament and law, and local government.

Who was Arnold Forster? Why cannot our bairns have the best? Why tell them all the stale lies about democracy, the freedom of the individual, the justice of our laws? Are Forster's ideas of citizenship as great as the ideas of Plato, of More, of Morris, of Wells? I intend to make an abridgement of Plato's *Republic,* More's *Utopia,* William Morris's *News from Nowhere,* Bacon's *A New Atlantis,* H. G. Wells' *A Modern Utopia,* and *New Worlds for Old.*

Arnold Forster was with the majority. Nearly every day I quote to my bairns Ibsen's words from *An Enemy of the People.* ...."The Majority *never* has right on its side. *Never* I say." Every lesson book shouts aloud the words: "The majority is always right."

Do I teach my bairns Socialism? I do not think so. Socialism means the owning of a State by the people of that State, and this State is not fit to own anything. For at present the State means the majority in Parliament, and that is composed of mediocre men. A State that takes up Home Rule while the slums of the East End exist is a State run by office boys for office boys.... to adapt Salisbury's description of a London daily. We could not have Socialism to-day; the nation is not ripe for it.

The Germans used to drink to "The Day"; every teacher in Britain should drink daily to "The Day" when there shall be no poor, when factory lasses will not rise at five and work till six. I know that I shall never see the day, but I shall tell my bairns that it is coming. I know that most of the seed will fall on stony ground, but a sower can but sow.

* * *

I have been image-breaking to-day, and I feel happy. It began with patent medicines, but how I got to them I cannot recollect. I remember commencing a lesson on George Washington. The word hatchet led naturally to Women's Suffrage; then ducks came up....Heaven only knows how, and the word quack brought me to Beans for Bibulous Britons. I told how most of these medicines cost half a farthing to make, and I explained that the manufacturer was spending a good part of the shilling profit in advertising. Then I told of the utter waste of material and energy in advertising, and went on to thunder against the hideous yellow tyre signs on the roadside.

At dinner-time I read in my paper that some knight had received his knighthood because of his interest in the Territorial Movement. "Much more likely that he gave a few thousands to the party funds," I said to my wondering bairns. Then I cursed the cash values that attach to almost everything.

I am determined to tear all the rags of hypocrisy from the facts of life; I shall lead my bairns to doubt everything. Yet I want them to believe in Peter Pan, or is it that I want them to believe in the beauty of beautiful stories? I want them to love the alluring lady Romance, but I think I want them to love her in the knowledge that she is only a Dream Child. Romance means more to the realist than to the romancist.

* * *

I wish I were a musician. If I could play

the piano I should spend each Friday afternoon playing to my bairns. I should give them Alexander's Ragtime Band and Hitchy Coo; then I should play them a Liszt Rhapsody and a Chopin waltz.

Would they understand and appreciate? Who knows what raptures great music might bring to a country child?

The village blacksmith was fiddling at a dance in the Hall last night. "Aw learnt the fiddle in a week," he told me. I believed him.

What effect would Ysaye have on a village audience? The divine melody would make them sit up startled at first, and, I think, some of them might begin to see pictures. If only I could bring Ysaye and Pachmann to this village! What an experiment! I think that if I were a Melba or a Ysaye I should say to myself:—"I have had enough of money and admiration; I shall go round the villages on an errand of mercy."

The great, they say, begin in the village hall and end in the Albert Hall. The really great would begin and end in the village hall.

III.

A VERY young calf had managed to get into the playground this morning, and when I arrived I found Peter Smith hitting it viciously over the nose with a stick. I said nothing. I read the war news as usual. Then I addressed the bairns.

" What would you do to the Germans who committed atrocities in Belgium ? " I asked. Peter's hand went up with the others.

" Well, Peter ? "

" Please sir, shoot them."

" Cruelty should be punished, eh ? " I said.

" Yes, sir."

" Then come here, you dirty dog ! " I cried, and I whacked Peter with a fierce joy.

I have often wondered at the strain of cruelty that is so often found in boys. The evolutionists must be right : the young always tend to resemble their remote ancestors. In a boy there is much of the brute.

I have seen a boy cut off the heads of a nest of young sparrows ; I wanted to hit him.... but he was bigger than I. This morning I was bigger than Peter ; hence I do not take any credit to myself for welting him.

I can see that cruelty does not disappear with youth. I confess to a feeling of unholy joy in leathering Peter, but I think that it was caused by a real indignation.

What made Peter hurt the poor wee thing I cannot tell. I am inclined to think that he acted subconsciously ; he was being the elemental hunter, and he did not realise that he was giving pain. I ought to have talked to him, to have made him realise. But I became elemental also ; I punished with no definite motive....and I would do it again.

* * *

We have had a return of wintry weather, and the bairns had a glorious slide made on the road this morning. At dinner-time I found them loafing round the door.

" Why aren't you sliding," I asked. They explained that the village policeman had salted the slide. After marking the registers I took up the theme.

" Why did he salt the slide ? " I asked.

"Because the farmers do not want their horses to fall," said one.

Then I took them to laws and their makers. "Children have no votes," I said, "farmers have; hence the law is with the farmers. Women have no votes and the law gives them half the salary of a man."

"But," said Margaret Steel, "would you have horses break their legs?" I smiled.

"No," I said, "and I would not object to the policeman's salting the slide if the law was thinking of animals' pain. The law and the farmers are thinking of property.

"Property in Britain comes before everything. I may steal the life and soul from a woman if I employ her at a penny an hour, and I may get a title for doing so. But if I steal Mr. Thomson's turnips I merely get ten days' hard."

"You bairns should draw up a Declaration of Rights," I added, and I think that a few understood my meaning.

* * *

I find that my bairns have a genuine love for poetry. To-day I read them Tennyson's *Lady of Shalott*; then I read them *The May Queen*. I asked them which was the better, and most of them preferred, *The Lady of Shalott.* I asked for reasons, and Margaret Steel said that the one was strange and mysterious, while the other told of an ordinary death-bed. The whole class seemed to be delighted when I called *The May Queen* a silly mawkish piece of sentimentality.

I have made them learn many pieces from Stevenson's *A Child's Garden of Verses,* and they love the rhythm of such pieces as *The Shadow March.*

Another poem that they love is *Helen of Kirkconnell;* I asked which stanza was the best, and they all agreed on this beautifully simple one :—

O Helen fair, beyond compare,
  I 'll mak a garland o' thy hair ;
Shall bind my heart for evermair,
  Until the day I dee,

I believe in reading out a long poem and then asking them to memorise a few verses. I did this with *The Ancient Mariner.* Long poems are an abomination to children ; to ask them to commit to memory a piece like Gray's *Elegy* is unkind.

I have given them the first verse of Francis Thompson's *The Hound of Heaven.* I did not expect them to understand a word of it ;

my idea was to test their power of appreciating sound. Great music might convey something to rustics, but great poetry cannot convey much. Still, I try to lead them to the greater poetry. I wrote on the board a verse of *Little Jim* and a verse of *La Belle Dame sans Merci,* and I think I managed to give them an inkling of what is good and what is bad verse.

I begin to think that country children should learn ballads. There is a beauty about the old ballads that even children can catch ; it is the beauty of a sweet simplicity. When I think of the orchestration of Swinburne, I think of the music of the ballads as of a flute playing. And I know that orchestration would be lost on country folk.

I hate the poems that crowd the average school-book. . . . *Little Jim, We are Seven, Lucy Gray, The Wreck of the Hesperus, The Boy stood on the Burning Deck,* and all the rest of them. I want to select the best of the Cavalier lyrists' works, the songs from the old collections like Davison's *Poetical Rhapsody* and *England's Helicon,* the lyrics from the Elizabethan dramatists. I want to look through moderns like William Watson,

Robert Bridges, George Meredith, Thomas Hardy, Henley, Dowson, Abercrombie, William Wilfred Gibson....there must be many charming pieces that bairns would enjoy.

I read out the old *Tale of Gamelyn* the other day, and the queer rhythm and language seemed to interest the class.

* * *

I think that the teaching of history in schools is all wrong. I look through a school-history, and I find that emphasis is laid on incident. Of what earthly use is the information given about Henry VIII.'s matrimonial vagaries? Does it matter a rap to anyone whether Henry I.—or was it Henry II.?—ever smiled again or not? By all means let us tell the younger children tales of wicked dukes, but older children ought to be led to think out the meaning of history. The usual school-history is a piece of snobbery; it can't keep away from the topic of kings and queens. They don't matter; history should tell the story of the people and their gradual progress from serfdom to......sweating.

I believe that a boy of eleven can grasp cause and effect. With a little effort he can understand the non-sentimental side ot the Mary Stewart-Elizabeth story, the result to Scotland of the Franco-Scottish alliance. He can understand why Philip of Spain, a Roman Catholic, preferred that the Protestant Elizabeth should be Queen of England rather than the Catholic Mary Stewart.

The histories never make bairns think. I have not seen one that mentioned that Magna Charta was signed because all classes in the country happened to be united for the moment. I have not seen one that points out that the main feature in Scots history is the lack of a strong central government.

Hume Brown's school *History of Scotland* is undoubtedly a very good book, but I want to see a history that will leave out all the detail that Brown gives. All that stuff about the Ruthven Raid and the Black Dinner of the Douglases might be left out of the books that the upper classes read. My history would tell the story of how the different parts were united to form the present Scotland, without mentioning more than half-a-dozen names of men and dates. Then it would go on to tell of the struggles to form a central government. Possibly Hume Brown does this. 1 don't know; I am met with so much detail about Perth Articles and murders that I lose the thread of the story.

Again, the school-histories almost always give a wrong impression of men and events. Every Scots schoolboy thinks that Edward I. of England was a sort of thief and bully rolled into one, and that the carpet-bagger, Robert Bruce, was a saint from heaven. Edward's greatness as a lawgiver is ignored; at least we ought to give him credit for his statesmanship in making an attempt to unite England, Scotland, and Wales. And Cromwell's Drogheda and Wexford affair is generally mentioned with due emphasis, while Charles I.'s proverbial reputation as "a bad king but a good father" is seldom omitted.

I expect that the school-histories of the future will talk of the "scrap of paper" aspect of the present war, and they will anathematise the Kaiser. But the real historians will be searching for deeper causes; they will be analysing the national characteristics, the economical needs, the diplomatic methods, of the nations.

The school-histories will say: "The war

came about because the Kaiser wanted to be master of Europe, and the German people had no say in the matter at all."

The historians will say....well, I'm afraid I don't know; but I think they will relegate the Kaiser to a foot-note.

* * *

The theorist is a lazy man. MacMurray down the road at Markiton School is a hard worker; he never theorises about education. He grinds away at his history and geography, and I don't suppose he likes geography any more than I do. I expect that he gives a thorough lesson on Canada, its exports and so on. I do not; I am too lazy to read up the subject. My theory says to me: "You are able to think fairly well, and a knowledge of the amount of square miles in Manitoba would not help you to think as brightly as H. G. Wells. So, why learn up stuff that you can get in a dictionary any day?" And I teach on this principle.

At the same time I am aware that facts must precede theories in education. You cannot have a theory on, say, the Marriage Laws, unless you know what these laws are. However, I do try to distinguish between facts and facts. To a child (as to me), the fact that Canada grows wheat is of less importance than the fact that if you walk down the street in Winnipeg in mid winter, you may have your ears frost-bitten.

The only information I know about Japan consists of a few interesting facts I got from a lecture by Arthur Diosy. I don't know what things are manufactured in Tokio, but I know that a Jap almost boils himself when he takes a bath in the morning.

I find that I am much more interested in humanity than in materials, and I know that the bairns are like me in this.

A West African came to the school the other day, and asked me to allow him to tell (for a consideration) the story of his home life. When I discovered that he did not mean his own private home life I gladly gave him permission. He talked for half-an-hour about the habits of his home, the native schools, the dress of the children (I almost blushed at this part, but I was relieved to find that they do dress after all); then he sang the native version of 'Mary had a little Lamb' (great applause).

The lecture was first-rate; and, in my lazy

—I mean my theoretical moments, I squint down the road in hopes that an itinerant Chinaman will come along. I would have a coloured band of geographers employed by the Department.

* * *

I am chuckling at myself to-night. A day or two ago I lectured about the policeman's action in salting the slide, and I certainly did not think of the farmer's position. To-day I wore a new pair of very light spats... and Lizzie Adam has a horrid habit of shaking her pen after dipping.

"Look what you've done!" I cried in vexation, "can't you stop that silly habit of chucking ink all over the school?" Then I laughed.

"Lizzie," I said sadly, "you won't understand, but I am the farmer who wants the slide salted. The farmer does not want to have his horse ruined, and I do object to having my new spats ruined."

The truth is that the interests of the young and of the old are directly antagonistical. I can argue with delightful sophistry that I am better than the farmer. I can say that throwing ink is a silly habit, with no benefit to Lizzie, while sliding brings joy to a schoolful of bairns; hence the joy of these bairns is of greater importance than the loss of a horse. But I know what I should think if it were my horse, yes, I know.

I find it the most difficult thing in the world to be a theorist . . . . and an honest man at the same time.

IV.

A JUNIOR Inspector called to-day His subject was handwriting, and he had theories on the subject. So have I. We had an interesting talk.

His view is that handwriting is a practical science ; hence we must teach a child to write in such a way as to carry off the job he applies for when he is fourteen.

My view is that handwriting is an art, like sketching My view is the better, for it includes his. I am a superior penman to him, and in a contest I could easily beat him. I really failed to see what he was worrying his head about. What does the style matter. It is the art that one puts into a style that makes writing good. I can teach the average bairn to write well in two hours ; it is simply a matter of writing slowly I like the old-schoolmaster hand, the round easy writing with its thick downstrokes and thin upstrokes. I like to see the m's with the joinings in the middle. The *Times* copy-book is the ideal one—to me. But why write down any more. The topic isn't worth the ink wasted.

* * *

I picked up a copy of a Popular Educator to-day. Much of the stuff seems to be well written, but I cannot help thinking that the words "low ideals" are written over the whole set of volumes. Its aim is evidently to enable boys and girls to gain success . . . as the world considers success. "Study hard," it blares forth, "and you will become a Whiteley or a Gamage. Study if you want wealth and position." What an ideal!

Let us have our Shorthand Classes, our Cookery Classes, our Typewriting Classes, but for any sake don't let us call them education. Education is thinking; it should deal with great thoughts, with the æsthetic things in life, with life itself. Commerce is the profiteer's god, but it is not mine. I want to teach my bairns how to live; the Popular Educator wants to teach them how to make a living. There is a distinction between the two ideals.

The Scotch Education Department would seem to have some of the Educator's aspirations. It demands Gardening, Woodwork,

Cookery; in short, it is aiming at turning out practical men and women.

My objection to men and women is that they are too practical. I used to see a notice in Edinburgh: "John Brown, Practical Chimney Sweep." I often used to wonder what a theoretical chimney sweep might be, and I often wished I could meet one. My view is that a teacher should turn out theoretical sweeps, railwaymen, ploughmen, servants. Heaven knows they will get the practical part knocked into them soon enough.

* * *

I have been experimenting with Drawing. I have been a passable black-and-white artist for many years, and the subject fascinates me. I see that drawing is of less importance than taste, and I find that I can get infants who cannot draw a line to make artistic pictures.

I commence with far-away objects—a clump of trees on the horizon. The child takes a BB pencil and blocks in the mass of trees. The result is a better picture than the calendar prints the bairns see at home.

Gradually I take nearer objects, and at length I reach what is called drawing. I ignore all vases and cubes and ellipses; my model is a school-bag or a cloak. The drawing does not matter very much; but I want to see the shadows stand out.

I find that only a few in a class ever improve in sketching; one is born with the gift.

Designing fascinates many bairns. I asked them to design a kirk window on squared paper to-day. Some of the attempts were good. I got the boys to finish off with red ink, and then I pasted up the designs on the wall.

I seem to recollect an Inspector who told me to give up design a good few years ago. I wouldn't give it up now for anyone. It is a delightful study, and it will bring out an inherent good taste better than any branch of drawing I know. Drawing (or rather, Sketching) to me means an art, not a means to cultivating observation. It belongs solely to Aesthetics. Sketching, Music, and Poetry are surely intended to make a bairn realise the fuller life that must have beauty always with it.

I showed my bairns two sketches of my own to-day. . . the Tolbooth and the Whitehorse Close in Edinburgh. A few claimed that the Whitehorse Close was the better, because it left more out. "It leaves something to the imagination," said Tom Dixon.

* * *

When will some original publisher give us a decent school Reader? I have not seen one that is worth using. Some of them give excerpts from Dickens and Fielding and Borrow (that horrid bore) and Hawthorne (another). I cannot find any interest in these excerpts; they have no beginning and no end. Moreover, a bairn does like the dramatic; prosiness deadens its wee soul at once.

I want to see a Reader especially written for bairns. I want to see many complete stories, filled with bright dialogue. Every yarn should commence with dialogue. I always think kindly of the late Guy Boothby, because he usually began with, "Hands up, or I fire!" or a kindred sentence.

I wish I could lay hands on a Century Reader I used as a boy. It was full of the dramatic. The first story was one about the Burning of Moscow, then came the tale of Captain Dodds and the pirate (from

Reade's novel, *Hard Cash,* I admit. An excerpt need not be uninteresting), then a long passage from *The Deerslayer*. . . . with a picture of Indians throwing tomahawks at the hero. I loved that book.

I think that dramatic reading should precede prosy reading. It is life that a child wants, not prosy descriptions of sunsets and travels; life, and romance.

I have scrapped my Readers; I don't use them even for Spelling. I do not teach Spelling; the teaching of it does not fit into my scheme of education.

Teaching depends on logic. Now Spelling throws logic to the winds. I tell a child that "cough" is "coff," and logic leads him to suppose that rough is "roff" and "through" is "throff." If I tell him that spelling is important because it shows whence a word is derived, I am bound in honesty to tell him that a matinee is not a "morning performance," that manufactured goods are not "made by hand." Hence I leave Spelling alone.

At school I "learned" Spelling, and I could not spell a word until I commenced to read much. Spelling is of the eye mainly.

Every boy can spell " truly " and " obliged " when he leaves school, but ten years later he will probably write " truely " and " oblidged." Why? I think that the explanation lies in the fact that he does not read as a growing youth. Anyway, dictionaries are cheap.

* * *

To-night I sat down on a desk and lit my pipe. Margaret Steel and Lizzie Buchan were tidying up the room. Margaret looked at me thoughtfully for a second.

" Please, sir, why do you smoke? " she said.

" I really don't know, Margaret," I said. " Bad habit, I suppose....just like writing notes to boys."

She suddenly became feverishly anxious to pick up the stray papers.

" I wonder," I mused, " whether they do it in the same old way. How do they do it, Margaret? " She dived after a piece of paper.

" I used to write them myself," I said. Margaret looked up quickly.

" You! " she gasped.

" I am not so old," I said hastily.

"Please, sir, I didn't mean that," she explained in confusion.

"You did, you wee bissom," I chuckled.

"Please, sir," she said awkwardly, "why—why are you not—not–m–married ?" I rose and took up my hat.

"I once kissed a girl behind the school door, Margaret," I said absently. She did not understand....and when I come to think of it I am not surprised.

* * *

To-day was prize-giving day. Old Mr. Simpson made a speech.

"Boys," he said, "study hard and you'll maybe be a minister like Mr. Gordon there." He paused. "Or," he continued, "if you don't manage that, you may become a teacher like Mr. Neill here."

Otherwise the affair was very pathetic : the medallist, a girl, had already left school and was hired as a servant on a farm. And old Mr. Simpson did not know it ; I thought it better not to tell the kindly soul. He spoke earnestly on success in life.

I hate prizes. To-day, Violet Brown and Margaret Steel, usually the best of friends, are looking daggers at each other. To-morrow I shall read them the story of the Judgment of Paris. And what rubbish these books are! There isn't a decent piece of literature in the bunch—*Matty's Present*, *The Girl Who Came to School*. Jerusalem!

V

THE more I see of it the more I admire the co-education system. To me it is delightful to see boys and girls playing together. Segregate boys and you destroy their perspective. I used to find at the university that it was generally the English Public School Boy who set up one standard of morals for his sisters and another for the shop-girls.

Co-education is the greatest thing in our State educational system. The bairns early learn the interdependence of the sexes ; boys and girls early begin to understand each other. All danger of putting women on a pedestal is taken away ; the boys find that the girls are ordinary humans with many failings ("Aw'll tell the mester !"), and many virtues. The girls find that boys....well, I don't exactly know what the girls find.

Seldom is there any over-familiarity. The girls have a natural protective aloofness that awes the boys ; the boys generally have strenuous interests that lead them to ignore the girls for long periods. At present the sexes are very friendly, for love-making (always a holy thing with bairns), has come with spring ; but in a few weeks the boys will be playing football or " bools," and they will not be seen in the girls' playground.

I can detect no striving after what is called chivalry (thank heaven !) If Maggie and Willie both lay hands on a ruler, they fight it out, but Maggie generally gets it ; she can say more. Mr. Henpeck begins life as a chick. I hate the popular idea of chivalry, and I want my boys to hate it. Chivalry to me means rising in the Tube to offer a typist your seat, and then going off to the city to boss a score of waitresses who are paid 6*s*. a week. As a nation we have no chivalry ; we have only etiquette. We hold doors open for nice women, and we tamely suffer or forget about a society that condemns poor women to slave for sixteen hours a day sewing shirts at a penny an hour. We say " Thank you " when the lady of the house stops playing, and we banish the prostitutes of Piccadilly from our minds. Chivalry has been dead for a long time now.

I want to substitute kindness for the word chivalry. I want to tell my bairns that the only sin in the world is cruelty. I do not preach morality for I hardly know what morality is. I have no morals, I am an a-moralist, or should it be a non-moralist? I judge not, and I mean to school my bairns into judging not. Yet I am not being quite consistent. I do judge cruelty and uncharitableness; but I judge not those who do not act up to the accustomed code of morals. A code is always a temptation to a healthy person; it is like a window by a railway siding: it cries out: "Chuck a chunk of coal through me." Codes never make people moral; they merely make them hypocritical. I include the Scotch code.

* * *

Until lately I thought that drill was unnecessary for rural bairns. It was the chief inspector of the district who converted me. He pointed out that country children are clumsy and slack. "A countryman can heave a sack of potatoes on his back," he said, "but he has no agility, no grace of movement."

I agree with him now. I find that drill makes my bairns more graceful. But I am far from being pleased with any system that I know. I don't really care tuppence whether they are physically alert or not, but I want them to be graceful, if only from an artistic point of view. The system I really want to know is Eurhythmics. I recently read an illustrated article by (or on ?) Jacques Dalcroze, the inventor of the method, and the founder of the Eurhythmics School near Dresden. The system is drill combined with music. The pupils walk and dance, and I expect, sit to music. The photographs were beautiful studies in grace ; the school appears to be full of Pavlovas. I think I shall try to found a Eurhythmics system on the photographs. I cannot surely invent anything more graceless than " 'Shun ! "

Grace is almost totally absent from rural dances. The ploughman takes off his jacket, and sweats his roaring way through " The Flowers o' Edinburgh " ; but the waltz has no attraction for him. Waltzing is a necessity in a rural scheme of education....and, incidentally, in a Mayfair scheme of education, now that the " Bunny Hug " and the " Turkey

Trot" and the "Tango" have come to these isles.

* * *

Robert Campbell left the school to-day. He had reached the age limit. He begins work tomorrow morning as a ploughman. And yesterday I wrote about introducing Eurhythmics! Robert's leaving brings me to earth with a flop. I am forced to look a grim fact in the face. Truly it is like a death; I stand by a new made grave, and I have no hope of a resurrection. Robert is dead.

Pessimism has hold of me to-night. I have tried to point the way to what I think best in life, tried to give Robert an ideal. Tomorrow he will be gathered to his fathers. He will take up the attitude of his neighbours: he will go to church, he will vote Radical or Tory, he will elect a farmer to the School Board, he will marry and live in a hovel. His master said to me recently: "Bairns are gettin' ower muckle eddication noo-a-days. What eddication does a laddie need to herd kye?"

Yes, I am as pessimistic as any Schopenhauer to-night, I cannot see the sun.

* * *

My pessimism has remained with me all day. I feel that I am merely pouring water into a sieve. I almost feel that to meddle with education is to begin at the wrong end. I may have an ideal, but I cannot carry it out because I am up against all the forces of society. Robert Campbell is damned, not because education is so very wrong, but because education is trying to adapt itself to commerce and economics and convention. I think I am right in holding that our Individualist, as opposed to a Socialist, system is to blame. "Every man for himself" is the most cursed saying that was ever said. If we are to allow an idle rich to waste millions yearly, if we are to allow profiteers to amass thousands at the expense of the slaving majority, what chance has poor Robert Campbell? I complete the saying—"and the Deil tak the henmost." Robert is the henmost.

O! the people are poor things. Democracy is the last futility. Yet I should not blame the people; they never get a chance. Our rulers are on the side of the profiteers, and the latter take very good care that Robert Campbell shall leave school when he is fourteen. It isn't that they want more cheap labour; they are afraid that if he is educated until he is nineteen he will be wise enough to say: "Why should I, a man made in the image of God, be forced to slave for gains that you will steal?"

Yet, the only way is to labour on, to strive to convey some idea of my ideal to my bairns. If every teacher in Scotland had the same ideal as I have I think that the fight would not be a long one. But how do I know that my ideal is the right one? I cannot say; I just *know*. Which, I admit, is a woman's reason.

* * *

I was re-reading *An Enemy of the People* last night, and the thought suddenly came to me: "Would my bairns understand it?" This morning I cut out Bible instruction and read them the first act. I then questioned them, and found to my delight that they had grasped the theme. It was peculiarly satisfying to me to find that they recognized Dr. Stockmann as a better man than his grovelling brother Peter. If my bairns could realise the full significance of Ibsen's play, "The

Day " would not be so far off as I am in the habit of thinking it is.

I must re-read Shaw's *Widowers' Houses;* I fancy that children might find much thought in it. It is one of his " Unpleasant Plays," but I see no reason for keeping the unlovely things from bairns. I do not believe in frightening them with tales of murder and ghosts. Every human being has something of the gruesome in his composition; the murder cases are the most popular readings in our press. I want to direct this innate desire for gruesome things to the realising of the most gruesome things in the world—the grinding of soul and body in order to gain profits, the misery of poverty and cold, the weariness of toil. If our press really wants to make its readers shudder, why does it not publish long accounts of infant mortality in the slums, of gin fed bairns, of back-doors used as fuel, of phthisical girls straining their eyes over seams? I know why the press ignores these things, the public does not want to think of them. If the public wanted such stories every capitalist owner of a newspaper would supply them, grudgingly, but with a stern resolve to get dividends. To-day the papers are mostly run for the rich and their parasites. The only way in which 'Enery Smith can get his photograph into the papers is by jumping on Mrs. 'Enery Smith until she expires. I wonder that no criminologist has tried to prove that publicity is the greatest incentive to crime.

When I read the daily papers to my bairns I try to tell them what is left out. "Humour at Bow Street," a heading will run. Ye Gods! Humour! I have as much humour as most men, but if anyone can find humour in the stupid remarks of a law-giver he must be a W. W. Jacobs, a Mark Twain, a George A. Birmingham, and a Stephen Leacock rolled into one .... with the Devil thrown in. Humour at Bow Street. I have been there. I have seen the poor Magdalenes and the pitiable Lazaruses shuffle in with terror in their eyes. I have seen the inflexible mighty law condemn them to the cells, I have heard their piteous cries for mercy. And the newspapers talk of the humour of the courts.

I once read that law's primary object is to protect the rich from the poor. The appalling truth of that saying dawned on me in Bow Street. Humour! Yes, there is humour in Bow Street. The grimmest, ugliest joke in the world is this.... Covent Garden Opera House stands across the street from the court.

* * *

To-day I told Senior II. to write up the following story, I advised them to add graces to it if they could.

" A farmer went to Edinburgh for the day. He was walking down the High Street with open mouth when the fire engine came swinging round the corner. The farmer gave chase down the North Bridge and Leith Street, and owing to the heavy traffic the engine's rate was so slow that he could easily keep up with it. But it turned down London Road, and in the long silent street soon outdistanced him. He ran until he saw that it was hopeless. Then he stopped and held up a clenched fist.

" Ye can keep yer dawmed tattie-chips," he cried, " Aw'll get them some other place."

Mary Peters began thus :—

" Mr. Peter Mitchell went to Edinburgh for the day...."

Mr. Peter Mitchell is Chairman of the School Board.

* * *

Why did I substitute "auld" for "dawmed" tattie-chips when I told the bairns the story. Art demands the "dawmed." I think I substituted the "auld" because I like a quiet life. I have no time to persuade indignant parents that "damn" is not a sin. But it was weakness on my part; I compromised, and compromise is always a lie.

VI.

THIS morning I had a note from a farmer in the neighbourhood.

"DEAR SIR,—I send my son Andrew to get education at the school not Radical politics.

I am,

Yours respectfully,

Andrew Smith."

I called Andrew out.

"Andrew," I said, with a smile, "when you go home to-night tell your father that I hate Radicalism possibly more than he does."

The father came down to-night to apologise. "Aw thocht ye was ane o' they wheezin' Radicals," he explained. Then he added, "And what micht yer politics be?"

"I am a Utopian," I said modestly.

He scratched his head for a moment, then he gave it up and asked my opinion of the weather. We discussed turnips for half-an-hour, at the end of which time I am sure he was wondering how an M.A. could be such an ignoramus. We parted on friendly terms.

* * *

I do not think that I have any definite views on the teaching of religion to bairns; indeed, I have the vaguest notion of what religion means. I am just enough of a Nietzschean to protest against teaching children to be meek and lowly. I once shocked a dear old lady by saying that the part of the Bible that appealed to me most was that in which the Pharisee said: "I thank God that I am not as other men." I was young then, I have not the courage to say it now.

I do, however, hold strongly that teaching religion is not my job. The parish minister and the U.F. minister get good stipends for tending their flocks, and I do not see any reason in the world why I should have to look after the lambs. For one thing I am not capable. All I aim at is teaching bairns how to live....possibly that is the true religion; my early training prevents my getting rid of the idea that religion is intended to teach people how to die.

To-day I was talking about the probable

formation of the earth, how it was a ball of flaming gas like the sun, how it cooled gradually, how life came. A girl looked up and said: " Please, sir, what about the Bible ? " I explained that in my opinion the creation story was a story told to children, to a people who were children in understanding. I pointed out a strange feature, discovered to me by the parish minister, that the first chapter of Genesis follows the order of scientific evolution....the earth is without form, life rises from the sea, then come the birds, then the mammals.

But I am forced to give religious instruction. I confine my efforts to the four gospels ; the bairns read them aloud. I seldom make any comment on the passages.

In geography lessons I often take occasion to emphasise the fact that Muhammudans and Buddhists are not necessarily stupid folk who know no better. I cannot lead bairns to a religion, but I can prevent their being stupidly narrow.

No, I fear I have no definite opinions on religion.

I set out to enter the church, but I think that I could not have stayed in it. I fancy that one fine Sunday morning I would have stood up in the pulpit and said: "Friends, I am no follower of Christ. I like fine linen and tobacco, books and comfort. I should be in the slums, but I am not Christlike enough to go there. Goodbye."

I wonder! Why then do I not stand up and say to the School Board: "I do not believe in this system of education at all. I am a hypocrite when I teach subjects that I abominate. Give me my month's screw. Goodbye." I sigh....yet I like to fancy that I could not have stayed in the kirk. One thing I am sure of: a big stipend would not have tempted me to stay. I have no wish for money; at least, I wouldn't go out of my way to get it. I wouldn't edit a popular newspaper for ten thousand a year. Of that I am sure. Quite sure. Quite.

Yet I once applied for a job on a Tory daily. I was hungry then. What if I were hungry now? The flesh is weak....but, I could always go out on tramp. I more than half long for the temptation. Then I should discover whether I am an idealist or a talker. Possibly I am a little of both.

I began to write about religion, and I find

myself talking about myself. Can it be that my god is my ego ?

* * *

I began these log-notes in order to discover my philosophy of education, and I find that I am discovering myself. This discovery of self must come first. Personality goes far in teaching. May it go too far? Is it possible that I am a danger to these bairns ? May I not be influencing them too much ? I do not think so. Anything I may say will surely be negatived at home; my word, unfortunately, is not so weighty as father's.

In what is called Spelling Reform we cannot have a revolution; all we can hope for is a reform within Spelling, a reform that will abolish existing anomalies. So in education we cannot have a revolution. All we can hope for is a reform wrought within education by the teacher. If every teacher were a sort of Wellsian-Shavian-Nietzschean-Webbian fellow, the children would be directly under two potent influences—the parents and teachers.

"What is Truth ?" millions of Pilates have asked. It is because we have no standard of Truth that our education is a failure. Each of us gets hold of a corner of the page of Truth, but the trouble is that so many grasp the same corner. It is a corner dirty with thumb-marks...." Humour in Bow Street," "Knighthood for Tooting Philanthropist," " Dastardly Act by Leeds Strikers," " Special Service of Praise in the Parish Kirk "....marks do not obliterate the page. My corner is free from thumbmarks, and anyone can read the clear type of " Christlessness in Bow Street," " Jobbery in the Sale of Honours," " Murder of Starving Strikers," " Thanksgiving Service for the Blessing of Whitechapel "....but few will read this corner's story; the majority likes the filthy corner with the beautiful news.

I have discovered my mission. I am the apostle of the clean corner with the dirty news written on it.

* * *

I began to read the second act of *An Enemy of the People* this morning, but I had to give it up; the bairns had lost interest. I closed the book. " Suppose," I said, " suppose that this village suddenly became famous as a health-resort. People would build houses and hotels, your fathers would grow richer; and suppose that the doctor discovered that the water supply was poisonous, that the pipes lay through a swamp where fever germs were. What would the men who had built hotels and houses say about the doctor? What would they do about the water supply?"

The unanimous opinion was that the water-pipes would be relaid; the people would not want visitors to come and take fever.

This opinion leads me to conclude that bairns are idealists; childhood takes the Christian view. Barrie says that genius is the power of being a boy again at will; I agree, but Barrie and I are possibly thinking of different aspects. Ibsen was a genius because he became as a little child. Dr. Stockmann (Ibsen) is a simple child; he cannot realise that self-interest can make his own brother a criminal to society.

I told my bairns what the men in the play did.

"But," said one in amazement, "they would not do that in real life?"

"They are doing it every day," I said. "This school is old, badly ventilated, over-crowded. It is a danger to your health and mine. Yet, if I asked for a new school, the whole village would rise up against me. 'More money on the rates!' they would cry, and they would treat me very much as the people in the play treated Dr. Stockmann."

* * *

I find it difficult to discuss the causes of the war with the bairns. I refuse to accept the usual tags about going to the assistance of a weak neighbour whom we agreed to protect. We all want to think that we are fighting for Belgium but are we?

I look to Mexico and I find it has been bathed in blood because the American Oil Kings and the British Oil Kings were at war. President Diaz was pro-English, Madero was pro-American, Huerta was pro-English.... and the United States supported the notorious Villa. Villa's rival, Carranzo, was pro-English. It is an accepted belief that the American Oil Kings financed the first risings in order to drive the British oil interests out of the country. Hence, widows and orphans in Mexico are the victims of a dollar massacre.

Can we trace the present war to the financiers? It is said that the Triple Entente is the result of Russia's receiving loans from France and Britain.

I cannot find a solution. I am inclined to attach little value to what is called national feeling. The workers are the masses, and I cannot imagine a German navvy's having any hatred of a British navvy. A world of workers would not fight, but at present the workers are so badly organised that they fight at the bidding of kings and diplomatists and financiers. War comes from the classes above, and by means of their press the upper classes convert the proletariat to their way of thinking.

A more important subject is that of the ending of wars. The idealistic vapourings of the I.L.P. with its silly talk of internationalism will do nothing to stop war. Norman Angell's cry that war doesn't pay will not stop war. But a true democracy in each country will stop it. I think of Russia with all its darkness and cruelty, and I am appalled; a true democracy there will be centuries in coming. For Germany I do not fear; out of her militarism will surely arise a great democratic nation. And out of our own great trial a true democracy is arising. Capitalism has failed; the State now sees that it must control the railways and engineering shops in a crisis. The men who struck work on the Clyde are of the same class as the men who are dying in Flanders. Why should one lot be heroes and the other lot be cursed as traitors? The answer is simple. The soldiers are fighting for the nation; the engineers are working primarily for the profiteers, and only secondarily for the nation. Profiteering has not stood the test, and the workers are beginning to realise the significance of its failure.

VII.

TO-DAY I have scrapped somebody's Rural Arithmetic. It is full of sums of the How-much-will-it-take-to-paper a-room ? type. This cursed utilitarianism in education riles me. Who wants to know what it will take to paper a room ? Personally I should call in the painter, and take my meals on the parlour piano for a day or two. Anyway, why this suspicion of the poor painter ? Is he worse than other tradesmen ? If we must have a utilitarian arithmetic then I want to see a book that will tell me if the watchmaker is a liar when he tells me that the mainspring of my watch is broken. I want to see sums like this :—How long will a plumber take to lay a ten foot pipe if father can do it at the rate of a yard in three minutes? (Ans., three days).

To me Arithmetic is an art not a science. I do not know a single rule ; I must always go back to first principles. I love catch questions, questions that will make a bairn think all the time. Inspectors' Tests give but little scope for the Art of Arithmetic; they are usually poor peddling things that smell strongly of materialism. In other words, they appeal to the mechanical part of a bairn's brain instead of to the imagination. I want to see a test that will include a sum like this:—$23.4 \times .065 \times 54.678 \times 0$. The cram will start in to multiply out; the imaginative bairn will glance along and see the nought, and will at once spot that the answer is zero.

* * *

I have just discovered an excellent song-book—Curwen's *Approved Songs*. It includes all the lovely songs of Cavalier and Puritan times, tunes like *Polly Oliver* and *Golden Slumbers*. At present my bairns are singing a Christmas Carol by Bridge, *Sweeter than Songs of Summer*. They sing treble, alto, and tenor, while I supply the bass. The time is long past Christmas, but details like that don't worry me. This carol is the sweetest piece of harmonising I have heard for a long time.

* * *

I have been re-reading Shaw's remarks on Sex in Education. I cannot see that he has anything very illuminating to say on the subject ; for that matter no one has. Most of us realise that something is wrong with our views on sex. The present attitude of education is to ignore sex, and the result is that sex remains a conspiracy of silence. The ideal some of us have is to raise sex to its proper position as a wondrous beautiful thing. To-day we try to convey to bairns that birth is a disgrace to humanity.

The problem before me comes to this : How can I bring my bairns to take a rational elemental view of sex instead of a conventional hypocritical one ? How can I convey to them the realisation that our virtue is mostly cowardice, that our sex morality is founded on mere respectability ? (It is the easiest thing in the world to be virtuous in Padanarum ; it is not so easy to be a saint in Oxford Street. Not because Oxford Street has more temptation, but because nobody knows you there.)

In reality I can do nothing. If I mentioned sex in school I should be dismissed at once. But if a philanthropist would come along and offer me a private school to run as I pleased, then I should introduce sex into my scheme of education. Bairns would be encouraged to believe in the stork theory of birth until they reached the age of nine. At that age they would get the naked truth.

A friend of mine, one of the cleverest men I know, and his wife, a wise woman, resolved to tell their children anything they asked. The eldest, a girl of four, asked one day where she came from. They told her, and she showed no surprise. But I would begin at nine chiefly because the stork story is so delightful that it would be cruel to deprive a bairn of it altogether. Yet, after all, the stork story is all the more charming when you know the bald truth.

Well, at the age of nine my bairns would be taken in hand by a doctor. They would learn that modesty is mainly an accidental result of the invention of clothes. They would gradually come to look upon sex as a normal fact of life; in short, they would recognise it as a healthy thing.

Shaw is right in saying that children must get the truth from a teacher, because parents find a natural shyness in mentioning sex to their children. But I think that the next generation of parents will have a better perspective ; shyness will almost disappear. The bairns must be told ; of that there is no doubt. The present evasion and deceit lead to the dirtiness which constitutes the sex education of boys and girls.

The great drawback to a frank education on sex matters is the disgusting fact that most grown-up people persist in associating sex with sin. The phrase " born in sin " is still applied to an illegitimate child. When I think of the damnable cruelty of virtuous married women to a girl who has had a child I want to change the phrase into " born into sin."

* * *

I have just discovered a section of the Code that deals with the subject of Temperance. I smile sadly when I think that my bairns will never have more than a pound a week to be intemperate on. I suspect that if I had to slave for a week for a pound I should trek for the nearest pub on pay night ; I should seek oblivion in some way.

Temperance ! Why waste time telling poor

bairns to be temperate? When they are fourteen they will learn that to be intemperate means the sack. If we must teach temperance let us begin at Oxford and Cambridge; at Westminster (I really forget how much wine and beer was consumed there last year; the amount raised a thirst in me at any rate).

Temperance! The profiteers see to it that the poor cannot afford to be intemperate. Coals are up now, the men who draw a royalty on each ton as it leaves the pit do not know the meaning of temperance.

I want to cry to my bairns: "Be intemperate! Demand more of the fine things of life. Don't waste time in the beershops, spend your leisure hours persuading your neighbour to help you to impose temperance on your masters."

The Code talks about food. But it does not do so honestly. I would insert the following in the Code:—

"Teachers in slum districts should point out to the children that most of their food is adulterated. Most of their boots are made of paper. Most of their clothes are made of shoddy"

* * *

The best thing I have found in the Code is the section on the teaching of English. I fancy it is the work of J. C. Smith, the Editor of the Oxford *Spenser*. I used to have him round at my classes; he was a first-rate examiner. If a class had any originality in it he drew it out. But I never forgave J. C. Smith for editing *Much Ado About Nothing*. He made no effort to remark on the absurdity of the plot and motives. To me the play is as silly as *Diplomacy* or *Our Boys*.

"No grammar," says the Code, "should be taught until written composition begins." I like that, but I should re-write it thus: "No grammar should be taught this side the Styx."

Grammar is always changing, and the grammar of yesterday is scrapped to-day. A child requires to know how to speak and how to write correctly. I can write passably well, and when I write I do not need to know whether a word is an adjective or an adverb, whether a clause is a nour clause or an adverbial clause of time modifying a certain verb....or is it a noun? Society ladies speak grammatically (I am told), and I'm quite sure that not three people in the Row could tell me whether a word is a verb or an adverb (I shouldn't care to ask). The fact that I really could tell what each word is makes absolutely no difference to me. A middle-class boy of five will know that the sentence "I and nurse is going to the Pictures" is wrong.

But I must confess that grammar has influenced me in one way. I know I should say "Whom did you see?" but I always say "Who did you see?" And I used to try not to split my infinitives....until I found out that you can't split an infinitive; "to" has nothing to do with the infinitive anyway.

I want to abolish the terms Subject, Predicate, Object, Extension, Noun, Verb, &c. I fancy we could get along very well without them. Difficulties might arise in learning a foreign tongue. I don't know anything about foreign tongues; all I know is the Greek alphabet and a line of Homer, and the fact that all Gaul is divided into three parts. Yet I imagine that one could learn French or German as a child learns a language.

Good speaking and writing mean the correct use of idiom, and idiom is the best phrasing of the best people—best according to our standards at the present time.

I have heard Parsing and Analysis defended on the ground of their being an exercise in reasoning. I admit that they do require reasoning, but I hold that the time would be better spent in Mathematics. I hope to take my senior pupils through the first and third books of Euclid this summer. Personally, I can find much pleasure in a stiff deduction, but I find nothing but intense weariness in an analysis of sentences. My theories on education are purely personal; if *I* don't like a thing I presume that my bairns dislike it. And the strange thing is that my presumptions are nearly always right.

* * *

Folklore fascinates me. I find that the children of Forfarshire and Dumfriesshire have the same ring song, *The Wind and the Wind and the Wind Blows High.* I once discovered in the British Museum a book on English Folksongs, and in it I found the same song obtaining in Staffordshire. Naturally, variations occur. Did these songs all spring from a common stock? Or did incomers bring them to a district?

When I am sacked....and I half expect to be some day soon....I shall wander round the schools of Scotland collecting the folk-songs. I shall take a Punch and Judy show with me, for I know that this is a long felt want in the country. That reminds me:—a broken-down fellow came to me to-day and told pathetically how he had lost his school ....“wrongous dismissal” he called it. I wept and gave him sixpence. To-night I visited the minister. “I had a sad case in to-day,” he began, “a poor fellow who had a kirk in Ross-shire. Poor chap, his wife took to drink, and he lost his kirk.”

“Chap with a reddish moustache?” I asked.

“Yes, did you see him?”

I ignored the question.

“Charity,” I said, “is foolish. I don't believe in charity of that kind. You gave him something?”

“Er—a shilling.”

“You have too much heart,” I said, and I took my departure.

If I have to go on tramp I shall try to live by selling sermons after school-hours.

VIII.

TO-DAY I discussed the Women's Movement with my class. They were all agreed that women should not have votes. I asked for reasons.

"They can't fight like men," said a boy.

I pointed out that they risk their lives more than men do. A woman risks her life so that life may come into the world; a soldier risks his life so that death may come into the world.

"Women speak too much," said Margaret Steel.

"Read the Parliamentary debates," said I.

"Women have not the brains," said a boy.

I made no reply, I lifted his last exam. paper, and showed the class his 21 per cent, then I showed him Violet Brown's 93 per cent. But I was careful to add that the illustration was not conclusive.

I went on to tell them that the vote was

of little use to men, and that I did not consider it worth striving for. But I tried to show them that the Women's Movement was a much bigger thing than a fight for political power. It was a protest against the system that made sons doctors and ministers, and daughters typists and shopgirls, that made girls black their idle brothers' boots, that offered £60 to a lady teacher who was doing as good work as the man in the next room with his £130. I did not take them to the deeper topics of Marriage, Inheritance, the economic dependence of women on men that makes so many marry for a home. But I tried to show that owing to woman's being voteless the laws are on the man's side, and I instanced the Corporation Baths in the neighbouring city. There only one day a week is set aside for women. Then it struck me that perhaps the women of the city have municipal votes, and I suggested that if this were the case, women are less interested in cold water than men, a circumstance that goes to show that women have a greater need of freedom than I thought they had.

On the whole it was a disappointing discussion.

* * *

I went up to see Lawson of Rinsley School to-night. I talked away gaily about having scrapped my Readers and Rural Arithmetic. He was amused; I know that he considers me a cheerful idiot. But he grew serious when I talked about my Socialism.

"You blooming Socialists," he said, with a dry laugh, "are the most cocky people I have yet struck. You think you are the salt of the earth and that all the others are fatheads."

"Quite right, Lawson," I said with a laugh. And I added seriously: "You see, my boy, that if you have a theory, you've simply *got* to think the other fellow an idiot. I believe in Socialism—the Guild Socialism of *The New Age*, and naturally I think that Lloyd George and Bonar Law and the Cecils, and all that lot are hopelessly wrong."

"Do you mean to tell me that you are a greater thinker than Arthur James Balfour?" Lawson sat back in his chair and watched the effect of this shot.

I considered for a minute.

"It's like this," I said slowly, "you really cannot compare a duck with a rabbit. You can't say that Shakespeare is greater than Napoleon or Burns than Titian. Balfour is a good man in his own line, and—"

"And you?"

"I sometimes think of great things," I replied modestly. "Balfour has an ideal; he believes, as Lord Roberts believed, in the Public Schools, in Oxford and Cambridge, in the type of Englishman who becomes an Imperialist Cromer. He believes in the aristocracy, in land, in heredity of succession. His ideal, so far as I can make out, is to have an aristocracy that behaves kindly and charitably to a deserving working-class—which, after all, is Nietzsche's ideal.

I believe in few of these things. I detest charity of that kind; I hate the type of youth that our Public Schools and Oxfords turn out. I want to see the land belong to the people, I want to see every unit of the State working for the delight that work, as opposed to toil, can bring. The aristocracy has merits that I appreciate. Along with the poor they cheerfully die for their country.... it is the profiteering class with its " Business as Usual " cant that I want to slay. I want to see all the excellent material that exists in our aristocracy turned to nobler uses than bossing niggers in India so that millionaires at home may be multi-millionaires, than wasting time and wealth in the social rounds of London."

" Are you a greater thinker than Balfour? "

I sighed.

" I think I have a greater ideal," I said. " And," I added, " I am sure that if Balfour were asked about it he would reply: 'I wish I could have got out of my aristocratic environment at your age.' "

" Lawson," I continued, " I gathered tatties behind the digger once. That is the chief difference between me and Balfour. When first I went through Eton on a motor-bus and saw the boys on the playing grounds, I said to myself, 'Thank God I wasn't sent to Eton!' "

" Class prejudice and jealousy," said Lawson. " Will the Rangers get into the Final?"

* * *

I met Wilkie the mason, on the road to-night. He cannot write his name, and he is the richest man in the village.

"What's this Aw hear aboot you bein' ane o' they Socialists?" he demanded. "Aw didna ken that when Aw voted for ye."

"If you had?"

"Not a vote wud ye hae gotten frae me. Ye'll be layin' yer bombs a' ower the place," he said half jocularly.

"Ye manna put ony o' they ideas in the bairns' heids," he continued anxiously. "Politics have no place in a schule."

I did not pursue the subject; I side-tracked him on to turnips, and by using what I had picked up from Andrew Smith I made a fairly good effort. When we parted Wilkie grasped my hand.

"Ye're no dozzent," he said kindly, "but, tak ma advice, and leave they politics alone. It's a dangerous game for a schulemester to play."

* * *

I find that I am becoming obsessed by my creed. I see that I place politics before everything else in education. But I feel that I am doing the best I can for true education After all it isn't Socialism I am teaching, it is heresy. I am trying to form minds that will question and destroy and rebuild.

Morris's *News from Nowhere* appeals to me most as a Utopia. Like him I want to see an artistic world.

I travelled to Newcastle on Saturday, and the brick squalor that stretches for miles out Elswick and Blaydon way sickened me. Dirty bairns were playing on muddy patches, dirty women were gossiping at doors, miners were wandering off in twos and threes with whippets at their heels. And smoke was over all. Britain is the workshop of the world. Good old Merrie England!

These are strange entries for a Dominie's Log. I must bring my mind back to Vulgar Fractions and Composition.

* * *

There was a Cinema Show in the village hall to-night. My bairns turned out in force. Most of the pictures were drivel . . . . the typist wrongly accused, the seducing employer; the weeping parents at home. The average cinema plot is of the same brand as the plots in a washerwoman's weekly. Then we had the inevitable Indian chase on horseback, and the hero pardoned after the rope was round his neck.

I enjoyed the comic films. To see the comic go down in diver's dress to wreck a German submarine was delightfully ludicrous. He took off his helmet under water and wiped the sweat from his brow. Excellent fun!

I have often thought about the cinema as an aid to education. At the present time it is a drag on education, for its chief attraction is its piffling melodrama. Yet I have seen good plays and playlets filmed....that is good melodramatic and incident plays.

I have seen *Hamlet* filmed, and then I understood what Tolstoi (or was it Shaw?) meant when he said that Shakespeare without his word music is nowhere. Yet I must be just; philosophy had to go along with music when the cinema took up *Hamlet.*

The cinema may have a future as an educational force, but it will deal with what I consider the subsidiary part of education—the facts of life. Pictures of foreign countries are undoubtedly of great use. The cinema can never give us theories and philosophy. So with its lighter side. *Charley's Aunt* might make a good film; *The Importance of Being Earnest* could not. The cinema can give us humour but not wit. What will happen when the cinema and the phonograph are made to work together perfectly I do not know. I may yet be able to take my bairns to a performance of *Nan* or *The Wild Duck* or *The Doctor's Dilemma.*

* * *

" Please, sir, Willie Smith was swearing." Thus little Maggie Shepherd to me to-day.

I always fear this complaint, for what can I do ? I can't very well ask Maggie what he said, and if he says he wasn't swearing.. well, his word is as good as Maggie's. I can summon witnesses, but bairns have but the haziest notion of what swearing is. (For that matter so do I.) If a boy shoves his fingers to his nose...." Please, sir, he swore ! "

I try to be a just man, and....well, I was bunkered at the ninth hole on Saturday, and I dismissed Willie Smith—without an admonition. But I am worried to-night, for I can't recollect whether Willie has ever caddied for me ; I have a shrewd suspicion that he has.

IX.

THE word "republican" came up today in a lesson, and I asked what it meant. Four girls told me that their fathers were republicans, but they had no idea of the meaning of the word. One lassie thought that it meant "a man who is always quarrelling with the Tories"....a fairly penetrating definition.

I explained the meaning of the word, and said that a republican in this country was wasting his time and energy. I pointed to America with its Oil Kings, Steel Kings, Meat Kings, and called it a country worse than Russia. I told of the corruption of politics in France.

Then I rambled on to Kings and Kingship. It is a difficult subject to tackle even with children, but I tried to walk warily. I said that the notion of a king was for people in an elementary stage of development. Intellectual folk have no use for all the pomp and pageantry of kingship. Royalty as it exists to-day is bad for us and for the royal family. The poor princes and princesses are reared in an atmosphere of make-believe. Their individuality and their loves are crushed by a system. And it is really a system of lies. "In the King's name!" Why make all this pretence when everyone knows that it is "In the Cabinet's name"? It is not fair to the king.

I am no republican; I do not want to see monarchy abolished in this land. I recognise that monarchy is necessary to the masses. But I want to bring my bairns to see monarchy stripped of its robes, its pageantry, its remoteness, its circumstance. Loyalty is a name to most of us. People sing the National Anthem in very much the same way as they say Grace before Meat. The Grace-sayer is thinking of his dinner; the singer is wondering if he'll manage to get out in time to collar a taxi.

I do not blame the kings; I blame their advisers. We are kept in the dark by them. We hear of a monarch's good deeds, but we never hear the truth about him. The unwritten law demands that the truth shall be kept secret until a few generations have passed. I know nothing about the king. I don't know what he thinks of Republicanism (in his shoes I should be a red-hot Republican), Socialism, Religion, Morals; and I want to know whether he likes Locke's novels or Galsworthy's drama. In short, I want to know the man that must of necessity be greater than the king. I am tired of processions and functions.

I became a loyalist when first I went to Windsor Castle. Three massed bands were playing in the quadrangle; thousands of visitors wandered around. The King came to the window and bowed. I wanted to go up and take him by the arm and say: "Poor King, you are not allowed to enjoy the sensation of being in a crowd, you are an abstraction, you are behind a barrier of nobility through which no commoner can pass. Come down and have a smoke with me amongst all these typists and clerks." And I expect that every man and woman in that crowd was thinking: "How nice it must be to be a king!"

Yet if a king were to come down from the pedestal on which the courtiers have placed him, I fear that the people would scorn him. They would cry: "He is only a man!" I am forced to the conclusion that pomp and circumstance are necessary after all. The people are to blame. The King is all right; he looks a decent, kindly soul with a good heart. But the people are not interested in good hearts; the fools want gilt coaches and crimson carpets and all the rubbish of show.

* * *

A lady asked me to-day whether I taught my children manners. I told her that I did not. She asked why. I replied that manners were sham, and my chief duty was to get rid of sham. Then she asked me why I lifted my hat to her....and naturally I collapsed incontinently. Once again I write the words, "It is a difficult thing to be a theorist....and an honest man at the same time."

On reflection I think that it is a case of personality *versus* the whole community. No man can be consistent. Were I to carry my convictions to their natural conclusion I should be an outcast....and an outcast is of no value to the community. I lift my hat to a lady not because I respect her

(I occasionally do. I always doff my hat to the school charwoman, but I am rather afraid of her), but because it is not worth while to protest against the little things of life. Incidentally, the whole case against hat-lifting is this :—In the lower and lower middle classes the son does not lift his hat to his mother though he does to the minister's wife.

No, I do not teach manners. If a boy " Sirs " me, he does it of his own free will. I believe that you cannot teach manners; taught manners are always forced, always overdone. My model of a true gentleman is a man with an innate good taste and artistry. My idea of a lady....well, one of the truest ladies I have yet known kept a dairy in the Canongate of Edinburgh.

I try to get my bairns to do to others as they would like others to do to them. Shaw says " No: their tastes may not be the same as yours." Good old G. B. S.!

I once was in a school where manners were taught religiously. I whacked a boy one day. He said, " Thank you, sir."

* * *

I wonder how much influence on observation the so-called Nature Study has. At one time I attended a Saturday class. We went botanising. I learned nothing about Botany, but that was because Margaret was there. I observed much....her eyes were grey and her eyelashes long. We generally managed to lose the class in less than no time. Yet we did pretend. She was pretending to show me the something or other marks on a horse-chestnut twig when I first kissed her. She is married now. I don't believe in Saturday excursions.

I got up my scanty Nature Study from Grant Allen's little shilling book on plants. It was a delightful book full of an almost Yankee imagination. It theorised all the way....grass developed a long narrow blade so that it might edge its way to the sun; wild tobacco has a broad blade because it doesn't need to care tuppence for the competition of other plants, it can grow on wet clay of railway bankings. I think now that Grant Allen was a romancer not a scientist.

I do not see the point in asking bairns to count the stamens of a buttercup (Dr. Johnson hated the poets who "count the streaks of the tulip"). But I do want to make them Grant Allens; I want them to make a theory. Nature Study has but little result unless bairns get a lead. No boy will guess that the lines on a petal are intended to lead bees to the honey; at least, I know I would never have guessed it. I should never have guessed that flowers are beautiful or perfumed in order to attract insects. But I am really no criterion. I could not tell at this moment the colour of my bedroom wall-paper; I can't tell whether my father wears a moustache or side-whiskers. Until I began to teach Woodwork I never observed a mortise, or if I did, I never wondered how it was made. I never noticed that the tops of houses sloped downward until I took up Perspective.

Anyway, observation is a poor attainment unless it is combined with genius as in Darwin's case. Sherlock Holmes is a nobody. Observation should follow fancy. The average youth has successive hobbies. He takes up photography, and is led (sometimes) to enquire into the action of silver salts; he takes up wood-carving, and begins to find untold discoveries in the easy-chair.

I would advocate the keeping of animals

at school. I would have a rabbit run, a pigeon loft, one or two dogs, and a few cats for the girls. Let a boy keep homers and fly them, and he will observe much. Apart from the observation side of the question I would advocate a live stock school-farm on humanitarian grounds; every child would acquire a sense of duty to animals. I am sure all my bairns would turn out on a Sunday to feed their pets. And what a delightful reward for kindness....make a boy or girl "Feeder-in-Chief" for the week! Incidentally, the study of pigeons and rabbits would conduce to a frank realisation of sex.

* * *

I have just bought the new shilling edition of H. G. Wells's *New Worlds for Old*, and I have come upon this passage...." ....Socialists turn to the most creative profession of all, to that great calling which, with each generation, renews the world's 'circle of ideas,' the Teachers!"

But why he puts the mark of exclamation at the end I do not know.

On the same page he says: "The constructive Socialist logically declares the teacher master of the situation."

If the Teachers are masters of the situation I wish every teacher in Scotland would get *The New Age* each week. Orage's *Notes of the Week* are easily the best commentary on the war I have seen. *The New Age* is so very amusing, too ; its band of " warm young men " are the kind who " can't stand Nietzsche because of his damnable philanthropy " as a journalist friend of mine once phrased it. They despise Shaw and Wells and Webb.... the old back-numbers. The magazine is pulsating with life and youth. Every contributor is so cock-sure of himself. It is the only fearless journal I know ; it has no advertisements, and with advertisements a journal is muzzled.

* * *

One or two bairns are going to try the bursary competition of the neighbouring Secondary School, and I have just got hold of the last year's papers.

" Name an important event in British History for each of any eight of the following years :—1314, 1688, 1759, &c."....and Wells says that teaching is the most creative profession of all !

" Write an essay of twenty lines or so on

any one of these subjects :—School, Holidays, Examinations, Bursaries, Books." The examiners might have added a few other bright interesting topics such as Truth, Morals, Faith, Courage.

"Name the poem to which each of the following lines belongs, and add, if you can, the next line in each case, &c." There are ten lines, and I can only spot six of them. And I am, theoretically, an English scholar ; I took an Honours English Degree under Saintsbury. But my degree is only a second class one ; that no doubt accounts for my lack of knowledge.

That the compilers of the paper are not fools is shown by the fact that they ask a question like this :—" A man loses a dog, you find it ; write and tell him that you have found it."

The Arithmetic paper is quite good. My bairns are to fail ; I simply cannot teach them to answer papers like these.

X.

I TRIED an experiment to-day. I gave an exam. in History, and each pupil was allowed to use a text-book. The best one was first, she knew what to select. I deprecate the usual exam. system of allotting a prescribed time to each paper. Blyth Webster, the racy young lecturer in English in Edinburgh University, used to allow us an indefinite time for our Old English papers. I generally required a half hour to give him all I knew about Old English, but I believe that some students sat for five hours. Students write and think at different rates, and the time limit is always unjust.

I wish the Department would allow me to set the Higher Grade Leavings English papers for once. My paper would certainly include the following :—

"If Shakespeare came back to earth what do you think would be his opinion of Women's Suffrage (refer to *The Taming of the Shrew*) Home Rule, Sweated Labour, the Kaiser ? "

" Have you read any Utopia ? If not, it doesn't matter ; write one of your own. (Note. . . . a Utopia is an ideal country—this side the grave.)

" Discuss Spenser's idea of chivalry, and state what you think would be his opinion on table manners, Soho, or any slum you know, " the Present State of Ireland."

" What would Burns have thought of the prevalence of the kilt among the Semitic inhabitants of Scotland ? Is Burns greater than Harry Lauder ? Tell me why you think he isn't or is."

" Discuss the following humorists and alleged humorists :—Dickens, Jacobs, Lauder, Jerome, Leacock, Storer Clouston, Wells (in *Kipps*, and *Mr. Polly*), Locke (in *Septimus*), Bennett (in *The Card*), Mark Twain, your class teacher, the average magistrate."

" If you have not read any humour at all, write a humorous dialogue between a brick and the mongrel dog it came in contact with."

I hold that my exam. paper would discover any genius knocking about in ignorance of his or her powers. I intend to offer it to the Department....when I am out of the profession.

* * *

It is extremely difficult for any teacher to keep from getting into a rut. The continual effort to make things simple and elementary for children is apt to deaden the intellect.

To-night I felt dull; I simply couldn't think. So I took up a volume of Nietzsche, and I now know the remedy for dullness. Nietzsche is a genius; he dazzles one....and he almost persuades. To-night I am doubting. Is my belief in a great democracy all wrong? Is it true that there is a slave class that can never be anything else? Is our Christian morality a slave morality which is evolving the wrong type of human?

I think of the pity and kindness which is making us keep alive the lunatic and the incurable; I am persuaded to believe that our hospitals are in the long run conducing to an unfit race. Unfit physically; but unfit mentally? Is Sandow the Superman? Will Nietzsche's type of Master man with his physical energy and warlikeness prove to be the best?

I think that the journalists who are anathematising Nietzsche are wrong ; I don't believe the Kaiser ever read a line of his. But I think that every German is subconsciously a believer in energy and " Master Morality " ; Nietzsche was merely one who realised his nature. The German religion is undoubtedly the religion of the Old Testament ; to them " good " is all that pertains to power ; their God is the tyrant of the Old Testament. Nietzsche holds that the New Testament code of morals was invented by a conquered race ; the poor were meek and servile, and they looked forward to a time when they would be in glory while the rich man frizzled down below.

No man can scorn Nietzsche; you are forced to listen to him. Only fools can dismiss him with the epithet " Madman ! "

But I cannot follow him ; I believe that if pity and kindness are wrong, then wrong is right. Yet I see that Nietzsche is wise in saying that there must always be one stone at the top of the pyramid. The question is this :—Will a democracy always be sure to choose the right man ? I wonder.

I found one arresting statement in the

book:—" If we have a degenerate mean environment, the fittest will be the man who is best adapted to degeneracy and meanness; he will survive." That is what is happening now. I believe that the people will one day be capable of altering this basis of society; Nietzsche believed that the people are mostly of the slave variety, and that a better state of affairs could only come about through the breeding of Supermen....masters. " The best shall rule," says he. Who are the best? I ask, and I really cannot answer myself.

* * *

As I go forward with these notes I find that I become more and more impelled to write down thoughts that can only have a remote connection with the education of children. I think the explanation lies in the fact that every day I realise more and more the futility of my school-work. Indeed, I find myself losing interest sometimes; I go through a lesson on Geography mechanically; in short, I drudge occasionally. But I always awake at Composition time.

I find it useless to do home correction; a bairn won't read the blue pencil marks. I must sit down beside him while I correct;

and this takes too much time....from a time-table point of view.

But the mistakes in spelling and grammar are minor matters, what I look for are ideas. I never set a dull subject of the How-I-spent-my-holidays type ; every essay must appeal to the imagination. " Suppose you go to sleep for a thousand years," I said, " and tell the story of your awaking." I asked my Qualifying to become invisible ; most of them took to thieving and spying. I gave them Wells's *The Invisible Man* and *When the Sleeper Wakes* to read later.

" Go to Mrs. Rabbit's Garden Party, and describe it." One boy went as a wolf, and returned with the party inside. A girl went as a weasel and left early because she could not eat the lettuce and cabbage on the table. One boy went as an elephant and could not get in.

" Write a child of seven's account of washing day," I said to my Qualifying, and I got some delightful baby-talk from Margaret Steel and Violet Brown.

" Imagine that you are the last man left alive on earth." This essay produced some good work ; most of the girls were concerned about the fact that there was no one to bury them when they died.

The best results of all came from this subject:—"Die at the age of ninety, and write the paragraph about yourself to the local paper." Most of them made the present minister make a few pious remarks from the pulpit; one girl was clever enough to name a strange minister.

A newspaper correspondence interests a class. "Make a Mr. James Smith write a letter to *The Scotsman* saying that he saw a cow smoking a cigar one night; then write the replies." One boy made a William Thomson suggest that a man must have been standing beside the cow in the darkness. Smith replied that this was impossible, for any man standing beside a cow would be a farmer or a cattleman, and "neither of them can afford to smoke cigars."

* * *

I notice that many School Boards insist on having Trained Teachers. Is it possible to "train" a teacher? Are teachers not born like poets? I think they are. I have seen untrained teachers at work, and I have seen trained teachers; I never observed a scrap of difference. All I would say to a young teacher is: "Ask questions. Ask why there is a fence round the field, ask why there is a fence round that tree in the field, then ask whether any plant or tree has a natural fence of its own."

And I think I should say this: "A good teacher will begin a lesson on Cromwell, touch, in passing, Jack Johnson, Charlie Chaplin, Votes for Women, guinea pigs, ghosts, and finish up with an enquiry into Protective Coloration of Animals."

The Code seems to be founded on the assumption that the teachers of Scotland don't know their business. Why specify that Nature Study will be taught? Any good teacher will refer to Nature every five minutes of the day. To me teaching is a ramble through every subject the teacher knows.

No, I don't think a teacher can be trained, but I am prejudiced; I took the Acting Teachers' Certificate Exam....and passed Third Class. In the King's Scholarship I was ninety-ninth in the list of a hundred and one. Luckily, the Acting Teachers' list was given in alphabetical order.

I had a friend at the university, Anderson

was his name, a medical. He had passed in Physics, and naturally his name was near the beginning of the list. His local paper had it "A Brilliant Student." Anderson got through at the ninth shot.

* * *

To-day I talked about crime and punishment. I told my bairns that a criminal cannot help himself; heredity and environment make a man good or bad. I spoke of the environment that makes millions of children diseased morally and physically, and of the law that punishes a man for the sins of the community. I told them that there should be no prisons; if a man is a murderer he is not responsible for his actions, and he must be confined....but not in prison.

Our present system is not justice; it is vengeance. I once saw a poor waif sent to prison for stealing a pair of boots, sent to the care of warders, sent to acquire a hatred of his fellowmen. Justice would have asked: "Why did he steal? Why had he no boots? What sort of life has he been forced to lead?" and I know that the waif would have been acquitted.

I told my bairns that to cure any evil you must get at the root of it, and I incidentally pointed to the Insurance Act, and said that it was like treating a man with a suppurating appendix for the headache that was one of the symptoms. I told them that their fathers have not tried to get at the root of evil, that their prisons and cats and oakum are cowardly expedients. The evil is that the great majority of people are poor slaves, while the minority live on their earnings. That isn't politics; it is truth. I told them that if I had been born in the Cowgate of Edinburgh I should have been a thief and a drunkard.... and society would have added to my curse of heredity and environment the pains and brutishness of a prison. And yet men accuse me of attaching too much importance to material reforms.

* * *

I have not used the strap for many weeks now. I hope that I shall never use it again. I found a boy smoking a cigarette to-day. Four years ago I should have run him into the school and welted him. To-day I spoke to him. "Joseph," I said, "I smoke myself, and at your age I smoked an occasional Woodbine. But it isn't really good for a boy, and I hope you won't get into the habit of buying cigs. with your pocket money." He smiled and told me that he didn't really like it; he just smoked for fun. And he tossed the cigarette over a wall.

A very clever friend of mine talks about the "Hamlet cramp." I've got it. Other men have a definite standard of right and wrong; I have none. The only original sin that I believe in is the cruelty that has come to man from the remote tree-dweller.

XI.

A VILLAGER stopped me on my way to school this morning. " Look at that," he cried, pointing to a broken branch on a tree in his garden, " that's what comes o' yer nae discipline ideas. That's ane o' yer laddies that put his kite into ma gairden. Dawm it, A'll no stand that ! Ye'll jest go doon to the school and gie that boy the biggest leathering that he's ever had in his life."

I explained patiently that I was not the village constable, and I told him that the broken branch had nothing to do with me. He became angry, but he became speechless when I said, " I sympathise with you. Had it been my garden I should have sworn possibly harder than you have done. On the other hand, had it been twenty years ago and my kite, well, I should have done exactly what the boy did. Good morning."

Although it was no concern of mine I called the boy out, and advised him to try to think of other people. Then I addressed the bairns. "You might convey to your parents," I said, "that I am not the policeman in this village; I'm a schoolmaster."

I think that many parents are annoyed at my giving up punishment. They feel that I am not doing their work for them; they think that the dominie should do the training of children....other people's children, not their own. I find that I am trying to do a very difficult thing. The home influence is bad in many cases; the children hear their parents slight the teacher, and they do not know what to think. The average parent looks upon the teacher as an enemy. If I hit a boy the parents side with him, if I don't hit the boy who hit their boy, they indignantly ask what education is coming to. Many a night I feel disheartened. I find that I am on the side of the bairns. I am against law and discipline; I am all for freedom of action.

* * *

At last I have attained my ambition. As a boy my great ambition was to possess a cavalry trumpet and bugle. I have just bought both. I call the bairns to school with "Stables" or the "Fall In," and I gleefully look forward to playtime so that I may have another tootle. The bairns love to hear the calls, but I think I enjoy them most.

I try hard to share the bairns' joys. At present I am out with them every day flying kites, and I never tire of this. The boys bring me their comic papers, but I find that I cannot laugh at them as I used to do. Yet, I like to see *Chips;* Weary Willie and Tired Tim are still figuring on the front page, but their pristine glory is gone. When I first knew them they were the creation of Tom Browne, and no artist can follow Tom in his own line.

I miss the old "bloods"; I used to glory in the exploits of Frank Reade and Deadwood Dick. I have sat on a Sunday with *Deadwood Dick* in the covers of a family Bible, and my old grandmother patted my head and told me I was a promising lad.

Then there was Buffalo Bill—tuppence coloured; I never see his name now. I wonder why so many parents and teachers cuff boys' heads when they find them reading comic papers and "bloods." I see no harm in either. I wish that people would get out of the absurd habit of taking it for granted that whatever a boy does is wrong. I hold that a boy is nearly always right.

I see in to-day's *Scotsman* that a Sheriff substitute in Edinburgh has sentenced two brothers of nine and ten to twelve stripes with the birch rod for stealing tuppence ha'penny. The account remarked that the brothers had previously had a few stripes for a similar theft. That punishment is no prevention is proved in this case.

The Sheriff Substitute must have a very definite idea of righteousness ; I envy him his conscience free from all remembrance of shortcomings in the past. For my part had I been sitting in judgment on the poor laddies I should have recollected the various times I have travelled first with a third ticket, sneaked into circuses by lifting the tent cover, laid farthings on the railway so that they might become ha'pennies, or, with a special piece of luck—a goods train—pennies. Then I should have invited the boys to tea, and sent them home with *Comic Cuts*, two oranges, and a considerable bit of chewing gum. Anyhow, my method would have brought out any good in the boys. The method of the judge will bring out no good; it may make the boys feel that they are enemies of society. And I should like to ask the gentleman what he would do if his young son stole the jam. I'm sure he would not send for the birch rod. The damnable thing about the whole affair is that he is probably a very nice kindly man who would not whip a dog with his own hand. His misfortune is his being part of a system.

* * *

I have just added a few volumes to my school library. I tried to recollect the books that I liked as a youth; then I wrote for catalogues of "sevenpennies." The new books include these:—*The Prisoner of Zenda* and its sequel, *Rupert of Hentzau, King Solomon's Mines, Montezuma's Daughter, The Four Feathers, A Gentleman of France, White Fang, The Call of the Wild, The Invisible Man, The War of the Worlds, The War in the Air, Dr. Nikola, A Bid for Fortune, Micah Clarke.* I find that the average bairn of thirteen cannot appreciate these stories. Margaret Steel was the only one who read *The Scarlet Pimpernel* and asked for the sequel. Most of them stuck half way with *Zenda*. Guy Boothby's novels, the worst of the lot possibly, appealed to them strongly. The love element bores the boys, but the girls rather like it. One boy sat and yawned over *King Solomon's Mines;* then he took out a coloured comic and turned to the serial. I took the book away and told him to read the serial. Violet Brown prefers a book about giants from the infant room to all the romantic stories extant. After all, they are but children.

* * *

I am delighted with my sketching results. We go out every Wednesday and Friday afternoon, and many bairns are giving me good work. We usually end up with races or wading in the sea. There was much wonder when first they saw my bare feet, but now they take my feet for granted.

Modesty is strong here. The other day the big girls came to me and asked if they could come to school slipshod.

"You can come in your nighties for all I care," I said, and they gasped.

We sit outside all day now. My classes take books and wander away down the road and lie on the banks. When I want them I call with the bugle. Each class has a "regimental call," and they come promptly. They most of them sit down separately, but the chatterers like to sit together.

I force no bairn to learn in my school. The few who dislike books and lessons sit up when I talk to the class. The slackers are not always the most ignorant.

I am beginning to compliment myself on having a good temper. For the past six weeks I have left the manual room open at playtime and the boys have made many toys. But they have made a woeful mess of the cutting tools. It is trying to find that your favourite plane has been cracked by a boy who has extreme theories on the fixing of plane irons. But it is very comforting to know that the School Board will have to pay for the damage. Yes, my temper is excellent.

* * *

On Saturday I went to a Bazaar, and various members of the aristocracy talked to me. They talked very much in the manner they talk to their gardeners, and I was led to muse upon the social status of a dominie. What struck me most was the fact that they imitate royalty in the broaching of topics of conversation; I knew that I presumed when I entered new ground of conversation. The ladies were very polite and very regal, and very well pleased with themselves. One of them said: "I hope that you do your best to make these children realise that there are classes in society; so many of their parents refuse to see the good in other classes!"

"For my part," I answered, "I acknowledge one aristocracy—the aristocracy of intellect. I teach my children to have respect for thinking." She stared at me, and went away.

I am not prejudiced against the county people, but any superiority of manner annoys me. I simply have no use for ladies who live drifting lives. The lady-bountifuls, or should it be the ladies-bountiful? of Britain would be much better as typists; in these days of alleged scarcity of labour they might come down and mix with the lower orders. Their grace and breeding would do much to improve us, and we might be able to help them in some ways. I am not being cynical, I have a genuine admiration for the breeding and beauty of some society women.

The doctor and the minister are seldom patronised. I cannot for the life of me see why it is more lowly to cure a child of ignorance than measles.

I have heard it said that the real reason of the teacher's low social status is the fact that very often he is the son of a humble labourer. There is some truth in this. At the Training College and the University the student meets men of his own class only; he never learns the little tricks of deportment that make up society's criterion of a gentleman. But for my part I blame the circumstances under which a dominie works. In Scotland he is the servant of a School Board, and a School Board is generally composed of men who have but the haziest notion of the meaning of education. That is bad enough, but very often there is a feud between one or two members and the teacher. Perhaps the teacher does not get his coals from Mr. Brown the Chairman, perhaps Mr. Brown voted for another man when the appointment was made. It is difficult for a man who is ruled by a few low-idealed semi-illiterate farmers and pig-dealers to emphasise his social position.

Larger areas have been spoken of by politicians. Personally, I don't want larger areas;

I want to see the profession run by the members, just as Law and Medicine are. It is significant that the medical profession has dropped considerably in the social scale since it allowed itself to work under the Insurance Act.

My ideal is an Education Guild which will replace the Scotch Education Department. It will draw up its own scheme of instruction, fix the salaries of its members, appoint its own inspectors, build its own schools. It will be directly responsible to the State which will remain the supreme authority.

I blame the teachers for their low social status. To-day they have no idea of corporate action. They pay their subscriptions to their Institute, and for the most part talk of stopping them on the ground that it is money wasted. The authorities of the Institute try to work for a better union, but they try clumsily and stodgily. They never write or talk forcibly; they resemble the Labour Members of Parliament in their having an eager desire to be respectable at any price. I don't know why it is, but when a professional man tries to put his thoughts on paper he almost always succeeds in saying nothing in many fine phrases.

What is really wrong with the Educational Institute of Scotland is hoary-headedness. It is run by old men and old wives. A big man in the Institute is usually a teacher with thirty years' experience as a headmaster. Well....if a man can teach under the present system for thirty years and retain any originality or imagination at the end of that time he must be a genius.

I object to age and experience; I am all for youth and empiricism. After all, what is the use of experience in teaching? I could bet my boots that ninety-nine out of a hundred teachers use the methods they learned as pupil-teachers. Experience! I have heard dominies expatiate on innovations like Kindergarten and Blackboard Drawing. I still have to meet a dominie of experience who has any name but "fad" for anything in education later than 1880.

I have never tried to define the word "fad." I should put it thus:—A fad is a half-formed idea that a sub-inspector has borrowed from a bad translation of a distinguished foreigner's treatise on Education, and handed on to a deferential dominie.

* * *

An inspector called to-day; a middle-aged kindly gentleman with a sharp eye. His chief interest in life was tables.

"How many pence in fifty-seven farthings?" he fired at my highest class. When he found that they had to divide mentally by four, he became annoyed.

"They ought to know their tables," he said to me.

"What tables?" I asked.

"O, they should learn up that; why I can tell you at once what sixty-nine farthings are."

I explained humbly that I couldn't, and should never acquire the skill.

I did not like his manner of talking *at* the teacher through the class. When an inspector says, "You ought to know this," the scholars glance at the teacher, for they are shrewd enough to see that the teacher is being condemned.

He fired his parting shot as he went out.

"You must learn not to talk in school," he said.

I am a peaceful man, and I hate a scene. I said nothing, but I shall do nothing. If he returns he will find no difference in the school.

The bairns did talk to each other when the inspector talked to me, but when he asked for attention he got it.

I am surprised to find that his visit does not worry me ; I have at last lost my fear of the terror of teaching—H.M.I.S.

XII.

I WENT "drumming" last night. I like the American word "drummer," it is so much more expressive than our "commercial traveller."

I made a series of postcards, and I went round the shops trying to place them. One man refused to take them up because the profits would not be large enough. As the profits work out at 41½ per cent I begin to wonder what he usually makes.

To-day I talked to the bairns about commerce, and I pointed out that much in commerce was thieving.

"This is commerce," I said: "Suppose I am a pig-dealer. I hear one day from a friend that pigs will rise in price in a few days. I at once set out on a tour of neighbouring farms, and by nightfall I have bought twenty pigs at the market price. Next morning pigs have doubled in price, and these farmers naturally want to shoot me. Why don't they shoot me?"

"They would be hanged," said Violet Brown.

"Because they would buy pigs in the same way if they had the chance," said Margaret Steel.

I went on to say that buying pigs like that is stealing, and I said that the successful business man is usually the man who is most unscrupulous.

I told them of the murderous system that allows a big firm to place a shop next door to a small merchant and undersell him till his business dies. It is all done under the name of competition, but of course there is no more competition about the affair than there is about the relationship between a wolf and a lamb.

I try very very hard to keep my bairns from low ideals. Some one, Oscar Wilde or Shaw, I think, says that love of money is the root of all good. That is the sort of paradox that isn't true, and not even funny. I see farmers growing rich on child labour: fifteen pence a day for spreading manure. I meet the poor little boys of thirteen and fourteen on the road, and the smile has gone from their faces; their bodies are bent and racked.

When I was thirteen I went to the potato-gathering at a farm. Even now, when I pass a field where potatoes are being lifted, the peculiar smell of potato earth brings back to me those ten days of misery. I seldom had time to straighten my back. I had but one thought all day: When will that sun get down to the west? My neighbour, Jock Tamson, always seemed fresh and cheerful, but, unfortunately, I did not discover the cause of his optimism until the last day.

"Foo are you feenished so quick, Jock?" I asked.

Jock winked and nodded his head in the direction of the farmer.

"Look!" he said, and he skilfully tramped a big potato into the earth with his right foot; then he surreptitiously happed it over with his left.

I have never forgiven Jock for being so tardy in spreading his gospel.

* * *

To-day I received from the Clerk the Report on my school.

"Discipline," it says, "which is kindly, might be firmer, especially in the Senior Division, so as to prevent a tendency to talk on the part of the pupils whenever opportunity occurs."

An earlier part runs thus: "The pupils in the Senior Division are intelligent and bright under oral examination, and make an exceedingly good appearance in the class subjects."

I scratch my head thoughtfully. If the inspector finds the bairns intelligent and bright, why does he want them to be silent in school? I cannot tell; I suspect that talking children annoy him. I fancy that stern disciplinarians are men who hate to be irritated.

"More attention, however, should be paid to neatness of method and penmanship in copybooks and jotters."

I wonder. I freely admit to myself that the jotters are not neat, but I want to know why they should be. I can beat most men at marring a page with hasty figures; on the other hand I can make a page look like copperplate if I want to. I find that my bairns do neat work on an examination paper.

The truth is that I am incapable of teaching neatness. My desk is a jumble; my sitting-room is generally littered with books and papers. Some men are born tidy: some have tidiness thrust upon them. I am of the latter crowd. Between the school charwoman and my landlady I live strenuously.

I object to my report. I hate to be the victim of a man I can't reply to, even when he says nice things. But the main objection I have to the report is this: the School Board gets not a single word of criticism. If I were not almost proud of my lack of neatness, I might argue that no man could be neat in an ugly school. It is always filthy because the ashed playground is undrained. Broken windows stand for months; the plaster of the ceiling came down months ago, and the lathes are still showing. The School Board does not worry; its avowed object is to keep down the rates at any price in meanness (some members are big ratepayers). The sanitary arrangements are a disgrace to a long-suffering nation. Nothing is done.

* * *

It would be a good plan to make teachers forward reports of inspectors' visits to the

Scotch Education Department. I should love to write one.

"Mr. Silas K. Beans, H.M.I.S., paid a visit to this school to-day, and he made quite a passable appearance before the pupils.

"It was perhaps unfortunate that Mr. Beans laboured under the delusion that Mrs. Hemans wrote *Come into the Garden, Maud*, but on the whole the subject was adequately treated.

"The geography lesson showed Mr. Beans at his best, but it might be advisable for him to consider whether the precise whereabouts of Seville possesses the importance in the scheme of things that he attributes to it. And it might be suggested that children of twelve find some difficulty in spelling Prsym—Prysem— Pryems——anyway, the name of the town that has kept the alleged comic weeklies alive during a trying period.

"The school staff would have liked Mr. Beans to have stayed long enough to discover that a few of the scholars possessed imagination, and it hoped that he will be able to make his visit longer than four hours next time.

"Mr. Beans's knowledge of dates is wonderful, and his parsing has all the glory of Early Victorian furniture."

XIII.

TO-NIGHT MacMurray invited me down to meet his former head, Simpson, a big man in the Educational Institute, and a likely President next year. Mac introduced me as " a chap with theories on education ; doesn't care a rap for inspectors and abominates discipline."

Simpson looked me over ; then he grunted.

" You'll grow out of that, young man," he said sagely.

I laughed.

" That's what I'm afraid of," I said, " I fear that the continual holding of my nose to the grindstone will destroy my perspective."

" You'll find that experience doesn't destroy perspective."

" Experience," I cried, " is, or at least, should be one of Oscar Wilde's Seven Deadly Virtues. The experienced man is the chap who funks doing a thing because he's had his fingers burnt. 'Tis experience that makes cowards of us all."

" Of course," said Simpson, " you're joking. It stands to reason that I, for instance, with a thirty-four years' experience of teaching know more about education than you do, if you don't mind my saying so."

" Man, I was teaching laddies before your father and mother met," he added.

" If you saw a lad and a lass making love would you arrange that he should sit near her ? "

" Good gracious, no ! " he cried. " What has that got to do with the subject."

" But why not give them chances to spoon? " I asked.

" Why not ? If a teacher encouraged that sort of thing, why, it might lead to anything ! "

" Exactly," I said, " experience tells you that you have to do all you can to preserve the morals of the bairns ? "

" I could give you instances— "

" I don't want them particularly," I interrupted. " My main point is that experience has made you a funk. Pass the baccy, Mac."

" Mean to tell me that's how you teach ? " cried Simpson. " How in all the world do you do for discipline ? "

"I do without it."

"My goodness! that's the limit! May I ask why you do without it?"

"It is a purely personal matter," I answered. "I don't want anyone to lay down definite rules for me, and I refuse to lay down definite rules of conduct for my bairns."

"But how in all the earth do you get any work done?"

"Work," I said, "is an over-rated thing, just as knowledge is overrated."

"Nonsense," said Simpson.

"All right," I remarked mildly, "if knowledge is so important, why is a university professor usually a talker of platitudes? Why is the average medallist at a university a man of tenth-rate ideas?"

"Then our Scotch education is all in vain?"

"Speaking generally, it is."

I think it was at this stage that Simpson began to doubt my sanity.

"Young man," he said severely, "some day you will realise that work and knowledge and discipline are of supreme importance. Look at the Germans!"

He waved his hand in the direction of the sideboard, and I looked round hastily.

"Look what Germany has done with work and knowledge and discipline!"

"Then why all this bother to crush a State that has all the virtues?" I asked diffidently.

"It isn't the discipline we are trying to crush; it is the militarism."

"Good!" I cried, "I'm glad to hear it. That's what I want to do in Scotland; I want to crush the militarism in our schools, and, as most teachers call their militarism discipline, I curse discipline."

"That's all rubbish, you know," he said shortly.

"No it isn't. If I leather a boy for making a mistake in a sum, I am no better than the Prussian officer who shoots a Belgian civilian for crossing the street. I am equally stupid and a bully."

"Then you allow carelessness to go unpunished?" he sneered.

"I do. You see I am a very careless devil myself. I'll swear that I left your garden gate open when I came in, Mac, and your hens will be all over the road."

Mac looked out at the window.

"They are!" he chuckled, and I laughed.

"You seem to think that slovenliness is a virtue," said Simpson with a faint smile.

"I don't, really, but I hold that it is a natural human quality."

"Are your pupils slovenly?" he asked.

"Lots of 'em are. You're born tidy or you aren't."

"When these boys go out to the workshop, what then? Will a joiner keep an apprentice who makes a slovenly job?"

"Ah!" I said, "you're talking about trade now. You evidently want our schools to turn out practical workmen. I don't. Mind you I'm quite willing to admit that a shoemaker who theorises about leather is a public nuisance. Neatness and skill are necessary in practical manufacture, but I refuse to reduce education to the level of cobbling or coffin-making. I don't care how slovenly a boy is if he thinks."

"If he is slovenly he won't think," said Simpson.

I smiled.

"I think you are wrong. Personally, I am a very lazy man; I have my library all over the floor as a rule. Yet, though I am lazy physically I am not lazy mentally. I hold that the really lazy teacher is your "ring the bell at nine sharp" man; he hustles so much that he hasn't time to think. If you work hard all day you never have time to think."

Simpson laughed.

"Man, I'd like to see your school!"

"Why not? Come up tomorrow morning," I said.

"First rate!" he cried, "I'll be there at nine."

"Better not," I said with a smile, "or you'll have to wait for ten minutes."

* * *

He arrived as I blew the "Fall in" on my bugle.

"You don't line them up and march them in?" he said.

"I used to, but I've given it up," I confessed. "To tell the truth I'm not enamoured of straight lines."

We entered my classroom. Simpson stood looking sternly at my chattering family while I marked the registers.

"I couldn't tolerate this row," he said.

"It isn't so noisy as your golf club on a Saturday night, is it?" He smiled slightly.

Jim Burnett came out to my desk and lifted *The Glasgow Herald,* then he went out to the playground humming *On the Mississippi.*

" What's the idea ? " asked Simpson.

" He's the only boy who is keen on the war news," I explained.

Then Margaret Steel came out.

" Please, sir, I took *The Four Feathers* home and my mother began to read them ; she thinks she'll finish them by Sunday. Is anybody reading *The Invisible Man ?* "

I gave her the book and she went out.

Then Tom Macintosh came out and asked for the Manual Room key ; he wanted to finish a boat he was making.

" Do you let them do as they like ? " asked Simpson.

" In the upper classes," I replied.

Soon all the Supplementary and Qualifying pupils had found a novel and had gone out to the roadside. I turned to give the other classes arithmetic.

Mary Wilson in the front seat held out a bag of sweets to me. I took one.

" Please, sir, would the gentleman like one, too ? "

Simpson took one with the air of a man on

holiday who doesn't care what sins he commits.

"I say," he whispered, "do you let them eat in school? There's a boy in the back seat eating nuts."

I fixed Ralph Ritchie with my eye.

"Ralph! If you throw any nutshells on that floor Mrs. Findlay will eat you."

"I'm putting them in my pooch," he said.

"Good! Write down this sum."

"What are the others doing?" asked Simpson after a time.

"Margaret Steel and Violet Brown are reading," I said promptly. "Annie Dixon is playing fivies on the sand, Jack White and Bob Tosh are most likely arguing about horses, but the other boys are reading, we'll go and see." And together we walked down the road.

Annie was playing fivies all right, but Jack and Bob weren't discussing horses; they were reading *Chips*.

"And the scamps haven't the decency to hide it when you appear!" cried Simpson.

"Haven't the fear," I corrected.

On the way back to the school he said: "It's all very pleasant and picnicy, but eating nuts and sweets in class!"

" Makes your right arm itch ? " I suggested pleasantly.

" It does," he said with a short laugh, " Man, do you never get irritated ? "

" Sometimes."

" Ah ! " He looked relieved. " So the system isn't perfect ? "

" Good heavens ! " I cried, " What do you think I am ? A saint from heaven ? You surely don't imagine that a man with nerves and a temperament is always able to enter into the moods of bairns ! I get ratty occasionally, but I generally blame myself." I sent a girl for my bugle and sounded the " Dismiss."

" What do you do now ? "

I pulled out my pipe and baccy.

" Have a fill," I said, " it's John Cotton."

* * *

To-night I have been thinking about Simpson. He is really a kindly man ; in the golf-house he is voted a good fellow. Yet MacMurray tells me that he is a very strict disciplinarian ; he saw him give a boy six scuds with the tawse one day for drawing a man's face on the inside cover of his drawing book. I suppose that Simpson considers that he is an eminently just man.

I think that the foundation of true justice is self-analysis. It is mental laziness that is at the root of the militarism in our schools. Simpson is as lazy mentally as the proverbial mother who cried: "See what Willie's doing and tell him he musn't." I wonder what he would have replied if the boy had said: "Why is it wrong to draw a man's face in a drawing book?" Very likely he would have given him another six for impertinence.

It is strange that our boasted democracy uses its power to set up bullies. The law bullies the poor and gives them the cat if they trespass; the police bully everyone who hasn't a clean collar; the dominie bullies the young; and the School Board bullies the dominie. Yet, in theory, the judge, the constable, the dominie, and the School Board are the servants of democracy. Heaven protect us from the bureaucratic Socialism of people like the Webbs! It is significant that Germany, the country of the super-official is the country of the super-bully.

Paradoxically, I, as a Socialist, believe that

the one thing that will save the people is individualism. No democracy can control a stupid teacher or a stupid judge. If our universities produce teachers who leather a boy for drawing a face, and judges who give boys the cat for stealing tuppence ha'penny, then our universities are all wrong. Or human nature is all wrong. If I admit the latter I must fall back on pessimism. But I don't admit it. Our cruel teachers and magistrates are good fellows in their clubs and homes; they are bad fellows in their schools and courts because they have never come to think, to examine themselves. In my Utopia self-examination will be the only examination that will matter.

H. G. Wells in *The New Machiavelli* talks of "Love and Fine Thinking" as the salvation of the world. I like the phrase, but I prefer the word Realisation. I want men like Simpson to realise that their arbitrary rules are unjust and cowardly and inhuman.

* * *

I saw a good fight to-night. At four o'clock I noticed a general move towards Murray's Corner, and I knew that blood was about to be shed. Moreover I knew that Jim Steel was to tackle the new boy Welsh, for I had seen Jim put his fist to his nose significantly in the afternoon.

I followed the crowd.

" I want to see fair play," I said.

Welsh kept shouting that he could " fecht the hale schule wi' wan hand tied ahent 'is back."

In this district school fights have an etiquette of their own One boy touches the other on the arm saying : " There's the dunt ! " The other returns the touch with the same remark. If he fails to return it he receives a harder dunt on the arm with the words, " And there's the coordly ! " If he fails to return that also he is accounted the loser, and the small boys throw divots at him.

Steel began in the usual way with his : " There's the dunt ! " Welsh promptly hit him in the teeth and knocked him down. The boys appealed to me.

" No," I said, " Welsh didn't know the rules. After this you should shake hands as you do in boxing."

Welsh never had a chance. He had no science ; he came on with his arms swinging in windmill fashion. Jim stepped aside and drove a straight left to the jaw, and before Welsh knew what was happening Jim landed him on the nose with his right. Welsh began to weep, and I stopped the fight. I told him that Steel had the advantage because I had taught my boys the value of a straight left, but that I would give him a few lessons with the gloves later on. Then I asked how the quarrel had arisen. As I had conjectured Steel and Welsh had no real quarrel. Welsh had cuffed little Geordie Burnett's ears, and Geordie had cried, "Ye wudna hit Jim Steel!" Welsh had no alternative but to reply: "Wud Aw no!" Straightway Geordie had run off to Steel saying: "Hi! Jim! Peter Welsh says he'll fecht ye!"

So far as I can remember all my own battles at school were arranged by disobliging little boys in this manner. If Jock Tamson said to me: "Bob Young cud aisy fecht ye and ca' yer nose up among yer hair!" I, as a man of honour, had to reply: "Aw'll try Bob Young ony day he likes!" And even if Bob were my bosom friend, I would have to face him at the brig at four o'clock.

I noticed that the girls were all on Steel's

side before the fight began, and obviously on Welsh's side when he was beaten, the bissoms!

XIV.

I GAVE a lecture in the village hall on Friday night, and many parents came out to hear what I had to say on the subject of *Children and their Parents.* After the lecture I invited questions.

" What wud ye hae a man do if his laddie wudna do what he was bidden ? " asked Brown the joiner.

" I would have the man think very seriously whether he had any right to give the order that was disobeyed. For instance, if you ordered your Jim to stop singing while you were reading, you would be taking an unfair advantage of your years and size. From what I know of Jim he would certainly stop singing if you asked him to do so as a favour."

" Aw dinna believe in askin' favours o' ma laddies," he said.

I smiled.

" Yet you ask them of other laddies. You don't collar Fred Thomson and shout :

'Post that letter at once!' You say very nicely: 'You might post that letter like a good laddie,' and Fred enjoys posting your letter more than posting a ton of letters for his own father."

The audience laughed, and Fred's father cried: "Goad! Ye're quite richt, dominie!"

"As a boy," I continued, "I hated being set to weed the garden, though I spent hours helping to weed the garden next door. A boy likes to grant favours."

"Aye," said Brown, "when there's a penny at the tail end o' them!"

"Yes," I said after the laughter had died, "but your Jim would rather have Mr. Thomson's penny than your sixpence. The real reason is that you boss your son, and nobody likes to be bossed."

"Believe me, ladies and gentlemen, I think that the father is the curse of the home. (Laughter.) The father never talks to his son as man to man. As a result a boy suppresses much of his nature, and if he is left alone with his father for five minutes he feels awkward, though not quite so awkward as the father does. You find among the lower animals that the father is of no importance; indeed, he is looked on as a danger. Have you ever seen a bitch flare up when the father comes too near her puppies? Female spiders, I am told, solve the problem of the father by eating him." (Great laughter.)

"What aboot the mothers?" said a voice, and the men cackled.

"Mothers are worse," I said. "Fathers usually imagine that they have a sense of justice, but mothers have absolutely no sense of justice. It is the mother who cries, 'Liz, ye lazy slut, run and clean your brother's boots, the poor laddie! Lod, I dinna ken what would happen to you, my poor laddie, if your mother wasna here to look after you.' You mothers make your girls work at nights and on Saturdays, and you allow your boys to play outside. That is most unjust. Your boys should clean their own boots and mend their own clothes. They should help in the washing of dishes and the sweeping of floors."

"Wud ye say that the mother is the curse o' the hame, too?" asked Brown.

"No," I said, "she is a necessity, and in spite of her lack of justice, she is nearer to the children than the father is. She is less aloof and less stern. You'll find that a boy will tell his mother much more than he will tell his father. Speaking generally, a stupid mother is more dangerous than a stupid father, but a mother of average intelligence is better for a child than a father of average intelligence.

"This is a problem that cannot be solved. The mother must remain with her children, and I cannot see how we are to chuck the father out of the house. As a matter of fact he is usually so henpecked that he is prevented from being too much of an evil to the bairns.

"The truth is that the parents of to-day are not fit to be parents, and the parents of the next generation will be no better. The mothers of the next generation are now in my school. They will leave at the age of fourteen—some of them will be exempted and leave at thirteen—and they will slave in the fields or the factory for five or six years. Then society will accept them as legitimate guardians of the morals and spiritual welfare of children. I say that this is a damnable system. A mother who has never learned to think has absolute control of a growing young mind, and an almost absolute control of a growing young body. She can beat her child; she can starve it. She can poison its mind with malice, just as she can poison its body with gin and bitters.

"What can we do? The home is the Englishman's castle! Anyway, in these days of high explosives, castles are out of date, and it is high time that the castle called home had some airing."

* * *

I cannot flatter myself that I made a single parent think on Friday night. Most of the villagers treated the affair as a huge joke.

I have just decided to hold an Evening School next winter. I see that the Code offers *The Life and Duties of a Citizen* as a subject. I shall have the lads and lasses of sixteen to nineteen in my classroom twice a week, and I guess I'll tell them things about citizenship they won't forget.

It occurs to me that married people are not easily persuaded to think. The village girl considers marriage the end of all things. She dons the bridal white, and at once she rises meteorically in the social scale. Yesterday she was Mag Broon, an outworker at

Millside; to-day she is Mrs. Smith with a house of her own.

Her mental horizon is widened. She can talk about anything now; the topic of child-birth can now be discussed openly with other married wives. Aggressiveness and mental arrogance follow naturally, and with these come a respect for church-going and an abhorrence of Atheism.

I refuse to believe those who prate about marriage as an emancipation for a woman. Marriage is a prison. It shuts a woman up within her four walls, and she hugs all her prejudices and hypocrisies to her bosom. The men who shout "Women's place is the home!" at Suffragette meetings are fools. The home isn't good enough for women.

A girl once said to me: "I always think that marriage makes a girl a 'has been.'"

What she meant was that marriage ended flirtation, poor innocent that she was! Yet her remark is true in a wider sense. The average married woman is a "has been" in thought, while not a few are "never wasers." Hence I have more hope of my evening school lasses than of their mothers. They have not become smug, nor have they concluded that they are past enlightenment. They are not too omniscient to resent the offering of new ideas.

A man's marriage makes no great change in his life. His wife replaces his mother in such matters as cooking and washing and "feeding the brute." He finds that he is allowed to spend less, and he has to keep elders' hours. But in essentials his life is unchanged. He still has his pint on a Saturday night, and his evening crack at the Brig. He has gained no additional authority, and he is extremely blessed of the gods if he has not lost part of the authority he had.

The revolution in his mental outfit comes later when he becomes a father. He thinks that his education is complete when the midwife whispers: "Hi, Jock, it's a lassie!" He immediately realises that he is a man of importance, a guide and preacher rolled into one; and he talks dictatorially to the dominie about education. Then he discovers that precept must be accompanied by example, and he aspires to be a deacon or an elder.

Now I want to get at Jock before the midwife gets at him. I don't care tuppence whether he is married or not....but he mustn't be a father.

* * *

To-day I began to read Mary Johnston's *By Order of the Company* to my bairns. I love the story, and I love the style. It reminds me of Malory's style; she has his trick of running on in a breathless string of "ands." When I think of style I am forced to recollect the stylists I had to read at the university. There was Sir Thomas Browne and his *Urn Burial.* What the devil is the use of people like Browne I don't know. He gives us word music and imagery I admit, but I don't want word music and imagery from prose, I want ideas or a story. I can't think of one idea I got from Browne or Fisher or Ruskin, or any of the stylists, yet I have found many ideas in translations of Nietzsche and Ibsen. Style is the curse of English literature.

When I read Mary Johnston I forget all about words. I vaguely realise that she is using the right words all the time, but the story is the thing. When I read Browne I fail to scrape together the faintest interest in burials; the organ music of his *Dead March* drowns everything else.

When a man writes too musically and ornately I always suspect him of having a paucity of ideas. If you have anything important to say you use plain language. The man who writes to the local paper complaining of "those itinerant denizens of the underworld yclept hawkers, who make the day hideous with raucous cries," is a pompous ass. Yet he is no worse than the average stylist in writing. I think it was G. K. Chesterton who said that a certain popular authoress said nothing because she believed in words. He might have applied the phrase to 90 per cent of English writers.

Poetry cannot be changed. Substitute a word for "felicity" in the line: "Absent thee from felicity awhile" and you destroy the poetry. But I hold that prose should be able to stand translation. The prose that cannot stand it is the empty stuff produced by our Ruskins and our Brownes. Empty barrels always have made the most sound.

* * *

There must be something in style after all. I had this note from a mother this morning.

"DEAR SIR,

Please change Jane's seat for she brings home more than belongs to her."

I refuse to comment on this work of art.

* * *

I must get a cornet. Eurhythmics with an artillery bugle is too much for my wind and my dignity. Just when the graceful bend is coming forward my wind gives out, and I make a vain attempt to whistle the rest. Perhaps a concertina would be better than a cornet. I tried Willie Hunter with his mouth-organ, but the attempt was stale and unprofitable, and incidentally flat. Then Tom Macintosh brought a comb to the school and offered to perform on it. After that I gave Eurhythmics a rest.

When the war is over I hope that the Government will retain Lloyd George as Minister of Munitions....for Schools. I haven't got a tenth of the munitions I should have; I want a player-piano, a gramophone, a cinematograph with comic films, a library with magazines and pictures. I want swings and see-saws in the playground, I want rabbits and white mice; I want instruments for a school brass and wood band.

I like building castles in Spain. The truth is that if the School Board would yield to my importunities and lay a few loads of gravel on the muddy patch commonly known as the playground I should almost die of surprise and joy. One learns to be content with small mercies when one is serving those ratepayers who control the rates.

XV.

MARGARET STEEL has left school, and to-morrow morning she goes off at five o'clock to the factory.

To-day Margaret is a bright-eyed, rosy-cheeked lassie; in three years she will be hollow-eyed and pale-faced. Never again will she know what it is to waken naturally after sleep; the factory syren will haunt her dreams always. She will rise at half-past four summer and winter; she will tramp the two mile road to the factory, and when six comes at night she will wearily tramp home again. Possibly she will marry a factory worker and continue working in the factory, for his wage will not keep up a home. In the neighbouring town hundreds of homes are locked all day....and Bruce the manufacturer's daughters are in county society. Heigh ho! It is a queer thing civilisation!

I wonder when the people will begin to

realise what wagery means. When they do begin to realise they will commence the revolution by driving women out of industry. To-day the women are used by the profiteer as instruments to exploit the men. Surely a factory worker has the right to earn enough to support a family on. The profiteer says "No! You must marry one of my hands, and then your combined wages will set up a home for you."

I spoke of this to the manager of Bruce's factory once.

"But," he said, "if we did away with female labour we'd have to close down. We couldn't compete with other firms."

"Not if they abolished female labour too?"

"I was thinking of the Calcutta mills where labour is dirt cheap," he said.

"I see," I said, "so the Scotch lassie is to compete with the native?"

"It comes to that," he admitted.

I think I see a very pretty problem awaiting Labour in the near future. As the Trade Unions become more powerful and show their determination to take the mines and factories into their own hands, capitalists will turn to Asia and Africa. The exploitation of the native is just beginning. At a time when Britain is a Socialistic State all the evils of capitalism will be reproduced with ten-fold intensity in India and China and Africa. I see an Asia ruled by lash and revolver; the profiteer has a short way with the striker in Eastern climes. The recent history of South Africa is sinister. A few years ago our brothers died presumably that white men should have the rights of citizenship in the Transvaal. What they seemed to have died for was the right of profiteers to shoot white strikers from the windows of the Rand Club. If white men are treated thus I tremble for the fate of the black man who strikes.

Yes, the present profiteering system is a preparation for an exploited East. Margaret Steel and her fellows are slaving so that a Persia may be "opened up," a Mexico robbed of its oil wells.

* * *

To-day I gave a lesson on Capital.

"If," I said, "I have a factory I have to pay out wages and money for machinery and raw material. When I sell my cloth I get more money than I paid out. This money is called profit, and with this money I can set up a new factory.

"Now what I want you to understand is this :—Unless work is done by someone there is no wealth. If I make a fortune out of linen I make it by using the labour of your fathers, and the machinery that was invented by clever men. Of course, I have to work hard myself, but I am repaid for my work fully. Margaret Steel at this moment standing at a loom, is working hard too, but she is getting a wage that is miserable.

"Note that the owner of the factory is getting an income of, say, ten thousand pounds a year. Now, what does he do with the money ?"

"Spends it on motor cars," said a boy.

"Buys cigarettes," said a girl.

"Please, sir, Mr. Bruce gives money to the infirmary," said another girl.

"He keeps it in a box beneath the bed," said another, and I found that the majority in the room favoured this theory. This suggestion reminded me of the limitations of childhood, and I tried to talk more simply. I told them of banks and stocks, I talked of luxuries, and pointed out that a man who lived by selling expensive dresses to women was doing unnecessary labour.

Tom Macintosh showed signs of thinking deeply.

"Please, sir, what would all the dressmakers and footmen do if there was no money to pay them?"

"They would do useful work, Tom," I said. "Your father works from six to six every day, but if all the footmen and chauffeurs and grooms and gamekeepers were doing useful work, your father would only need to work maybe seven hours a day. See? In Britain there are forty millions of people, and the annual income of the country is twenty-four hundred million pounds. One million of people take half this sum, and the other thirty-nine millions have to take the other half."

"Please, sir," said Tom, "what half are you in?"

"Tom," I said, "I am with the majority. For once the majority has right on its side."

* * *

Bruce the manufacturer had an advertisement in to-day's local paper. "No encumbrances," says the ad. Bruce has a family of at least a dozen, and he possibly thinks that he has earned the right to talk of "encumbrances." I sympathise with the old chap.

But I want to know why gardeners and chauffeurs must have no encumbrances. If the manorial system spreads, a day will come when the only children at this school will be the offspring of the parish minister. Then, I suppose, dominies and ministers will be compelled to be polygamists by Act of Parliament.

I like the Lord of the Manor's damned impudence. He breeds cattle for showing, he breeds pheasants for slaughtering, he breeds children to heir his estates. Then he sits down and pens an advertisement for a slave without "encumbrances." Why he doesn't import a few harem attendants from Turkey I don't know; possibly he is waiting till the Dardanelles are opened up.

* * *

I have just been reading a few schoolboy howlers. I fancy that most of these howlers are manufactured. I cannot be persuaded that any boy ever defined a lie as "An abomination unto the Lord but a very present help in time of trouble." Howlers bore me; so do most school yarns. The only one worth remembering is the one about the inspector who was ratty.

"Here, boy," he fired at a sleepy youth, "who wrote *Hamlet?*"

The boy started violently.

"P—please, sir, it wasna me," he stammered.

That evening the inspector was dining with the local squire.

"Very funny thing happened to-day," he said, as they lit their cigars.

"I was a little bit irritated, and I shouted at a boy, 'Who wrote *Hamlet?*' The little chap was flustered. 'P—please, sir, it wasna me!' he stuttered."

The squire guffawed loudly.

"And I suppose the little devil had done it after all!" he roared.

* * *

Lawson came down to see me to-night, and as usual we talked shop.

"It's all very well," he said, "for you to talk about education being all wrong. Any idiot can burn down a house that took many men to build. Have you got a definite scheme to put in its place ? "

The question was familiar to me. I had had it fired at me scores of times in the days when I talked Socialism from a soap-box in Hyde Park.

" I think I have a scheme," I said modestly.

Lawson lay back in his chair.

" Good ! Cough it up, my son ! "

I smoked hard for a minute.

" Well, Lawson, it's like this, my scheme could only be a success if the economic basis of society were altered. So long as one million people take half the national yearly income you can't have any decent scheme of education."

" Right O ! " said Lawson cheerfully, " for the sake of argument, or rather peace, we'll give you a Utopia where there are no idle rich. Fire away ! "

" Good ! I'll talk about the present day education first.

" Twenty years ago education had one aim——to abolish illiteracy. In consequence the Three R.'s were of supreme importance. Nowadays they are held to be quite as important, but a dozen other things have been placed beside them on the pedestal. Gradually education has come to aim at turning out a man or a woman capable of earning a living. Cookery, Woodwork, Typing, Book-keeping, Shorthand....all these were introduced so that we should have better wives and joiners and clerks.

"Lawson, I would chuck the whole blamed lot out of the elementary school. I don't want children to be trained to make pea-soup and picture frames, I want them to be trained to think. I would cut out History and Geography as subjects."

"Eh?" said Lawson.

"They'd come in incidentally. For instance, I could teach for a week on the text of a newspaper report of a fire in New York."

"The fire would light up the whole world, so to speak," said Lawson with a smile.

"Under the present system the teacher never gets under way. He is just getting to the interesting part of his subject when Maggie Brown ups and says, 'Please, sir, it's Cookery now.' The chap who makes a religion of his teaching says 'Damn!' very forcibly, and the girls troop out.

"I would keep Composition and Reading

and Arithmetic in the curriculum. Drill and Music would come into the play hours, and Sketching would be an outside hobby for warm days."

"Where would you bring in the technical subjects?"

"Each school would have a workshop where boys could repair their bikes or make kites and arrows, but there would not be any formal instruction in woodwork or engineering. Technical education would begin at the age of sixteen."

"Six what?"

"Sixteen. You see my pupils are to stay at school till they are twenty. You are providing the cash you know. Well, at sixteen the child would be allowed to select any subject he liked. Suppose he is keen on mechanics. He spends a good part of the day in the engineering shop and the drawing room—mechanical drawing I mean. But the thinking side of his education is still going on. He is studying political economy, eugenics, evolution, philosophy. By the time he is eighteen he has read Nietzsche, Ibsen, Bjornson, Shaw, Galsworthy, Wells, Strindberg, Tolstoi, that is if ideas appeal to him."

"Ah!"

"Of course, I don't say that one man in a hundred will read Ibsen. You will always have the majority who are averse to thinking if they can get out of it. These will be good mechanics and typists and joiners in many cases. My point is that every boy or girl has the chance to absorb ideas during their teens."

"Would you make it compulsory? For instance, that boy Willie Smith in your school; do you think that he would learn much more if he had to stay at school till he was twenty?"

"No," I said, "I wouldn't force anyone to stay at school, but to-day boys quite as stupid naturally as Smith stay at the university and love it. A few years' rubbing shoulders with other men is bound to make a man more alert. Take away, as you have done for argument's sake, the necessity of a boy's leaving school at fourteen to earn a living and you simply make every school a university."

"And it isn't three weeks since I heard you curse universities!" said Lawson with a grin.

"I'm thinking of the social side of a university," I explained. "That is good. The educational side of our universities is bad because it is mostly cram. I crammed Botany and Zoo for my degree and I know nothing about either; I was too busy trying to remember words like Caryophylacia, or whatever it is, to ask why flowers droop their heads at night. So in English I had to cram up what Hazlitt and Coleridge said about Shakespeare when I should have been reading *Othello*. The university fails because it refuses to connect education with contemporary life. You go there and you learn a lot of rot about syllogisms and pentameters, and nothing is done to explain to you the meaning of the life in the streets outside. No wonder that Oxford and Cambridge dons write to the papers saying that life has no opening for a university man."

"But I thought that you didn't want education to produce a practical man. You wanted a theoretical chimney-sweep, didn't you?" said Lawson smiling.

"The present university turns out men who are neither practical nor theoretical. I want a university that will turn out thinkers.

The men who have done most to stimulate thought these past few years are men like Wells and Shaw and Chesterton; and I don't think that one of them is a 'varsity man.'"

"You can't run a world on thought," said he.

"I don't know," I said, "we seem to run this old State of ours *without* thought. The truth is that there will always be more workers than thinkers. While one chap is planning a new heaven on earth, the other ninety-nine are working hard at motors and benches.

"H. G. Wells is always asking for better technical schools, more research, more invention. All these are absolutely necessary, but I want more than that; along with science and art I want the thinking part of education to go on."

"It goes on now."

"No," I said, "it doesn't. Your so-called educated man is often a stupid fellow. Doctors have a good specialist education, yet I know a score of doctors who think that Socialism means 'The Great Divide.' When Osteopathy came over from America a few years ago thousands of medical men pronounced it 'damned quackery' at once; only a few were wide enough to study the thing to see what it was worth. So with inoculation; the doctors follow the antitoxin authority like sheep. At the university I once saw a raid on an Anti-Vivisection shop, and I'm sure that not one medical student in the crowd had ever thought about vivisection. Mention Women's Freedom to the average lawyer, and he will think you a madman.

"Don't you see what I am driving at? I want first-class doctors and engineers and chemists, but I want them to think also, to think about things outside their immediate interests. This is the age of the specialist. That's what's wrong with it. Somebody, Matthew Arnold, I think, wanted a man who knew everything of something and something of everything. It's a jolly good definition of education."

"That is the idea of the Scotch Code," said Lawson.

"Yes, perhaps it is. They want our bairns to learn tons of somethings about everything that doesn't matter a damn in life."

* * *

My talk with Lawson last night makes me realise again how hopeless it is to plan a system of education when the economic system is all out of joint. I believe that this nation has the wealth to educate its children properly. I wonder what the Conscriptionists would say if I hinted to them that if a State can afford to take its youth away from industry to do unprofitable labour in the army and navy it can afford to educate its youth till the age of twenty is reached.

The stuff we teach in school leads nowhere; the Code subjects simply lull a child to sleep. How the devil is a lad to build a Utopia on Geography and Nature Study and Woodwork? Education should prove that the world is out of joint, and it should point a Kitchener finger at each child and say, " Your Country Needs *You*....to set it Right."

XVI.

THIS has been a delightful day. About eleven o'clock a rap came at the door, and a young lady entered my class-room.

" Jerusalem ! " I gasped. " Dorothy ! Where did you drop from ? "

" I'm motoring to Edinburgh," she explained, " on tour, you know, old thing ! "

Dorothy is an actress in a musical comedy touring company, and she is a very old friend of mine. She is a delightful child, full of fun and mischief, yet she can be a most serious lady on occasion.

She looked at my bairns, then she clasped her hands.

" O, Sandy ! Fancy you teaching all these kiddies ! Won't you teach me, too ? " And she sat down beside Violet Brown. I thanked my stars that I had never been dignified in that room.

" Dorothy," I said severely, " you're talking to Violet Brown and I must give you the strap."

The bairns simply howled, and when Dorothy took out her wee handkerchief and pretended to cry, laughter was dissolved in tears.

It was minutes time, and she insisted on blowing the "Dismiss" on the bugle. Her efforts brought the house down. The girls refused to dismiss, they crowded round Dorothy and touched her furs. She was in high spirits.

"You know, girls, I'm an actress and this big bad teacher of yours is a very old pal of mine. He isn't such a bad sort really, you know," and she put her arm round my shoulders.

"See her little game, girls?" I said. "Do you notice that this woman from a disreputable profession is making advances to me? She really wants me to kiss her, you know. She—" But Dorothy shoved a piece of chalk into my mouth.

What a day we had! Dorothy stayed all day, and by four o'clock she knew all the big girls by their Christian names. She insisted on their calling her Dorothy. She even tried to talk their dialect, and they screamed at her attempt to say "Guid nicht the noo."

In the afternoon I got her to sing and play; then she danced a ragtime, and in a few minutes she had the whole crowd ragging up and down the floor.

She stayed to tea, and we reminisced about London. Dear old Dorothy! What a joy it was to see her again, but how dull will school be tomorrow! Ah, well, it is a workaday world, and the butterflies do not come out every day. If Dorothy could read that sentence she would purse up her pretty lips and say, "Butterfly, indeed, you old bluebottle!" The dear child!

* * *

The school to-day was like a ballroom the "morning after." The bairns sat and talked about Dorothy, and they talked in hushed tones as about one who is dead.

"Please, sir," asked Violet, "will she come back again?"

"I'm afraid not," I answered.

"Please, sir, you should marry her, and then she'll always be here."

"She loves another man, Vi," I said ruefully, and when Vi whispered to Katie Farmer, " What a shame ! " I felt very sad. For the moment I loved Dorothy, but it was mere sentimentalism, Dorothy and I could never love, we are too much of the pal to each other for emotion to enter.

" She is very pretty," said Peggy Smith.

" Very," I assented.

" P—please, sir, you—you could marry her if you really tried ? " said Violet. She had been thinking hard for a bit.

" And break the other man's heart ! " I laughed.

Violet wrinkled her brows.

" Please, sir, it wouldn't matter for him, we don't know him."

" Why ! " I cried, " he is a very old friend of mine ! "

" Oh ! " Violet gasped.

" Please, sir," she said after a while, " do you know any more actresses ? "

I seized her by the shoulders and shook her.

" You wee bissom ! You don't care a rap about me ; all you want is that I should marry an actress. You want my wife to come and teach you ragtimes and tangoes ! " And she blushed guiltily.

* * *

Lawson came down to see me again to-night ; he wanted to tell me of an inspector's visit to-day.

" Why don't you apply for an inspectorship ? " he asked.

I lit my pipe.

" Various reasons, old fellow," I said. " For one thing I don't happen to know a fellow who knows a chap who lives next door to a woman whose husband works in the Scotch Education Department.

" Again, I 'm not qualified ; I never took the Education Class at Oxford."

" Finally, I don't want the job."

" I suppose," said Lawson, " that lots of 'em get in by wire-pulling."

" Very probably, but some of them probably get in straight. Naturally, you cannot get geniuses by wire-pulling ; the chap who uses influence to get a job is a third-rater always."

Lawson reddened

" I pulled wires to get into my job," he said.

"That's all right," I said cheerfully, "I've pulled wires all my days."

"But," I added, "I wouldn't do it again."

"Caught religion?"

"Not quite. The truth is that I have at last realised that you never get anything worth having if you've got to beg for it."

"It's about the softest job I know, whether you have to beg for it or not. The only job that beats it for softness is the kirk," he said.

"I wouldn't exactly call it a soft job, Lawson; a rotten job, yes, but a soft job, no. Inspecting schools is half spying and half policing. It isn't supposed to be you know, but it is. You know as well as I do that every teacher starts guiltily whenever the inspector shoves his nose into the room. Nosing, that's what it is."

"You would make a fairly decent inspector," said Lawson.

"Thanks," I said, "the insinuation being that I could nose well, eh?"

"I didn't mean that. Suppose you had to examine my school how would you do it?"

"I would come in and sit down on a bench and say: 'Just imagine I am a new boy, and give me an idea of the ways of the school. I warn you that my attention may wander. Fire away! But, I say, I hope you don't mind my finishing this pie; I had a rotten breakfast this morning.' "

"Go on," said Lawson laughing.

"I wouldn't examine the kids at all. When you let them out for minutes I would have a crack with you. I would say something like this: 'I've got a dirty job, but I must earn my screw in some way. I want to have a wee lecture all to myself. In the first place I don't like your discipline. It's inhuman to make kids attend the way you do. The natural desire of each boy in this room was to watch me put myself outside that pie, and not one looked at me.

" 'Then you are far too strenuous. You went from Arithmetic to Reading without a break. You should give them a five minutes chat between each lesson. And I think you have too much dignity. You would never think of dancing a ragtime on this floor, would you? I thought not. Try it, old chap. Apart from its merits as an antidote to dignity it is a first-rate liver stimulator.' Hello! Where are you going? Time to take 'em in again?

"'O, I say, I'm your guest, uninvited guest, I admit, but that's no reason why you should take advantage of me. Man, my pipe isn't half smoked, and I have a cigarette to smoke yet. Come out and watch me play footer with the boys.'"

"You think you would do all that," said Lawson slowly, "but you wouldn't you know. I remember a young inspector who came into my school with a blush on his face. 'I'm a new inspector,' he said very gingerly, 'and I don't know what I am supposed to do.' A year later that chap came in like whirlwind, and called me 'young man.' Man, you can't escape becoming smug and dignified if you are an inspector."

"I'd have a darned good try, anyway," I said. "Getting any eggs just now?"

* * *

To-night I have been glancing at *The Educational News*. There is a letter in it about inspectors, it is signed "Disgusted." That pseudonym damns the teaching profession utterly and irretrievably. Again and again letters appear, and very seldom does a teacher sign his own name. Naturally, a letter signed with a pseudonym isn't worth reading, for a moral coward is no authority on inspectors or anything else. It sickens me to see the abject cringing cowardice of my fellow teachers. "Disgusted" would no doubt defend himself by saying, "I have a wife and family depending on me and I simply can't afford to offend the inspector."

I grant that there is no point in making an inspector ratty, or for that matter making anyone ratty. I don't advise a man to seize every opportunity for a scrap. There is little use in arguing with an inspector who has methods of arithmetic different to your methods; it is easier to think over his advice and reject it if you are a better arithmetician than he. But if a man feels strongly enough on a subject to write to the papers about it, he ought to write as a man not as a slave. Incidentally, the habit of using a pseudonym damns the inspectorate at the same time. For this habit is universal, and teachers must have heard tales of the victimising of bold writers. Most educational papers suggest by their contributed articles that the teachers of Britain are like a crowd of Public School boys who fear to send their erotic verses to the school magazine lest the Head flays them. No wonder the social status of teachers is low; a profession that consists of "Disgusted" and "Rural School" and "Vindex" and their kind is a profession of nonentities.

* * *

Once in my palmy days I told a patient audience of Londoners that the Post Office was a Socialist concern.

"Any profits go to the State," I said.

A postman in the crowd stepped forward and told me what his weekly wage was, and I hastily withdrew my statement. To-day I should define it as a State Concern run on the principles of Private Profiteering, *i.e.*, it considers labour a commodity to be bought.

The School Board here is theoretically a Socialistic body. Its members are chosen by the people to spend the public money on education. No member can make a profit out of a Board deal. Yet this board perpetrates all the evils of the private profiteer.

Mrs. Findlay gets ten pounds a year for cleaning the school. To the best of my knowledge she works four or five hours a day, and she spends the whole of each Saturday morning cleaning out the lavatories. This sum works out at about sixpence a day or three ha'pence an hour. Most of her work consists of carrying out the very considerable part of the playground that the bairns carry in on their boots. Yet all my requests for a few loads of gravel are ignored.

The members do not think that they are using sweated labour; they say that if Mrs. Findlay doesn't do it for the money half a dozen widows in the village will apply for the job. They believe in competition and the market value of labour.

A few Saturdays ago I rehearsed a cantata in the school, and I offered Mrs. Findlay half a crown for her extra trouble in sweeping the room twice. She refused it with dignity, she didn't mind obliging me, she said. And this kindly soul is merely a "hand" to be bought at the lowest price necessary for subsistence.

Sometimes I curse the Board as a crowd of exploiters, but in my more rational moments I see that they could not do much better if they tried. If Mrs. Findlay had a pound a week the employees of the farmers on the Board would naturally object to a woman's getting a pound a week out of the public funds for working four hours a day while they slaved from sunrise to sunset for less than a pound. A public conscience can never be better than the conscience of the public's representatives. Hence I have no faith in Socialism by Act of Parliament ; I have no faith in municipalisation of trams and gas and water. Private profit disappears when the town council takes over the trams, but the greater evil—exploitation of labour remains.

Ah ! I suddenly recollect that Mrs. Findlay has her old age pension each Friday. She thus has eight and six a week. I wonder did Lloyd George realise that his pension scheme would one day prevent fat farmers from having conscience qualms when they gave a widow sixpence a day ?

* * *

As I came along the road this morning I saw half a dozen carts disgorging bricks on one of Lappiedub's fields. Lappiedub himself was standing by, and I asked him what was happening.

"Man," he cried lustily, "they've fund coal here and they're to sink pits a' ower the countryside."

When I reached the school the bairns were waiting to tell me the news.

" Please, sir," said Willie Ramsay, " they're going to build a town here bigger than London."

" Bigger than Glasgow even," said Peter Smith.

A few navvies went past the school.

" They're going to build huts for thousands of navvies," said a lassie.

" Please, sir, they'll maybe knock down the school and have a mine here," suggested Violet Brown.

" They won't," I said firmly, " this ugly school will stand until the countryside becomes as ugly as itself. Poor bairns! You don't know what you're coming to. In three years this bonny village will be a smoky blot on God's earth like Newcastle. Dirty women will gossip at dirty doors. You, Willie, will become a miner, and you will walk up that road with a black face. You, Lizzie, will be a trollop of a wife living in a brick hovel. You can hardly escape."

" Mr. Macnab of Lappiedub will lose all his land," said a boy.

"He didn't seem sad when I saw him this morning," I remarked.

"Maybe he's tired of farming," suggested a girl.

"Perhaps," I said, "if he is he doesn't need to worry about farming. He will be a millionaire in a few years. He will get a royalty on every ton of coals that comes up from the pit, and he will sit at home and wait for his money. Simply because he is lucky he will be kept by the people who buy the coals. If he gets sixpence a ton your fathers will pay sixpence more on every ton. I want you to realise that this is sheer waste. The men who own the mines will take big profits and keep up big houses with servants and idle daughters. Then Mr. Macnab will have his share. Then a man called a middleman will buy the coals and sell them to coal merchants in the towns, and he will have his share. And these men will sell them to the householders. When your father buys his ton of coals he is paying for these things:—the coalowner's income, Mr. Macnab's royalty, the middleman's profit, the town coal merchant's profit, and the miners' wages. If the miners want more wages and strike, they will get them, but these men won't lose their profits; they will increase the price of coals and the householders will pay for the increase.

"Don't run away with the idea that I am calling Mr. Macnab a scoundrel. He is a decent, honest, good-natured man who wouldn't steal a penny from anyone. It isn't his fault or merit that he is to be rich, it is the system that is bad."

Thomas Hardy somewhere talks about "the ache of modernism." I adapt the phrase and talk about the ache of industrialism. I look out at my wee window and I see the town that will be. There will be gin palaces and picture houses and music-halls—none of them bad things in themselves, but in a filthy atmosphere they will be hideous tawdry things with horrid glaring lights. I see rows of brick houses and acres of clay land littered with bricks and stones thrown down any way. Stores will sell cheap boots and frozen meat and patent pills, packmen will lug round their parcels of shoddy and sheen. And education! They will erect a new school with a Higher Grade department, and the Board will talk of turning out the type of scholar the needs of the community require. They will have for Rector a B.Sc., and technical instruction will be of first importance. When that happens I shall trek inland and shall seek some rural spot where I can be of some service to the community. I might be able to stand the smoke and filth, but before long there would be a labour candidate for the burgh, and I couldn't stand hearing him spout.

XVII.

I have been considering the subject of school magazines, and I wonder whether it would be possible to run a school magazine here. I have had no experience with a school magazine, but I edited a university weekly for a year. It wasn't a success. I wrote yellow editorials and placarded the quadrangles with flaring bills which screamed "Liars!" "Are School Teachers Socially Impossible?" "The Peril and the Pity of the Princes Street Parade," at the undergraduates passing by. It was of no use. No one bothered to reply to my philippics, and I had to sit down and write scathing replies to my own articles. I could never bring my circulation up to the watermark of a previous editor who had written editorials on such bright topics as "The Medical Congress" and "The Work of the International Academic Committee."

In Edinburgh the students are indifferent to their 'varsity magazine, but in St. Andrews the publication of *College Echoes* is the event of the week. The reason is that the St. Andrew's students form a small happy family; if a reference is made to Bejant Smith everyone understands it. If you mentioned Bejant Smith in the Edinburgh *Student* no one would know whom you were referring to.

The success of *College Echoes* gives me the idea of a school magazine that would succeed. A magazine for my hundred and fifty bairns would be useless; what I want is a magazine for parents and children. It would be issued weekly, and would mingle school gossip with advice. If Willie Wilson knew that Friday's edition might contain a paragraph to the effect that he had been discovered murdering two young robins, I fancy that he would think twice before he cut their heads off.

I imagine entries like the following:—

"Peter Thomson said on Thursday that it was Lloyd George who said 'Father, I cannot tell a lie,' and he was caned by the master who, by the way, has just been appointed President of the Conservative Association."

"Mary Brown was late every morning this week."

" John Mackenzie is at present gathering potatoes at Mr. Skinnem's farm, and is being paid a shilling a day of ten hours. Mr. Skinnem has been made an elder of the Parish Kirk."

Someone has said that the most arresting piece of literature is your own name in print. That is true, although I suppose that the thrill wears off when you become as public as Winston Churchill or Charlie Chaplin. Why shouldn't the bairns experience this thrill? When I write the report of a local concert for the local papers I always give prominence to the children who performed. Incidentally, when I have sung at a concert I omit all reference to my part; I hate to remind the audience that I sang. I am a true altruist in both cases.

Publicity is the most pleasing thing in life, and that's why patent medicines retain their popularity. At present the village cobbler is figuring in the local paper as a " Cured by Bunkum's Bilious Backache Bunion Beans " example, and beneath his photograph (taken at the age of nineteen; he is fifty-four now) is a glowing testimonial which begins with these words :—" For over a decade I have suffered from an excess of Uric Acid, from Neurotic Dyspepsia, and from Optical Derangements. Until I discovered that marvellous panacea...."

I marvel at his improved literary style; it is only a month since he wrote me as follows :—" Sir, i will be oblidged if you will let peter away at three oclock tonight hoping that you are well as this leaves me i am your obidt servent peter Macannish."

The magazine would also contain interesting editorials for the parents. Art would have a prominent place; if a bairn made a good sketch or a bonny design it would be reproduced.

Of course, the idea cannot be carried out for lack of funds. Yet I fancy that the money now spent on hounds and pet dogs would easily run a magazine for every school in Scotland.

The technical difficulties could easily be overcome. The bigger bairns could read the proofs and paste up the magazine, and the teachers would revise it before sending it to the printers.

I must get estimates from the printers, and

if they are moderate I shall try to raise funds by giving a school concert.

*   *   *

I see that the Educational Institute is advertising for a man who will combine the post of Editor of *The Educational News* with the office of Secretary to the Institute. The salary is £450 per annum.

This combining of the offices seems to me a great mistake. For an editor should be a literary man with ideas on education, while a good secretary should be an organizer. Because a man can write columns on education, that is no proof that he is the best man to write to the office washerwoman telling her not to come on Monday because it is a holiday.

I could edit the paper (I would take on the job for a hundred a year and the sport of telling the other fellow that his notions of education were all wrong), but I couldn't organise a party of boys scouts. Kitchener is a great organiser, but I shouldn't care for the editorials of *The New Statesman* if he were editor.

I think that the Institute does not want a

man with ideas. It wants a man who will mirror the opinions of the Institute. To do this is a work of genius, for the Institute has no opinions. No man can represent a body of men. Suppose the Institute decides by a majority that it will support the introduction of "Love" as a subject of the curriculum. The editor may be a misogynist, or he may have been married eight times, yet the poor devil has to sit down and write an editorial beginning: "Love has too long been absent from our schools. Who does not remember with holy tenderness his first kiss?...."

A paper can be a force only when it is edited by a man of force and personality. A man who writes at the dictation of another is a tenth-rater. That, of course, is why our press says nothing.

* * *

Little Mary Brown was stung by a wasp the other day as she sat in the class.

"Henceforward," I said, "the wasp that enters this room is to be slain. Tom Macintosh I appoint you commander in chief."

I begin to think that I prefer the wasp to the campaign against it. To-day I was in the midst of a dissertation on Trusts when Tom started up.

" Come on lads, there's a wasp ! "

They broke a window and two pens ; then they slew the wasp.

The less studious boys keep one eye on the window all day, and I found Dave Thomson chasing an imaginary wasp all round the room at Arithmetic time. Dave detests Arithmetic. But when I found that Tom Macintosh was smearing the inside window-sill with black currant jam, I disbanded the anti-wasp army.

* * *

The Inspectors refuse to allow teachers to use slates nowadays on the ground that they are insanitary.

To-day I reintroduced slates to all classes. My one reason was that my bairns were missing one of the most delightful pastimes of youth—the joy of making a spittle run down the slate and back again. I always look back with tenderness to my old slate. It was such a serviceable article. By running my slate-pencil up it I got all the beats of a drum ; its wooden sides were the acknowledged tests for a new knife, as a hammer it had few rivals. Then you could play at X–es and O–ies with impunity; you simply licked your palm and rubbed the whole game out when the teacher approached.

In the afternoon half a dozen bairns brought sponges, and I sighed for the good old days when sanitary authorities were plumbers on promotion.

* * *

I have given my bairns two songs—*Screw-Guns* and *Follow Me Home,* both by Kipling. I prefer them to the usual "patriotic" song that is published for school use. I don't see the force of teaching children to be patriotic; the man who imagines that a dominie can teach a bairn to love his neighbour or his country is fatuous. Flag-waving is the last futility of noble minds. The queer thing is that all these titled men who spout about Imperialism and Patriotism, and "Make the Foreigner Pay" are enemies of the worker. They don't particularly want to see a State where slums and slavery will be no more; they are so busy thinking out a scheme to extend the Empire abroad that they haven't time to think about the Empire at home. What is the use of an India or a South Africa if East Ham is to remain ?

No, I refuse to teach my bairns to sing, " Britons never, never, never shall be slaves." My sense of humour won't allow me to introduce that song.

Although I like Kipling's verses I abominate Kipling's philosophy and politics. He is always to be found on the same platform with the Curzons and Milners and Roosevelts. He believes in " the big stick" ; to him Britain is great because of her financiers, her viceroys, her engineers. He glories in enterprise and big ships. He believes with the late Lord Roberts that the Englishman is the salt of the earth. I should define Kipling as a Grown-up Public School Boy.

I always think that the " Patriot's " main contention is that a man ought to be ready to die for his country. I freely grant that it is a great thing to die for your country, but I contend that it is still greater to live for your country ; and the man who tries to live for his country usually earns the epithet " Traitor."

" What do they know of England who only England know ? " Kipling says this, or words to this effect. That's the worst of these travelled Johnnies; they go out to India or Africa, and two months after their arrival they pity the narrow vision of the people at home. After having talked much to travelled men I have come to the conclusion that travel is the most narrowing thing on earth.

"If I went out to India," I remarked one day to an Anglo-Indian friend at College, "and if I started to talk about Socialism in a drawing-room, what would happen?"

"Oh," he said with a smile, "they would listen to you very politely, but, of course, you wouldn't be asked again."

When I went down to Tilbury to see this friend off to India I looked at the crowd on the first-class deck.

"Dick," I said, "these people are awful. Look at their smugness, their eagerness to be correct at any expense. They are saying good-bye to wives and mothers and sweethearts, and the whole blessed crowd of 'em haven't an obvious emotion among 'em. I'll bet my hat that they won't even wave their hands when the tender goes off."

As I left the boat the first-class passengers

stood like statues, but one fat woman, with a delightfully plebeian face cried: "So long, old sport!" to a man beside me.

"Good!" cried Dick to me with a laugh.

"Lovely!" I called, and waved my hat frantically to the fat woman. Poor soul, I fear that society out East will be making her suffer for her lapse into bad form.

Travel is like a school-history reader; it forces you to study mere incident. The travelled man is an encyclopædia of information; but I don't want to know what a man has seen; I want to know what he has thought. I am certain that if I went to live in Calcutta I should cease to think. I should marvel at the colour and life of the streets; I should find great pleasure in learning the lore of the native. But in a year I should very probably be talking of "damned niggers," and cursing the India Office as a crowd of asses who know nothing about India and its problems.

I once lent *Ann Veronica* to a clever young lady. Her father, an engineer who had been all over the world, picked up the book. Two days later he returned it with a final note dismissing me as a dangerous character for his daughter to know. The lady was clever, and had mentality enough to read anything with impunity.

No, travel doesn't broaden a man's outlook.

My writing is like my teaching, it is an irresponsible ramble. I meant to write about songs all the time to-night.

I curse my luck in not being a pianist. I want to give my bairns that loveliest of tenor solos—the *Preislied* from *The Meistersingers.* I want to give them Lawrence Hope's *Slave's Song* from her *Indian Love Lyrics*—"*Less than the Dust beneath thy Chariot Wheel.*" And there are one or two catchy bits in *Gipsy Love* and *The Quaker Girl* that I should like them to know. I am sure that they would enjoy *Mr. Jeremiah, Esquire,* and *The Gipsy's Song.*

XVIII.

THE essay I set to-day was this :—" Imagine that you are an old lady who ordered a duck from Gamage's, and imagine that they sent you an aeroplane in a crate by mistake. Then describe in the first person the feelings of the aviator who found the duck awaiting him at breakfast time."

One girl wrote :—" Dear Mr. Gamage, I have not opened the basket, but it seems to be an ostrich that you have sent. What will I feed it on ? "

A boy, as the aviator, wrote : " If you think I am going to risk my life on the machine you sent you are wrong. It hasn't got a petrol tank."

The theme was too difficult for the bairns ; they could not see the ludicrous side. I don't think one of them visualised the poor old woman gazing in dismay on the workmen unloading the crate. H. M. Bateman would have made an excellent drawing of the incident.

I tried another theme.

"A few days ago I gave you a ha'penny each," I said. "Write a description of how you spent it, and I'll give sixpence to the one who tells the biggest lie."

I got some tall yarns. One chap bought an aeroplane and torpedoed a Zeppelin with it; one girl bought a thousand motor-cars But Jack Hood, the dunce of the class, wrote these words: "I took it to the church on sunday and put it in the clecshun bag."

I gave him the tanner, although I knew that he had won it by accident. I don't think that Jack will ever get so great a surprise again in this life.

* * *

We rambled out to sketch this afternoon. It was very hot, and we lay down under a tree and slept for half-an-hour. Suddenly Violet Brown started up.

"Here's Antonio!" she cried, and the Italian drew his van to the side of the road.

"A slider for each of us," I said, and he began to hustle. My turn came last.

"You like a glass, zir, instead of a zlider?" said Antonio.

"Yes," I replied, "a jolly good suggestion; I haven't had the joy of licking an ice-cream glass dry for many a long day."

It was glorious.

On the way back a girl bought sweets at the village shop. She gave me one.

"Please, sir, it's one of them changing kind," she said.

"Eh?" I hastily took it out and looked at it.

"By George, so it is, Katie!" I cried, "I thought they were dead long since." It was white at first but it changed to blue, then red, then green, then purple. Unfortunately, I bit it unthinkingly, and I never discovered its complete spectrum.

I call this a lucky day; ice cream and changing balls in one afternoon are the quintessence of luck. But man is insatiable; to-night I have a great craving for a stick of twisted sugarelly—the polite call it liquorice.

* * *

A couple of Revivalists came to the village a week ago, and they have made a few converts. One of them stopped me on the road to-night and asked if I were saved.

"I am, or, at least, was, a journalist," I said, and walked on chuckling. Of course he gaped, for he did not know why I chuckled. I was thinking of the reporter sitting in the back seat at a Salvationist Meeting. A Salvation lass bent over him. "Are you saved, my friend?" she whispered. He looked up in alarm.

"I'm a journalist," he said hastily.

"O! I beg your pardon," she said, and moved on.

I don't like Revivalism. A couple of preachers came to our village when I was a lad, and for a month I thought of nothing but hell. "Only believe!" one of them used to say when he met you on the road; the other one had a shorter salutation: "Glory!" he shouted at you fiercely. Incidentally, the village was a hotbed of petty strife when they departed. And the young women who had stood up to give their "Testimony" were back to the glad-eye phase again within three weeks.

Lizzie Jane Gunn was a typical convert. Lizzie Jane used to describe the night of her testimony-giving thus:—"Mind you, Aw was gaein' alang the road, and Aw had just been gieing ma testimony, and it was gye dark and Aw was by ma leensome. Weel, a' at eence something fell into ma hand, and Aw thocht that it was a message frae the Loard; so Aw just grippit ma hand ticht, an' Aw didna look to see fat it wuz. Fan Aw got hame Aw lookit to see fat wuz in ma hand, an' d'ye ken fat it wus?....a button aff ma jaicket!"

I have no sympathy with all this "saving" business. It's a cowardly selfish religion that makes people so anxious about their tuppence-ha'penny souls. When I think of all the illiterate lay preachers I have listened to I feel like little Willie at the Sunday School.

"Hands up all those who would like to go to Heaven!" said the teacher. Willie alone did not put his hand up.

"What! Mean to tell me, Willie, that you don't want to go to Heaven?"

Willie jerked a contemptuous thumb towards the others.

"No bloomin' fear," he muttered, "not if that crowd's goin'."

Shelley says that "most wretched men

are cradled into poetry through wrong." I think that most wretched preachers are cradled into preaching through conceit. It is thrilling to have an audience hang upon your words ; we all like the limelight. Usually we have to master a stiff part before we can face the audience. Preaching needs no preparation, no thinking, no merit ; all you do is to stand up and say : "Deara friendsa, when I was in the jimmynasium at Peebles, a fellow lodger of mine blasphemeda. From that daya, deara friendsa, that son of the devila nevera prospereda. O, friendsa ! If you could only looka into your evila heartsa. . . . ."

I note that when Revivalists come to a village the so-called village lunatic is always among the first to give his testimony. Willie Baffers has been whistling *Life, Life, Eternal Life* all the week, but I was glad to note that he was back to *Stop yer Ticklin', Jock,* to-night.

* * *

I have introduced two new text-books—*Secret Remedies,* and *More Secret Remedies.* These books are published by the British

Medical Association at a shilling each, and they give the ingredients and cost of popular patent medicines.

These books should be in every school. Everyone should know the truth about these medicines, and unless our schools tell the truth, the public will never know it. No daily newspaper would think of giving the truth, for the average daily is kept alive by patent medicine advertisements.

I marvel at the mentality of the man who can sell a farthing's worth of drugs for three and sixpence. I don't blame the man ; I merely marvel at him. What is his standard of truth ? What does he imagine the purpose of life to be ?

Poor fellow ! I fancy he is a man born with a silver knife in his mouth, as Chesterton says in another context ; either that, or he is born poor in worldly goods and in spirit. He is dumped down in an out-of-joint world where money and power are honoured, where honesty is never the best policy ; the poor, miserable little grub realises that he has not the ability to earn money or power honestly; but he knows that people are fools, and that a knave always gets the better of a fool.

Our laws are really funny. I can swindle thousands by selling a nostrum, but if I sign Andrew Carnegie's name on a cheque I am sent to Peterhead Prison. Britain is individualistic to the backbone. The individual must be protected, but the crowd can look after itself. If I steal a pair of boots and run for it, I am a base thief; if I turn bookie and become a welsher I have entered the higher realms of sport, and I get a certain amount of admiration....from those who didn't plunge at my corner. I have seen a cheap-jack swindle a crowd of Forfarshire ploughmen out of a month's earnings, but not one of them thought of dusting the street with him.

Honesty must be a relative thing. Personally I will "swick" a railway company by travelling without a ticket on any possible occasion; yet, when a cycle agent puts a new nut on my motor-bike and charges a shilling I call him a vulgar thief. Of course he is; there is no romance in making a broken-down motor-cyclist pay through the nose, but a ten mile journey without a ticket is the only romantic experience left in a drab world.

I once saw an article on *Railway Criminals* in, I think, *Tit-Bits*. It pointed out that the men who are convicted of swindling the railway companies have well marked facial characteristics I recollect going to the mirror at the time and saying " Tu quoque ! "

In these days I had a firm belief in physiognomy ; I believed that you had only to gaze into a person's eyes to see whether he was telling the truth or not. I am wiser now that I know Peter Young. Pete is ten, and he has a clear, honest countenance. To-night I found him tinkering with the valve of my back tyre.

" Who loosened that valve ? " I demanded.

" Please, sir, it was Jim Steel," he said unblushingly, and he looked me straight in the eyes.

" All right, George Washington," I remarked. " There's a seat in the Cabinet, waiting for you, my lad." And I meant it too. I believe in the survival of the fittest, and I know that Peter is the best adapted to survive in a modern civilisation. It is said of his father that he bought an old woman's ill-grown pig, a white one, and promised her a fine piebald pig in a week's time. He brought her the piebald. Then rain came....

I often condemn the press for not seeking truth, yet no man has a greater admiration for a good liar than I have. When I hear a fellow break in on a conversation with the words: "Talking of Lloyd George, when I was in the Argentine last winter...." I grapple him to my soul with hoops of steel. I can't stand the common or garden liar with his trite expressions...."So the missis is keeping better, old man? Glad to hear it." "Your singing has improved wonderfully, my dear." "I was kept late at the office," and all that sort of lie. All the same I recognise that we are all liars, and few of us can evade the trite manner of lying.

I met a man on the road to-night, and he stopped to talk. I hate the fellow; he is one of those mean men who would plant potatoes on his mother's grave if the cemetery authorities would allow it. Yet I shook his greasy hand when he held it out. If I had had the tense honesty of Ibsen's *Brand* I should have refused to see his hand. But we all lie in this way; indeed, life would be intolerable if we were all *Brands* and cried

"All or Nothing!" We all compromise, and compromise is the worst lie of all. Compromise I can pardon, but not gush. I know men who could say to old greasy-fist: "Man, I'm glad to see you looking so well!" men who would cut his throat if they had the pluck. Nevertheless gush is not one of the Scot's chief characteristics.

There is a shepherd's hut up north, and George Broon lives there alone. Once another shepherd came up that way, and he thought he would settle down with George for a time. The newcomer, Tam Kennedy, came in after his day's work, and the two smoked in silence for two hours. Then Tam remarked: "Aw saw a bull doon the road the nicht."

Next morning George Broon said: "It wasna a bull; it was a coo."

Tam at once set about packing his bag.

"Are ye gaein' awa?" asked George in surprise.

"Yus," said Tam savagely, "there's far ower much argy-bargying here."

* * *

Summer holidays at last! Many a day I have longed for them, but now that they are here I feel very very sad. For to-day some of these bairns of mine sat on these benches for the last time. When I blow my bugle again I shall miss familiar faces. I shall miss Violet with her bonny smile; I shall miss Tom Macintosh with his cheery face. Vi is going to the Secondary School, and Tom is going to the railway station. They are sweethearts just now, and I know that both are sad at leaving.

"Never mind, Tam," I heard her say, "Aw'll aye see ye at the station, ilka mornin' and nicht."

"We'll get merried when Aw'm station mester, Vi," said Tom hopefully, and she smiled and blushed.

Poor Tom! I'm sorry for you my lad. In three years you will be carrying her luggage, and she won't take any notice of you, for she is a lawyer's daughter.

Confound realism!

Once I felt as Tom feels. I loved a farmer's daughter, and I suffered untold agony when she told me that her father's lease expired in seventeen years.

"Then we're flittin' to Glesga," she said,

and I was wretched for a week. She was ten then ; now she is the mother of four.

Annie and her seventeen years reminds me of the professor who was lecturing on Astronomy to a village audience.

"In seven hundred million years, my friends," he said solemnly, "the sun will be a cold body like the moon. There will be no warmth on earth, no light, no life.... nothing."

A chair was pushed back noisily at the back of the hall, and a big farmer got up in great agitation.

"Excuse me, mister, but hoo lang did ye say it wud be till that happened ? "

"Seven hundred million years, my friend."

The farmer sank into his chair with a great sigh of relief.

"Thank Goad ! " he gasped, "Aw thocht ye said seven million."

They say that when a man dies after a long life he looks back and mourns the things that he's left undone. I suppose that some teachers look back over a year's work and regret their sins of omission. I do not.

I know that I have had many lazy days this session ; I know that there were exercises that I failed to correct, subjects that I failed to teach. I regret none of these things, for they do not count.

Rachel Smith is leaving the district, and to-day Mary Wilson shook her hand. " Weel, by bye, Rachel, ye'll have to gang to anither schule, and ye'll maybe have to work there," she said.

" Eh ? " I cried, " do you mean to say, Mary Wilson, that Rachel hadn't to work in this school ? "

" No very much," said Mary, " ma father says that we just play ourselves at this school."

Mary's father is right ; I have converted a hard-working school into a playground. And I rejoice. These bairns have had a year of happiness and liberty. They have done what they liked ; they have sung their songs while they were working at graphs, they have eaten their sweets while they read their books. They have hung on to my arms as we rambled along in search of artistic corners. It was only yesterday that Jim Jackson marched up the road to meet me at dinner-time with his gun team and gun, a log of wood mounted on a pair of perambulator wheels. As I approached I heard his command: "Men, lay the gun!" and when I was twenty yards off he shouted "Fire!"

"Please, sir," he cried, "you're killed now, but we'll take you prisoner instead." And the team lined up in two columns and escorted me back to the school to the strains of *Alexander's Ragtime Band* played on the mouth-organ.

"Is it usual, Colonel," I asked, "for the commander of the gun team to act as the band?"

Jim scratched his head.

"The band was all killed at Mons," he said, "and the privates aren't musical." Then he struck up *Sister Susie's Sewing Shirts for Soldiers*.

I know that I have brought out all the innate goodness of these bairns. When Jim Jackson came to the school he had a bad look; if a girl happened to push him he turned on her with a murderous scowl. Now that I think of it I realise that Jim is always a bright cheery boy now. When I knew him first I could see that he looked upon me as a natural enemy, and if I had thrashed him I might have made him fear me, but the bad look would never have left his face.

If I told anyone that I had made these bairns better I should be met with the contemptuous glance that usually greets the man who blows his own horn. Stupid people can never understand the man who indulges in introspection ; they cannot realise that a man can be honest with himself. If I make a pretty sketch I never hesitate to praise it. On the other hand I am readier than anyone else to declare one of my inferior sketches bad. Humility is nine-tenths hypocrisy.

I do have a certain amount of honesty, and I close my log with a solemn declaration of my belief that I have done my work well.

As for the work that the Scotch Education Department expected me to do....well, I think the last entry in my official Log Book is a fair sample of that.

"The school was closed to-day for the summer holidays. I have received Form 9b from the Clerk."

A Dominie in Doubt

A.S. NEILL

Author of
A DOMINIE'S LOG

To Homer Lane, whose first lecture convinced me that I knew nothing about education. I owe much to him, but I hasten to warn educationists that they must not hold him responsible for the views given in these pages. I never understood him fully enough to expound his wonderful educational theories.

A. S. N.

FORFAR,
AUGUST 12, 1920.

A DOMINIE IN DOUBT

I.

"JUST give me your candid opinion of *A Dominie's Log;* I'd like to hear it."

Macdonald looked up from digging into the bowl of his pipe with a dilapidated penknife. He is now head-master of Tarbonny Public School, a school I know well, for I taught in it for two years as an ex-pupil teacher.

Six days ago he wrote asking me to come and spend a holiday with him, so I hastily packed my bag and made for Euston.

This evening had been a sort of complimentary dinner in my honour, the guests being neighbouring dominies and their wives, none of whom I knew. We had talked of the war, of rising prices, and a thousand other things. Suddenly someone mentioned education, and of course my unfortunate *Log* had come under discussion.

I had been anxious to continue my discussion with a Mrs. Brown on the subject of the relative laying values of Minorcas and Buff Orpingtons, but I had been dragged into the miserable business in spite of myself.

Now they were all gone, and Macdonald had returned to the charge.

"It's hardly a fair question," said Mrs. Macdonald, "to ask an author what he thinks of his own book. No man can judge his own work, any more than a mother can judge her own child."

"That's true!" I said. "A man can't judge his own behaviour, and writing a book is an element of behaviour. Besides, there is a better reason why a writer cannot judge his own work," I added.

"Because he never reads it?" queried Macdonald with a grin.

I shook my head.

"An author has no further interest in his book after it is published."

Macdonald looked across at me. It was clear that he doubted my seriousness.

"Surely you don't mean to say that you have no interest in *A Dominie's Log*?"

"None whatever!" I said.

"You mean it?" persisted Macdonald.

"My dear Mac," I said, "an author dare not read his own book."

"Dare not! Why?"

"Because it's out of date five minutes after it's written."

For fully a minute we smoked in silence. Macdonald appeared to be digesting my remark.

"You see," I continued presently, "when

I read a book on education, I want to learn, and I certainly don't expect to learn anything from the man I was five years ago."

"I think I understand," said Macdonald. "You have come to realise that what you wrote five years ago was wrong. That it?"

"True for you, Mac. You've just hit it."

"You needn't have waited five years to find that out," he said, with a good-natured grin. "I could have told you the day the book was published—I bought one of the first copies."

"Still," he continued, "I don't see why a book should be out-of-date in five years. That is if it deals with the truth. Truth is eternal."

"What is truth?" I asked wearily. "We all thought we knew the truth about gravitation. Then Enstein came along with his relativity theory, and told us we were wrong."

"Did he?" inquired Macdonald, with a faint smile.

"I am quoting from the newspapers," I added hastily. "I haven't the remotest idea what relativity means. Perhaps it's Epstein I mean—no, he's a sculptor."

"You're hedging!" said Macdonald.

"Can you blame me?" I asked. "You're trying to get me to say what truth is. I am not a professor of philosophy, I'm a dominie. All I can say is that the *Log* was the truth . . . for me . . . five years ago; but it isn't the truth for me now."

"Then, what exactly is your honest opinion of the *Log* as a work on education?"

"As a work on education," I said deliberately, "the *Log* isn't worth a damn."

"Not a bad criticism, either," said Macdonald dryly.

"I say that," I continued, "because when I wrote it I knew nothing about the most important factor in education—the psychology of children."

"But," said Mrs. Macdonald in surprise—hitherto she had been an interested listener—"I thought that the bits about the bairns were the best part of the book."

"Possibly," I answered, "but I was looking at children from a grown-up point of view. I thought of them as they affected me, instead of as they affected themselves. I'll give you an instance. I think I said something about wanting to chuck woodwork and cookery out of the school curriculum. I was wrong, hopelessly wrong."

"I'm glad to hear you admit it," said Macdonald. "I have always thought that every boy ought to be taught to mend a hen-house and every girl to cook a dinner."

"Then I was right after all," I said quickly.

Macdonald stared at me, whilst his wife looked up interrogatively from her embroidery.

"If your aim is to make boys joiners and girls cooks," I explained, "then I still hold that cookery and woodwork ought to be chucked out of the schools."

"But, man, what are schools for?" I saw a combative light in Macdonald's eye.

"Creation, self-expression . . . . the only thing that matters in education. I don't care what a child is doing in the way of creation, whether he is making tables, or porridge, or sketches, or—or—"

"Snowballs!" prompted Macdonald.

"Or snowballs," I said. "There is more true education in making a snowball than in listening to an hour's lecture on grammar."

Mrs. Macdonald dropped her embroidery into her lap, with a little gasp at the heresy of my remark.

"You're talking pure balderdash!" said Macdonald, leaning forward to knock the ashes from his pipe on the bars of the grate.

"Very well," I said cheerfully. "Let's discuss it. You make a class sit in front of you for an hour, and you threaten to whack the first child that doesn't pay attention to your lesson on nouns and pronouns."

"Discipline," said Macdonald.

"I don't care what you call it. I say it's stupidity."

"But, hang it all, man, you can't teach if you haven't got the children's attention."

"And you can't teach when you have got

it" I said. "A child learns only when it is interested."

"But surely, discipline makes them interested," said Mrs. Macdonald.

I shook my head. "It only makes them attentive."

"Same thing," said Macdonald.

"No, Mac," I replied. "It is not the same thing. Attention means the applying of the conscious mind to a thing; interest means the application of both the conscious and the unconscious mind. When you force a child to attend to a lesson for fear of the tawse, you merely engage the least important part of his mind—the conscious. While he stares at the blackboard his unconscious is concerned with other things."

"What sort of things?" asked Macdonald.

"Very probably his unconscious is working out an elaborate plan to murder you," I said, "and I don't blame it either," I added.

"And the snowballs?" queried Mrs. Macdonald.

"When a boy makes a snowball, he is interested; his whole soul is in the job, that is, his unconscious and his conscious are working together. For the moment he is an artist, a creator."

"So that's the new education . . . making snowballs?" said Macdonald.

"It isn't really," I said; "but what I want to do is to point out that making snowballs is nearer to true education than the spoon-feeding we call education to-day."

* * * * * *

Duncan does not like me. He is a young dominie of twenty-three or thereabouts, a friend of Macdonald, and he has just been demobilised. He was a major, and he does not seem to have recovered from the experience. He has got what the vulgar call swelled head. Last night he was dilating upon the delinquencies of the old retired teacher who ran the school while Duncan was on active service. It seems that the old man had allowed the school to run to seed.

"Would you believe it," I overheard Duncan say to Macdonald, "when I came back I found that the boys and girls were playing in the same playground. Why, man, some of them were playing on the road! And the discipline! Awful!"

Poor children! I see it all; I see Duncan line them up like a squad of recruits, and march them into school with never a smile on their faces or a word on their lips. Macdonald tells me that he makes them lift their slates by numbers.

And the amusing thing is that Duncan thinks himself one of the more advanced teachers. He reads the educational journals, and eagerly devours the articles about new methods in teaching arithmetic and geography. His school is only a mile and a half away, and I hope that he will come over to see Mac a few times while I am here.

I have seen the old type of dominie, and I have seen the new type. I prefer the former. He had many faults, but he usually managed to do something for the human side of the children. The new type is a danger to children. The old dominie leathered the children so that they might make a good show before the inspector ; the new dominie leathers them because he thinks that children ought to be disciplined so that they may be able to fight the battle of life. He does not see that by using authority he is doing the very opposite of what he intends ; he is making the child dependent on him, and for ever afterwards the child will lack initiative, lack self-confidence, lack originality.

What the new dominie does do is to turn out excellent wage-slaves. The discipline of the school gives each child an inner sense of inferiority . . . . what the psycho-analysts call an inferiority complex. And the working-classes are suffering from a gigantic inferiority complex . . . . otherwise they would not be content to remain wage-slaves. The fear that Duncan inspires in a boy will remain in that boy all his life. When he enters the workshop he will unconsciously identify the foreman with Duncan, and fear him and hate him. I believe that many a strike is really a vague insurrection against the teacher. For it is well known that the unconscious mind is infantile.

* * * * * *

To-night I dropped in to see my old friend Dauvit Todd the cobbler. Many an evening have I spent in his dirty shop. Dauvit works on after teatime, and the village worthies gather round his fire and smoke and spit and grunt. I have sat there for an hour many a night, and not a single word was said. Peter Smith the blacksmith would give a great sigh and say: "Imphm!" There would be silence for ten minutes, and then Jake Tosh the roadman would stare at the fire, shake his head, and say: "Aye, man!" Then a ploughman would smack his lips and say: "Man, aye!" A southerner looking in might have jumped to the conclusion that the assembly was collectively and individually bored, but boredom never enters Dauvit's shop. We Scots think better in crowds.

To-night the old gang was there. The hypothetical southerner again would have marvelled at the reception I received. I walked into the shop after an absence of five years.

"Weel, Dauvit," I said, and sat down in the basket chair. Dauvit and I have never shaken hands in our lives. He looked up.

"Back again!" he said, without any evident surprise; then he added: "And what like a nicht is 't ootside?"

Gradually other men dropped in, and the same sort of greeting took place. The weather continued to be discussed for a time. Then the blacksmith said: "Auld Tam Davidson's swine dee'd last nicht."

Dauvit looked up from the boot he was repairing.

"What did it dee o'?" and there followed an argument about the symptoms of swine fever.

An English reader of *The House with the Green Shutters* would have concluded that these villagers were deliberately trying to put me in my place. By ignoring me might they not be showing their contempt for dominies who have just come from London? Not they. They were glad to see me again, and their method of showing their gladness was to take up our friendship at the point where it left off five years ago.

The only time a Scot distrusts other Scots is when they fuss over him. The story goes in Tarbonny that when young Jim Lunan came home unexpectedly after a ten years' farming in Canada, his mother was washing the kitchen floor.

"Mother!" he cried, "I've come hame!"

She looked over her shoulder.

"Wipe yer feet afore ye come in, ye clorty laddie," she said.

But there is a garrulous type of Scot . . . or rather the type of Scot that tries to make the other fellow garrulous. In our county we call them the speerin' bodie. To speer means to ask questions. The speerin' bodie is common enough in Fife, and I suppose it was a Fifer who entered a railway compartment one morning and sat down to study the only other occupant—an Englishman.

"It's a fine day," said the Scot, and there was a question in his tone.

The Englishman sighed and laid aside his newspaper.

"Aye, mester," continued the inquisitive Fifer, "and ye'll be——"

The Englishman held up a forbidding hand.

"You needn't go on," he said; "I'll tell you everything about myself. I was born in Leeds, the son of poor parents. I left school at the age of twelve, and I became a draper. I gradually worked my way up, and now I am traveller for a Manchester firm. I married six years ago. Three kids. Wife has rheumatism. Willie had measles last month. I have a seven room cottage; rent £27. I vote Tory; go to the Baptist church, and keep hens. Anything else you want to know?"

The Scot had a very dissatisfied look.

"What did yer grandfaither dee o'?" he demanded gruffly.

When the argument about swine fever had died down, Dauvit turned to me.

"Aye, and how is Lunnon lookin'?"

"Same as ever," I answered.

"Ye'll have to tak' Dauvit doon on a trip," laughed the smith.

Dauvit drove in a tacket.

"Man, smith, I was in Lunnon afore you was born," he said.

"Go on, Dauvit," I said encouragingly, "tell us the story." I had heard it before, but I longed to hear it again. Dauvit brightened up.

"There's no muckle to tell," he said, as he tossed the boot into a corner and wiped his face with his apron. "It'll be ten years come Martimas. Me and Will Tamson gaed up by boat frae Dundee. Oh! we had a graund time. But there's no muckle to tell."

"What about Dave Brownlee?" I asked.

Dauvit chuckled softly.

"But ye've a' heard the story," he said, but we protested that we hadn't.

"Aweel," he began, "some of you will no doubt mind o' Dave Broonlee him that stoppit at Millend. Dave served his time as a draper, and syne he got a good job in a Lunnon shop. Weel, me and Will Tamson was walkin' along the Strand when Will he says to me, says he: 'Cud we no pay a veesit to Dave Broonlee?' Then I minded that Dave's father had said something aboot payin' him a call, but I didna ken his address. All I kent was that he was in a big shop in Oxford Street.

"Weel, Will and me we goes up to a bobby and speers the way to Oxford Street. When we got there Will he goes up to another bobby and says: 'Please cud ye tell me whatna shop Dave Broonlee works intil?' At that I started to laugh, and syne the bobby he started to laugh. He laughed a lang time and syne when I telt him that it was a draper's shop he directed us to a great big muckle shop wi' a thousand windows.

"'Try there first,' says the bobby.

"Weel, in we goes, and a mannie in a tail coat he comes forart rubbin' his hands.

"'And what can I do for you, sir?' he says to Will.

"'Oh,' says Will, 'we want to see Dave Broonlee,' but the man didna ken what Will was sayin'. It took Will and me twenty meenutes to get him to onderstand.

"'Oh,' says he, 'I understand now. You want to see Mr. Brownlee?'

"'Ye're fell quick in the uptak,' says Will, but of coorse the man didna ken what he was sayin'.

"He went to the backshop to speer aboot Dave, and when he cam back he says, says he: 'I'm sorry, but Mr. Brownlee has gone out to lunch. Will you leave a message?'

"Will turned to the door.

"'Never mind,' says he, 'we'll see him doon the toon.'"

*   *   *   *   *   *

In reading my *Log* I am appalled by the amount of lecturing I did in school. Since writing it I have visited most of the best schools in England, and I found that I was not the only teacher who lectured. But we are all wrong. I fancy that the real reason why I lectured so much was to indulge my showing-off propensities. To stand before a class or an audience; to be the cynosure of all eyes; to have a crowd hanging on your words . . . . all showing off! Very, very human, but . . . . bad for the audience.

When a teacher lectures he is unconsciously giving expression to his desire to gain a feeling of superiority. That, I fancy, is the deepest wish of every one of us . . . . to impress others, to be superior. You see it in the smallest child. Give him an audience, and he will show off for hours. The boy at the top of the class gains his feeling of superiority by beating the others at arithmetic, while the dunce at the bottom of the class gains his in more original ways . . . punching the top boy at playtime, scoring goals at football, spitting farther than anyone else in school. I have seen a boy smash a window merely to draw attention to himself, and thus to gain a momentary feeling of superiority.

And we grown-ups are boys at heart. The boy is the father to the man. Take, for instance, a childish trait—exhibitionism. Most children at an early age love to run about naked, to show off their bodies. Later the conventions of society make the child repress this wish to exhibit himself. But we know that a repressed wish does not die ; it merely buries itself in the unconscious. Many years later the exhibition impulse comes out in sublimated form as a desire to show off before the public . . . . hence our politicians, actors, actresses, street-corner revivalists, and—er—dominies.

Now I hasten to add that there is nothing to be ashamed of in being a politician or a dominie. But if I lecture a class I am making the affair my show, and I am not the most important actor in the play ; I am the scene-shifter ; the real actors who should be declaiming their lines are sitting on hard benches staring at me and wondering what I am raving about. Each little person is thirsting to show his or her superiority, and he never gets the chance. Occasionally I may ask a sleepy-looking urchin what are the exports to Canada, and he may gain a slight feeling of superiority if he can tell the right answer. Yet I fancy that his unconscious self despises me and my question. Why in all the earth should I ask a question when I know the answer ? The whole thing is an absurdity. The only questions asked in a school should be asked by the pupils.

The truth is that our schools do not give

education ; they give instruction. And it is so very easy to instruct, and so very easy to go on talking, and so very easy to whack Tommy when he does not listen. Our prosy lectures are wasted time. The children would be better employed playing marbles.

Of course if a child asks for information that is a different story. He is obviously interested . . . . . that is if he isn't trying to tempt you into a long explanation so that you will forget to hear his Latin verbs. Children soon understand our little vanities, and they soon learn to exploit them.

* * * * * *

" I had a scene in school to-day," remarked Mac while we were at tea to-night.

" What happened ? " I asked.

" Tom Murray was wrong in all his sums, and he wouldn't hold out his hand," and by Mac's grim smile I knew that the bold Tom had been conquered.

" What would you have done in a case like that ? " asked Mac.

" I would never have a case like that, Mac. If he had all his sums wrong I should sit down and ask myself what was wrong with my teaching."

" I didn't mean that," he said ; " what I meant was : what would you do if Tom defied you ? "

"That wouldn't happen either, Mac. Tom couldn't defy me because you can only defy an authority, and I'm not an authority."

Mac shook his head.

"You won't convince me, old chap. A boy like Tom has to be dealt with with a firm hand."

I studied his face for a time.

"You know, Mac," I said, "you puzzle me. You're one of the kindest decentest chaps in the world, and yet you go leathering poor Tom Murray. Why do you do it?"

"You must keep discipline," he said.

I shook my head.

"Mac, if you knew yourself you wouldn't ever whack a child."

This seemed to tickle him.

"Good Lord!" he laughed, "I could write a book about myself! I'm one of the most introspective chaps ever born."

"And you understand yourself?"

"I have no illusions about myself at all, old chap. I know my limitations."

"Well, would you mind telling me why you are a bit of a nut?" I asked. "It isn't usual for a country dominie to wear a wing collar, a bow tie, and shot-silk socks."

"That's easy," he said quickly. "I think that teachers haven't the social standing they ought to have, and I dress well to uphold the dignity of the profession. Don't you believe me?" he demanded as I smiled.

"Quite! I believe you're quite honest in your belief, but it's wrong you know. There must be a much more personal reason than that."

"Rot!" he said. "Anyway, what is the reason?"

"I don't know, Mac; it would take months of research to discover it. I can't explain your psychology, but I'll tell you something about my own. These swagger corduroys I'm wearing . . . . . when I bought them someone asked me why I chose corduroy, and I at once answered: 'Economy! They'll last ten years!' But that wasn't the real reason, I bought them because I wanted to have folk stare at me. I've got an inferiority complex, that is an inner feeling of inferiority. To compensate for it I go and order a suit that will make people look at me; in short, that I may be the centre of all eyes, and thus gain a feeling of outward superiority."

This sent Mac off into a roar of laughter.

"You're daft, man!" he roared.

After a minute or two he said; "But what has all this to do with Tom Murray?"

"A lot," I said seriously. "You think you whack Tom because you must have discipline, but you whack him for a different reason. In your deep unconscious mind you are an infant. You want to show your self-assertion just as a kid does. You leather Tom because you've never outgrown your seven-year-old stage. On market-day, when Tom walks behind a drove and whacks the stots over the hips with a stick, he is doing exactly what you did this afternoon. You are both infants."

I have had to give up lecturing Mac, for he always takes me as a huge joke. He is a good fellow, but he has the wonderful gift of being blind to anything that might make him reconsider his values. Many people protect themselves in the same way—by laughing. I have more than once seen an alcoholic laugh heartily at his wrecked home and lost job.

II.

WHAT an amount of excellent material Mac and his kind are spoiling. Tom Murray is a fine lad, full of energy and initiative, but he has to sit passive at a desk doing work that does not interest him. His creative faculties have no outlet at all during the day, and naturally when free from authority at nights he expresses his creative interest anti-socially. He nearly wrecked the five-twenty the other night ; he tied a huge iron bolt to the rails. Mac called it devilment, but it was merely curiosity. He had had innumerable pins and farthings flattened on the line, and he wanted to see what the engine really could do.

There is devilment in some of Tom's activities, for example in his deliberate destruction of Dauvit's apple tree. Mac and the law would give him the birch for that, but fortunately Mac and the law don't know who did it. Tom's destructiveness is only the direct result of Mac's authority. Suppression always has the same result ; it turns a young god into a young devil. Had I Tom in a free school all his activities would be social and good.

And yet nearly every teacher believes in Mac's way. They suppress all the time, and what is worst of all they firmly believe they are doing the best thing.

"Look at Glasgow!" cried Mac the other night when I was talking about the crime of authority. "Look at Glasgow! What happened there during the war? Juvenile crime increased. And why? Because the fathers were in the army and the boys had no control over them; they broke loose. That proves that your theories are potty."

I believe that juvenile crime did increase during the war, and I believe that Mac's explanation of the phenomenon is correct. The absence of the father gave the boy liberty to be a hooligan. But no boy wants to be a hooligan unless he has a strong rebellion against authority. No boy is destructive if he is free to be constructive. I think that the difference between Mac and myself is this: he believes in original sin, while I believe in original virtue.

I wonder why it is so difficult to convert the authority people to the new way of thinking. There must be a deep reason why they want to cling to their authority. Authority gives much power, and love of power may be at the root of the desire to retain authority. Yet I fancy that it is deeper than that. In Mac, for instance, I think that his quickness in becoming angry at Tom's insubordination is due to the insubordination within himself. Like most of us Mac has a father complex, and he fears and hates any authority exercised over himself. So in squashing Tom's rebellion he is unconsciously squashing the rebellion in his own soul. Tom's rebellion could not affect me because I have got rid of my father complex, and his rebellion would touch nothing in me.

Authority will be long in dying, for too many people cling to it as a prop. Most people like to have their minds made up for them; it is so easy to obey orders, and so difficult to live your own life carrying your own burden and finding your own path. To live your own life . . . . . that is the ideal. To discover yourself bravely, to realise yourself fully, to follow truth even if the crowd stone you. That is living . . . . . but it is dangerous living, for that way lies crucifixion. No one in authority has ever been crucified; every martyr dies because he challenges authority. . . . . Christ, Thomas More, Jim Connolly.

* * * * * *

Duncan and McTaggart the minister were in to-night, and we got on to the subject of wit and humour. Having a psycho-analysis complex I mentioned the theory that we laugh so as to give release to our repressions. The others shook their heads, and I decided to test my theory on them. I told them the story of the golfer who was driving off about a foot in front of the teeing marks. The club secretary happened to come along.

"Here, my man!" cried the indignant secretary, "you're disqualified!"

"What for?" demanded the player.

"You're driving off in front of the teeing mark."

The player looked at him pityingly.

"Away, you bletherin' idiot!" he said tensely, "I'm playing my third!"

"Now," I said to the others, "I'm going to tell you one by one what your golf is like. You, McTaggart, are a scratch man or a plus man. Is that so?"

"Plus one," he said in surprise. "How did you guess?"

"I didn't guess," I said with great superiority. "I found out by pure science. You didn't laugh at my joke; you merely smiled. That shows that bad golf doesn't touch any complex inside you. The man who takes three strokes to make one foot of ground means nothing to you because, as I say, there's nothing in yourself it touches."

"Wonderful!" cried the minister.

"It's quite simple," I crowed, "and now for Mac! You, Mac, are a rotten player; you take sixteen to a hole."

'Only ten," protested Mac hastily. "How the devil did you know? I've never played with you."

"Deduction, my boy. You roared at my

joke, because it touched your bad golf complex. In fact you were really laughing at yourself and your own awful golf."

"What about me?" put in Duncan.

Now there was something in Duncan's eye that should have warned me of danger, but I was so proud of my success that I plunged confidently.

"Oh, you don't play golf," I said airily.

"Wrong!" he cried, "I do! And I'm worse than Mac too!"

I was astounded.

"Impossible!" I cried. "You never laughed at my story at all; that is it touched nothing whatsoever inside you."

Duncan shook his head.

"You're completely wrong this time."

"Well, why *didn't* you laugh?" I asked.

He grinned.

"I dunno. Possibly it is because I first heard that joke in my cradle."

* * * * * *

Mac's infant mistress was off duty to-day owing to an attack of influenza, and he gladly accepted my offer to take her place.

Half-an-hour after my entry into the room Mac came in to see how I was getting on. Most of the infants were swarming over me, and Mac frowned. At his frown they all crept back silently to their seats.

"You seem to have the fatal gift of demoralising children," he growled.

It hadn't struck me before, but it is a fact; I do demoralise children. Not long ago I entered a Montessori school, and I spoke not one word. In five minutes the insets and long stairs were lying neglected in the middle of the floor, and the kiddies were scrambling over me. I felt very guilty for I feared that if Montessori herself were to walk in she would be indignant. I cannot explain why I affect kiddies in this way. It may be that intuitively they know that I do not inspire fear or respect; it may be that they unconsciously recognise the baby in me. Anyway, as Mac says, it is a fatal gift.

I think Miss Martin the infant mistress is a good teacher. Her infants do not fear her, and I am sure they love her. The only person they fear is Mac, poor dear old Mac, the most lovable soul in the world. He tries hard to show his love for the infants but somehow they know that behind his smile is the grim head-master who leathers Tom Murray. I sent wee Mary Smith into Mac's room to fetch some chalk to-day, and she wept and feared to enter. Occasionally, I believe, Mac will enter the room, seize a wee mite who is speaking instead of working, and give him or her a scud with the tawse. I wonder how a good soul like Mac can do it.

I have an unlovely story of a board school.

An infant mistress lay dying, and in her delirium she cried in terror lest her head-master should come in again and strap her dear, wee infants. It is a true story, and it is the most damning indictment of board school education anyone could wish for. She was a good woman who loved children, and if fear of her head-master brought terror to her on her deathbed, what terrors are such men inspiring in poor wee infants? The men who beat children are exactly in the position of the men who stoned Jesus Christ; they know not what they do, nor do they know why they do it.

* * * * * *

There was a stranger in Dauvit's shop when I entered to-day, a seedy-looking whiskered man with a threadbare coat and extremely dirty linen. Shabby genteel would be the Scots description of him.

Dauvit asked me a casual question about London, and the stranger became interested at once.

"Ah," he said, "you're from London, are ye? Man, yon's a great place, a wonderful place!"

I nodded assent.

"Man," he continued, "yon's the place for sichts! Could anything beat the procession at the Lord Mayor's show, eh?"

I meekly admitted that I had never seen the Lord Mayor's show, and he raised his eyebrows in surprise.

"But I'll tell ye what's just as good, mister, and that's the King and Queen opening Parliament. Man, yon's a sicht, isn't it?"

"I—er—I haven't had the opportunity of seeing it," I said.

He looked more surprised than ever.

"But, man, I'll tell ye what's just as good, and that's a big London fire. Man, to see the way the firemen go up the ladders like monkeys. Yon's a sicht for sair een!"

"I never had the luck to see a fire in London," I said hesitatingly. "When were you last in town?"

He did not seem to hear my question; he was evidently thinking of other London thrills.

"Man," he said ruminatingly, "often while I sit in the Tarbonny Kirk I just sit and think aboot Westminster Abbey. Man, yon's a kirk! I suppose you'll be there ilka Sunday?"

I found it difficult to tell him that I had never been in the Abbey, but I managed to get the words out, and then I avoided his reproachful eye. He knocked out his pipe, and I took the action to be a symbolic one meaning: You are an empty sort of person. He studied me critically for a time, then he brightened.

"Aye," he said cheerfully, "London's a graund place, but, for sichts give me New York."

I felt more humble than ever, for I had never travelled. He seemed to guess that by the look of me, for he never asked my opinion of New York.

"Man," he said warmly, "yon's a place! Yon skyscrapers! Phew!" and he whistled his wonder and admiration. "And the streets! Man, ye canna walk on the sidewalk at the busy times. A wonderfu' place, New York, but, as for me, give me the West, California and 'Frisco."

"You have travelled much, sir," I said reverently. The "sir" seemed to come naturally; my inferiority complex was touched on the raw.

Again he ignored me.

"To see yon cowboys! Man, yon's what I call riding! And the Indians!"

He sighed; it was obvious that he was living over again his life in the western wilds. A wistful look crept into his eyes, and I began to construct his sad story. He loved a maid, but the bruiser of the camp loved her also . . . . . hence the broken-down clothes, the dirty collar. But anon he cheered up again.

"Yes," he said, "I love the West, but for colour and climate give me Japan."

I was so confused now that I had to blow out my pipe vigorously. I glanced at Dauvit, but he was sharpening his knife on the emery hone, and did not appear to be interested. I felt a vague anger against Dauvit; why wasn't he helping me in my trial?

"Japan," continued the irrepressible stranger, "is one of the finest countries in the world, but, for climate give me Siberia."

I hastily thought to myself that if I were Lenin I . . . . . but I did not follow out my daydream, for the stranger brought me back to earth by inquiring what was my honest and unbiassed opinion of the Peruvians. I very cleverly pretended that I had swallowed some nicotine, and, after a polite pause for my answer, he went off to the subject of pearl fishing at Thursday Island. Then he looked at Dauvit's clock.

"Jerusalem!" he gasped, "the pub shuts at twa o'clock!" and he rushed out of the shop. I heaved a great sigh of relief, and then I heaved a greater sigh of relief.

I seized Dauvit by the arm.

"Dauvit," I gasped, "who—who is your cosmopolitan friend?"

"My what kind o' a friend?"

"Your world-travelled friend, Dauvit. Tell me who he is."

Dauvit laughed softly.

"That," he said, "was Joe Mill. He bides wi' his old mother in that cottage at the foot o' the brae. To the best o' my knowledge he hasna been further than Perth in his life."

"But!" I cried in amazement, "he has been everywhere!"

"He hasna," said Dauvit shortly, "but he works the cinema lantern at the Farfar picter hoose."

* * * * * *

I had a long talk to-night with Macdonald about self-government in schools, and I told him of my plans for running a self-governing school in Highgate. At the end of the discussion I had the biggest surprise of my life. Mac smoked for a long time in silence, then he turned to me suddenly.

"Look here, old chap, I'll have a shot at introducing self-government to-morrow," he said with enthusiasm.

I grasped his hand.

"Excellent! Mac, you're a wonder! You're a brave man!"

"I don't feel brave," he said nervously. "It's going to be a very difficult job."

"It is," I said grimly, "and the most difficult part is for you to keep out of it."

"What do you mean?"

"I mean that you have been an authority for so long that you'll find yourself issuing orders unthinkingly. More than that the kiddies are so much dependent on you that they will wait to see how you vote."

"What's the best way to begin it?" he asked.

"Simply walk in to-morrow and say : 'Look here, you are going to govern yourselves. I have no power ; I won't order anyone to do anything ; I won't punish anyone. Now, do what you like'."

Mac looked frightened.

"But, good Lord, man, they'll—they'll wreck the school !"

"Funk !" I laughed.

His eyes were full of excitement.

"It'll be an awful job to keep my hands off them," he said half to himself.

"Funk !" I said again

"It's all very well, but . . . . . well, I'm rather strict you know."

"So much the better ! All the better a row !"

"You Bolshevist !" he laughed. He was like a boy divided between two desires—to steal the apples and to escape the policeman. I half feared that his courage would desert him.

"Here," he said, "why not come over to school ?"

The temptation was great and I wavered.

"No," I said at last, "I can't do it. My presence would distract the children, and . . . . they won't smash all the windows in front of a stranger. You want my support, you dodger!"

But I would give ten pounds to be in Mac's schoolroom to-morrow morning.

* * * * * *

I went out this morning and sat on the school wall and smoked my pipe. I strained my ears for the first murmur of the approaching storm. Not a sound came from the schoolroom.

"Mac has funked it after all," I groaned, and went in to help Mrs. Macdonald to pare the potatoes.

When Mac came over at dinner-time his face wore a thoughtful look.

"You coward!" I cried.

"Coward!" he laughed. "Why, man, the scheme is in full swing!"

Then I asked him to tell me all about it.

"Your knowledge of children is all bunkum," he began. "You said there would be a row when I announced that I gave up authority."

"And wasn't there?"

"Not a vestige of one. The kids stared at me with open mouth, and . . . . ."

"And what?"

"Oh, they simply got out their books and began their reading lesson. As quiet as mice too."

"And do you mean to tell me that it made no difference?" I asked.

"None whatever. I tell you they just went on with the timetable as usual."

"But didn't they talk to each other more?"

"There wasn't a whisper."

I considered for a minute.

"What exactly did you say to them when

you announced that they were to have self-government ? "

" I just said what you told me last night."

" Did you add anything ? "

He avoided my eye.

" Of course I said that I trusted them to carry on the school as usual," he admitted reluctantly.

" Thereby showing them that you didn't trust them at all," I explained. " Mac, you must have been a thundering strict disciplinarian. The kiddies are dead afraid of you. I fear that you'll never manage to have self-government. This fear of you must be broken, and you've got to break it."

" But how ? " he asked helplessly.

" By coming down off your pedestal. You must become one of the gang. One dramatic exhibition will do it."

" What do you mean ? "

" Smash a window ; chuck books about the room . . . . . anything to break this idea that you are an exalted being whose eye is like God's always ready to see evil."

Mac looked annoyed and injured.

" What good will my fooling do ? " he asked.

" But," I protested seriously, " it's essential. You simply must break your authority if you are to have a free school. There can be no real self-expression if you are always standing by to stamp out slacking and noise."

"But," he protested, "didn't I tell 'em I was giving up my authority?"

"Yes, but they don't believe you. You've got the eye of an authority."

He was by this time getting rather indignant.

"I can't go the length you do," he said sourly. "I'm not an anarchist."

"In that case I'd advise you to chuck the experiment, Mac," I said with an indifferent shrug of my shoulders. The shrug nettled Mac; he is one of the bull-dog breed, and I saw his lips set.

"I've begun it, and I won't chuck it," he said firmly. "And I hope to prove that your methods are all wrong. Let it come gradually; that's what I say."

When he came over at four o'clock his face glowed with excitement. He slapped me on the back with his heavy hand.

"Man," he cried, "it's going fine! We had our first trial this afternoon."

"Go on," I said.

"Oh, it was a first class start. Jim Inglis threw his pencil at Peter Mackie."

"I hope he didn't miss," I said flippantly.

Mac ignored my levity.

"And then I didn't know what to do. My first impulse was to haul him out and strap him, but of course I didn't. I just said to the class: 'You saw what Jim Inglis did? You have to decide what is to be done about it'."

"And they answered: 'Please, sir, give him the tawse'?" I said.

Mac laughed.

"That's exactly what they did say, but I told them that they were governing themselves, and suggested that they elect a chairman and decide by vote."

"Bad tactics," I commented. "You should have left them to settle their own procedure. What happened then?"

"They appointed Mary Wilson as chairman, and then John Smith got up and proposed that the prisoner get six scuds with the tawse from me. The motion was carried unanimously."

"You refused of course?" I said.

"Man, I couldn't refuse. I was alarmed. because six scuds are far too many for a little offence like chucking a pencil. I made them as light as possible."

I groaned.

"What would you have done?" he asked.

"Taken the prisoner's side," I said promptly, "I should have chucked every pencil in the room at the judge and jury. Then I should have pointed out that I refused to do the dirty work of the community."

"But where does the self-government come in there?" he protested. "Chucking things at the jury is anarchy, pure anarchy."

"I know," I said simply. "But then anarchy

is necessary in your school. You don't mean to say that the children thought that throwing a pencil was a great crime? What happened was that they projected themselves on to you; unconsciously they said: 'The Mester thinks this a crime and he would punish it severely.' They were trying to please you. I say that anarchy is necessary if these children are to get free from their dependence on you and their fear of you. So long as you refuse to alter your old values you can't expect the kids to alter their old values. Unless you become as a little child you cannot enter the kingdom of — er — self-government."

I know that Mac's experiment will fail, and for this reason; he wants his children to run the school themselves, but to run it according to his ideas of government.

* * * * * *

I think of an incident that happened when I was teaching in a school in London. I had a drawing lesson, and the children made so much noise that the teacher in the adjoining room came in and protested that she couldn't make her voice heard. The noise in my room seemed to increase . . . . . and the lady came in again. The noise increased.

Next day I went to my class.

"You made such a noise yesterday that

the teacher next door had to stop teaching. She rightly complained. Now I want to ask you what you are going to do about it."

"You should keep us in order," said Findlay, a boy of eleven.

"I refuse," I said; "it isn't my job."

This raised a lively discussion; the majority seemed to agree with Findlay.

"Anyway," I said doggedly, "I refuse to be your policeman," and I sat down.

There was much talking, and then Joy got up.

"I think we ought to settle it by a meeting, and I propose Diana as chairman."

The idea was hailed with delight, and Diana was elected chairman and she took my desk seat and I went and sat down in her place.

Joy jumped up again.

"I propose that Mr. Neill be put out of the room."

The motion was carried.

"Righto!" I said, as I moved to the door, "I'll go up to the staff-room and have a smoke. Send for me if you want me."

I smoked a cigarette in the staff-room, and as I threw the stump into the grate Nancy came in.

"You can come down now."

I went down.

"Well," I said cheerily, "have you decided anything?"

"Yes," said the chairman, "we have decided that——"

Joy was on her feet at once.

"I propose that we don't tell Mr. Neill what we have decided. We can ask him at the end of the week if he notices any difference in our behaviour."

Others objected, and the matter was put to the vote. The voting was a draw, and Diana gave the casting vote in favour of my being told. Then she said that the meeting had agreed that if anyone made a row in class, he or she was to be sent to Coventry for a whole day.

"What will happen if I speak to the one that has been sent to Coventry?" asked Wolodia.

"We'll send you to Coventry too," said Diana, and the meeting murmured agreement.

No one was ever sent to Coventry, but I had no further complaints against the class. One interesting feature in the affair was this: Violet, a lively girl full of fun, one day got up and, as a joke, proposed that Mr. Neill be sent to Coventry. The others, usually willing to laugh with Violet, protested.

"That's just silly, Violet," they said. "If you propose silly things like that we'll send you to Coventry."

Then someone got up and proposed that Violet be sent to Coventry for being silly, and Diana at once took the chair. I got up and moved the negative, pointing out that I made no charge against her, and she was acquitted by a majority of one. I mention this to show that children of eleven and twelve can take their responsibilities seriously.

When I told the story to Macdonald he said : " But why didn't you join in their noise ? "

" For two reasons, Mac," I said. " Firstly these children were not under the suppression of government schools : secondly it wasn't my school."

III.

THE servant girl at the Manse has had an illegitimate child, and Meg Caddam, the out-worker at East Mains is cutting her dead. Thus the gossip of Mrs. Macdonald. Meg Caddam is the unmarried mother of three.

I have noticed again and again that the most severe critic of the unmarried mother is the unmarried mother, and I have many a time wondered at the fact. Now I know the explanation; it is the familiar Projection of a Reproach. Meg feels guilty because of her three children, but her guilt is repressed, driven down into the unconscious.

She dare not allow her conscious mind to face the truth, for then the truth would lower her self-respect; it would be unpleasant, out of harmony with her ego-ideal. But it is easy for her to project this inner reproach on to someone else, hence her blaming of the Manse lassie. Meg Caddam is really condemning herself, but she does not know it.

I used to despise the Meg Caddams as hypocrites, but, poor souls, they are not hypocrites. Their condemnation of their fallen sisters is genuine. It is wonderful how we all manage to divide our minds into compartments. Sandy

Marshall of Brigs Farm is a most religious man, yet the other day he was fined for watering his milk. It is unjust to say that his religion is hypocritical. What happens is that his religion is shut up in one compartment of his mind, and his dishonesty is shut up in another compartment . . . . . and there is no direct communication between the compartments.

The mind is like one of the older railway carriages; education's task is to convert the old carriage into a new corridor carriage with communication between the compartments. Meg Caddam's own transgression against current morality is locked up in one compartment; her condemnation of the Manse girl is in another compartment. There is an unconscious communication, but there is no conscious communication. I don't know what Meg would say if a cruel friend pointed out to her that she also was a fallen woman.

I think that the gossip of this village mostly consists of projected reproaches. Liz Ramsay, an old maid and the super-gossip of Tarbonny, came into the schoolhouse this morning.

"Do ye ken this," she said to Mrs. Macdonald, "it's my opeenion that Mrs. Broon died o' neglect. I went to the door the day afore she died to speer hoo she was, and her daughter cam to the door, and do ye ken this? That lassie was smiling. . . . . *smilin'* . . . . . and her auld mother upstairs at death's door.

Eh, Mrs. Macdonald, she's a heartless woman that Mary Broon. She killed her mother by neglect, that's what she did."

After she had gone I said to Mrs. Macdonald : " Who nursed Liz's mother when she died last June ? "

" Nobody," said Mrs. Macdonald grimly. " Liz had too much gossip to retail in the village, and I'm told that Liz was seldom in the house."

I think I am guessing fairly rightly when I say that Liz feels guilty of neglecting her own mother, and like Meg Caddam she projects the reproach on to someone else.

* * * * * *

Last Friday night I gave a lecture to the Literary Society in Tarby, our nearest town. I chose the subject of forgetting, and I told the audience of Freud and his great work in connection with the unconscious. To-day's *Tarby Herald* in reporting the lecture prints phonetically the spelling " Froid," but the *Tarby Observer* goes one better when it says : " Mr. Neill is an exponent of the new science of Cycloanalysis."

Which reminds me of a painful episode that took place when I was eighteen. I was much enamoured of a young university student, and I always strove to gain her favour by being interested in the things she liked. One day she informed me that she intended to take the Psychology class at St. Andrews the following session. I had never heard the word before, and I made a bold guess that it had something to do with cycles. In consequence we talked at cross purposes for a while.

"I'd love a subject like that," I said warmly.

"Most of it will be experimental psychology," she said.

My enthusiasm increased. I thought of the many experiments I had tried with my old cushion-tyred cycle.

"Excellent!" I cried. "A sort of training in inventing. Cranks, eh?" At that time my one ambition in life was to invent a folding crank that would give double power on hills.

The lady looked at me sharply.

"Why cranks?" she demanded. "I don't see it. Psychology has nothing to do with crystal-gazing you know."

I was gravelled.

"But what's the idea?" I asked. "Improvement of design?"

This made her think hard.

"H'm, yes, I think I know what you mean," she said slowly. "But remember that before you can improve the psyche you must know the psyche."

I hastened to agree.

"Certainly, but all the same there is much room for improvement. You don't want to come off at every hill, do you?"

This seemed to make her more thoughtful still.

" No," she said, " but don't you think that the mind makes the hill ? "

This staggered me.

" Eh ? " I gasped. " Mean to say that I broke my chain on Logie Brae yesterday because——"

" I'm afraid it is too difficult for me," she said apologetically. " I get lost in metaphors."

Then I asked her something about ball bearings, and she threw me a grateful smile . . . . for changing the subject—as she thought.

The most amusing joke is the joke about the innocent or ignorant. Everyone is tickled at the Hamlet joke I referred to in my *Log*. The school inspector was dining with the local squire.

" Funny thing happened in the village school to-day," he said. " I was a little bit ratty, and I fired a question at a sleepy-looking boy at the bottom of the class.

" Here, boy, who wrote *Hamlet ?* "

The little chap got very flustered.

" P—please, sir, it wasna me ! "

The squire laughed boisterously.

" And I suppose the little devil had done if after all ! " he cried.

We laugh at that story because we have all made mistakes owing to ignorance, and blushed for them a hundred times later. When we laugh at the squire, we are really laughing at ourselves ; we are getting rid of our pent-up self-shame. That's why a good laugh is a medicine ; it allows us to get rid of psychic poison, just as a good sweat rids us of somatic poison. Charlie Chaplin has possibly cured more people than all the psycho-analysts in the world.

* * * * * *

Public speaking is a most difficult thing. It is difficult enough when you know your subject, and it is almost impossible if you don't. At a dinner someone asks you to get up and propose the health of the ladies. I tried proposing that toast once ; luckily most of the diners were under the table by that time. What can one say about the ladies ?

When you have a definite subject to talk about, and when you know everything about it, even then public speaking is difficult. You stand up before a sea of faces. You see no one ; you dare not catch anyone's eye. The best plan is to fix your eye on the blurred face of the man at the back of the hall. You feel that the audience is vaguely hostile.

At one time I used to go straight into my subject . . . "Ladies and gentlemen, the subject of evolution has occupied the minds of—" Then the audience began to rustle, and the women turned to look at the hats behind them.

Nowadays I am more wary. I stand up and gaze over the sea of faces for a full minute. There is absolute silence. I put my hands into my trouser pockets and gaze at the ceiling, as if I were considering whether I should go on or give it up and go home. Even the boys at the back of the hall begin to look towards the platform.

Then I look down and find that my tie is hanging out of my waistcoat, and I adjust it. A girl of ten giggles.

"What can you expect for fivepence halfpenny?" I ask, and the audience gasps.

"Why doesn't someone invent a long tie that won't come out at the ends?" I ask wearily, and there is a laugh. I go on from ties to collars, and there is another laugh. After that I can speak on education for two hours, and everyone in the hall will listen with great attention.

The first thing in public speaking is to get on good terms with your audience, and I claim that the best way to do this is to show them the human side of yourself. Some of your hearers are agin you; they have come out to criticise you. You disarm them at once by treating yourself as a joke. Of course you must suit your tactics to your audience. The tie remark will put me on good terms with a rural audience, but it would fail in a lecture to teachers in the Albert Hall.

An important thing to remember is that

crowd humour is quite different from individual humour. A crowd will roar with delight if the lecturer accidentally knocks over the drinking glass on the table, but no individual ever laughs when a similar accident happens in a private room. Read the reports of speeches in the House of Commons. You will read that Lloyd George, in a speech, says: "And now let us turn to Ireland (loud laughter)." But in cold print it isn't a very good joke.

Quite a good way of commencing a lecture is to tell a short story . . . . about the chairman if possible. But you must be careful. Keep off the topic of the chairman's marital affairs; he may have lodged a divorce petition the week before.

On second thoughts I think it better not to mention the chairman at all. Last winter the local mayor was presiding at a lecture I gave in an English town. After I had delivered the lecture, he got up.

"I came to this meeting feeling dead tired," he said, "but after Mr. Neill's lecture I feel as fresh as a daisy."

I rose in alarm.

"Ladies and gentlemen," I said hastily, "the mayor has been sitting behind me. Do tell me: has he been asleep?"

In the ante-room afterwards he assured me solemnly that he hadn't been asleep.

On Friday night I began thus: "Mr. Chairman, ladies and gentlemen, I am going to talk about Forgetting." Then I put my hand in my inside coat pocket; then I tried another pocket, and got very excited while I rummaged every pocket I had.

"I must apologise," I said, "but I have forgotten my notes."

The audience laughed, and we became the best of friends.

* * * * * *

Forgetting is very often intentional. We forget what we do not want to remember. Brown writes to me saying that he is taking the wife and kids to the seaside, and would I please pay him the fiver I owe him? I at once sit down and write: "My dear Brown, I enclose a cheque for five quid. Many thanks for the loan. Hope you all have a good time at the sea."

Three days later Brown replies.

"Thanks for your letter, old man, but you forgot to enclose the cheque."

Why did I forget the cheque? Because I did not want to pay up. Consciously I did want to pay, for I wrote out the cheque all right, but my unconscious did not want to pay, and it was my unconscious that made me slip the cheque under the blotter.

Last summer I was invited to spend the week-end with some people at Stanmore. I did not want to go; a previous week-end with them had been most boring. However, I reluctantly consented to go out on the Saturday morning. When Saturday morning came I was not very much surprised to find that I had forgotten to put out my boots to be cleaned the night before.

"It looks as if I weren't keen on this trip," I said to myself.

I went down to Baker Street and got into the train. We stopped at many stations, and after an hour's journey I began to wonder what was wrong. I asked another man in the compartment when we were due at Stanmore, and he looked surprised.

"Why," he said, "you're on the wrong line; you ought to have changed at Harrow."

I got out at the next station and found that I had an hour to wait for the return train to Harrow. As I sat on the platform I took from my pocket my host's letter.

"Remember," it ran, "to change at Harrow," and the words were underlined.

I arrived four hours late . . . . and spent a pleasant week-end.

One night I was dining out in London, and I told my host the new theory of forgetting.

"That's all bunkum," he said. "Why, there is a flower growing at the front door there, and I can never remember the name of it. I am fond of flowers and never have any difficulty in remembering their names as a rule."

"What flower is it?" I asked.

He tried to recall it, and had to give it up.

"It's the joke of the family," said his wife. "He can never remember the name Begonia."

"Begonia!" cried my host, "that's the name! But surely you don't mean to tell me that I want to forget it? Why should I?"

"It may be associated with something unpleasant in your life," I said.

"Nonsense!" he laughed. "The name conveys nothing to me."

We began to talk about other things. Ten minutes later my host suddenly exclaimed: "I've got it!"

"What?" I asked.

"That Begonia business. When I began business as a chartered accountant over twenty years ago, the first books I had to audit were the books of a company calling itself The Begonia Furnishing Company. I glanced through the books and soon concluded that they were swindlers. I worried over that case for a week; you see it was my first case, and I felt a little superstitious about it. However, at the end of a week I sent the books back saying that I couldn't see my way to undertake the auditing. I've never given them a thought since."

I explained the mechanisms to him. The

whole idea of this Begonia Company was so painful to him that he repressed it, that is, drove it down into the unconscious. Twenty years later he was unconsciously afraid to recall the name of the flower, because the name might have brought back the painful memories of the questionable books.

On Friday night during question time one man got up.

"Why is it, then," he asked, "that I cannot forget the painful time when my wife died?"

I explained that a big thing like that cannot be forgotten, but pointed out that in a case like that the tendency is to forget little things in connection with the big pain. I told him of a case I had myself known. A lady of my acquaintance lived for a few years in Glasgow; then she moved to Edinburgh, where she lived for almost thirty years. Now she lives in London. When she talks of her old home in Edinburgh she always says: "When we were in Glasgow." Invariably she makes this mistake. The reason is almost certainly this: just before she left Edinburgh she lost the one she loved most in life. She says: "When we were in Glasgow" because the word Edinburgh would at once bring back the painful memories connected with her loved one's death.

When I was teaching in Hampstead one of my pupils, a boy of sixteen, came to me one day.

"That's all rot, what you say about wanting to forget things," he said. "I went and left my walking-stick in a bus yesterday."

"Were you tired of it?" I asked.

"Tired of it?" he said indignantly. "Why, it was a beauty, a silver-topped cane, got it from mother on my birthday. That proves your theory is all wrong."

"Tell me about yesterday," I said.

"Well, I was going to a match at Lord's, and it looked rather dull, so mother told me I'd better take a gamp. I said it wasn't going to rain, and took my cane, but I had just got on the top of a bus when down came the rain in bucketfuls and I tell you I was wet to the skin."

"So you did mean to leave your cane behind?" I asked, with a smile.

"But I tell you I didn't!"

"You did, all the same. You kicked yourself because you hadn't taken your mother's advice and brought a gamp. You deliberately left your cane behind you because it had proved useless."

I must add that I failed to convince him.

Connected with forgetting are what Freud calls symptomatic acts. I leave my stick or gloves behind when I am calling at a house: I conclude that I want to go back there. I go to dinner at the Thomsons', and at their front door I absent-mindedly take out my latch-key. This may mean that

I feel at home there; on the other hand, it may mean that I wish I were at home. It is dangerous to dogmatise about the unconscious.

I was sitting one night with Wilson, an old college friend of mine. We talked of old times, and I remarked that he had been very lucky in his lodgings during his college course.

"Yes," he said, "I was in the same digs all the five years. She was a ripping landlady was Mrs.—Mrs.—Good Lord! I've forgotten her name!"

He tried to recall the name, but had to give it up. Two hours later, as he rose to go, he exclaimed: "I remember the name now! Mrs. Watson!"

"What are your associations to the name Watson?" I asked.

"Associations? What do you mean?"

"What's the first thing that comes into your head in connection with the name?" I asked.

He made an effort to concentrate his mind, then suddenly he laughed shortly.

"Good Lord!" he cried, "that's my wife's name!"

I felt that I could not very well ask him anything further, but I suspected that Wilson and his wife were not getting on well together.

* * * * * *

Macdonald's self-government scheme has fizzled out. Yesterday his scholars besought him to return to the old way of authority.

"They were fed up with looking after themselves," explained Mac to me. "They were always trying each other for misdemeanours, and they got sick of it."

I tried to explain to Mac why his attempt had failed. Self-government always fails unless it is complete self-government. Mac was the director and guide; it was he who decided the time-table; it was he who rang the bell and decided the length of the intervals. The children had nothing to do but to keep themselves in order, hence they came to spy on each other. All their energies were directed to penal measures. Their meeting degenerated into a police court. That was inevitable; Mac, by laying down all the laws, prevented their using their creative energy on things and ideas. Naturally they put all the energy they had into the only thing open to them—the trial of offenders. In short, they were employing energy in destruction when they ought to have been employing it in construction. Mac seems indifferent now. "The thing is unworkable," he says.

* * * * * *

Duncan came over to-night. I decided to let him do most of the talking, and he did it well. He has been doing a lot of Regional Geography, and I learned much from his conversation. As the evening wore on he became very affable, and he treated me with the greatest kindness. When Mac was seeing him out Duncan remarked to him: "That chap Neill isn't such a bad fellow after all." Now that I have shown Duncan that I am his inferior in Geography he will listen to me with less irritation.

After supper I went over to see Dauvit. His shop was crowded. Conversation was going slowly, and Dauvit seemed to welcome my entrance.

"Man, Dominie," he said, "I am very glad to see ye, cos the smith here has been tellin' his usual lees aboot the ten pund troot that he nearly landed in the Kernet."

"I doot ye dreamt it, smith," said the foreman from Hillend. "I ken for mysell that the biggest troot I ever catched were in my dreams."

"Dreams is just a curran blethers," said the smith in scorn.

Dauvit looked at him thoughtfully.

"That's a very ignorant remark, smith," he said gravely. "There's naebody kens what a dream is. Some o' thae spiritualist lads say that when ye are asleep yer spirit goes to the next plane, and that maks yer dreams."

The smith laughed loudly.

"Oh, Dauvit! Why, man, I dreamed last nicht that I was sittin' we a great muckle pint o' beer in my hand. Do ye mean to tell me that there is beer in heaven?"

There was a laugh at Dauvit's expense, but the laugh turned against the smith when Dauvit remarked dryly: "I didna mention heaven; I said the next plane, and onybody that kens you, smith, kens that the plane you're gaein' to is the doon plane."

"Naturally, a muckle pint o' beer will be the exact thing ye need doon there," he added.

"It's my opeenion," said old John Peters, "that dreams is just like a motor car withoot the driver. Or like a schule withoot the mester; the bairns just run aboot whaur they like, nae control as ye micht say. Weel, that's jest what happens in dreams; the mester is sleepin' and the bairns do all sorts o' mad things."

"Aye, man, John," said Dauvit, who seemed to be struck with the idea, "there's maybe something in that. Just as bairns when they get free do a' the things they're no meant to do, we do the same things in oor dreams. Goad, but I've done some awfu' things in my dreams!"

Here Jake Tosh the roadman began to cough, and Jake's cough always means that he is about to say something.

"You're just a lot o' haverin' craturs," he said with conviction. "If ye had ony sense ye wud ken that the dream is just cheese and tripe for supper."

Dauvit's eyes twinkled.

"And does the cheese wander frae yer stammick up to yer heid, Jake?"

"I wudna go so far as that," said Jake seriously, "but what I say is that a' the different parts o' the body work thegether. If the stammick has to work a' nicht to digest the cheese, the heid has to keep workin' at the same rate, and that's why ye dream."

"Aye, man, Jake," said Dauvit, "it's a bonny theory, but wud ye jest tell me exactly what work yer toes and fingers and hair are doin' a' nicht to keep upsides wi' yer stammick?"

Jake dismissed the question with an airy wave of his hand.

"Onybody kens that," he said; "they grow. Yer hair and yer nails grow at nichts, and that's why ye need a shave in the mornin'!"

"What if you don't dream at all, Jake?" I asked.

"Ye're needin' some grub," said Jake shortly.

On thinking it over I feel that Jake's theory throws some light on Jung's theory of the libidō.

IV.

THIS morning I had a letter from a friend in London asking when I am going to set up my "Crank School" in London. I began to think about the word Crank. What is a Crank? Usually the name is applied to people who wear long hair, eat vegetarian diet, wear sandals . . . . or something in that line. A Crank therefore is someone who differs from the crowd, and I am led to conclude that the Crank not only differs from the crowd but is usually ahead of the crowd.

According to Sir Martin Conway the crowd has no head; it can only feel. Hence it comes that the main feature of a crowd is its emotion. When we study the street crowd, the mob, this fact is evident; but can we say the same of other crowds . . . the Public School crowd, the Church, the Miners, the Doctors? I think so. The anger that Alec Waugh's book, *The Loom of Youth*, aroused in the public schools was not a thought-out anger; it came from the public school emotion. So with vivisection; the doctors' rage at the anti-vivisectionists is not an intellectual rage; it is simply a professional emotion. Just before I left London I happened one night to be in a company of men who were arguing about Re-incarnation. I had no special views on the subject, but I soon found myself supporting the crowd that was sceptical about Re-incarnation. The reason was that the leader of the anti-reincarnation crowd happened to be a man called Neill. It is highly probable that if two rag-and-bone men got into a scrap in a public house they would support each other simply out of a professional crowd emotion.

That the crowd has no head is evident when we read the popular papers or see the popular films. The most successful papers are those that touch the passions of the mob. I proved this one week last spring. Judges were beginning to introduce the "cat" for criminals, as a means to stem the crime wave. I sat down and wrote an article on the subject, pointing out that this was a going back to the days of barbarism when lunatics were whipped behind the cart's tail. I made a strong plea for the psychological treatment of the criminal, basing my plea on the fact that crime is the result of unconscious workings of the mind, and stating that instead of sending a poor man to penal servitude we ought to analyse his mind and cure him of his anti-social tendencies.

I thought it a jolly good article, and when a prominent Sunday paper returned the manuscript to me I was surprised. My surprise left me on the following Sunday when the same paper blared forth an article by Horatio Bottomley. His title was: "Wanted—the Cat!"

My article was more thoughtful, more humane, more scientific. Why, then, was it suppressed? The answer is simple: it did not fit in with the passions of the crowd. It becomes clear why our best public men—editors, cabinet ministers, publicists are not great thinkers. They must keep in touch with the crowd; they must express the emotions of the crowd.

The attitude of the crowd to the anti-crowd person, the Crank, is never one of contemptuous indifference. It is always distinctly hostile. If I travel by tube from Hampstead to Piccadilly without a hat the other travellers stare at me with mild hostility. Why? Conway, in *The Crowd in Peace and War*, an excellent book, says that this hostility comes from fear. A crowd is always afraid of another crowd, because the only force that can destroy a crowd is a rival crowd. Every individual who differs from the herd is suspect because he is perhaps the nucleus of a rival crowd. That is why the world always crucifies its Christs.

The Crank School, then, is a school where anti-crowd people send their children. It is the school *par excellence* of the Intelligentsia. The tendency of every Crank School is to exaggerate the difference between the crank and the crowd; hence its adoption of an ideal and its concomitant crazes. I cannot for the life of me see why ideals are associated with vegetarianism, long hair, Grecian dress, and sandals, just as I cannot see why art should attach itself to huge bow-ties, long hair, and foot-long cigarette holders.

The Crank School holds up an ideal. It plasters its walls with busts of Walt Whitman and Blake; it hangs bad reproductions of Botticelli round the walls; it sings songs to Freedom; it rhapsodises about Beethoven and Bach. The children of the Crank Schools are, I rejoice to say, not cranks. They leave the boredom of Bach and seek the jazz record on the gramophone; they ignore the pictures of Whitman and Blake and study *The Picture Show* or *Funny Bits*. Many of them think more highly of Charlie Chaplin than of William Shakespeare.

I say again that I rejoice in this; it serves the Crank School people jolly well right. I cannot see by what right educators force what they consider good taste down the children's throats. That is a return to the old way of authority, of treating the child's mind as a blank slate. If the Crank Schools are to improve, they must drop their high moral purpose tone and come down to earth. They must realise that Charlie Chaplin and *John Bull* have their place in education just as Shakespeare and Beethoven have their place. We do not want to turn out cranks who will form a new superior crowd; we want to turn out men and women who will readily join the conventional crowd and help it to reach better ideals.

This question of good taste is a sore one with me. I think it fatal to impose good taste on any child; the child must form his own taste. I know that it is possible to cultivate good taste and to become a very superior cultivated person, but I know that the human, erring, vulgar, music-hall, Charlie Chaplin part of such a person's make-up is not annihilated; it is merely repressed into the unconscious.

I have a theory that each of us has a definite amount of human nature, some of it high, some of it low, or, to phrase it differently, some of it animal, some of it spiritual. We can repress one part, and then we become either a saint or a sinner; the better way is to be both saint and sinner, to look life straight in the face, condemning no one, judging no one.

* * * * * *

Macdonald was re-reading *A Dominie Dismissed* to-night, and he looked up and said: "Look here, you've got an awful lot of swear-words in this book!"

"That," I said, "has a cause, Mac. They aren't really swear-words; the world has grown out of being shocked at a 'damn,' but I am willing to admit that there are more damns and hells than is usual. They are symptomatic; they date back to my early days when swearing was a crime punishable with the strap. They are simply symbols of my freedom. Most bad language is from a like cause. When you foozle on the first tee there is no earthy reason why you should say 'Hell' rather than 'Onions'! But if onions had been taboo when you were a child you would find yourself using the word as a swear. The curse word is the link that joins your foozle with the nursery; whenever you curse you regress, that is, you go back to the infantile."

"But," said Mac, "you don't mean to say that if swearing were permitted to children that they wouldn't curse when they were grown up?"

"I don't think they would," I said. "Nor would there be any unprintable stories if we had a frank sex education. It's a sad fact, Mac, but nine-tenths of humour is due to early suppression and repression."

"Seems to me," said Mac with a laugh, "that if everybody were psycho-analysed, the world would be a pretty dull place."

* * * * * *

A few days ago I found a pot of light paint in Mac's workshop, and, impelled by heaven only knows what unconscious process, I painted my bicycle blue. This morning, the paint being dry, I rode forth into an unsympathetic world. Women came to their doors to stare at my machine, and as they stared they broke into laughter. When I reached the village of Cordyke the school was coming out, and I was greeted with a howl of derision. I thought it a good instance of crowd psychology; I was different from the crowd, and I evoked laughter and derision.

After cycling a few miles, I came to an old man breaking stones at the bottom of a hill. On my approaching he threw down his hammer and turned to stare at my cycle. I dismounted.

"Almichty me!" he said with surprise. "That's a michty colour!"

"It's unusual," I said, as I lit a cigarette.

He fumbled for his clay pipe.

"I've seen black anes, and I wance saw a silver-plated ane, but I never heard tell o' a blue bike afore," he said. "Did you pent it?"

I acknowledged that it was my very own handiwork.

"But," he said in puzzled tones, "what was yer idea?" and he stared at it again. "A michty colour that!"

I threw my bike down on the grass and sat down on the cairn.

"Between you and me," I said mysteriously, "I had to paint it blue."

He raised his eyebrows.

"Yea, man!"

"Government orders," I said carelessly, and began to throw stones at a tree trunk at the other side of the road.

"Government orders?" He looked very much surprised.

"Yes," I said airily. "You see, it's like this. The Coalition Government isn't very firmly placed these days, and, well, I'm an agent for it. Of course, you know that it is really a Tory government, and my bike, as it were, invites the electorate to vote True Blue."

"Yea, man! I thocht that you was maybe ane o' thae temperance lads frae Americky."

"Ah!" I said solemnly, "that reminds me; Pussyfoot tried to induce me to make my tour a sort of joint thing. He suggested that I might carry on my Tory work, and at the same time take part in the blue ribbon campaign. Of course I refused."

"Of coorse," he nodded.

"Officially I am doing Coalition work," I continued conversationally, "but I have motives of my own."

"You don't say!"

"Oh, yes. I am a great admirer of Lord Fisher and the Blue Water school, sometimes spoken of as the Blue Funk school. Again, I find that the Great War has left many people in the blues, and by means of homeopathy I cure 'em ; I mean to say that they come to their doors and laugh at my blue bike. My blue dispels their blues."

The old man did not seem to follow this.

"Of course," I went on, "the Bluebells of Scotland have something to do with my selection of the colour."

"A verra nice sang," he commented.

"An excellent song ! Then there is the well-known phrase 'Once in a Blue Moon,' and innumerable songs about the pale moonlight. Also I once knew a man who had the blue devils."

I tried to think of other phases of blueness, but my stock was almost exhausted.

"Of course," I added, "I am not forgetting the other blues, the Oxford blues, Reckitt's Blue, Blue Coupons, and—and—I'm afraid I can't think of any other blues just at the moment."

The old man drew the back of his hand over his mouth.

"There's the 'Blue Bonnets' up at the tap o' the brae," he suggested thirstily.

"Good idea !" I cried, "come on !" and together we climbed the brae.

* * * * * *

A friend of mine in London has written me asking if I will write an article on Coeducation for an educational journal, in which she is interested. I replied: "I can't see where the problem comes in; to a Scot co-education is not a thing that has to be supported by argument; he accepts it as he accepts the law of gravitation."

I wonder why English people are so afraid of co-education. To this day schools like Bedales, King Alfred's, Harpenden, and Arundale are reckoned as crank schools. The great middle-class of England believes in segregation. Even Dr. Ernest Jones, the most prominent Freudian psycho-analyst in England, appears to be afraid of it.

I can only conjecture that Jones agrees with the middle and upper classes in associating sex with sin. I have never tried to think out my reasons for believing in co-education; possibly the true reason is that having grown up in a co-education atmosphere, co-education has become a part of me just as my Scots accent has. In other words, I may have a co-education complex. If that is so, my arguments will be mere rationalisations, but I give them for what they are worth.

We are all born with a strong sex instinct, and this instinct must find expression in some way. We know that the sex energy can be sublimated, that is, raised to a higher power. For instance, the creative sex urge may be directed to the making of a bookcase, or the making of a century at cricket.

But I know of no evidence to prove that all the instinct can be sublimated. An adolescent may spend his days at craftwork and games, but he will have erotic dreams at nights. All the drawing and painting in the world will not prevent his having emotion when he looks at the face of a pretty girl.

In our segregation schools boys and girls see nothing of each other. The unsublimated sex instinct finds expression in homosexuality, that is the emotion that should go to the opposite sex is fixed on a person of the same sex. I admit that we are all more or less homosexual; otherwise there could be no friendship between man and man, or woman and woman. In our boarding schools the sex instinct often takes the road of auto-eroticism.

In a co-education school the sex impulse is directed to one of the opposite sex. This attachment is nearly always a romantic ideal attachment. I have never known a case that went the length of kissing; among little children at a rural school, yes; at the age of seven I kissed my first sweetheart; but among adolescents I find that neither the boy nor the girl has the courage to kiss. Theirs is a sublimated courtship; they never use the word Love; they talk about "liking So-and-so."

That at many co-education schools this romantic attachment is more or less an underground affair is due to the moral attitude of teachers. They pride themselves on the beautiful sexless attachments of their pupils; they give moral lectures on the subject of kissing, and naturally every pupil in school at once becomes painfully self-conscious on the subject. The truth is that many co-educationists do not in their hearts believe in the system; they still see sin in sex.

To be a thorough success the co-education school must include sex education in its curriculum. The children of the most advanced parents seldom get it at home, and they come to school with the old attitude to sex. Sex education does not mean telling children where babies come from; it should dwell mostly on the psychological side of the question. The child ought to learn the truth about its sex instinct. Most important of all, the child who has indulged in autc-eroticism ought to be helped to get rid of his or her sense of guilt. This sense of guilt is the primary evil of self-abuse; abolish it, and the child is on the way to a self-cure.

How many children can go to their teacher and make confession of sex troubles? Very few. It is the teachers' fault; they set themselves up as moralists, and a moralist is a positive danger to any child.

Not long ago I was addressing a meeting of teachers in south London. At question time a woman challenged me.

"You have condemned moralists," she said;

"do you mean to say that you would never teach a child the difference between right and wrong?"

"Never," I answered, "for I do not know what is right and what is wrong."

"Then I think you ought not to be a teacher," she said.

"I know what is right for me, and wrong for me," I went on to explain, "but I do not know what is right and wrong for you. Nor do I presume to know what is right or wrong for a child."

I was pleasingly surprised to find that the meeting roared approval of my reply.

* * * * * *

Macdonald had to attend a funeral to-day, and he asked me if I would take his classes for an hour. I gladly agreed.

"Give them a lesson on psychology," he said; "it will maybe inprove their behaviour."

I went over to the school at two o'clock, and Mac introduced me, although I had already made friends with most of the children in the playground and the fields. Mac then went away and I sat down at his desk.

"We'll have a talk," I said, "just a little friendly talk between you and me. I want to hear your opinions on some things."

They looked at me with interest.

"Why," I said, "why do you sit quiet in school?"

Andrew Smith put up his hand.

"Please, sir, 'cause if we don't the mester gies us the strap."

"A very sound reason, too," I commented. "And now I want to ask you why you sometimes want to throw papers or slate-pencils about the room."

"Please, sir, we never do that," said little Jeannie Simpson.

"The mester wud punish us," said another girl.

"But," I cried, "surely one of you has thrown things about the room?"

Tom Murray, the bad boy of the school (according to Mac), put up his hand.

"Please, sir, I did it once, but the mester licked me."

"Why did you do it, Tom?"

Tom thought hard.

"I didna like the lesson," he said simply.

I then went on further.

"Now I want you all to think this out: was Tom being selfish when he threw paper, or was he unselfish?"

Everyone, Tom included, judged that the paper-throwing was a selfish act.

"I don't agree," I said. "Tom was trying to do a service to the others; you were all bored by a lesson, and Tom stepped in and took your attention. Unfortunately he also attracted the attention of Mr. Macdonald, but that has nothing to do with Tom's reason for doing it. Tom was the most unselfish of the lot of you; he showed more good than any of you."

"The mester didna think that!" said Tom, with a grin.

Peter Wallace carefully rolled a paper pellet and threw it at Tom.

"Now," I said with a smile, "let's think this out; why did Peter throw that pellet just now?"

"Because the class is bored," said a little girl, and there was a good laugh at my expense.

"Righto!" I laughed, "shall we do something else?" but the class shouted "No!" and I proceeded.

"Peter, do tell us why you threw that pellet."

"For fun," said Peter, blushing and smiling.

"He did it so's the class wud look at him," said Tom Murray, and Peter hid his diminished head.

"A wise answer, Tom," I said; "but we are all like that; we all like to be looked at. Who is the best at arithmetic?"

"Willie Broon," said the class, and Willie Broon cocked his head proudly.

"And who is the best fighter?"

"Tom Murray," answered the boys, and one little chap added: "Tom cud fecht Willie Broon wi' one hand."

Tom tried to look modest.

I went round the class and with one exception every child had at least one branch of life in which he or she found a sense of superiority. The exception was Geordie Wylie, a small lad of thirteen with a white face and a starved appearance. The class were unanimous in declaring that Geordie had no talent.

"He canna even spit far enough," said one boy.

Geordie's embarrassment made me change the subject quickly, but I made up my mind to have a talk with him later.

Some of the reasons for individual pride were strange. Jake Tosh's feeling of superiority lay in the circumstance that his father had laid out a gamekeeper while poaching. Jock Wilson had once found a shilling; another boy had seen "fower swine stickit a' in wan day;" another could smoke a pipe of Bogie Roll without sickening (but I had to promise not to tell the Mester). The girls seemed to find their superiority mostly in lessons, although a few were proud of their needlework.

I then went on to ask them what their highest ambition in life was. The boys showed less imagination than the girls. Six of them wanted to be ploughmen like their fathers. To a townsman this might appear to be a very modest ambition, but to a boy it means power and position; to drive a pair of horses tandem fashion as they do on the East Coast, with the tracer prancing on the braes ; that is what being a ploughman means to a village lad. One boy wanted to be an engineer, another a clerk (" 'cos he doesna need to tak' aff his jaicket to work ! "), another a soldier.

" Not a single teacher ! " I said.

" We're no clever enough," said Tom Murray.

I turned to the girls.

" Now, let's see what ambition you have," I said hopefully. The result was good ; three teachers, two nurses, one typist, one lady doctor, one . . . . lady. This was Maggie Clark. She just wanted to be like one of thae ladies in the picters with a motor car.

" And husband ? " I asked.

" No, I dinna want a man, but I wud like a lot of bairns," she said, and there was a snigger from the boys who had got their sex education from the ploughmen at the Brig of evenings.

Another girl remarked that Maggie's ambition was a selfish one.

" But are you not all selfish ? " I asked. The class indignantly denied it.

" Right," I said, " what do you say to a composition exercise ? "

They obediently got out their composition books, but I told them that my exercise was an easy one. I tore up a few pages into slips and distributed them.

" Now," I said, " suppose I give you five pounds to do what you like with. Write down what you would do with it, fold the paper, and hand it in to me."

They eagerly agreed, and at the end of five minutes I had a hatful of slips. I then drew a line down the centre of the blackboard. On one side I wrote the word Selfish; on the other Unselfish. The class groaned and laughed.

"Now," I said cheerfully, "this will prove whether the class is unselfish or not," and I unfolded the first slip.

"But you'll say we are selfish!" said a boy.

"I have nothing to do with it," I said; "you are to decide by vote. First person . . . . 'I would buy a bicycle': selfish or unselfish?"

"Selfish!" roared the class, and I put a mark in the first column.

"Next paper . . . . 'Scooter, knife, and the rest on ice-cream.'"

"Selfish!" and I put down another mark.

"Next: . . . . 'Buy a pair of boots' . . . . selfish or unselfish?"

The class had to stop and think here.

"Selfish!" said a few.

"Unselfish," said others, "'cos he wud be helpin' his mother."

"Then we'll vote on it," I said, and by a majority of two the act was declared to be unselfish.

We then had a run of knives, tops, candy,

cycles, and no vote was necessary. Then came a puzzler.

"I would send every penny to the starving babies of Germany."

"Unselfish!" cried the class in one voice. I was just about to put the mark in the unselfish column when a boy said: "That's selfish, cos she'd feel proud of being so—so unselfish."

"How do you know it is a she?" I asked.

"'Cause I ken it's Jean Wilson," he answered promptly; "she has took a reid face."

There followed a breezy debate on Jean's act.

"It is selfish," said Mary, "because when you do a kind action you feel pleased with yourself, and it was selfish because if it hadna pleased her she wud never ha' done it."

I asked for a vote and to my astonishment the act was declared selfish by a majority of three. I suspect that conventional Hun Hatred had something to do with the voting.

The voting over I totted up the marks.

"You have judged yourselves," I said, "and according to your own showing you as a class are 87 per cent. selfish and 13 per cent. unselfish."

This essay in composition was not original; I got the idea from Homer Lane, who claimed that it was the best introduction to school psychology. "It is the best way to make children think of their own behaviour," he said, and my experiment has shown this.

When Mac came back I said to him ; " You've got a fine lot of bairns, Mac."

" Had you any difficulty ? " he asked.

" What do you mean ? "

" Oh, I half thought they would try to pull your leg, especially a boy like Tom Murray He is a most difficult chap, you know."

" Tom's a saint," I said ; " every child is a saint if you treat him as an equal. No, I had no difficulty, but I want you to send over Geordie Wylie to me this afternoon. There is something wrong with that boy ; he has no ambition and he has one of the worst inferiority complexes I have ever struck. I want to have a quiet talk with him."

Mac promised, and at three o'clock Geordie came over to the schoolhouse. I took him into the parlour, and he sat nervously on the edge of a chair.

" Tell me about yourself, Geordie," I said, but he did not answer.

" Do you keep rabbits ? "

" Aye."

" What kind ? "

" Twa Himalayas and a half Patty."

" Keep doos ? "

" No."

It was like drawing blood from a milestone.

" What do you do when you go home at nights ? "

It was a long difficult task to get anything out of him. The only fact of value I got was that he was a great reader of Wild West stories. I asked him to come to me again, and he said he would.

To-night I asked Mac about him.

" He's a dreamer, "said Mac, " and he's lazy. I am always strapping him for inattention. He's not a manly boy, never plays games, always stands in a corner of the playground."

" Does he ever fight ? " I asked.

" He's a great coward, but there's one queer thing about him ; when any boy challenges him to fight he goes white about the gills but he always fights . . . . . and gets licked."

" Mac," I said, " will you do me a favour ? Don't whack him again ; it is the worst treatment you can give him. He is a poor wee chap, and he is badly in need of real help."

" All right," said the kindly Mac, " I'll try not to touch him, but he irritates me many a time."

* * * * * *

I had Geordie for an hour this morning. He was taciturn at first, but later he talked freely. He is very much afraid of his father, and he weeps when his father scolds him. This makes the father angrier and he calls Geordie a lassie, a greetin' lassie. This jeer wounds the boy deeply. He is afraid in the dark. He told me that he was puzzled about one thing ; when he goes for his milk at night he is never afraid on the outward journey, but when he leaves the dairy to come home he is always in terror. I asked him what he was afraid of and he told me that he always imagined that there was a man in a cheese-cutter cap waiting to murder him.

"What is a cheese-cutter?" I asked.

"It is a bonnet with a big snout, something like a railway porter's. My father's a porter and he has ane."

Evidently the man he is afraid of is his father. This may account for his lack of fear when he is walking from his home to the dairy. Then he is leaving his father; when he starts to return he is going back to his father and is afraid.

I asked him about his fights with other boys. He always feared a fight but he went through with it so that the other boys should not call him a coward. Naturally he always lost the battle; he fought with a divided mind; while his less imaginative opponent thought only of hitting and winning, Geordie was picturing the end of the fight.

I asked him if he had a sweetheart, and he blushed deeply. He told me that he often took fancies for girls, but they would not have him. Frank Murray always cut him out; Frank was a big hefty lad and the girls like the beefy manly boy.

He does much day-dreaming, phantasying it is called in analysis. His dreams always take the form of conquests; in his day-dream he is the best fighter in the school, the best scholar, the most loved of the girls. His night dreams are often terrifying, and he has more than once dreamt that his father and Macdonald were dead. He finds compensation for his weaknesses in his day-dreams and his reading. He likes tales of heroes who always kill the villians and carry off the heroines.

It is difficult to know what to do in a case like this. The best way would be to change the boy's environment, but that is out of the question. Even then the early fears would go with him; he would transfer his father-complex to another man.

I tried to explain to Mac the condition of Geordie. The boy is all bottled up; his energy should be going into play and work, but instead it is regressing, going back to early ways of adaptation to environment.

"But what can I do with him?" asked Mac.

"Give him your love," I said. "He fears you now, and your attitude to him makes him worse. You must never punish him again, Mac."

"That's all very well," said Mac ruefully, "but what am I to do? Suppose Tom Murray and he talk during a lesson, am I to whack Tom and allow Geordie to get off?"

"Chuck punishment altogether," I said. "You don't need it; it is always the resort of a weak teacher."

"I couldn't do without it," he said.

"All right then," I said wearily, "but I

want you to realise that your punishments are making Geordie a cripple for life."

*   *   *   *   *   *

I went down and had a talk with Geordie's father. He was not very pleasant about it; indeed he was almost unpleasant.

"There's nothing wrong wi' the laddie," he said aggressively. "He's a wee bit lassie-like and he has no pluck."

Here Geordie entered the kitchen, and his father turned on him harshly.

"Started to yer lessons yet?" he demanded.

Geordie muttered something about having had to feed his rabbits.

"I'll rabbit ye! Get yer books oot this minute!" and Geordie crept to a corner and rummaged among some old clothes for his school-bag.

I tried to be as amiable as I could, and avoided controversy. I soon saw that father and mother were not pulling well together, and I suspected that the father's harshness to Geordie was often a weapon to wound the fond mother. I saw that nothing I could say would do any good, and I took my departure.

Later I went to see Dauvit, and found him alone. I asked him to tell me about the Wylies.

"Tam Wylie is wan o' the stupidest men in a ten mile radius," said Dauvit. "But he's no stupid whaur money is concerned; they tell me that he drinks aboot half his weeks' wages, and his puir wife has to suffer. That laddie o' theirs, he was born afore the marriage, and they tell me that Tam wud never ha' married her if he hadna been fell drunk the nicht he put in the banns."

This case of poor Geordie shows what a complexity there is in human affairs. His father has a mental conflict, and he drinks so that he may get away from reality. The father's drinking and the son's reading of romances are fundamentally the same thing; each is trying to get away from a reality he dare not face. No treatment of Geordie could be satisfactory unless at the same time the parents were being treated.

V.

CARROTTY BROON, one of my old scholars, came to Dauvit's shop to-night, and he talked about his pigeons . . . . . his doos he calls them. He keeps a pigeon loft of homers, and he spends a considerable amount in training them.

"Some fowk think," he said, "that a homer will flee hame if ye throw it up five hunder miles awa."

"I've read of flights of seven hundred miles," I said.

Carrotty Broon chuckled.

"I mind o' a homer I had," he went on. "He was a beauty, a reid chequer. His father had flown frae London to Glasgow, and his mither was a flier too. Weel, I took him doon to Monibreck on my bike, and let him off. I never saw him again; five mile, and he cudna find his way hame!"

"He must ha' been shot," said Dauvit, "for thae homers find their way hame by instinct."

"Na, na, Dauvit," said Broon, "they flee by sicht. When ye train a homer ye tak it a mile the first day, syne three miles, syne maybe seven, ten, twenty, fifty, and so on. Send the purest bred homer fower mile without trainin' and ye'll never see him again."

Carrotty Broon told us many interesting things about doos and their ways. We listened to him because he was an authority and we knew little about the subject.

"The only thing I ken aboot doos," said Dauvit with a laugh, "is that when I was a laddie auld Peter Smith and John Wylie keepit homers and they were aye trying competitions in fleein'. John was gaein' to London for his summer holiday, and so him and Peter made a bargain that they wud flee twa homers from London. Weel, John he got to London, and he thocht to himsell that seein' they had a bet o' twa pund on the race, he wud mak sure o' winnin', and so what does he do but tak a pair o' shears and cut the wing o' Peter's doo.

"When John cam hame after a fortnight's trip he met auld Peter at the station.

"'Weel, Peter,' says he, 'wha won the race?'

"'You,' said Peter; 'your doo cam hame the next day, but mine only got hame this mornin'. And it has corns on its feet like tatties.'"

* * * * * *

To-day was Macdonald's Inspection Day, and at dinner time he brought over Mr. J. F. Mackenzie, H.M.I.S., a middle-aged man and Mr. L. P. Smart, assistant I.S., a cheery youth fresh from Oxford. When inspectors dine with the village dominie they never mention the word education. These two talked a lot, and all their conversation was about mountain-climbing in Switzerland. They swopped long prosy yarns about dull incidents, and I was very much bored. So was Mac, but he pretended to be interested, but then he was to see them again, and I wasn't . . . . . at least I prayed that I might not. After a time I began to feel that I was being left out of the conversation, and I waited until Mackenzie paused for a breath.

"Switzerland is very beautiful," I remarked, "but you should see the Andes."

Mackenzie looked at me coldly.

"I haven't been to South America," he said.

"Same here," said I cheerfully, "but I remember seeing pictures of them in the geography book at school."

Mackenzie looked at me more coldly than before. I don't think he liked me, and when the younger man chuckled Mackenzie glared at him. Smart had a sense of humour.

"I'm afraid we have been boring you," he said to me with a smile.

"I'd rather listen to you two talking education," I confessed.

Mackenzie waved the suggestion away.

"I leave education behind when I walk out of the school," he said in grand manner. "Most excellent rhubarb, Mrs. Macdonald.

Home grown? " And then we had ten minutes of garden products versus shop greens. I admit that this inspector had a genius for small talk. We dismissed greens and I led the conversation to hens and ducks. Mackenzie did not know much about them, and he confirmed my opinion of his genius for small talk by saying: " Buff Orpingtons! They are named after Orpington in Kent. I remember staying a night there before I went to Switzerland . . . . ." and the dirty dog took the conversation back to his mountain climbing.

I made a gesture to the younger man and got him out into the garden.

" Why does he waste precious time talking about cabbages and dreary Swiss inns? " I asked.

Smart laughed shortly.

" You know how rich folk talk at table when the servants are present? "

I nodded.

" Well, that's the Chief's attitude to teachers; he never says anything of any importance whatever."

" But why? "

" He is of the old school. He has been inspecting schools for forty years. In the olden days an inspector was a sort of Almighty; teachers quaked before him because with a stroke of his pen he could reduce their money grant. To this day the old man treats teachers as a king treats his subjects—with kindness but with distance."

"Has he any views on education?" I asked. Smart shook his head.

"None, but he has heaps of views on instruction and discipline. By the way, he thinks that Macdonald's discipline is very good."

"And you?"

"I think it rotten," he said ruefully, "but what can I do? A junior inspector is a nobody; if he has any views of his own he has to pocket them. I would chuck out all this discipline rot and go in for the Montessori stunt. Take my tip and never accept an inspectorship."

"I won't," I said hastily.

I liked Smart, and I wish we had more of his stamp in the inspectorate.

When we returned to the dining-room Mackenzie looked at me with interest.

"I didn't know that you were the *Dominie's Log* man till Mr. Macdonald told me two minutes ago," he said. "I am delighted to meet you. I enjoyed your book very much indeed. Very amusing."

He was quite affable now. Writing a book gives a man a certain standing. I fancy it is the dignity of print that does it, and we all have the print superstition. I find myself accepting statements in books, whereas if someone said the same things to me over a dinner-table I should refute them with scorn. "If it is in *John Bull* it is so!" Mr. Bottomley is a sound psychologist.

When they were departing I said to Smart: "Yes, he's very amiable and all that, but I am jolly glad I had Frank Michie and not him as my chief inspector when I wrote my *Log*."

Smart laughed.

"My dear chap, Mackenzie would have let you run your school in your own way."

"But," I cried, "he doesn't believe in freedom!"

"He doesn't, but don't you see that he simply couldn't have jumped on you? He would have thought you either a lunatic or a genius, and he would have feared to condemn you in case you might turn out to be the latter. I know an art critic in London, and, believe me, the poor devil lives in terror lest he should damn the work of a new Augustus John. The Futurists aren't flourishing on their merits; they are flourishing because the critics are in a holy funk to condemn them in case they might be artists after all."

I want to meet Smart again. I like his style.

* * * * * *

I am indeed a Dominie in Doubt. What is education striving after? I cannot say, for education is life and what the aim of life is no one knows. Psycho-analysis can clear up a life; it can release bottled up energy, but it cannot say how the released energy is to be used. The analyst cannot advise, because no man can tell another how to live his life. Freud clears up the past, but he cannot clear up the future.

Is there such a thing as Re-incarnation? I wonder. Am I living the life that my past lives on earth fitted me for? If so analysis is wrong. If I am suffering from a severe neurosis it is because I earned this punishment in my past lives, and Freud has no right to cure me. He is interfering with the plans of the Almighty. If, as I have heard a Theosophist declare, the children in the slums are miserable because they failed to learn their lesson in previous lives, then the people who try to abolish slums are all wrong. I think my Theosophist would argue that the charitable person is growing in grace, thereby rising above his previous lives. And thus one soul helps another to rise to perfection. It may be, and I hope it is so, for then life would have a meaning. Pain and war would then be less terrible, for they would be but incidents in the eternal unfolding of perfection.

Yet I find myself doubting. If I am William Shakespeare born again I do not know it, and I am left in doubt as to whether I may not have been Charles Peace instead. Possibly I was both.

Then there is psychical research. I have been to a medium and have heard things that all the psycho-analysis in the world cannot account for. I want to believe that the dead can speak to us, but where are the dead? I have read Sir Oliver Lodge's *Raymond*, and the description of the next world given there. Frankly I don't fancy it, and I have no desire to go there.

How then can I attempt to educate children when the ultimate solution of life is denied me? I can only stand by and give them freedom to unfold. I do not know whither they are going, but that is all the more a reason why I ought not to try to guide their footsteps. This is the final argument for the abolition of authority. We may beat and break a horse because we selfishly require a horse's service, and according to the accepted view a horse has no immortal soul. We dare not beat and break a child, for a child is going to an end that we cannot know.

I like the Theosophist schools, although I do not like all Theosophists. Some of them seem to be living the higher life consciously, and repressing their lower natures. Most of them do not smoke or drink or eat meat or swear or go to music-halls. That may be living on a higher plane, but it is not living fully. Still, in many ways they are broad-minded. In their schools they do not force Theosophy down the children's throats; they allow a great amount of freedom, but their schools are not free schools. There is a definite attempt to mould character chiefly by insisting on good taste. I am quite sure that no head-master of a Theosophical School would take his children to see a Charlie Chaplin film. Charlie is not obviously living the higher life; he stands for the vulgar side of life; he picks up girls and gets drunk (in the play) and is sea-sick and very vulgar about soda-water.

I find myself insisting on the inclusion of Charlie in any scheme of education because no one ought to be taught to be shocked at sea-sickness and soda-water squirting. Charlie to me is the antidote to the higher-plane crowd; he and his kind are as essential as Shelley. I admit that reading Shelley is a higher kind of pleasure than watching "Champion Charlie," but no human being can safely live on the higher plane, and no child wants to. Education must deal with *all* life; a higher plane diet will produce hot-house plants, beautiful perhaps, but delicate and artificial.

* * * * * *

Old Willie Murray the cobbler had been bedridden for over a year, and when I dropped into Dauvit's shop this morning Mary Rickart was telling Dauvit that his old master was dead.

"Aye, Dauvit," she was saying when I entered, "I'm no the kind that speaks ill o' the deid, but I will say this, that Wull Murray had his faults. Aye, and though he's a corp the day, I canna pertend that he was ony freend o' mine."

When Mary had gone Dauvit turned to me with a queer smile.

"Dominie, you tell me that you have studied the science o' the mind, psy—what is't you call it?"

"Psychology," I said.

"That's the word. Weel then, dominie, just tell me why Mary Rickart had sic a pick at auld Willie Murray."

I smoked for a time thoughtfully.

"It's difficult, Dauvit. I haven't got enough evidence. However I think I can make a good guess."

"Weel?"

"Mary and Willie sat in the same class at school?"

"Good!" said Dauvit, "they did."

"And Mary was Willie's first sweetheart?"

"Imphm!"

"Mary loved Willie and he loved her. They were sweethearts for a long time, but another damsel came and stole Willie's heart away. Mary wept bitter tears, but in time she repressed her love . . . . . and it changed into hate."

Dauvit chuckled.

"A very nice story," he said, "but, ye ken, it's just a story. You cudna guess the real reason why Mary hated him so much."

"Then what was the real reason, Dauvit?"

He laughed.

"Mary hated Willie Murray because he aince telt her that she was a silly woman to think that she cud wear a number fower shoe on a number acht foot."

We laughed together, and then I said: "Dauvit, why did you never marry? You like women I fancy."

My remark made him thoughtful.

"Man," he said, "I've often speered the same question o' mysel. As a young man I was gye fond o' the lassies, but . . . . . I dinna ken!" and he broke off suddenly and took up a boot. "Thae soles are just paper noo-a-days," he growled.

I refused to let him run away from the subject.

"Had you a sweetheart?" I asked.

He laughed boisterously to hide his confusion.

"Dozens o' them!" he cried.

"Then why didn't you marry one of them?"

He shook his head.

"Dominie, that's the question." He stared at the grate for a while. "There was Maggie Adams, a bonny lassie she was. Man, I mind when I took her to Kirriemair Market . . . . ." He sighed. "Aye, man, dominie, I liked Maggie mair than ony o' the others."

"Did she love someone else?" I asked softly.

Dauvit took some time to reply.

"No, man, Maggie wanted me."

"Then the fault lay on your side? You didn't love her!"

Dauvit brought his hand down on the board.

"Goad, man, but I did!"

I could not understand.

"Man, on the road hame frae Kirrie Market I was to speer if she wud marry me . . . . . but I didna."

We smoked silently for a long minute.

"Ye see," he went on slowly, "Maggie was a bonny lassie and I liked to kiss and cuddle her, but kissin' and cuddlin' are a very sma' part o' marriage, dominie. There was something in Maggie that I was aye lookin' for, but cud never find. Aye, I tried to find it in other lassies, but I never fund it."

"What was it you wanted to find, Dauvit?"

Dauvit paused.

"Ye micht call it a soul," he said. "Oh, aye," he went on, "Maggie was a bonny lassie wi' a heart o' gold, but she hadna a soul. Wud ye like to ken what stoppit me speerin' her that nicht as we cam through Zoar? Man, I said to mysel: When we come to the toll bar I'll tak Maggie in my arms and say: 'Maggie, I want ye, lassie!'"

He had to light his pipe here.

"Weelaweel, we got to the toll bar and I said: 'Maggie, we'll sit doon on the bank for a while.' So we sat doon, and I was just tryin' to screw up my courage when she pointed to the settin' sun. 'I'd like a dress like that, only bonnier,' she said. Man, dominie, I looked at that sunset wi' its gold and purple . . . . . and syne I kent that Maggie was nae wife for me. I kent that she had nae soul."

After a time I remarked : " And so, Dauvit, you are a bachelor because you were a poet ! "

He busied himself with the paper sole.

" Maggie married Bob Wilson the farmer o' East Mains. Aye, and the marriage turned oot a happy one, for Bob never rose abune neeps and tatties in his life." Dauvit sighed. " But I sometimes used to look at the twa o' them when their bairns were roond their knees, and syne I used to gie a big *Dawm !* and ging back to my wee hoose and mak my ain tea."

"It doesna pay to hae a soul, dominie," he added with a short laugh.

" Perhaps you could have given her a soul, Dauvit," I said.

He shook his head with decision.

" Na, dominie, a soul is something ye're born wi' ; if it isna there it canna be put there. You say that I'm a poet, and you may be richt ; there may be a wee bit o' the artist in me, and ye never heard o' an artist that was happily married. Wumman and art are opposites, and a man canna marry both."

" That is true, Dauvit. But art is the feminine side of a man's nature ; it is the woman in him . . . . . and the woman is superfluous to him, for she becomes the rival of the woman in himself."

This thought impressed Dauvit.

"Noo I understand Rabbie Burns," he cried. "Rabbie cudna love a wumman because he loved the wumman in himsel. She was the wife that bore his bairns—his poems." He paused, and a pained look came to his face. "There may be a poet in me, dominie," he said ruefully, "but she has borne me nae bairns. I am ane o' the mute inglorious Miltons . . . . . and I wud ha' been better if I had married Maggie and talked aboot neeps and tatties a' my life."

"You couldn't have done it, Dauvit," I said as I rose to go.

From the door I looked back at the old man as he stared at the fender.

* * * * * *

One of the analysts says that the flirt is suffering from a mother complex. He has never got over his infantile love for his mother, and he is always trying to find the mother again in women. Hence he is like a bee, sipping at one flower and then flying on to another.

I suspect that many a bachelor is a bachelor because his early love is fixed on the mother. Few mothers realise the danger of coddling their children. I have heard grown men dying in pain call on their mothers. It is a hard task for parents, but they must always try to break their children's fixation upon them.

Women having father-complexes are common. The other day I met a girl who had no interest in young men; all her interest was in men with beards. No matter what the conversation was about she managed to mention her father. . . . . "Father says!" She will probably marry a man twice her age. It is well-known that boys of seventeen often fall in love with women of thirty, while adolescent girls usually fall in love with men of thirty. They are not really in love; they are looking for a substitute for the mother or father.

The psychology of the man of forty who falls in love with the girl of sixteen is more difficult to grasp. I think that in most cases the man's love interest is fixed away back in childhood; often the girl of sixteen is a substitute for a beloved sister. Perhaps on the other hand, a man of forty's paternal instinct has been starved so long that he wants to find at once a wife and a child.

Few of us realise how much of our love interest is fixed in the past. Think of the men who want to be mothered by their wives . . . . . they generally address their wives as "Mother." I know happily married men who are psychically children; "mother" won't allow them to carry coals or wash dishes or brush clothes;

she treats them as they unconsciously desire to be treated—as babes.

It may be that Dauvit has a strong mother complex. He often talks of his mother, and more than once I have heard him say that she was the best woman he had ever known. It may be that he was unconsciously looking for the mother in Maggie and the other girls, and failed to find her. Maggie's remark about the sunset and the dress was not enough to stifle his love declaration. The soul he longed to find in Maggie may have been the soul of the mother he knew as an infant . . . . . the soul of his ideal woman.

The more I see of men the less importance I pay to their conscious reasons for attitudes. "I hate Brown; he never washes"; "I dislike Mrs. Smith; she uses bad language." "Murphy is a rotter; he has no manners." Statements like these are rationalisations; the real reason for the dislike lies deeper in every case.

VI

THE law courts have re-introduced flogging for criminals. To the best of my knowledge no member of the law profession has protested. If there is a reform movement within the law I never heard of it.

The curse of law is that it works according to precedent, and it is therefore conservative. Our judges hand out sentences in blissful ignorance of later psychology. Last week a boy of eleven was birched for holding up another boy of nine on the highway and demanding tuppence or his life. The attitude of the bench is that fear of another flogging will prevent that boy from turning highwayman again. I admit that fear will cure him of that special vice, but what the bench does not know is that the boy's anti-social energy will take another form. Every act of man is prompted by a wish, and very often this wish is unconscious. And all the birching in the world will not destroy a wish; the most it can do is to change its form.

Without an analysis of the boy no one can tell what unconscious wish impelled him to turn highwayman, but speaking generally a boy expresses his self-assertion in terms of anti-social behaviour only when his education has been bad. I believe that all juvenile delinquency is due to bad education. Our schools enforce passivity on the child; his creative energy is bottled up. No boy who has tools and a bench to work with will express himself by smashing windows. Delinquency is merely displaced social conduct; the motive of the little boy who turned highwayman was essentially the motive of the boy who builds a boat.

Ah! but we have Industrial Schools for bad boys!

I spent an evening with an Industrial School boy of thirteen not long ago. It was an unlovely tale he told me of his life in school. I got the impression of a building half-prison, half-barracks. No one was allowed to go out unless to football matches when the school team was playing. Punishment was stern and frequent.

"One old guy, 'e sends you to the boss for punishment and says you gave 'im an insubordinate look, and you ain't allowed to deny wot 'e says."

"Look here, Jim," I said, "suppose I took you to a free school to-morrow, a school where you could do what you liked, what's the first thing you would do?"

A wild look came into his eyes.

"I'd lay out the blarsted staff," he said tensely.

"But," I laughed, "what would be the point

of laying me out if I gave you freedom? What have you got against *me?*"

"Oh," he said, "I thought you meant if I got freedom in the Industrial School!"

That school is condemned; if a school produces one boy who hates and fears its teachers, it is a bad school.

I think of the other way, the Homer Lane way.

Homer Lane was superintendent of the Little Commonwealth in Dorset. He attended the juvenile courts and begged the magistrates to hand over to him the worst cases they had. He took the children down to Dorset and gave them freedom. He refused to lay down any laws, and naturally the beginning of the Commonwealth was chaos. Lane joined in the anti-social behaviour; he became one of the gang. When the citizens thought that their best way of expressing themselves was to smash windows, Lane helped them to smash them. His marvellous psychological insight will best be illustrated by the story of Jabez.

Jabez was a thoroughly bad character; he had been thief and highwayman, a bully who could fight with science. He came to the Commonwealth and was astonished. He found boys and girls working hard all day, and making their own laws at their citizen meetings at night. Jabez could not understand it, and not understanding he felt hostile.

The citizens lived in cottages, and one night Lane went over to the cottage in which Jabez lived. They were having tea, and Lane sat down beside Jabez.

"What are you always grousing about, Jabez?" he asked. "Don't you like the Commonwealth?"

"No," said Jabez viciously.

"What's wrong with it?"

"It's too respectable for me," said Jabez, and his eyes wandered to the table. "Them fancy cups and saucers! Wot's the good o' things like that to me? I'd like to smash the whole lot o' them."

Lane rose from the table, walked to the fire-place, took up the poker and handed it to Jabez.

"Smash them," he said.

Jabez had all eyes turned towards him. He seized the poker and smashed his cup and saucer.

"Excellent!" cried Lane, "Jabez is making the Commonwealth a better place," and he pushed forward another cup and saucer. These were at once smashed, and Lane proceeded to shove forward the other dishes. But by this time Jabez was beginning to feel queer. Breaking dishes was good fun when you were breaking laws, but here there was no law to break, and Jabez felt that he was doing a foolish thing. He wanted to stop, but he could not see how he was to stop with dignity. Fortunately one of the other inmates of the cottage came to his aid.

"It's all very well for you, Mr. Lane," she

said, "but this isn't your cottage, and you are making Jabez break our dishes."

Jabez hailed the idea with delight; he now had an excellent excuse for stopping.

"Right you are!" cried Lane cheerfully, "Jabez will break something else," and he took out his gold watch and placed it on the table. "Smash that, Jabez."

"No," said Jabez, "I won't smash your watch."

Now Jabez had a saying that if a man were dared to do a thing and he didn't do it he was a coward.

"I dare you to smash the watch."

Jabez seized the poker again.

"What! You dare me!"

"Yes, I dare you."

He looked at the watch for a few seconds; then he threw down the poker and rushed from the room.

Poor Jabez was killed in France. I saw the letters that he wrote to Lane from the front, and they were the letters of a decent, good boy.

The early history of Jabez was one of constant suppression. Authority was always stepping in and saying: "Don't do that!" As a result Jabez at the age of seventeen was psychically an infant. The infantile desire to break things was suppressed, but it lived on in the unconscious, and years later Jabez found himself behaving like a child of three.

The cure was to encourage him to act in his infantile way ; by smashing a few cups Jabez got rid of his long pent up infantile wish to destroy. Discipline would have kept the childish wish underground ; freedom led to the expression of the wish.

Homer Lane is the apostle of Release. He holds that Authority is fatal for the child ; suppression is bad ; the only way is to allow the child freedom to express itself in the way it wants to. And because I count among my friends boys and girls who once went to the Little Commonwealth as criminals, I believe that Lane is right. I also believe that the schools will come to see that he was right . . . . . somewhere about the year 2500.

* * * * * *

Conversation to-night in Dauvit's shop turned on Spiritualism. Dauvit is a firm believer, and he often goes to Dundee and Aberdeen to attend séances.

" It's just a lot o' blethers," said Jake Tosh contemptuously. " When ye're deid ye're deid, and that's a' aboot it. Na, na, Dauvit, them that sees ghosts is either drunk or daft."

" That's just yer ignorance, Jake," said Dauvit. " Do ye ken whaur Brazil is ? "

" Wha is he ? " asked Jake puzzled.

" It's no a he ; it's a place. I asked ye that question just to prove that a man that doesna ken his ain world canna speak wi' ony authority o' the next world. Yer mind's ower narrow, Jake; ye've no vision."

"Na, na, Dauvit," laughed Jake, "it winna do. Spooks and things is just a curran nonsense, and no sane man wud believe in them. What do you say, dominie?"

"I am willing to believe that the dead do communicate," I said.

Jake was thoroughly amused.

"It's a queer thing," he said musingly, "that the more eddication a man has the more be believes in rubbish. Here's Dauvit here, a man that reads Shakespeare and Burns and Carlyle, and the dominie there that went through a college, and the both o' you believe things that I stoppit believin' when I was sax year auld. Then there's Sir Oliver Lodge, and Conan Doyle. Oh, aye, the Bible was quite richt when it said: Much learning hath made them mad."

"What do you think happens to the dead, Jake?" I asked.

"As the tree falleth so it lies," quoted Jake. "There's only the twa places after death; if ye're good ye go to Heaven; if ye're bad ye go to Hell. And that's why I say that thae messages from the deid are rubbish, cos if a man's in Heaven he's no going to leave a place like that to come doon to speak to a daft auld cobbler like Dauvit in a wee room doon in Dundee. And if a man's in Hell the Devil will tak good care that he doesna get oot."

I wondered to find that Dauvit had no answer to this. I guessed that Dauvit's silence was due to his early training. He was brought up in the old stern Scots way, and although he has now rejected the old beliefs intellectually; his unconscious still clings to them emotionally. I fancy that if I were very very ill I might go back to my childish fear of Hell-fire, for, in illness old emotions return, and intellect flees. Dauvit would no doubt react in the same way.

* * * * * *

Many people seem to have a decided fear of psycho-analysis. A mother writes me from London saying that she would like to send her girl to my new school, only she is afraid that I shall attempt to analyse the children.

The fear of psycho-analysis comes from the general belief that Freud traces every neurosis to early sex experiences. Whether Freud is right or not does not concern the teacher; he deals with normal children, and to try to analyse a normal child appears to me to be unnecessary. The teacher's job is to see that the children are free from fear and free to create; if he does his task well he is preventing neurosis.

A neurosis is the outcome of repression; the neurotic is a person whose libido or life force is bottled up; he can be cured only by letting his pent up emotions free. The aim of education is to allow emotional release, so that there will be no bottling up, and no future neurosis ; and this release comes through interest. The boy who hates algebra and has to work examples is getting no release whatever, for his mind is divided ; his attention goes to his quadratic equations, but his interest is elsewhere.

Hence I do not think analysis is necessary when children are being freely educated. In an exceptional case a little analysis will do good. If I see a child unhappy, moody, anti-social, a thief, a bully, I consider it my job to make an attempt to find out what is at the back of his mind. With a young boy it is not advisable to tell him the whole truth about himself ; the teacher discovers the truth by watching the child at play, by studying his wishes as expressed in his writing, by noting his attitude to his playmates. When he has made his diagnosis the teacher can then make the necessary changes in the boy's environment.

I recall the case of Tommy, aged ten. His class was constructing a Play Town after the fashion set by Caldwell Cook in his delightful book *The Play Way*. Tommy worked with enthusiasm, too much enthusiasm, for he pinched the girls' sand for his railway track. The girls objected, and a regular wordy battle took place. Tommy felt that he was beaten, and he ceased work.

I was not very much surprised when the girls

came and told me that Tommy was shying bricks at the railway line he had been so keen on constructing. Tommy was brought up before the assembled class, and they voted unanimously that he be forbidden to approach within ten yards of Play Town. Tommy grinned maliciously. That night the town appeared to have been the victim of an earthquake.

I went to Tommy.

" Why don't you like the Play Town ? " I asked.

" Because the girls are too bossy," he said. " It was my town ; I began it, and I don't see why they should be in it at all."

" And you want a Play Town all to yourself?" I asked.

" Yes."

" Right ho," I said easily. " Why not start to build one ? "

His eyes lit up, and away he ran to lay his foundations. He worked eagerly all day, but at night he seemed dissatisfied.

" I haven't got any railway or houses ; Christo won't lend me a bit of his railway, and Gerda has all the houses."

I left him to work out his problem. In the morning he solved it ; Christo wouldn't lend him any rails, but if Tommy liked he, Christo, would run his line up to Tommy's town from the class town. Tommy readily agreed. In a week's time Tommy's town was a suburb of the bigger town, and Tommy was appointed President of the whole state. He spent many an hour building his bridges and digging his tunnels. At first he would allow no one to enter his suburb, but in a few days he ceased to claim it as his own, and he worked as a member of the gang.

I think that most anti-social children are like Tommy: when their self-assertion is threatened they react with hostility. The cure for them is to direct their self-assertion to things instead of people. No boy will try to break up a ball game if he has a rabbit hutch to construct.

The danger is that the teacher will often step in when the boy ought to be left to his companions. The gang is the best disciplinarian.

One day a class and I were writing five-minute essays. I would call out a word or a phrase, and we would all start to write. The children loved the method; it allowed so much play for originality. For example, when I gave the word "broken" one girl wrote of her broken doll, another of a broken tramp, another of a broken heart; a boy wrote a witty essay on being stoney broke, another wrote of a broken window.

On this day Wolodia, a boy of eleven, did not want to write essays. I called out a word, and we started to write. Wolodia began to talk loudly.

" Stop it, man," I said impatiently, " you're spoiling our essay."

He grinned and went on talking.

" Oh, shut up ! " cried Joy.

" Shan't ! " he snapped, and he went on talking.

Diana rose with a determined air.

" We'll chuck him out," she said grimly, and the class seized him and heaved him out. Then they barricaded the door with desks. Wolodia made a big row by hammering on the door, and as a result we could not proceed with our writing.

" Let him in," I suggested.

The class protested.

" He'll sit like a lamb for the rest of the period," I said.

They took away the desk and Wolodia came in. He went to his seat . . . . and not a sound came from him during the rest of the period. This incident impressed me greatly ; my complaint, Joy's complaint did not affect him, but when the gang was against him he was defeated. It was a beautiful instance of the force of public opinion.

Cases of stealing should be treated by analysis. Moral lectures are useless ; the cause lies in the unconscious, and the moral lecture does not touch the unconscious. Nor does punishment affect the root cause of the delinquency. The teacher must dig down into the child's unconscious in order to find the cause.

An illuminating book for all teachers and parents to read is Healy's *Mental Disorders and Misconduct*. He shows that stealing is very often a symptomatic act. The mechanism of many cases is something like this: a child has been punished for sexual activities; later he breaks into a store and steals an article. Sex activities and thieving have this in common, that they are both forbidden, but the boy has found that much more ado is made about sex activities than about stealing. So when he is actuated by a sexual urge he dare not indulge it; but his sexual wish finds a substitute; it goes out to the associated forbidden thing . . . . the article on the store counter.

We see the same sort of mechanism in the neurotic patient; she fears her own sex impulses, and because she dare not admit her sex wishes into consciousness she projects her fear on to dogs or mice or rats. All phobias—fear of closed places, fear of open places, fear of heights—are displaced fears; the sufferer is really afraid of his own unconscious wishes.

I do not say that all juvenile stealing is due to repressed sex. Stealing may mean to a boy a method of self-assertion; it may mean that thus he rebels against authority of father and teacher; it may be the result of any one of a dozen causes. But whatever the cause stealing is always associated with unhappiness, and the teacher must try to cure the unhappiness.

In my *Dominie's Log* I confessed that I liked to cheat the railway company, and I excused it on the ground that "a ten-mile journey without a ticket is the only romantic experience left in a drab world." That was a delightful bit of rationalisation. The real reason for my delinquency lay in my unconscious. As a child I impotently rebelled against the authority of parents and teachers. Later in life I unconsciously identified the railway company with the authorities of my infancy. Authority said: "Don't do that or you will be smacked"; the railway company put up a notice saying: "Don't travel without a ticket or you'll be fined forty shillings."

My rebellion was really a rebellion against authority. This may seem to be a far-fetched explanation, but the fact remains that now that I have discovered the reason I have no more desire to cheat the railway company.

* * * * * *

Old Jeems Broon was buried to-day, and Dauvit went to the funeral. He came back chuckling.

"What's the joke, Dauvit?" I asked.

"The burial service," laughed Dauvit. "You ken what sort o' a man Jeems was; an auld sinner if there ever was a sinner in Tarbonny, a bad auld scoondrel. Weel, Jeems hadna been at the kirk for twenty years, and of coorse the minister didna ken onything aboot him. So when he gave the funeral prayer he referred to auld Jeems as 'this holy man whose life stands as an example to those still tarrying in the flesh.' Goad, but I burst oot laughin'! I did that!"

"Had I been the minister," said I, "I should certainly have made a few inquiries about Jeems."

"But there's a better story than that aboot the minister," went on Dauvit with a laugh. "Mag Currie's little lassie had the diphtheria, and at the end o' the week the minister was asked to come oot to tak' a burial service in Mag's bed room. Man, he was eloquent! He spoke earnestly aboot this flower plucked before it had reached its full bloom, this innocent life so sadly cut off; he was most touchin' when he turned to Mag and her man and said: 'Mourn not for those hands that never did wrong, the lisping tongue that never spoke evil, the wide pure eyes that looked their love for you.'"

"I suppose the parents broke down at that," I said.

"Not they!" chuckled Dauvit, "for the corpse wasna their lassie ava; it was auld Drucken Findlay the lodger."

I always like to hear Dauvit talk about ministers, and I encouraged him to go on.

"It's a very queer thing, dominie, that

a body ay wants to laugh at the wrong time. In the kirk and at a funeral—that's when I want to laugh.

"I mind when the minister was awa' for his holidays, and there was an auld minister frae the Heelands cam' to tak' his place. This auld man had a habit o' readin' a verse and syne stoppin' to explain it to the congregation.

"Weel aweel, wan Sunday he was readin' a chapter frae the Auld Testament, and he cam' to the words: 'And the Angel of the Lord appeared unto Hosea.' So he looks at the congregation ower his specs and he says: 'The Angel of the Lord appeared unto Hosea.' Now, prethren, we must ask ourselves this important question: Was Hosea afraid? No, Hosea was not afraid. *You* would have been afraid, prethren; *I* would have been afraid. You and I would have begun to quake and tremble, but Hosea was not afraid; he was a prave man, a pold man. When we are in trouble let us remember that Hosea was not afraid.'

"So the auld man he turns ower the page and reads the next verse: 'And Hosea was sore afraid.'"

"What did he say then?" I asked.

"He was a cunnin' auld deevil," said Dauvit, "for he gave a bit cough and says: 'Prethren, that is a wrong translation from the original Hebrew.'"

"I don't think you like ministers, Dauvit," I said.

He paused in his efforts to place a new needle in his sewing-machine.

"No, man, I do not," he said slowly. "Nowadays the kirk is just a job like anything else; men go in for it for the loaves and fishes mostly, and their prayers never get past the roof. And as for the congregation, the kirk is just a respectable sort o' society. I tell ye, dominie, that releegion is deid. At least, Christianity is deid. That was bound to come; flowers, folk, hooses, trees, horses, aye, and nations, have a birth, a youth, middle age, auld age, and then death. It's the law o' nature, and a religion is no exception."

"True, O philosopher!" I said, "but there is always new life, and new life comes from the old. The flower dies and its seed lives; man dies and his seed inherit the earth. Christianity dies and—and what?"

"That may be," he said thoughtfully. "It may be that the new religion will grow from the seed o' the deid Christianity; that I canna say. What I do say is that ministers are oot-o'-date; they are doin' useless labour . . . . when they're no fishin' and curlin'."

VII.

DUNCAN came over to-night, and he asked my advice about books.

"What books would you advise a teacher to buy?" he asked.

"There are scores of good books," I replied, "but no teacher can afford to buy them."

"I know," he said crossly; "I've had a row with the Income Tax people. I asked for a rebate of ten pounds for necessary school books, and they wouldn't allow it, although I'm told that if a London merchant buys a London Directory he gets a rebate for the amount."

"I agree that it is unjust," I said, "but the new Income Tax proposals allow twenty pounds a year for teachers' books."

"Just tell us what you would advise a teacher to spend his twenty quid on," said Macdonald.

"It depends on his tastes," I said. "If his subject is History he will buy history books; if his subject is behaviour, he'll buy psychology books."

"Give us an idea of your own library," said Duncan.

I sat down and wrote out a list from memory. It ran as follows :—

BOOKS ON EDUCATION :—

The Play Way, by Caldwell Cook.

The Path to Freedom in the School, by Norman MacMunn.

What Is and What Might Be, by Edmond Holmes.

Montessori's three volumes.

An Adventure in Education, by J. H. Simpson.

BOOKS ON PSYCHO-ANALYSIS AND PSYCHOLOGY :

Freud's *Interpretation of Dreams, Psycho-pathology of Everyday Life, Three Contributions to the Sexual Theory.*

Jung's *Psychology of the Unconscious, Studies in Word Association, Analytical Psychology.*

Frink's *Morbid Fears and Compulsions.*

Maurice Nicoll's *Dream Psychology.*

Morton Prince's *The Unconscious.*

Pfister's *The Psycho-analytic Method.*

Ernest Jones' *Psycho-analysis.*

Ferenczi's *Contributions to Psycho-analysis.*

Wilfred Lay's *The Child's Unconscious Mind.*

Moll's *The Sexual Life of the Child.*

Adler's *The Neurotic Constitution.*

Bernard Hart's *The Psychology of Insanity.*

CROWD PSYCHOLOGY :—

The Crowd in Peace and War, Martin Conway.

Instincts of the Herd in Peace and War, Trotter.

The Crowd, Gustave le Bon.

GENERAL PSYCHOLOGY :—

Psychology and Everyday Life, Swift.
Textbook of Psychology, James.
The Boy and His Gang, Puffer.
Mental Conflicts and Misconduct, Healy.
The Individual Delinquent, Healy.
Rational Sex Ethics, Robie.
Social Psychology, McDougall.
The Play of Man, Groos.

"That's too much for me," said Duncan. "I couldn't afford a quarter of these books. What books would you recommend if you had to choose half a dozen for a hard-up dominie ?"

I thought for a little, and then I replied : "Bernard Hart's *The Psychology of Insanity*, two bob ; Frink's *Morbid Fears and Compulsions*, a first-rate book on analysis, a guinea ; *The Crowd in Peace and War*, by Sir Martin Conway, eight and six ; Healy's *Mental Conflicts and Misconduct*, ten and six ; and Wilfred Lay's *The Child's Unconscious Mind*, ten and six."

"But," cried Duncan, "I don't want to set up an asylum ! What's the good of books on insanity and morbid fears to a teacher ?"

I explained that the titles of Hart's and Frink's books were misleading, although the difference between the mind of the lunatic and the mind of the average man is merely one of degree. Bernard Hart shows that the lunatic has the same faults as we have, only more so. Frink's book is badly named; it is an excellent work on mind mechanisms. Any teacher who reads these six books with understanding will never again use a strap on a pupil. If I were Education Minister, I should present every school in Britain with a copy of each of the six.

Macdonald asked if I had any books on hypnotism and suggestion.

"No," I said, "but I have read them through a library. I don't believe in either because they do not touch root causes. We are all suffering from bottled up infantile emotion, and analysis goes to the root of the matter; it makes what is unconscious conscious, and enables the patient to re-educate himself, to use the old repressed emotion up in his daily life. Analysis means release. Suggestion does not touch the root repressed emotion, and I fancy that after suggestion the symptom merely changes. A man has a phobia of cats. By suggestion I can dispel his fear of cats, but the fear is transferred to something else, and he then has an exaggerated fear of catching tuberculosis. Unless the ancient cause becomes conscious it is not released.

"We see suggestion working in our schools daily. By suggestion parents and teachers force the child to inhibit his gross sexual wishes, and in a short time the child accepts the ideals of his masters. At first he inhibits a desire because father thinks it naughty; later he inhibits it because he himself thinks it naughty. But the gross sexual wish lives on in the unconscious . . . . hence the neurosis, hence the respectable old men who are imprisoned for showing gross pictures to children, hence the frequent indecent assaults on children. All these unfortunate people are suffering from the results of early suggestion —the suggestion that sex is sin. That primitive sex impulses can be sublimated I admit, but the teacher's job is not to preach that sex activities are evil; his job is to help the child to use up his primitive sex energy in creative work."

* * * * * *

What is education's chief aim? The reply generally given is that education's aim is to help a child to live its life fully. Yet it seems to me that that reply does not go far enough; I think that the aim should be to help a child to live its cosmic life fully, to live for others. Every human is egocentric, selfish. No human ever rises above selfishness, only there are degrees of selfishness. I buy a motor-cycle because I am selfish; and you found a hospital for orphans because you are selfish. It is my pleasure to have a Sunbeam; it is yours to help the poor.

Your selfishness has become altruism; that is, in pleasing yourself you have managed to please others. The aim in education is not to abolish selfishness; it is to educe the selfishness that is altruistic. Hence it may be said that education's chief aim is to teach one how to love. No, that won't do; no one can teach another how to love; the teacher's job is to evoke love. This he can do only by loving. If I hate my pupils I evoke hate from them; if I love them I evoke love from them in return.

Is it possible to love your neighbour as yourself? It is when you know yourself. You hate in others what you hate in yourself, and you love in others what is lovable in yourself. So that in loving your neighbour you are loving yourself.

If, then, the teacher's first aim is to evoke the love of his pupils, he must know himself, and knowing must love himself. Every day pupils are suffering because of the teacher's hatred of himself.

Dominie Brown rises in the morning surly and unhappy. He complains about the bacon and eggs at breakfast . . . . no, the red herring; dominies cannot afford bacon and eggs . . . . and Mrs. Brown makes unpleasant remarks. Brown crosses the road to school with thunder on his face, and the children shiver in terror all morning.

If Brown could sit down calmly to think

out his bad mood, he would realise that he was punishing the children because he was worsted in his word battle with his wife. And *he would be quite wrong.* The truth would be that he was punishing the children because he was at war with himself. His early morning ugly mood betrayed a mental conflict. Hating himself, he hated his wife; his hate evoked her hate . . . . and thus the circle was completed.

We might trace all the futilities, all the stupidities of mankind, all the wars and crimes and injustices to man's ignorance of self. To know all is to forgive all. Christ condemned no one because he was at peace with himself. Yet, I suddenly remember that He whipped the money-changers out of the Temple. This incident is comforting, for it shows that the most lovable man who ever lived betrayed one human frailty on one occasion at least. But now I am preaching again.

* * * * * *

I went to see Charlie Chaplin in "Shoulder Arms" last night. Charlie is an artist of high quality; for once I think as the crowd thinks. But I leave the crowd when it comes to appreciating the "moving human dramas" in five parts.

The cinema must be reckoned with in any educational scheme. One may learn more about crowd psychology from attendance at cinemas than from reading books on crowd psychology. The cinema is popular because it encourages day-dreaming or phantasy. There are two kinds of thinking, reality thinking and phantasy or day-dreaming. Phantasying is the easier of the two ; I can sit for hours building castles in Spain, and I never grow tired ; but if I have to sit down and think out the Theory of Quadratics I soon become weary. In reality thinking the intellect is active, but in day-dreaming emotion is in control. Day-dreaming gets nowhere ; the asylums are full of day-dreamers who spend their hours constructing beautiful phantasies. In childhood phantasy is supreme. Bobby turns the nursery into a jungle ; the sofa is a tiger, the chairs are lions, the rocking-horse is an elephant. It is all real to him. And in later years Bobby often returns to his childish phantasying. We all do. What young lover has not phantasied a burning mansion where his lady love is imprisoned ? Have we not all clambered up the water pipes and rescued her from the flames ?

The world of the theatre is a phantasy world. With the rising of the curtain we forget our outside life ; we live the part of the hero or the heroine. To this day I always leave a theatre with a vague depression of spirits ; everyday humdrum life chills me when I come out to the street. Reality is always difficult to face. The great popularity of the cinema is due to this human desire for make-believe. Cinema-going is a regression to the infantile; we return to the childish phase where the wish was all powerful. In the cinema the villain is always worsted; the wronged heroine always falls into the hero's arms at the end. Life for most of us means trials and sorrows and conflicts, and we long to return to the nursery phase where life was what we wished it to be. The cinema and the public-house are the most convenient doors by which we can regress.

The "moving drama" is the other side of the industrial picture. Life for the masses means dirt and disease, ugly factories, sordid homes, mean streets. The moving drama takes the masses away from grim reality; they see beautifully gowned women in drawing-rooms; they see the King reviewing his regiments; they see wild and free cowboys chasing Red Indians. For two hours they live . . . and then they go out again into their world of mere existence. And it is all wrong, tragically wrong. The cinema craze means that life is too ugly to face; it means that the masses are fleeing from reality and to flee from reality is fatal. Day-dreams are laudable only when they come true. If the masses day-dreamed of an economic Utopia and forthwith set about building a New Jerusalem, their phantasies would become realities; but the moving human drama never leads to building; it is raw whisky swallowed to bring oblivion. The moving human drama will live and flourish so long as mankind tolerates the slavery of industrialism. It is a powerful weapon for capitalism; like the church and the public-house, it keeps the wage-slaves quiet.

* * * * * *

To-night the conversation in Dauvit's shop turned to the subject of honours.

"They tell me," said Jake Tosh, "that you can buy a knighthood, or a peerage for that matter."

"Yea, man!" said Willie Simpson, the joiner and undertaker from Tillymains.

"So there's no muckle chance o' you getting ane, Willie," said Dauvit.

The joiner smoked thoughtfully for a while.

"Na, Dauvit," he said, "there's little chance o' an undertaker gettin' a title. You would think na that the man that coffined the likes o' Lloyd George wud get a knighthood."

Dauvit cackled.

"Honours are sold, as Jake says; they are never given for public services."

I am afraid the joke was lost on most of the assembly. Jake failed to see it. It is said that Jake has been known to laugh at a joke only once, and that was when the earth gave way beneath the minister's feet when he was conducting a service at a grave-side, and he fell into the open grave.

"Undertakin'," continued the joiner, "is a verra queer trade."

Jake shivered.

"I dinna ken how ye can do it," he said; "man, it wud gie me the scunners."

"Man, ye soon get accustomed to it," said the joiner. "Of course, it has its limitations; ye canna verra weel advertise in the front page o' *The Daily Mail,* but, man, it's what ye micht call a safe trade."

"How safe?" I asked.

"Oh, ye never need to worry aboot yer custom; it's aye there. Noo in other lines the laws o' supply and demand are tricky. I mind a gey puckle years syne there was a craze for walkin'-sticks wi' ebony handles. Weel, I went doon to Dundee and bocht ten pund worth o' ebony, and afore the wood was delivered the fashion had changed, and the men were all buyin' cheese-cutter bonnets, so here was I left wi' ten pund worth o' ebony on my hands . . . . and if I hadna sold it to Davie Lamb the cabinet-maker for thirteen pund I micht ha' lost the money. Noo, in my trade there's no sudden change o' fashion as ye micht say; the demand is what ye micht call constant, and that's what makes me say it is a safe trade."

Dauvit winked to me surreptitiously.

"Noo, joiner," he said, "will ye tell me wan thing? I want to ken the inner workin's o' an undertakker's mind. When somebody is verra ill, what's your attitude? I mean to say, do ye sort o' look on the illness wi' hope or what? When ye see a fine set-up man on the road, do ye look at him wi' a professional eye and say to yersell: 'Sax feet by twa; a bonny corp!'?"

"I'm no so bad as that, Dauvit," he laughed, "though I dinna mind sayin' that I've sometimes been a wee bit disappointed when somebody got better. On the other hand, when big Tamson was badly, I keepit prayin' that he wud get better."

"An unbusinesslike thing to do," I laughed.

"Aweel," said the joiner, "big Tamson weighed aboot saxteen stone, and at the time I hadna the wood."

"I dinna like to hear aboot things like that," said Jake Tosh nervously; "things like that give me the creeps, and besides it's no a proper way to speak."

Dauvit turned to me.

"Man, dominie, it's a queer thing, but the more religious a man is the less he likes to hear aboot death. Jake here is an elder o' the auld kirk; he's on the straight and narrow path; he's going straight to heaven when he dees . . . . and I never saw onybody so feared o' death as Jake is. How wud ye explain that?"

"I think," I replied, "that it is due to the fact that Jake has been brought up in the fear of the Lord."

"Exactly," nodded Dauvit. "It's my belief that most religious fowk are religious not becos they want specially to play harps in the next world, but becos they dinna want to be roasted."

Dauvit's philosophy comes pretty near that of Edmond Holmes. In *What Is and What Might Be* Holmes argues that our education system is founded on the Old Testament. Man is a sinner, prone to evil; a stern angry God chastises him when he trangresses. Education treats children as sinners; it punishes the wrongdoer. I believe Holmes is right, only he does not trace back education far enough. The God of the Old Testament was a man-made God (Jung says that man makes his God in his own image; his God is his ego-ideal).

The genesis of education is not the God of the Old Testament; it is the unconscious wish of the primitive men who invented that God. The religion of the Old Testament is a father complex religion; God is the hated and feared father, the authority who punishes, the provider of food and clothing, the maker of laws. Authority always makes the governed inferior and dependent; the man with a father complex cannot stand alone; he must always flee to his father or father substitute when he meets a difficulty. Thus does the Christian act ; he seeks the Father ; he places his burden on the Lord ; he avoids responsibility. The Hebraic religion and our modern education both demand that the individual shall avoid responsibility ; the good Christian and the good schoolboy must obey the Law. I think that if the world is to be free the church and the school must aim at breaking the power of the Father.

* * * * * *

"Look here, Mac," I said last night, "I am going to pay you for my board."

Mac protested vigorously.

"You'll do nothing of the kind," he said firmly.

I went to the kitchen and made the offer to his wife, and she also protested.

This morning I cycled to Dundee and bought a knife-cleaner and a vacuum cleaner. They arrived to-night, and Mrs. Mac gave a gasp of delight. Mac tried to frown, but he could not manage it. Both protested against what they called my idiotic kindness, but their protests were half-hearted.

It is a strange thing that money itself is considered a sordid thing. Why should Mac refuse five pounds with anger, and accept a ten pound gift with pleasure? If anyone wants to study the psychological meaning of money I recommend Chapter XL. in Dr. Ernest Jones' *Psycho-analysis*. In the unconscious, at any rate, money is assuredly "filthy lucre."

* * * * * *

A teacher should know very little about the subject he professes to teach. In my London school I succeeded a line of excellent teachers of drawing. I had not been long in the school when Di, aged 15, looked over my shoulder one day and said: "Rotten! You can't draw for nuts!"

A week later Malcolm looked at a water colour of mine.

"You've got a horrible sense of colour," he said brightly.

Then I began to wonder why everyone in school was much more keen on drawing and painting than they had ever been in the days of the skilled teachers. The conclusion I came to was that my bad drawing encouraged the children. I remembered the beautiful copy-book headlines of my boyhood, and I recalled the hopelessness of ever reaching the standard set by the lithographers. No child should have perfection put before him. The teacher should never try to teach; he should work alongside the children; he should be a co-worker, not a model.

Most teachers set themselves on a pedestal. They think that they lose dignity if they are not able to answer every question that a child puts to them. One result is that the child develops a dangerous inferiority complex. I knew one boy who was a duffer at mathematics. His weakness was due to the inferiority he felt when he saw the learned mathematical master juggle with figures as easily as a conjurer juggles with billiard balls. The little chap lost all hope, and when he worked problems he worked solely to escape punishment.

The difficulty is that if a teacher works at a subject year after year he is bound to become an expert. The only remedy I can think of is to make each teacher take up a new subject at the beginning of every school year. By the time that he had been master of Mathematics, History, Drawing, English, French, German, Latin, Geography, Chemistry, Physics, Psychology, Physiology, Eurhythmics, Music, Woodwork, it would be time to retire . . . . with a pension or a psychosis. The late Sir William Osler said that a man was too old at forty; my experience leads me to conclude that many a teacher is too old at twenty.

I sometimes think that every man has a certain definite psychic age fixed for him by the Almighty before he is born. I know a man of seventy who is psychically five years old, and he will never grow older. I know a boy of ten who is psychically sixty years dold, an he will never grow younger.

Psycho-analysis is doing a lot of good, but I fear that it may do a lot of harm, for, one fine day Professor Freud or Dr. Jung will get hold of Peter Pan, take him by the back of the neck, and say: "My lad, you've got a fixation somewhere; you are the super-regression-to-the-infantile specimen; you've got to be analysed." And then Peter will grow up and read *The Daily News* and own an allotment and a season ticket.

When we know all about psychology, the world will be rather dull. The Freudians have said that the play of *Hamlet* is the result of Shakespeare's Œdipus Complex. If Shakespeare had not had an unconscious hatred of his father, *Hamlet* would never have been written. In other words, if Bacon had discovered the psychology of the unconscious, Shakespeare might have been analysed and forthwith might have gone in for keeping bees instead of writing plays.

It is the neurotic who leads the world; he is a rebel and he is an idealist. Yet when you analyse him you find what a poor devil he is. His noble crusade against vivisection is due to the abnormal strain of cruelty he is repressing in himself; his passion for Socialism comes from his infant fear of and rebellion against his father. The ardent suffragette who smashes windows in a just cause is merely doing so because the vote is a symbol of freedom from an arrogant husband.

What I want to know is this: In the year 5000, when everyone is free from repressions and suppressions, will there be any rebels to spur humanity on? But then if humanity is free from unconscious urges there will be no need for rebels, for there will be no crime or prison or wars or politicians. Every man will be a superman.

I firmly believe that Freud's discovery will have a greater influence on the evolution of humanity than any discovery of the last ten centuries. Freud has begun the road that leads to superman, and, although Jung and Adler and others have begun to lead sideroads off the main track, the sideroads are all leading forward. Theirs is a great message of hope.

And yet, nineteen hundred years ago Jesus Christ gave the world a New Psychology . . . and none of us have tried to apply it to our souls.

VIII.

MAC came across a vulgar word in a composition he was correcting to-night, and it seemed to alarm him. He could not understand why I laughed, and I explained to him that I liked vulgarity.

I remember when a high-minded mother came into my class-room in Hampstead. The highest class was writing essays. On her asking what the subject was, I replied that each pupil had a different subject. She walked round and looked over their shoulders. I saw the lady's eyebrows go up as she read titles such as these :—" I Grow Forty Feet high in One Night " ; " I Edit the Greenland *Morning Frost* " (the news this boy gave was delightful) ; " I Interview Noah for the *Daily Mail* " (photos on back page). She nodded approvingly when she read the titles of the more serious essays. Then I saw her adjust her spectacles in great haste ; she was looking over Muriel's shoulder.

" Mr. Neill," she gasped, " do you think this a suitable subject for a girl ? "

I glanced at the title ; it was : " Autobiography of My Nose."

"Er—what's wrong with it?" I said falteringly.

"It lends itself too readily to vulgarity," she said.

I picked up the book, and together we read the opening words.

"When first I began to run . . . .

The high-minded lady left the room hurriedly.

I loved that class. Often I wish that I had kept their essays. One day we had a five minute essay on the subject: Waiting for My Cue. Lawrence wrote of standing on the steps in a cold sweat of fear. He had only five words to say—"The carriage waits, my lord," but he had never acted before. His cue was: "Ho! Who comes here?"

"At last," he wrote, "I heard the fateful words: 'Ho! Who comes here?' I could not move; I stood trembling on the stairs.

"'Get on, you idiot!' whispered the stage manager savagely, but still I could not move.

"'Ho! Who comes here?' repeated the fool on the stage. Still I could not move a step.

"'Ho! Who comes here?'

"Suddenly I became aware of a disturbance in the auditorium. The noise increased, and then I heard the agonising words: 'Fire!

Fire!' Panic followed, and cries of terror rang out.

"But I . . . I jumped on the stage and cried: 'Hurrah! Hoo-blinking-rah!' It was the happiest moment of my life."

Sydney took a different line. Her cue was the sound of a stage kiss. Boldly she walked on, and the stage lovers glared at her, for she arrived before the kiss was finished or rather properly begun. The audience chuckled. At the next performance she determined to be less punctual. She heard the smack of the kiss, but she did not move. As she waited she heard the audience roaring with laughter, and then she realised that the poor lovers had been standing kissing each other for a full five minutes.

I must write to these dear old children to ask if they kept their essays.

* * * * * *

Duncan was in to-night, and he told a school story that was new to me.

In a certain council school it was the custom for teachers to write down on the blackboard any instructions they might have for the janitor before they left at night. One night he came in and read the words: Find the L.C.M.

"Good gracious!" he growled, "has that darn thing gone and got lost again?"

That version was new to me. My own version ran thus :—

Little Willie is doing his home lessons, and he asks his father to help him with a sum. The father takes the slate in his hand and reads the words: Find the G.C.M.

"Good heavens!" he cries, "haven't they found that blamed thing yet? They were hunting for it when I was at school."

I think both versions are very good.

* * * * * *

I have a strong Montessori complex. I find myself being critical of her system, and I have often wondered why. I used to think that my dislike of Montessori was a projection: I disliked a lady who raved about Montessori, and I fancied that I had transferred my dislike of the lady to poor Montessori. But now I refuse to accept that explanation; it is not good enough for me; there must be something deeper. I shall try to discover that something deeper.

When I first read Montessori's books I said to myself: "She is devoid of humour." This to me suggests a limitation in art, and I feel that Montessori is always a scientist but never an artist. Her system is highly intellectual, but sadly lacking in emotionalism. This is seen in her attitude to phantasy. She would probably argue that phantasy is bad for a child, but it is a fact that much of a child's life is lived in phantasy. Phantasy is a means of gratifying an unfulfilled wish. The kitchen-maid in her day-dream marries a prince, and, as Maurice Nicoll says in his *Dream Psychology,* to destroy her phantasy without putting something in its place is dangerous.

To a child, as to Cinderella, phantasy is a means of overcoming reality. Father bullies Willie and the boy retires into a day-dream world where he becomes an all-powerful person . . . . hence the fairy tales of giants (fathers) killed by little Jacks. In later life Willie takes to drink or identifies himself with the hero of a cinema drama.

The extreme form of phantasy is insanity, where the patient completely goes over to the unreal world and becomes the Queen of the World. And it might be objected that phantasying is the first stage of insanity. Yes, but it is the last stage of poetry. Coleridge's *Kubla Khan,* one of the most glorious poems in the language, is pure phantasy. I rather fear that one day a grown-up Montessori child will prove conclusively that the feet of Maud did not, when they touched the meadows, leave the daisies rosy.

No, the Montessori world is too scientific for me; it is too orderly, too didactic. The name "didactic apparatus" frightens me.

I quote a sentence from *The New Children*, by Mrs. Radice.

"'Per carita! Get up at once!' she (Montessori) has exclaimed before now to a conscientious teacher found dishevelled on the ground with a class of little Bolshevists sitting on top of her."

In heaven's name, I ask, why get up? Life is more than meat, and education is more than matching colours and fitting cylinders into holes.

Montessori was thinking of the conscious mind of the child when she evolved her system, and the apparatus does not satisfy the whole of the child's unconscious mind. Noise is suppressed in a Montessori school, but every child should be allowed to make a noise, for noise means power to him, and he will use it only as long as it means power to him. I have watched Norman MacMunn's war orphans at Tiptree Hall at work. MacMunn, the author of *A Path to Freedom in the School*, did not say "Hush!"; his boys filled the room with noisy talk as they worked, and never have I seen children do more work with so much joy.

The Montessori teacher, when she finds that Jimmy is interfering with the work of Alice, segregates the bad Jimmy, and treats him as a sick person. But the right thing to do is to solve Jimmy's problem as well as Alice's. What is behind Jimmy's aggressiveness? Jimmy does not know, nor does the Montessori teacher, because she has been trained in the psychology of the conscious only.

Another reason why I am not wholly on the side of Montessori is, I fancy, that her religious attitude repels me. She is a church woman; she has a definite idea of right and wrong. Thus, although she allows children freedom to choose their own occupations, she allows them no freedom to challenge adult morality. But for a child to accept a ready-made code of morals is dangerous; education in morality is a thousand times more important than intellectual education with a didactic apparatus.

* * * * * *

To-night Duncan came in, and as usual we talked education. I took up the subject of punishment, and condemned it on the ground that it treats effect instead of cause. After a little persuasion Duncan seemed inclined to agree with me.

"I see what you mean," he said, "but what I say is that if you abolish punishment you must also abolish reward."

"Why not?" I said. "The case against rewards is just as simple. A child should do a lesson for the joy of doing it. Milton certainly did not write *Paradise Lost* for the five pounds he got for it."

"Yes, I see that," said Duncan thoughtfully, "but what about competition? The prize at the end introduces a breezy struggle for place."

I shook my head.

"No competition! I won't have it. It makes the chap at the top of the class a prig, and gives the poor chap at the bottom an inferiority complex. No, we want to encourage not competition but co-operation. Competition leads naturally to another world war, as competition between British and American capital is doing now."

Then Duncan floored me.

"And would you discourage football because it introduces the idea of competition?" he asked.

"Of course not," I replied

"Then why discourage it in arithmetic?" he asked.

It was an arresting question, and I had to grope for an answer that would convince not only Duncan but myself. That every healthy boy likes to try his strength against his fellows is a fact that we cannot ignore. Mr. Arthur Balfour's desire to beat his golfing partner and Jock Broon's desire to spit farther than Jake Tosh are fundamentally the same desire, the desire for self-assertion. And I see that the man who comes in last in the quarter-mile race is in the same position of inferiority as the boy who is always at the bottom of the class. Yet I condemn competition in school-work while I appreciate competition in games. Why?

I think I should leave it to the children. Obviously they like to compete in games and races, but they have no natural desire to compete in lessons. It appears that some things naturally lend themselves to competition—racing, boxing, billiards, jumping, football and so on. Other things do not encourage competition. Bernard Shaw and G. K. Chesterton do not compete in the output of books; Freud and Jung do not struggle to publish the record number of analysis cases; George Robey and Little Tich do not appear together on the stage of the Palladium and try to prove which is the funnier. Rivalry there always is, but it remains only rivalry until *The Daily Mail* offers a prize for the biggest cabbage or sweet-pea, and then competition seizes suburbia.

I should therefore leave the children to discover for themselves what interests lend themselves to competition, and what interests do not. I know beforehand that of their own accord they will not introduce it into school subjects. This is in accord with my views on the authority question. I insist that the teacher will impose nothing; that his task is to watch the children find their own solution.

* * * * * *

I must write down a wise saying that came

from Dauvit. A rambling and ill-informed discussion of Bolshevism arose in his shop to-night. Dauvit took no part in it, but when we rose to go he said: "Tak' my word for it, Bolshevism is wrong."

"How do you make that out, Dauvit?" I asked.

"Because it's a success," he said shortly.

* * * * * *

To-night the Rev. Mr. Smith, the U.F. minister, came in. He is one of the unco' guid, and to him all pleasures are sinful. It happened that I was telling Macdonald the Freudian theory of dreams when he entered, and when Mac told him what the conversation had been about, he begged me to continue. It was evident that he had never heard of dream interpretation, and he was surprised.

"And every dream has a meaning?" he asked.

"Yes," I said.

"I had a dream last night," he began, but I held up a warning hand.

"You shouldn't tell your dreams in public," I said hastily; "they may give things away that you don't want others to know."

He laughed.

"I don't mind that," he said, "I'll take the risk. Last night I dreamt that I was in a public-house among a lot of men who were telling most obscene stories. According to Freud every dream is the fulfilment of a wish. Do you mean to tell me that I *wish* to be in such a company?"

I explained that the dream as told is not the dream in reality, the meaning lies behind the symbolism, and it can be got at by the method of free association. I also explained that I did not believe the Freud theory, that the dream is always a wish, and suggested that Jung was a surer guide.

"According to Jung," I said, "the dream is often compensatory. In your own case you are consciously living the higher life, but there is another side of life that you are ignoring, and that is the vulgar pub side. Your dream is a hint that the vulgar side of life cannot be ignored. You may ignore it consciously, but your unconscious will seek the other side in your dreams."

This seemed to make him think.

"But the saints and martyrs!" he cried. "Think of the thousands who crucified the flesh so that they might win the everlasting crown! Do you tell me that they were all wrong?"

I lit my pipe.

"I think they were," I said, "for they merely repressed their animal life. They thought that they had conquered it, but they only buried it. The real saint is the man who faces his flesh boldly and loves it too, just as much as he loves his God."

Then the minister fled.

The interpretation of dreams is one of the most fascinating studies in the world. The method as evolved by Freud is simple, although the interpretation is anything but simple. Obviously the average dream has no meaning. You dream that a horse speaks to you, and then it turns into your brother. It is all nonsense, yet behind the nonsense is a serious meaning. Not long ago I was analysing a girl of sixteen. About a week after the analysis began she brought a dream which began thus: "I am invisible, and I have a tail that I can take off or put on."

Following the method of free association I said to her: "What comes into your mind about being invisible?"

"Oh, I've often wanted to be invisible, for then I could do what I liked; then I would be free."

Being invisible therefore meant being free.

Then I asked her associations to the tail part.

"Tail . . . . . monkeys at the Zoo; they are poor things always kept behind bars. Just like me. I forgot to say that my tail wasn't on in the dream."

Tail therefore meant something associated with confinement and restriction. It is significant that her tail was unattached. I took it to mean a wish-fulfilment dream; in it she got free from her neurosis.

The following night she dreamt that she was being driven in a motor car by a swanky chauffeur. They came to the bottom of a hill, and the car stopped, and she got out and walked. Her first association was: "The chauffeur had a big green coat on, one just like the coat you wear."

"So I was the chauffeur?" I asked.

She brightened at once.

"I see it!" she cried. "The car is the analysis; you are driving me away from my old life!"

"Excellent!" I said, "but don't forget that the car stopped at the bottom of the hill. What does the word hill give you?"

"Something difficult to climb. I hated climbing it and thought it a shame that the motor didn't take me up."

"Well?"

"I've got to climb to get better, haven't I?"

"That's right," I said. "I told you the other night that no analyst should give advice, and I refused when you asked me for it. In your unconscious you realise that the chauffeur is not going to take you up the hill; in other words you've got to do most of the work."

Freud holds that there is a censor standing between the conscious and the unconscious. Primitive wishes seek to come from the unconscious, but the censor holds up his hand. "No," he says, "that's too disgusting; the conscious mind couldn't stand that; it would be shocked. You must disguise yourself in harmless form!" And so the infantile sex wish is changed into a harmless dog or cycle. But if this is the case why should my little girl dream of me as a chauffeur? There was nothing disgusting about me, nothing that her conscious mind could not face.

I prefer Jung's theory. He says that we dream in symbols because symbolism is the oldest language in the world, and, as the unconscious is primitive it uses this language. We all dream of shocking things, and if the endopsychic censor were really on duty he would never allow these disgusting dreams to get through.

If I dream that my father is dead the Freudians declare that I either wish or, in the past, have wished unconsciously for my father's death. But surely so alarming a wish would be changed into a harmless form if there were a censor. One night I dreamt that an acquaintance, Murray, was dead. The first association to Murray was: "He's a lazy sort of chap." I think that all he stood for was laziness, and he was merely my own laziness symbolised. The dream was a hint to me to be up and doing, for I had been neglecting a task that I should have undertaken.

There is what might be called the cheese-and-tripe supper theory of the dream held by many people.

"There's nothing in dreams," they say, "nothing but the disorders following late supper."

A cheese-and-tripe supper will cause queer dreams, but the advocates of this theory cannot explain why a tripe supper should make me dream of—say—a tiger. Why not a lion or a mouse?

It is an accepted fact now in psychology that the dream is the working of the unconscious. Some theosophists claim that during sleep your spirit leaves your body and seeks the astral plane, but I have never seen anything resembling evidence of this. It may be a fact for all that.

Concerning the prophetic aspect of dreams I know nothing. I have heard that the night before the Tay Bridge disaster a woman dreamt that it was to take place, and she persuaded her husband not to travel by that ill-fated train, but I cannot vouch for the story. I believe, however, that the dream is prophetic in that the unconscious during the night is working out the problems of the next day. The popular saying about sleeping over a problem shows that there is a real belief in this aspect. I know a lady who was undergoing analysis. She was suffering from a father complex, that is, her infantile fixation on the father had remained with her, and unconsciously she was approving or disapproving of every man she met according as he did or did not in some way resemble her father.

For a few weeks after the analysis began she was always dreaming that she was back in her childhood home, and in her dreams she was always trying to get away from home and he· father was always restraining her from going. Often the figure in the dream was not the father, but the associations always showed that the figure was standing for the father. One night the figure was the King, and her first association was : " The King's name is George. . . . . . That's father's name too."

This seems to be a case where the unconsc:ous is striving to find a solution.

The way the unconscious does things is wonderful. I remember one night listening to a lecture by Homer Lane. He brought forward a new theory about education, and it was so deep that I did not quite grasp its meaning. At the time Alan, Homer Lane's youngest child, was one of the pupils in the school in which I taught. That night I dreamt that I was standing before a class. Alan was sitting in the front seat, and behind him was a boy whom in the dream I called "Homer Lane's youngest child." The new theory had become in the language of symbolism Alan's younger brother. . . . . in short, Lane's latest. Here again I cannot see why any censor should change a theory into a child.

* * * * * *

In my *Log* I make a very, very poor statement about sex instruction. I say that children should be encouraged to believe in the stork theory of birth until the age of nine. That was a wrong belief, but then at that time I had not read Freud or Bloch or Moll. I see now that the child should be told the truth about sex whenever he asks for information. But I fear, that many modern mothers think that they have sexually educated their child when they tell him where babies come from. The physiological side of sex is the less important; you can take a child through all the usual stages—pollination of plants, fertilisation of eggs, right up to human birth, but the child will find no help in these informations when he faces his sex instinct at adolescence. Sex instruction should be psychological; it should deal with the sex instinct as one form of life force or libido. The child should be led to face it openly. It should be entirely dissociated from sin, and moral lectures should not be given.

Who is to give the instruction? That is the difficulty. Most parents and teachers cannot do it because their own sex instinct is all wrong. Make a remark about sex in the company of adults, and it will be reacted to in two ways; some will grin and laugh; others will be shocked. I hasten to add that the shocked ones are worse than the laughers. The laugh is a release of sex repressions; the shocked appearance is a compensation for an unconscious over-interest in sex. Anyway neither type is capable of talking about sex to children, and since humanity is roughly divided into prudes and sinners (not *saints* and sinners), there is little hope of a frank sex education for kiddies.

Many people say: "Oh, leave it to the doctors," but personally I haven't enough faith in doctors. Their attitude to sex is usually no better than the attitude of the layman. I know doctors who could give excellent instruction to children on the physiology of sex, but the only doctors of my acquaintance who could teach the psychological side are psycho-analysts or psycho-therapists of some sort.

Teachers can tackle the sex problem negatively. Sex activity is a form of life force or interest, and if a child is not finding life interesting enough there is a danger that he will regress to what is called auto-eroticism. When we remember that the sexual instinct is the creative instinct, and that creation in dancing or music or poetry or art of any kind is sublimated sex, that is sex raised to a higher power, we can readily see that one of the most important parts of a teacher's job is to provide ways and means for creation. I realise that this is not enough, but, as I say, I cannot see the way to a good sex education, until every teacher and parent has discovered his or her own sex complexes. Co-education helps, for then the commingling of the sexes affords a harmless and unconscious outlet for sex interest. But co-education is no panacea, for the sex problems of the individual child in a co-educational school are almost as immediate as those of the child from the segregated school.

IX.

THIS morning I was setting off for Dundee when Willie Marshall entered the compartment. He was dressed in his Sunday best, and I wondered why he was going to Dundee on a Wednesday.

"Hullo, Willie!" I cried, "what's on to-day?"

He looked troubled and angry.

"I've been summoned to serve on the jury that's tryin' that dawmed rat that stailt ten pund frae the minister," he said viciously, "and I had little need to lose a day, for I hae far mair work than I can dae. Mossbank's twa cairts cam in yestreen, and he's swearin' like onything that he maun hae them by the nicht." Willie is a joiner, and most of his work is building and repairing carts.

"So you think that Nosie Broon is guilty?" I said with a smile.

"Of coorse he is," he cried with emphasis

"But," I said seriously, "you'll maybe alter your mind when you hear the evidence."

He grunted.

"Dawn nae fear! I'll show him that he's

no to drag me awa frae ma work for nothing!"

He opened his *Dundee Courier*, and I sat and thought of the trial by jury method. I would not condemn it on the strength of Willie's dangerous misunderstanding of what it means, but I do condemn it on other grounds. Weighing evidence is a difficult enough business even for the specialist, for it is almost impossible to eliminate emotion in forming a judgment. With a jury of citizens, some of them possibly illiterate, too much depends on the advocates, or on outside causes.

During the war there was a glaring instance of this. A soldier shot the man who had been trying to steal his wife's love . . . . . and the verdict of the jury was Not Guilty. The emotional factor in this case was that the dead man was a German. I am not arguing that the prisoner should have been hanged or imprisoned, for I think both procedures are bad; I merely point out that in the eyes of legalism the soldier was guilty, yet the jury threw legalism overboard.

Another instance of the emotional factor over-ruling legalism is seen in the trial of the man who shot Jaures. He was acquitted. . . . . . Not Guilty . . . . . the man who slew one of the best men in Europe. On the other hand the youth who attempted to assassinate Clemenceau was sentenced to death, pardoned, and sent to penal servitude. In

France therefore it is a crime to kill a politician of the right, but a virtue to kill one of the Socialist left.

Abstract justice is a figment. No jury and no judge can be impartial. The other day a man was charged with striking a Socialist orator with an ice-pick. The judge lectured the orator on his Bolshevism, and then gave the accused imprisonment for a short term in the second division. Suppose that the Bolshevist had used an ice-pick on a Cabinet Minister !

I do not think that our judges and magistrates ever consciously show partiality. They are an upright class of men, men above suspicion. It is their unconscious that shows partiality, just as mine does. The army colonels who tried Conscientious Objectors were upright men, but it was wrong to imagine that they could possibly see the C.O.'s point of view. So it was with the regular R.A.M.C. doctors. To some of them the neurotic patient was a swinger of the lead, a malingerer. They had never heard of the new psychiatry, and the neurotic was a strange creature to them. Their ignorance supplemented their prejudice, and they could not possibly have treated these men with justice.

The truth is that we all make up our minds according as our buried complexes impel us. If I saw a Frenchman fighting a Scot I should take the Scot's side, because I have a Scot complex. Occasionally our complexes work in the opposite way. I fancy that the few people who sided with the Germans in the war were suffering from an " agin the government " complex, which, if you trace it deep enough is usually found to be an infantile rebellion against the father. In this case the State represented the father, and Germany was the outside helper who should conquer the father (or mother) country. Had Germany won, the unpatriotic man would immediately have turned his hate against Prussia, for then Prussia would have been the father substitute.

Our loves and hates and fears are within ourselves. I know a man who has a nagging wife; she has a constant wish for new things. He bought her a hat, and for two days she was happy; then she nagged, and he bought her a dress. Three days later she demanded a necklace, and he gave her a necklace. He may continue giving her everything she asks for, but if he buys her a Rolls Royce and a house in Park Lane she will be a dissatisfied woman, for " the fault, dear Brutus, lies not in our stars but in ourselves." I advised him to spend his money on having her psycho-analysed.

* * * * * *

To-night Tammas Lownie the joiner came into Dauvit's shop. He is an infrequent attender at Dauvit's parliament, and Dauvit seemed slightly surprised at his entry.

"Weel, Tammas," he said, "it's no often that we see you here. What's brocht ye here the nicht?"

Tammas spat in the grate.

"Oh, it was a fine nicht, and I thought I'd just tak a daunder yont," he said easily.

Dauvit looked at him searchingly.

"Na, na, Tammas, it winna dae! It wasna the fine nicht that brocht ye yont. Ye've got some news I'm thinkin'."

Tammas laughed loudly.

"Dauvit, ye're oncanny!" he cried. "Ye seem to read what's at the back o' a man's heid. But I have nae news to gie ye."

Dauvit chuckled.

"I wudna wonder if ye didna come yont to tell me aboot the eldership," he said slowly.

The expression on Tammas's face showed that he *had* come to tell us that the minister had asked him to become an elder.

"'Od, Dauvit, noo that ye come to mention it I wud like to hear yer advice aboot the matter. I dinna see how I can tak an eldership, Dauvit."

"How no?" asked Dauvit in surprise. Then he added: "But maybe ye ken whether ye've got a sinfu' heart or no."

"It's no that," said Tammas hastily, "I'm nae worse than some other elders I ken," and he glanced at Jake Tosh. " No, it's no the sin I'm thinkin' o' ; it's my trade."

" But," I put in, " why shouldn't a joiner be an elder ? "

Tammas bit off a chunk of Bogie Roll.

" That may as may be, dominie, but I'm mair than a joiner ; I'm an undertakker."

" Weel," said Dauvit, " what aboot that ? "

Tammas shook his head sadly.

" An undertakker canna be an elder, Dauvit. Suppose the minister was awa preachin' or at the Assembly, and ane o' his congregation was deein', me as an elder micht hae to ging to the bedside and offer up a bit prayer."

" There's nothing in that," said Jake proudly ; " I've offered up a bit prayer afore noo when the minister was awa."

" Aye, Jake," said Tammas, " but ye see you're a roadman. But an undertakker is a different matter. Goad, lads, I canna gie a man a bit prayer at sax o'clock and syne measure him for his coffin at acht. That wud look like mixin' religion wi' business."

The assembly thought over this aspect.

" All the same," said the smith, " Dr. Hall is an elder, and naebody ever thinks o' accusin' him o' mixin' religion wi' his business."

We all considered this statement.

" Tammas," said Dauvit, " if ye want to be an elder tak it, and never mind the under-takkin'. But if ever ye have to gie a prayer just get Jake here to tak on the job."

He began to laugh here.

"I mind o' Jeemie Ritchie when he got his eldership. The minister gaed awa to the Assembly in Edinbro, and as it happened auld Jess Tosh was deein', so Jeemie was asked to come up and gie her a prayer. Jeemie was in my shop when the lassie Tosh cam for him, and I never saw a man in sic a state.

"'Dauvit,' he cries, 'I canna dae it! I never offered up a prayer in my life!'

"'Hoots, Jeemie,' says I, 'it's easy; just bring in a few bitties frae the Bible.'

"Auld Jeemie he scarted his heid.

"'Man, Dauvit,' says he, 'I cudna say twa words o' the Bible.'

"Weel-a-weel, I had to shove him oot o' the shop, and I tell ye, boys, he was shakin' like a shakky-trummly.

"Weel, in aboot half-an-hour Jeemie cam back, and he was smilin' like onything.

"'Hoo did ye get on?' I speered.

"'Graund!' he cried, '. . . . . she was deid afore I got there!'"

* * * * * *

When I published my *Log* a correspondent wrote accusing me of being disloyal to my colleagues in the teaching profession.

"Where is your professional etiquette?" he wrote.

I had lots of letters from teachers, some flattering, some not. One man wrote me from Croydon :—

"Dear Sir,— Are you a fool or merely a silly ass ? "

"Both," I replied, "else I should not have paid 2d. for your letter."

In haste the poor man hastened to forward two penny stamps, and to apologise for not having stamped the letter he sent me.

"I really thought that I had stamped it," he wrote.

Then I wrote him a nice letter telling him that the mistake was mine, for his first letter had had a stamp on it after all. He never replied to that, and I suppose that now he goes about telling his friends that I am a fool, a silly ass, and a typical Scot.

Authors hear queer things about themselves. The other day a friend of mine asked for my *Log* in a West End library. As the librarian handed over the book she shook her head sadly.

"Isn't it sad about the man who wrote that book ? " she said.

My friend was startled.

"Sad ! What do you mean ? "

"Oh, haven't you heard ? " asked the librarian in surprise ; "he's a confirmed drunkard now."

"Impossible ! " cried my friend, "with whisky at ten and six a bottle ! "

But I meant to write about colleagues.

One day a class was holding a self-government meeting, and they sent for me. I was annoyed because I was having my after-dinner smoke in the staff-room. However I went up.

"Hullo!" I said as I entered, "what do you want?"

Eglantine the chairman said: "A member of this class has insulted you."

"Impossible!" I cried.

Then Mary got up.

"I did," she blurted out nervously; "I said you were just a silly ass."

"That's all right!" I said cheerfully, "I am," and I made for the door. Then the class got excited.

"Aren't you going to do anything?" asked Ian in surprise.

"Good Lord, no!" I cried. "Why should I?"

"You're on the staff," said Ian.

"Look here," I said impatiently, "I hereby authorise the crowd of you to call me any name you like."

The class became indignant.

"You can't criticise the staff," said one.

"Why not?" I asked, and they looked at each other in alarm. This was carrying self-government too far.

Suddenly Mary jumped up.

"Then if we can criticise the staff here goes! I accuse Miss Brown of favouritism."

It was a bombshell. Everyone jumped up, and some cried : " Shame ! Withdraw ! " The chairman appealed to me.

" I have nothing to do with it," I protested.

Then bitter words flew. They told me that I, as a member of the staff, should squash Mary. Voices became louder, but then the bell rang and the class had to go to its own class-room to work.

My colleagues when they heard the story agreed with the children ; they held that I acted wrongly in listening to an accusation against a colleague. My argument was that I was a guest at a meeting ; I had no vote, nor would I have interfered had I been a member of the meeting. I was quite sure that if the bell had not broken up the meeting somebody would have made the discovery that Miss Brown was the proper person to make the accusation to. When they thought that Mary insulted me they sent for me, and I fully expected they would send for Miss Brown. Again I argued that if Miss Brown had favourites the class had a right to criticise her. If she had no favourites let her arraign the class before a meeting of the whole school and accuse them of libel.

Looking back I still think my attitude was right, for unless the staff can lay aside all dignity and become members of the gang education is not free. Yet I see now that I was secretly exulting in the discomfiture of a colleague . . . . . a common human failing which none of us care to recognise in ourselves. It is a sad fact but a true one that however much Dr. A. protests when a patient tells him that Dr. B. is a clumsy fool, unconsciously at least Dr. A. is gratified at the criticism of his rival. Psycho-analysts, that is people who are supposed to know the contents of their unconscious, are just as guilty in this respect as other doctors, and if anyone doubts this let him ask a Freudian what he thinks of the Jungian in the next street.

My earliest memory of professional jealousy goes back to the age of seven. I lived next door to a dentist, a real qualified L.D.S. Across the street lived a quack dental surgeon. When trade was dull these two used to come to their respective doors and converse with each other in the good old simple way of putting the fingers to the nose. They never spoke to each other. Life in a northern town was simple in these days.

* * * * * *

Helen Macdonald is four years old, and her mother and I have some breezy discussions about her upbringing. Mrs. Mac has a great admiration for her own mother, and she is bent on bringing up her daughter in the way that she was brought up.

"Mother made me obey and I'll make Helen obey," she said to-day with decision.

"It's dangerous," I said.

"No it isn't; it worked well enough in my case anyway."

"Don't blow your own trumpet, madam!"

She smiled.

"I don't think I am a bad product of the good old way," she said with a self-satisfied air.

"Madam, shall I tell you the truth about yourself?"

She bubbled and drew her chair closer to mine.

"Do!" she cried, and then added: "But I won't believe the nasty bits."

Mac chuckled.

"To begin with," I said pompously, "you are an awful example of a bad education."

She bowed mockingly and Mac guffawed. He is a wee bit afraid of his wife and he marvels at my courage in ragging her.

"You," I continued, "were made to obey as a child, and as a result you became dependent on your mother. In short you are your own mother."

"Don't be silly," she said with a frown; "I want your serious opinion."

"And you are getting it," I replied. "Because you had to obey you never lived your own life, and naturally you never had a mind of your own. To this day you act as your mother acted. She made her daughter obey; you follow her example; she made scones in such and such a way; you make scones in exactly the same way."

"That's right!" laughed Mac.

Mrs. Mac looked thoughtful.

"Anyway," she said quickly, "they are excellent scones."

"Most excellent scones," I hastened to add, "but my point is that if we all follow our parents there will be no progress."

"Progress will never bring better scones," said Mac and he patted his wife's cheek.

"Mac," I said gallantly, "your wife has brought scones to their perfect and utmost evolution. She has made the super-scone. Only, Helen isn't a scone you know."

At this point Helen was found trying to pull the marble clock down from the mantlepiece. Her mother rescued the clock as it was falling, and she scolded the fair Helen.

"You are all theory," she cried to me. "What would you do in a case like this?"

"Same as you did," I answered hastily, and then added: "Only I would try to give her so many interesting things to play with that she'd forget to want the clock."

Then Mrs. Mac indignantly dragged out Helen's toys from a cupboard.

"Dozens of them!" she cried, "and she is tired of every one."

Then I discoursed on toys. The toys of the world are nearly all bad. Helen has a beautiful sleeping doll that cost five pounds; rather I should say that Helen *had* a beautiful sleeping doll that cost five pounds. On the one occasion that Helen was allowed to play with it she made a careful attempt to open the head with a pair of scissors to see what made the eyes close and open. Then her mother put the doll in a box, packed the box in a trunk, and explained to Helen that the doll was to lie in that trunk until Helen had a little baby girl of her own.

I explained to Mrs. Mac that the toy a child needs is one that will take to pieces. Every toy should be a mine of discovery. The only good toys that I know of are Meccano and Primus, but there is much need for constructive toys for younger children.

"Mac," I said, "if you were even a passably good husband you would be making Montessori apparatus for your offspring."

We have many arguments like this. Mrs. Mac's problem is that of a million mothers; she has to fit the child into an adult environment. Yesterday she was painting in oils. The baker whistled outside and she ran out to get the bread. On her return she found that Helen was busily painting the pink wall-paper a prussian blue.

Wealthy mothers solve the problem by employing nurses, but the solution is a poor one. Few nurses know enough about children, and many do positive harm by frightening the child.

Nor can the hired nurse give the infinite amount of love that a child demands. If she could it is probable that she would be sacked, for no mother likes to see her child lavish his love on another. On more than one occasion I have discovered that the parents of children who loved me were hostile to me. That is natural. If a father is continually hearing his daughter say: "Mr. Neill says this; Mr. Neill says that," I have every sympathy with him when he growls: "Damn this Neill blighter!" On the other hand I have no sympathy with him if he expects me to ask his little Ada how her dear charming papa is.

* * * * * *

A book of ten volumes might well be written on the subject of parents and teachers. If a teacher were the author no publisher would look at it, for the language would be unprintable.

To the teacher the parent is an enemy. When Mrs. Brown comes to school she and the dominie chat pleasantly about the weather, while the children look on and marvel. Little Willie is amazed to see his mother smile as she talks, for it was only last night that he heard her say: "That Mr. Smith is by no means a gentleman. Did you see his nails?" Poor little Willie does not know that his mother and the dominie are using fair smiles to cover a real hostility. Mrs. Brown will talk agreeably all through her visit, but as she is shaking hands on the doorstep she will say, " Oh, by the way, Mr. Smith, Willie came home last night saying that he wasn't allowed to play hockey yesterday. I want him to play every Wednesday."

" But," says Mr. Smith deferentially, " I—er—well, Wednesday is the day when the Seniors play, and—er—since Willie is a Junior I—er—I—"

" Oh, thank you so much," she gushes, " I knew that you would arrange that he will play on Wednesdays," and she sails away.

Or perhaps Mrs. Brown will put it on to her husband.

" The way things are done at that school are disgraceful, Tom. You must go and see Smith and insist that the boy has his hockey."

Well, the poor father comes up to school, and he and the dominie discuss the weather and Lloyd George. All the time Brown is trying to muster up enough courage to tackle the hockey question.

" Er," he begins after clearing his throat, " my wife was saying something about—er—what a splendid view you have from here ! "

" First rate," nods the dominie. " Your wife was saying ? "

" Er—something about hockey." He coughs. " Splendid game ! I—er—I must go . . . . . er—good-bye."

No mere man can badger a dominie.

From the parent's point of view a teacher is a rival when he isn't a sort of under-gardener. The parent would never think of arguing with the doctor when he says that Willie has measles; the doctor is a specialist in disease, and the parent is not. But it is different with the dominie. He is a specialist in education, but then so is the parent. That is possibly one of the reasons that the teaching profession is such a low-class one, for a teacher is merely a specialist in a world of specialists. Everybody knows how a child ought to be brought up. In justice to parents I must confess that there are only two teachers in Britain to whom I should trust the education of any child of mine. Most teachers are instructionists only, and the parent has some ground for suspicion.

X.

DUNCAN was talking about awkward moments to-night, and he told of the shock he got when he joined the army and found that the sergeant of his squad was an old pupil of his.

" I think I can beat that, Duncan," I said, and told him the story of an army lecture. I had a commission in the R.G.A. for a short time, and one morning I had to give a lecture to the men of the battery on lines of fire. They were mostly miners, and I tried to make the lecture as simple as possible. I began with the definition of an angle and went on to circular measurement. I noticed that one man stared at the blackboard in bewilderment, a very stupid looking fellow he was. When the lecture was over I approached him.

" I don't think you understood what I was trying to tell you," I said.

" I did have some difficulty in following it, sir," he said.

" H'm ! What were you in civil life ? "

" Mathematical master in a secondary school, sir."

I could not rise to the occasion. I fled to the mess and ordered a brandy and soda.

Speaking about rising to the occasion brings to my mind another army incident in which I did not shine. I was a recruit in the infantry, and a gym sergeant was putting us through physical jerks. He told us the familiar tale that although we had broken our mothers' hearts we wouldn't break his ; in short he put the wind up us. I got very nervous.

"Right turn!" he roared, and I thought he said "Right about turn."

He told the squad to stand easy, and then he eyed me curiously.

"You! Big fellow! Take that smile off your face!"

I don't know why he said that for I couldn't have smiled at that moment for anything less than my ticket. He studied me carefully for a bit, then enlightenment seemed to dawn on him.

"I got it!" he exclaimed triumphantly. "I know wot's wrong with you! You've got a stupid face ; you can't think ; you never thought in yer life."

I looked on the ground.

"*Did* yer ever think in yer life?"

"No, sergeant," I said humbly.

"I blinkin' well thought so!" he said and moved away.

Then the worm turned. Who was he that he should bully a scholar and a gentleman? I would lower him to the dust.

"Sergeant!"

He turned quickly.

"Wot d'ye want?" and he tried to freeze me with his look.

"It isn't my fault I can't think, sergeant; I was unfortunate enough to spend five years at a university."

His mouth gaped, and his eyes stared, but only for a moment. Then he rose to the occasion.

"I blinkin' well thought so!" he cried. "Squad! . . . . . Tshun!"

* * * * * *

It is Sunday night, and I have just been to town. At the Cross I stood and listened to a revivalist bellowing from a soap-box. His message was Salvation but I was more interested in the man than his message. Consciously he is out to save sinners, but I suspect that unconsciously he is out to draw attention to himself. I do not blame him. I do the same thing when I publish a book; Lloyd George and George Robey and the revivalist and I are all striving each in his little corner to draw attention to ourselves.

The exhibition impulse is in every child. A child loves to run about naked, but then society in the form of the mother steps in and says: "You must not do that!" But we know that every wish lives on in the depths of the mind, and the childish wish to exhibit the body appears in later years as a desire to preach or sing or act or lecture.

This is the psychology of the testimonials for liver pills which appear in every local paper. It is the psychology of much crime. Many a slum youth glories in having been birched, simply because his gang looks on him as a hero.

I hasten to state that exhibitionism alone does not make a Cabinet Minister or a comedian. There are other motives from infancy, an important one being the desire for power. I recall that as a boy I delighted in following a drove of cattle and smiting the poor creatures hard with a cudgel. Freud would say that in this way I was releasing sex energy, but I think that the infantile sense of power was at the root of my cruelty ; here was I, a wee boy, controlling a big heavy stot. It is love of power that makes little boys want to be engine-drivers.

To the teacher this love of power is the most vital thing in a child's make-up. Discipline thwarts the boy at every turn, and our adult authority is fatally injuring the boy's character. Our task is to provide the child with opportunity to wield his power. We suppress it and the lad shows his power in destructive instead of constructive activities. I find that I keep returning to this subject of suppression, but it is the most important evil in education. It does not matter how perfect a teacher makes his instruction in arithmetic ; if he has not come to see that suppression of a child is a tragedy, his instruction is of no value. From an examination point of view, yes ; from a spiritual point of view, no.

* * * * * *

Parents and teachers fail because they cannot see the world as the child sees it. The child of three is a frank egoist. He cares for no one but himself, and the world is his. Anger him and he would have you drawn and quartered if he had the power. His instincts prompt him to master his environment, and to begin with, when he is a few weeks old, his environment and his own person are indistinguishable.

Homer Lane gives a delightful description of the child's first efforts and how they are frustrated by ignorant adults.

"At a very early age the child becomes aware through various processes that his own hand which he has seen moving across his line of vision is a part of himself, and that he can move it himself. He has discovered power. He then enters upon his career. The same motive that will govern his behaviour for the rest of his life comes into operation, and he wants to use this new-found power for some purpose that will increase his enjoyment of life. Up to this time he has had only one pleasure, and that was to do with the commissariat. Having discovered power over his fist he therefore wants to put it in his mouth . . . . . a difficult task requiring much practice and patient perseverance.

"As he goes on working he learns that his power increases with effort, and now his motive is modified. At first it was purely materialistic; he wanted to have his fist in his mouth. Now he wants to put it there. His interest is in doing the thing rather than in having it.

"This is the spiritual element in his present desire, and now comes the first mistake in education. The mother, analysing the behaviour of the child, has noticed his complaint at the difficulty of the task as fatigue sets in, and, misunderstanding the motive of the child she helps him to put his fist in his mouth. But that is just what the child did not want, and he protests violently against this interference with his purpose in life.

"The mother again makes a false analysis of the situation, and concludes that his protest is the result of his disappointment that there is no nourishment in the fist. She then gives him food or paregoric, whatever may be her method of dealing with the spiritual unrest of her child, and thus drugs his creative faculties."

I have said that the infant is an egoist. If his egoism is allowed full scope he will enter upon the next stage of life, the self-assertive stage, with a huge capacity for being altruistic.

This stage comes on about the age of six or seven. But if the child has had parents who believe in moulding character he will have had many severe lectures about his selfishness. These lectures will not have cured his selfishness; they will have driven it underground for the moment. The selfishness of adults is one result of the moral lecture in childhood, for no wish or emotion will remain buried for ever.

The age of self-assertion is the rowdy age, and naturally it is now that father uses his authority. The child is still ego-centric, but in a different way. At the age of three he was the king of the world; at the age of seven he is the king of the other boys who play with him. He is now reckoning with society, and he uses society as a background against which he may play the hero. Thus be bleeds Jack's nose for no reason in the world other than that he thus asserts himself. If he plays horses with the boy next door he insists upon being the driver.

It is at this period that he should be free from authority. If authority in the shape of father or teacher or policeman steps in to suppress his self-assertion the boy becomes an enemy of all authority and very often anti-social. The "rebel" in the Socialist camp is a good specimen of the man whose self-assertive period was injured by authority, and I suspect that the truculent drunk is letting off the steam that he should have let off at the age of eight.

The third stage in the evolution of a child is the adolescent stage. For the first time the boy becomes a unit in society. Hitherto he has played for his own hand; his games have been games in which personal prowess was the desired aim. Now he feels that he is one of a team. Even before puberty the team-forming impulse is seen; Puffer, for instance, in *The Boy and his Gang*, gives ten to sixteen as the gang age.

These divisions are purely arbitrary, and children differ much in evolution. The teacher, however, should have a general knowledge of these three phases. I have often seen a school prescribe cricket or hockey for boys who are still in the self-assertive stage. The result was that, having no team impulse, each boy had no further interest in the game when the umpire shouted: "Out!"

I used to umpire for boys and girls of eight to eleven, and it was a tiresome business. Quite often when a boy had been bowled with the first ball, he would throw down the bat in disgust and refuse to give the other side an innings. There was nothing wrong with the children; what was wrong was that a team phase game was being forced on a self-assertive phase group.

*   *   *   *   *   *

Duncan and two other dominies were in

to-night and we got on to golf yarns. I remarked that there were very few good ones, and they all trotted out their favourites. I liked Duncan's best.

An oldish man was ploughing his way to the tenth hole at St. Andrews, and, when he ultimately holed out in nineteen, he turned to his caddie.

" Caddie," he cried in disgust, " this is the worst game I ever played."

The caddie stared at him open-mouthed.

" So ye *have* played afore, have ye ? " he gasped in amazement.

Why are there no cricket or football stories, I wonder ? Possibly because they are team games ; a team is a crowd, and I never heard of a joke against a crowd. A crowd is an impersonal thing, and no one can joke about an impersonal thing. I never heard of a joke about the moon or a turnip. Yet are there not jokes against a nation, and a nation is a crowd ? Take the joke about the Scot who was brought up at Bow Street for being drunk and disorderly. The magistrate, before passing sentence, asked the accused if he had anything to say for himself.

" Weel, ma lord, it was like this. I travelled frae Glesga to London yesterday, and I got into bad company in the train."

" Bad company ? "

" Aye, ma lord. When I got into the train at Glesga Central I had twa bottles o' whuskey in my bag, and . . . . . a' the other men in my compartment was teetotal."

That looks like a joke against a long-suffering race, but is it so in reality ? Make the traveller an 'Oodersfield' man on his way to see the Cup-tie Final at Chelsea, and it is not changed in essence. Only it has become a convention that the Scot is a hard drinker. It is the personal touch that makes the joke, and it is the individual that we laugh at.

I presume that the typical joke about Scots' meanness appeals to Englishmen because Englishmen are mean themselves. No joke appeals to a man unless it releases some repressed wish of his own. No one expects a devout Roman Catholic to see the point of a joke about extreme unction. The professional comedian to be a success must know what the crowd repressions are. Dickens is a great humorist because he knew by intuition what the crowd would laugh at. And that brings me to the subject of human types.

Broadly speaking there are two types of man. One is called an extrovert (Latin, to turn outwards) ; he identifies himself with the crowd, and he lives the life of the crowd. Lloyd George and Horatio Bottomley are typical extroverts ; they seem to know instinctively what the crowd is thinking, and unconsciously they speak and act as the crowd wants them to speak and act. Dickens was another, and that is why he has so universal an appeal.

The other type, the introvert type, turns inward. They do not identify themselves with the crowd. What the public wants does not concern them ; they give the crowd what they think it ought to want. This class includes the thinkers, the men who are in advance of their time. An introvert is never popular with the crowd because the crowd never understands him. He can never get away from himself, and he sums up events according to the personal effect they have on himself. Yet to the unconscious of the introvert crowd opinion is of the greatest importance.

In the realm of humour the extrovert is a success ; what amuses him amuses the crowds. But the introvert laughs alone, and in some cases he decides that the crowd has no sense of humour, and he becomes a cynic.

It is necessary that the teacher should be able to recognise the different types . The extrovert is popular ; he it is who leads the gang. Doubts and fears do not trouble him ; life is pleasant and he laughs his way through it. But the introvert is the boy who stands apart in a corner of the playground ; he is timid and fears the rough and tumble of team games. He feels inferior and he turns in upon himself to find superiority. Thus he will day-dream of situations in which he is a hero like David Copperfield when he stood at Dora's garden gate and saw himself rescuing her from the burning house.

I think that the job of the teacher is to help each type to a position midway between introversion and extroversion. The boy who lives in the crowd might well be tempted to take more interest in his own individuality, and the introvert might well be encouraged to project his emotions outward.

* * * * * *

To-night Mac told me a story about old Simpson the dominie over at Pikerton. Last summer an English bishop was touring Scotland, and one morning he drove up to Simpson's school in a big car, flung open the door and walked in.

"*Good* morning, children," he cried.

The bairns sat gazing at him in awe. He turned to Simpson.

"My good sir," he protested, "when I enter a village school in England, the children all rise and say: 'Good morning, sir'!"

"Possibly," said Simpson dryly, "but in Scotland children are not accustomed to see strangers walk into a school. Scots visitors always knock at the door and await the headmaster's invitation to enter."

* * * * * *

Mac and I were talking about education to-night.

"I never heard you mention the teaching

side of education," he remarked. "Giving a child freedom isn't enough, you know. What about History and Geography and so on?"

"I think they are jolly well taught in many schools, Mac," I said. "It is the psychological side of education that is a thousand years behind the times."

"Yes," said Mac doubtfully, "but suppose you have a school of your own, I presume you'd teach the English yourself?"

I nodded.

"How would you do it?"

I thought for a while.

"I'd reverse the usual process, Mac," I said. "Usually the teacher begins with Chaucer and works forward to Dickens; I would begin with *Comic Cuts* and *Deadwood Dick* and work back to Chaucer."

"Oh, do be serious for once," he said impatiently.

"I am quite serious, Mac," I said. "The only thing that matters in school work is interest, and I know from experience that the child is interested in *Comic Cuts* but not in the *Canterbury Tales*. My job is to encourage the boy's interest in *Comic Cuts*."

I ignored Macdonald's reference to idiocy, and went on.

"You see, Mac, what you do is this: you see a boy reading *Deadwood Dick*, and you take his paper away from him and possibly whack the little chap for wasting his time.

But you don't kill his interest in penny dreadfuls, and the result is that in later years he reads the Sunday paper that supplies the most lurid details of murders and outrages. My way is to encourage the lad to devour tales of blood and thunder so that in a short time blood and thunder have no more interest for him. The reason why most of the literature published to-day is tripe is that the public likes tripe, and it likes tripe because its infantile interest in tripe was suppressed in favour of Chaucer and Shakespeare."

"But," cried Mac, "isn't Shakespeare better for him than tripe?"

"Yes and no. If every poet were a Shakespeare the world would be a dull place; you need the tripe to form a contrast. The best way to enjoy the quintessence of roses, Mac, is to take a walk through the dung-heaps first."

"What books would you advise your pupils to read?" asked Mac.

"In their proper sequence . . . . . *Comic Cuts, Deadwood Dick, John Bull, Answers, Pearson's Weekly, Boy's Own Paper, Scout, Treasure Island, King Solomon's Mines, White Fang, The Call of the Wild, The Invisible Man,* practically anything of Jack London, Rider Haggard, Conan Doyle, Kipling."

"And serious literature?"

"All literature is serious, Mac."

"I mean Dr. Johnson, Swift, Bunyan, Milton, Dryden, and that lot," said Mac.

I smiled.

" Mac, I want you to answer this question: have you read Boswell's *Life of Johnson?*"

" Extracts," he admitted awkwardly.

" Bunyan's *Life and Death of Mr. Badman?*"

" No."

" Milton's *Areopagitica?*"

' Er—no."

' Swift's *Tale of a Tub?*"

" No."

I sighed.

" Would you like to read them ? " I asked.

" I don't think they would interest me," he admitted.

" Then in heaven's name, why expect children to have any interest in them ? If these classics weren't shoved down children's throats the adult population of this country would be sitting of an evening reading and enjoying Milton instead of *John Bull.*"

Mac would not have this.

" Children must read the classics so that they may get a good style," he said.

" Style be blowed ! " I cried. " The only way to get a style is by writing. Mac, I should cut out all the lectures about Chaucer and Spenser and Shakespeare, and let the children write during the English period . . . . . if I had periods, which I wouldn't. I don't want style from kiddies ; I want to see them create in their own way. If they are free to create they will form their own style."

In a conversation one always has a tendency to overstate a case, and as the argument went on I found myself saying wild things. Writing calmly now I still hold to my attitude concerning style. I love a book written in fine style, but I refuse to impose style on children. In every child there is a gigantic protest. Thus the son of praying parents often turns out to be a scoffer. I had a good instance of the danger of superimposition of style.

I had a class of boys and girls of fifteen, sixteen, and seventeen years of age. For one period a week we all wrote five minute essays, and then we read them out. Sometimes we would make criticisms ; for instance one girl used the word " beastly " in a serious essay, and we all protested against it. Then one day the head-master decided that they should write essays for him. He set a serious subject—The Function of Authority, I think it was—and then he went over their books with a blue pencil and corrected their spelling and style.

Three days later my English period came round. I entered the room and found the class sitting round the fire.

" Hullo ! " I said, " aren't you going to write?"

" No," growled the class.

" Why not ? "

" Fed up with writing. We want to talk about economics or psychology."

A fortnight later they made an attempt to write short essays, but it was a miserable failure ; all the joy in creation had been killed by that blue pencil.

I can give an example of the other way, the only way. One boy of fifteen hated writing essays, and when I began the five minute essay game he sat and read a book. After a time I gave out the subject " Mystery," and I saw him look up quickly with flashing eyes.

" Phew ! What a ripping subject ! " he cried, " I must have a shot at that ! "

His shot was promising, and he continued to make shots, until some of his essays were praised by the class. Then one day he came to me.

" I don't know anything about stops and things," he said, " and I want you to tell me about them."

This is my ideal of education ; no child ever learns a thing until he wants to learn it. That lad picked up all he wanted to know about stops in half-an-hour. He was interested in stops because he wanted to write better essays. I need hardly say that he had listened to hundreds of lessons on stops during his school career.

* * * * * *

To-morrow I return to London, and to-night I went over to say good-bye to Dauvit.

" Aye, dominie, and so ye're gaein' back to London ! " he said.

" I don't want to leave this lazy life, Dauvit,"

I said, " but I must go back and start my school."

" It'll cost ye some bawbees to gang to London," put in Jake Tosh. " Penny three ha'pennies a mile noo-a-days I onderstand."

" A shullin' a mile for corps," remarked the undertaker.

Dauvit chuckled.

" So ye'll better no dee in London, dominie," he laughed.

" And that reminds me of Peter Wilson, him that passed into the Civil Service and gaed to London. He came hame onexpectedly wan mornin' and his father he says : ' What in a' the earth brocht ye hame in the month o' February, Peter ? Surely ye dinna hae a holiday the noo ? '

" ' No,' says Peter, ' but I had a cauld and I thocht I was maybe takkin' pewmonia, and, weel father, corpses is a bob a mile on the railway.' "

" Dauvit," I said, " I don't care where I am buried."

" Is that so ? " asked Jake in surprise. " What's become o' yer patriotism, dominie ? I canna onderstand a man no wanting to be buried in his ain country. For my pairt I wudna like to be buried ony place but the wee kirkyaird up the brae there."

Dauvit grunted.

" What does it matter, Jake, whaur ye're buried ? "

"Goad," said Jake, "it matters a lot. The grund up in the kirkyaird is the best grund in Scotland. It's a' sand, and they tell me that yer corp will keep for years in that grund."

Dauvit laughed, but the others seemed to take Jake's preservation argument seriously.

"Jake," said Dauvit, "does it no strike ye that to be buried in yer native place is a disgrace?"

"Hoo that, na?" said Jake.

"Because the man that bides in the place he was born in is of nae importance. A' the best men leave their native village, aye, and their native country. Aye, lads, the best men and the worst women leave their native country."

"I sincerely trust that you are not insinuating that they leave together, Dauvit," I put in hastily.

"No, they dinna do that, dominie; but whether they meet in London I dinna ken," and he smiled wickedly.

Jake spat in the grate.

"I dinna see what the attraction o' London is," he said with a touch of contempt.

It is rather difficult to describe," I said. "For one thing you feel that you are in the centre of things. You are in the midst of all the best plays and concerts and processions . . . . . and you never think of going to see them. Then all the important people are there, the King and Lloyd George and Bernard Shaw

. . . . . but you never see them anywhere. Then there are the places of historic interest, the Tower, Westminster Abbey, St. Paul's . . . . . and you don't know where they are until your cousins come up for a week's trip, and then you ask a policeman where the Tower is. And the strange thing is that you get to love London."

"There will be a fell puckle funerals I daresay," said the undertaker.

"To tell the truth," I answered, "I have never seen a funeral in London. In the suburbs, yes, but never in the centre of the West End. I've often seen them at the crematorium in Golders Green."

The undertaker frowned.

"That crematin' business shud be abolished by act o' Parliament," he said gruffly. "It's just a waste o' guid wood and coal. They tell me it taks twa ton o' coal ilka time."

I was surprised to find that the broad-minded Dauvit agreed with the undertaker in condemning cremation. I suspect that early training has something to do with it, and there may be an unconscious connecting of cremation with hell-fire. Dauvit's argument that cremation would destroy the evidence in poisoning cases was a pure rationalisation.

I wondered why the topic of funerals kept coming up, and I laughingly put the matter to Dauvit.

"Maybe it's because we're sad because ye're

gaein' awa," he said half-seriously. "We'll miss yer crack at nichts."

At last I got up to go.

"Aweel, Dauvit, I'll be going," I said.

"Aweel, so long," said Dauvit without looking up. The others said "Guidnicht" or "So Long," and I went out. I was sorry to leave these good friends, and they were sorry to lose me; yet we parted, it may be, for years, just as if we were to see each other to-morrow. We are a queer race.

XI.

WHEN I arrived in London to-night I received a blow. A letter awaited me saying that the landlord of the school I was taking over had decided to sell the property. Thus all my dreams of a free school vanished in smoke. There isn't a house to rent in London; thousands are for sale, but I have no money to buy. If I had money I should hesitate to buy, for if a school is a success it expands, and the ideal thing to do is to take it out to the country where there is fresh air and space to grow.

To-night I feel pessimistic; it is difficult to be an optimist when a long-planned scheme suddenly falls to pieces.

I think of my capitalist friend Lindsay. He could buy me a school to-morrow, and never miss the money, but I don't think I should accept it. He would always have a big say in the running of it, and his ideals are not mine. I know other people with money, but I fancy that they have no faith in me. That is one of the disadvantages of writing light books like *A Dominie's Log*. The adult reads it and says: "Funny chap this!" But people have little faith in funny chaps. You can be a funny chap if you are a magistrate or a cabinet minister, but a teacher must be a staid dignified person. He must be a man who by his serious demeanour will impress the children and lead them out of the morass of original sin in which they were born. Montessori is catching on in the educational world not entirely because of her excellent system; part of her success is due to the fact that she never makes a joke; she is always the dignified moral model teacher.

Poor Montessori! Here I am transferring my irritation at the landlord who sold my school to her. I beg her pardon. Nor am I really annoyed with the landlord; the person I am annoyed with is myself. I bungled that school business.

Now I feel better. When I am irritated I always think of the traveller from St. Andrews. He arrived at Leuchars Junction and had five minutes to wait for the Edinburgh train. He entered the bar and had a drink. He had a second drink, and then awoke to the fact that he had missed the train. The next train was due in two hours. The barmaid shut the bar between trains and the traveller went out on the platform. It was a cold rainy November night. He went to the waiting room, but there was no fire there.

"Anyway," he said, "I'll have a smoke," and he filled his pipe. Then he found that he had but one match left. He struck it, and it went out. He went out to the platform and found an old porter screwing down the lamps. The porter knelt down to tie his lace and the traveller approached him.

"Could you oblige me with a match?"

The old porter eyed him dispassionately.

"I dinna smoke. I dinna believe in smokin.' I dinna hae a match."

The traveller walked wearily forward to an automatic machine and inserted his last penny . . . . and drew out a bar of butter-scotch. He tossed it over the line, and then he threw his pipe after it. He walked along the platform, and then he came back. The old porter was again tying his lace. The traveller suddenly rushed at him and kicked him as hard as he could.

"What did ye do that for?" demanded the poor old man when he picked himself up.

The traveller turned away in disgust.

"Och, to hell wi' you; ye're ay tying your lace!" he said.

Lots of people cannot see the joke in this yarn, and I challenge anyone to explain the point.

* * * * *

Good fortune came to rescue me from sorrowing over my lost school. It sent me to Holland thuswise: about five hundred Famine Area children were coming from Vienna to

England, and I was invited to become one of the escort. Then it struck me that I might go over earlier and have a look at the Dutch schools. I hastened to get a few passport photographs ; I looked at them . . . . . and then I thought I shouldn't risk going. However, on second thoughts, I decided to risk it, and went to the passport office. There a gentleman with a big cigar looked at the photograph ; then he looked at me.

"The face of a criminal," his eyes seemed to say as he studied the photo.

"Isn't it like me ? " I asked in alarm.

"Quite a good likeness," he said brusquely, and passed me on to the next pigeonhole.

At last I landed in Flushing, and a kind guard found me a carriage. There I began to learn the Dutch language. "Niet rooken." Scots *reek* means *smoke ;* hurrah ! "do not smoke ! "

"Verbodden te spuwen." "It is forbidden to——" no, that wouldn't be nice ! Got it ! "Do not spit ! "

At this juncture a pretty Scheveningen lassie entered and greeted me. Alas ! I knew but five words of Dutch, and when I thought the matter over I concluded that they were not very appropriate for carrying on a mild flirtation. Still, it's wonderful how much you can do with facial expression. Just before the train started a man entered. He knew English, and with more kindness than knowledge of humanity he offered to act as interpreter. The ass! as if a fellow can tell a girl through an interpreter that her hair is just the shade he admires. This fisher lassie was the only pretty girl I saw in Holland in ten days.

Rotterdam. My first and abiding impression was that never before had I seen so many badly-dressed people. If I had money and a profiteering complex I should set up a Bond Street shop in the centre of Rotterdam. No, that's wrong; that wasn't my first impression at all: my first impression was of a window filled with cigars at six cents each—one and a fifth pence. From that moment I loved Holland and the Dutch. What did it matter if their clothes were badly cut? What did anything matter? I dived into that shop and bought twenty . . . . . and ten yards farther on discovered a shop with fatter and longer cigars at *five* cents each. Three days later in the Hague I walked round the cigar shops for two hours, dying for a smoke, but not daring to buy a cigar at five cents lest in the next street I should find a shop offering them at four cents.

It was in Rotterdam that I discovered how bad my manners were. I was sitting in a cafe when a gentleman entered. He swept off his hat and bowed graciously . . . . . and I hastily put a protecting hand on the pocket containing my pocket-book. But every man who entered greeted me in the same way, and I realised that I was in a polite country. By the end of the week I was beating the Dutch at their own game, for I swept off my hat to every policeman, shopkeeper, tramwayman I spoke to.

On a Monday morning I walked forth to inspect the Dutch schools. I saw a troop of little girls following a mistress, and I joined the procession. They turned into a playground, and I followed. I approached the lady.

"Do you speak English?"

"Engelish! Ja!" she said with a smile.

"I am an English—no, Scots teacher," I explained, "and I should like to see the school."

"I will ask the head-mistress," she said, and entered the school, while I stood and admired the bonny white dresses of the girls. She returned shaking her head.

"The head-mistress says that it is not allowed to visit a school in Holland without a permit from the Mansion House."

"A rotten country!" I growled, and went away.

In the street I ran into a group of boys led by a master who was smoking a fat cigar.

"Speak English?" I asked, lifting my hat gracefully.

"Nichtenrichtilbricht," he said; at least that's how it sounded.

"Thank you," I said, lifted my hat again, and fell in behind the boys. I was determined to see this thing through.

I tackled him again when we reached the playground.

"I the head would see," I began, "the ober-johnny, the chef."

"Ja!" he exclaimed with an enlightened grin, and nodded. In ten seconds the chief stood before me. He could speak a broken English, and said he would be glad to show me round. It was a third class school, and I gathered that in Holland there are three grades of State school; the first class is attended by the rich, the second by the middle class, and the third by the poor.

The school was very like a Board School in England. The children sat in the familiar desks and were spoon-fed by the familiar teacher. There was nothing new about it. I noticed that hand writing seemed to be the most important thing, and each class teacher proudly showed me exercise books filled with beautiful copper-plate writing. Most obliging class teachers they were. Would I like to hear some singing? It was wonderful singing in three parts; what surprised me was that the boys seemed to be just as keen on singing as the girls. I have always found it otherwise in Scotland and England.

In this school I got the gratifying news that corporal punishment is not allowed in Dutch schools, and later I learned that this applies to all reformatories also.

I think the Dutch are fond of children. Children seem to be everywhere. I went to the police-station to register as an alien, and as the inspector was examining my passport his wee girl of three toddled in and climbed on his knees. He laid down his pen and fondled the child. Then his wife came in; she had been out shopping, and wanted him to admire the big potatoes she had bought. I was delighted to see the human element mingle with the official. A country that allows wives and children to mix up with its red-tape is on the right road to health if not wealth.

I went to the Hague next day, and English friends met me at the station and piloted me to their home. Next morning I visited an establishment called the Observatiehuis, and found that the superintendent had spent six years in England and had an English wife. The observation house, he explained, is a home for bad boys. When convicted they are sent there and are "observed." If a boy is well-behaved he is sent to live with a family and learn a trade; if he is incorrigible he is sent to a reformatory.

I looked in vain for the new psychological way of treating delinquents. There was discipline here, but it was kindly discipline, for Mr. Engels is a kindly man; the boys sang as they swept the stairs. That was good, yet, it was Mr. Engels that brought freedom into the school; his successor may be a bully.

From Mr. Engels I got a letter of introduction to a real reformatory in Amersfoort, and off I set. Amersfoort is inland and I expected to find much language difficulty there, for I thought it unlikely that English would be spoken so far inland.

Amersfoort is a beautiful old town, and I at once set out to find the Coppleport mentioned in my guide-book. I suppose I looked a lost soul. A youth of eighteen jumped off his cycle and lifted his cap. Then he pointed to a badge he wore in his coat.

"Boy scout!" he said.

"Excellent!" I cried, "you speak English?"

He held out his hand.

"Good bye!" he said; "pleased you to meet!"

"How do you do?" I said.

He grinned.

"God damn!" he said sweetly.

After that conversation seemed to die down. I managed to convey to him that I was looking for the Coppleport, and he led me to it. Gradually his English improved, and he told me of his brother in England. A nice lad. I told him that I had once had a long conversation with the great B.P., but he looked blank.

"Baden Powell, your chief," I explained.

He shook his head ; he had never heard of B.P. I think now that what was wrong was that he did not understand the name as I pronounced it ; possibly he knows B.P. under the sound of Bahah Povell or something similar.

On the following morning I went to the reformatory. It was a beautiful building fitted with every appliance necessary . . . . . and one not necessary — a solitary confinement room. A young teacher, Mr. Conijn, a very decent chap, who could speak excellent English, showed me round. Every door we came to had to be opened with a key and locked behind us. Here there was more of military discipline than in the Observatiehuis, but none of the boys looked sulky or unhappy. The relations of the boys and the teachers were fine ; as Conijn passed a lad he would pull his hair or pass a funny remark, and the boy would grin and reply.

" Any self-government ? " I asked.

" We tried it but it was no good. It may work with English boys but not with Dutch," said Mr. Conijn.

" Did you have locked doors ? " I asked.

" Oh, yes."

" Then self-government hadn't the ghost of a chance to succeed," I remarked.

We entered a class where an old man of about eighty was teaching a group.

" Why do these lads keep their eyes on the

ground?" I asked. "Is their spirit crushed out of them?"

Conijn laughed.

"They are admiring your boots!" he cried.

I wore a pair of ski-ing boots on my trip, and all Holland stared open-mouthed at them. If I had been wanted for a murder I don't think anyone in Holland could have identified me, for their eyes never got above my boots.

One of the masters, Mr. van Something-or-other, very trustingly lent me his bike, and on the following day I cycled to Laren to see the Humanitarian School there. Nearly every road has a cycle path on one side and a riding path on the other, but in spite of the excellent roads I did not enjoy cycling in Holland; a free wheel was of little value on the flat surface. One delightful feature about cycling in Holland is that there are no mid-day closing times for pubs, but on the other hand you cannot raise much of a thirst in a flat country.

Well, I reached Laren after many narrow escapes, for I was continually forgetting that you keep to the right in Holland. A postman came along, and I jumped off.

"Humanitaire School?" I asked as I doffed my hat.

By his expression I judged that he did not know the institution under that name.

"School," I said, and he nodded and pointed to the village State school.

"Nay! School Humanitaire!" I persisted.

At this juncture another man came forward, and the two of them jawed away gutturally for some time. I began to grow weary.

"Hell!" I murmured to myself half aloud.

The postman brightened, and enlightenment came to him.

"Engelissman!" he exclaimed.

"Liar!" I cried, "I'm a Scot," and I left the two of them discussing Engelissmen.

After much trouble and many bitter words I found the school. A gentleman who looked extremely like Bernard Shaw before Shaw's hair turned grey, was digging in a garden with a lot of boys and girls. He was Mr. Elbrink, the head-master. He could speak English and he showed me round.

The school is rather like what is known as the crank school in England. In a manner it is the super-crank school, for everyone on the staff is teetotal, vegetarian, and a non-smoker. Here it was that I heard of Lightheart for the first time, and I blushed for my ignorance of the gentleman. It appears that he was a great educational reformer, a sort of Froebel I fancied, for handwork seemed to be the main consideration in the school. But I regret to say that the school did not impress me much. Too many children were doing the same sort of work; they sat in desks and held themselves more or less rigid. Here was benevolent authority again, not true freedom. All schools in Holland are State schools, and the Humanitarian School is one of them. It is almost impossible for a State school to be very much advanced; I think it is impossible, for the State is the national crowd, and a large crowd has little use for the crank.

I returned to Amersfoort, where by this time I had become the guest of the International School of Philosophy. This is a building standing in about twenty acres of ground amid the pine forests two miles south of the town. I was the sole guest, for the summer classes had not started. This school is the beginning of a great movement. Here students from every country will meet and discuss life and education. Mr. Reiman, the president, talked long and earnestly to me about the scheme, but I found myself challenging his insistence on spiritual education.

The aim of the school is to develop the spiritual side of man, an excellent aim . . . . . so long as man does not imagine that by living on the higher plane he is annihilating his earthly self. Everyone there was very, very kind to me, but I did not feel quite in my element, for I am not an obviously spiritual person. I find that I can discuss the higher life best when I have a glass of Pilsener at my elbow and a penny cigar in my mouth. It is clear that I have a complex about the higher life, and it may be a sour-grapes complex. All the same I should like to attend a summer course at Amersfoort and listen to the wise men dilate on the Bhagavadgita, Psycho-analysis and Religion, Plato, Sufism, and other subjects on the programme; anyway I would have no prepossessions and prejudices in listening to Dr. G. R. S. Meads' course of lectures on The Mystical Philosophy and Gnosis of the Trismegistic Tractates.

From Amersfoort I went to Amsterdam.

"Umsterdum, dree klasse, returig," I said to the ticket office girl.

"Third class return?" she asked with a smile and gave me the ticket.

I was indignant.

It is the most humiliating thing in the world to ask a question in Dutch and to be answered in English. In Rotterdam I had stopped a seafaring looking man and tried to ask him in Dutch what was the way to the Hotel de France. He listened patiently while I struggled with the language; then he spat on my boot.

"Hotel de France?" he replied in broad Cockney, "damned if I know."

On the way to Amsterdam I got into a carriage full of farmers and one of them made a remark to me. I shook my head.

"Engelissman?" he said.

I nodded.

Then those men began to talk about Engelissmen, and they talked and laughed all the way to Amsterdam. Every now and then one of them would jerk his thumb in my direction. It was a trying journey.

Arrived in Amsterdam I made for the Rijks Museum. At the door a seedy-looking man touched me on the arm.

"Guide, sir?"

"No thank you."

"Two hundred rooms, sir! Official guide."

"No thank you."

He kept pace with me, and in a weak moment I inquired his charge. It was three guilden (five shillings), and I saw at once that the dirty dog had won, for he took on an air of possession.

"Righto," I said resignedly, and he led me into the building.

He began his tiresome patter.

"Thees picture was painted in 1547; beautiful ees eet not? Wonderful arteest!"

I sighed.

"Take me to the Rembrandts," I said.

I cannot describe this incident. I hated the beast because I had been so weak as to accept his services. The beauty of Rembrandt and Franz Hals was lost on me; all I could see was the dirty face of that guide. Rembrandt's *Night Watch* made me forget the creature for a moment, but when he began to describe it I fled in horror. We finished up in the modern section, and as I looked at van Gogh and Cézanne and Whistler's *Effie Deans* his squeaky voice kept up a running commentary. I rushed from the building after a ten minutes' tour, paid the worm his three guilden . . . . and then went back and enjoyed the gallery. But I nearly committed murder in the Rijks Museum that day. If ever I am hanged it will be for murdering an official guide. This particular specimen spoiled my visit to Amsterdam. I could not get away from the thought of my weakness, and I fled the city.

In the train going back to Amersfoort a genial Dutchman made a remark to me. I resolved that I should pretend to be a fellow-countryman.

"Ja!" I said, and the answer seemed to satisfy him. He went on to say other things, and when his facial expression seemed to demand an affirmative I said "Ja!"

After a time he frowned as he said a sentence.

"Nay!" said I.

That did it. He became white with anger, and swore at me all the way to Amersfoort. He had a fine command of language, too, and I was extremely sorry that I could not understand it.

On the Saturday I set off on my return journey to Rotterdam, doing a tour in American fashion of Leiden on the way. It was like going home, for I liked Rotterdam. I think it was the gay paint on the barges that attracted me so much.

On the Sunday morning the Austrian kiddies arrived, and my sight-seeing ended.

XII.

THE Austrian kiddies arrived at the Maas station on Sunday morning, and the Dutch folk gave them a kindly welcome. The Rotterdam committee was in charge, and I stood back because it was not my job. The kiddies came tumbling out of the train with great relief, for they had travelled for two nights. All had heavy rucksacks, many of them the packs of their dead fathers and brothers.

My eye lit on little Hansi. She stood on the platform crying, and I went forward to comfort her. Alas ! I knew less German than I did Dutch, and I knew not what she said; but one of the Austrian escort told me that she had been homesick all the way. There is, however, a universal language that all children understand, and I took wee Hansi in my arms and cuddled her. The flow of tears stopped and she took from a small basket slung to her neck a tiny naked doll. I included Puppe in the cuddle, and Hansi smiled. A dear wee mite she was, very very thin, with great big eyes that were sunken. Her tears did not affect me, but when she smiled I found myself weeping, and I had to blow my nose hard.

The four hundred and fifty-eight children were bundled across the road to a ship, which took them in two parts across the Maas to the large building used by the Cunard Line for emigrants. Many of them thought they were on the way to England, and ten minutes later I found a wee chap gazing round in wonder on the land of England.

"This aint England, anywye," he said at last in evident disgust; "look at them clogs! This is Holland."

The boy was a Londoner resident in Vienna. There were about a dozen English children in the party. Later I found one standing in front of a group of Austrian boys.

"Any one o' you," he was shouting, "I'll box the whole gang o' you!"

This Cockney, his little brother, and their sister were the thorn in the flesh of the escort.

"Absolute terrors," declared everyone, but I liked them.

Many of the children were middle class, children of doctors, lawyers, architects, and so on; nice kiddies they were. The bigger girls could speak English, and I used them as interpreters.

On the Monday morning the English escort took charge. The first task was medical inspection, and the two English doctors and four or five Dutch doctors prepared for action. Our job was to marshal the kiddies, help them to take their shirts off, and then bundle them into the inspection room. It sounds easy, but it was a weary business. You looked down the list for No. 258, and you found a name.

"Mitzi Dvoracek!" you called, and wondered whether a boy or a girl would appear. There was no answer . . . . and an hour later you found a little girl who had lost her identity card, and you concluded that she was Dvoracek, but she wasn't; her name was Leopoldine Czsthmkyghw, or something resembling that.

I was greatly troubled by their questions. Following a method I had used with indifferent effect while conversing with garrulous Dutchmen in railway carriages, I answered "Ja" and "Nay" alternately. Many of the children stared at me in wonder and I marvelled . . . until I discovered that most of them had been asking me the way to the lavatory. After that I just pointed to a door in the wall when a boy asked me a question, and when one lad didn't seem to understand, I took him by the back of the neck and shoved him through the door. Then I found that he had been asking the time.

I gave up replying to questions after that.

The children had all been examined, and one lad stood alone; he had no card and no one could place him. Then he confessed that he was a stowaway who had been too old to join the batch, and had boarded the train quietly at Vienna. Mrs. Ensor, the secretary of the Famine Area Committee. proved herself a sport by declaring that she would take him to England. The good Dutch folk also rose to the occasion, and went out and bought him a pair of short trousers.

In the afternoon I sat down beside a few boys. And then I did a fatal thing. A boy dropped his pencil and I picked it up, threw it over the house . . . . and then produced it from another lad's pocket. That did it. In two seconds I had a hundred children round me roaring at me. An Austrian lady explained that they were calling me a magician and asking for more. I blushingly told her to explain to them that it was my only trick. Sighs of disgust followed, and I was on the point of losing my popularity when I hastily got the lady to explain to them that I had a better talent . . . . I could make anyone laugh merely by looking at him. Fifty of them at once challenged me to begin, and I had a great time. One lad beat me, but then he had toothache, a blistered heel, and was homesick.

After a time I asked them to sing to me, and they sang sweet folk songs of their home. They were delightful singers, and the boys sang as eagerly and as well as the girls. In England boys usually hate singing. I marvelled at their all knowing the same songs, and one of the girls explained to me that in Austria every school has the same songs; more than that, every school has the same class-books, and if two children living a hundred miles apart meet on the street they can say to each other: "I'm at page 67 of my Geography. What page are you at?"

They demanded a song from me, and I sang *Now is the Month of Maying*, and, by special request, *Tipperary*. Then I asked them to sing their National Anthem, and the lady began it, but the children did not follow her. At my look of surprise the lady said: "They cannot sing it because now they feel that they have no Austria left to sing about."

A man's voice sounded from inside the building, and they rushed indoors, for it was the voice of their beloved Ministry of Health doctor, who had brought them from Vienna, and they all loved him. They forgot me at once and left me . . . . all but one. Little Hansi put her wee hand in mine and snuggled closer . . . . and that's why I love her so very much.

On Tuesday morning they all took up their packs, and we set off for England via the Maas boat and station. We packed into carriages and set off. There was no water on the train, but we laughed and said: "We'll be in Flushing in two hours! We are a special!" We were. We left the Maas station at one o'clock, and we travelled until three. Then we drew up . . . . and found we were back at the Maas station. Where we had been I don't know, but it was the biggest mystery of my life. Well, we crawled along past picturesque villages where women with white caps and red arms smiled on us and gave us water to drink. And at eight o'clock we reached Flushing all very weary and extremely dirty. The kiddies had a good meal set out on white tablecloths, and the doctor and I had the best Pilsener of our lives. We handed over the kiddies to the ship stewards and the fresh escort from England, and retired to rest.

I awoke at six and found that all the children were on deck, and the bad English boy almost in the water, for his heels were off the ground and his head far down towards the water. He was looking for fish, he said. None of the children had seen the sea before, but I think they were too tired to be excited about it. They did become excited when they saw the cliffs of Dover.

Much to my annoyance a gentleman had been teaching them *God Save the King* on the way over. I was annoyed because I knew it was a piece of jingoism meant for the journalists at Folkestone. When we drew up at the pier, sure enough the gentleman struck up the tune, and the kiddies sang it. But the girls who could speak English sang *God Save YOUR Gracious King*. I thought it a beautiful touch; the finest piece of good taste I have ever come across.

I didn't like the well-dressed ladies who came bossing around at Folkestone. Frankly I was jealous. As I was leading the children off the steamer, one of them touched me on the arm and asked me to make way for the children. And I smiled to see that the women in rich dresses managed somehow to get in front of the camera.

We took the children to Sandwich by rail and then to a camp by motor lorry. It was a tiresome job loading and unloading the lorry, but after six trips I found that every child was in camp. I went off to have a wash and some tea, and then, glowing with self-satisfaction at all I had done, I lit a cigar and walked outside. A gentleman passed me.

"Are you a worker?" he demanded.

"I—er—I suppose I am—in a way," I said modestly.

"Well, don't you think you might find something to do?" he asked. "There's plenty to do, you know."

Then for the first time in my life I understood the old Mons Ribbon men who used to annihilate the recruit with the terse phrase: "Afore you came up!"

The pressmen passed by, a dozen of them with the stowaway in their midst. Presently they posed him and a dozen cameras snapped while a cinema burred. And next day the papers told a romantic story; the stowaway had crept into the train at Vienna, and, foodless, had hid until he arrived in Rotterdam. Then darkly he had crept on board the ship and had been discovered at Folkestone. Also when next day I saw in the pictorial papers a photograph of a boy violinist playing to his chums, I was not very much surprised to find the title of the photo was: *The Stowaway Entertains His Companions.* As a matter of fact, the fiddler wasn't the stowaway at all, but this incident makes me think hard about history. If a Fleet Street reporter changes one boy into another, why, we may be all wrong in our history. Henry VIII. may only have had one wife, and the reporter who interviewed him may have had so much sack to drink that his vision along with the journalistic touch may have manufactured the other five. The tale of King Harold being shot through the eye at the Battle of Hastings may have arisen from a reporter's using the figurative expression that William the Conqueror "put his eye out." Nor, after reading the account of the landing of the Austrian children, can I believe the tale of the minstrel Taillifer who sprang into the water to lead the Normans in landing. And as for the time-honoured phrases, "Take away that bauble!" and "England expects every man to do his duty," I don't believe they were ever uttered—not now.

I am not singling out journalists as special misreporters. Not one of us can report an incident truly. There is a good example of this truth in Swift's *Psychology and Everyday Life*, just published. Swift prepared a stunt as a test for his adult class. In the midst of a serious lecture two men and two women students created a disturbance outside in the lobby, then they burst into the room. One held a banana pistol-wise at another's head. Swift dropped a toy bomb, and one of the students staggered back crying: "I'm shot!"

One student dropped a parcel containing a brick, and all yelled and made much noise. The class was seriously alarmed until they were assured that the whole affair was a put-up job. Each student was asked to write an account of what had happened, and the result of their attempts is so astounding that the reader becomes uncertain whether any witness in a law-court ever tells the truth. Few, if any, students could identify one of the wranglers; every account said that the banana was a real pistol; only one or two saw the brick drop. The strangest thing was that many were quite sure of the identity of the actors . . . . and one or two of the accounts named students who had long since left the college. I write from memory, but the facts were as arresting as the ones I have given.

This makes one uneasy about the methods the police adopt to identify a prisoner. If

I saw a man shoot another in Piccadilly, it is a thousand to one chance that I should not be able to identify him later. Yet many a man has been hanged on identification.

But I meant to finish my account of the Austrian kiddies. The time came when I had to leave them and return to London. I set out to find my Hansi to say good-bye to her. I saw her in the distance . . . . and then I ran away, for I hate saying good-bye.

I liked those kiddies, dear wee souls, just as sweet as any English kiddies, but then children have no nationality ; they are lovable for they all belong to the Never Never Land. Barrie proved himself a genius when he created Peter Pan, for Peter symbolises man's highest wish—to become a little child and never grow up. "Genius," he says, "is the power of being a boy again at will." It is true in his case. Yet this kind of genius is retrospective ; it is a regression. The genius who will help man to look forward instead of backward must not return to boyhood ; he must go forward to superman. To put it psychologically, Barrie's genius comes from the unconscious, but what the world needs is a man whose genius will come from the superconscious, the divine.

XIII.

I HAVE just been reading Jack London's *Michael, Brother of Jerry,* and I am full of righteous rage. What a picture! It is the story of how performing animals are trained, and before I had read half the book I made a vow that never again will I sit through a performance of animals.

The tale of Ben Bolt the tiger, if known by the masses, would kill every animal turn on the stage. Ben Bolt, fresh from the jungle, is broken by the trainers. The method is unspeakable; he is lashed with iron bars and stabbed with forks until in agony he falls senseless in the arena. This treatment goes on for weeks . . . . and in the end many good, kindly people see Ben Bolt, a miserable, broken animal, sit up in a chair like a human. And they laugh. My God!

Then there is Barney the good-natured mule that was once a family pet. Later he becomes the celebrated bucking mule, and a prize is offered to anyone who will keep on his back for one minute. Audiences go into fits of laughter at his antics. But the audiences do not know that Barney was trained with a spiked saddle, and that for months life was one long agony of pain.

Is my anger due to the cruelty I am repressing in myself? I don't care whether it is sadism or the spark of the divine in me. All I care about is that this inferno of pain must cease.

Never has any book affected me as this one has done. By word of mouth and by my pen I shall try my hardest to send dear old Jack London's message round the world. Public opinion is the only thing that can stop the misery of these broken creatures, and I suggest that the anti-vivisectionists turn their energies to this infinitely worse evil. The vivisectionists, at any rate, are working for humanity, but the brutes who break performing animals are merely amusing crowds of good people who know nothing about what goes on behind the scenes.

* * * * * *

I see in the newspaper that Mary Pickford and Douglas Fairbanks held up the traffic in Piccadilly. They appeared on a balcony at the Ritz, and the crowd went frantic. The super-hero and the super-heroine of the cinema drew the crowd's emotion to them, and Tagore the Indian poet arrived in town at the same time unnoticed. It would seem that the crowd responds to the presence of the unimportant person only. London went mad over Hawker and Jack Johnson, and Georges Carpentier;

and if Charlie Chaplin were to come over, I fancy London would take a general holiday.

No one will contend that these people are of supreme importance in the scheme of life. Charlie is a funny little man; Douglas Fairbanks is a fine lump of a fellow; Mary Pickford is a sweet little woman. But Tagore will live longer; Thomas Hardy, Bernard Shaw, Bertrand Russell, Sigmund Freud are of greater moment to humanity, yet each could walk out of Paddington Station and be unrecognised by the crowd.

The morning paper shows well that the crowd is interested only in unessentials. "Punish the profiteers!" was the press cry a few months ago. Well, they punished the profiteers . . . . and prices continued to rise. A few years ago the cry was: "Flog the white slave traffickers!" They flogged them, and yet I still see thousands of white slaves in the West End of London. And while Europe is sinking into anarchy and bankruptcy to-day, the only remedies the crowd representatives—the press—can think of are remedies of the Hang-the-Kaiser type. I believe that the crowd still thinks that juvenile crime is mainly caused by cinema five-part dramas.

The crowd is rather like the individual unconscious; it is primitive, and like the unconscious it can only wish. The crowd that welcomed Mary and Douglas was closely akin to the personal unconscious. Douglas stands to each individual in the crowd as the eternal hero, the man who always wins. Each man in the crowd sees in Douglas his own ideal self, so that when the office boy cheers Douglas he is cheering himself. Mary has been well named "the world's sweetheart"; she is the ideal heroine, beautiful, wronged, protected by six foot of masculinity. Both come from the world of make-believe, the world of phantasy. Their arrival in England simply made a dream come true.

Now I am certain that if any individual in the great Piccadilly crowd had met Douglas and Mary on the boat, he or she would have looked at them with interest, but there would have been no cheering and throwing of roses. What the crowd does is to raise an emotion to a superlative degree. In a full hall you will laugh at a joke that would not bring a smile to your face in a room. You become absorbed in your crowd, and you are fully open to your crowd's suggestion. I generally laugh at Charlie Chaplin, but one night a cinema manager, a friend of mine, gave me a private view of Charlie's latest production. I sat alone in the large cinema palace . . . . and I couldn't even smile. Had a crowd been there to share my laugh, I should have roared.

The Douglas-Mary episode makes me pessimistic about the future of democracy. For democracy is crowd rule, and the crowd is a baby when it isn't a savage. Yet we have no real democracy in this country. We have a slave state, the exploiters and the exploited, the "haves" and the "have nots." Douglas and Mary came over, and the poor beauty-starved populace forgot for the moment its poverty, and showered all its pent-up emotion on the people from picture-book land.

In Elizabethan times the world was a place of wonder; every mariner was coming home with wondrous tales of Spanish gold and men with necks like bulls. All you had to do to find a reality that was more wonderful than fancy was to sail away across the sea. But to-day the world holds no mystery; there are no pirates to overcome, no prisoned maidens to rescue. Reality means toil and taxes and trouble. But there is a land where men are dew-lapped like bulls . . . . the land of phantasy. There is a society where the villain always gets his deserts . . . . the land of film pictures. And when your hero and heroine walk out of the picture and become real flesh and blood, what are you to do? After all, you cannot pour all your emotion into your looms and office-desks and counters. Sweet-faced Mary does not know it, but she is one of the best allies that our capitalist system could have; for if the crowd were not showering its emotion on her it might well be using it up in the smashing of all the ugly things in our civilisation.

* * * * * *

I have been thinking of the crowd in another aspect. Last year in a merry mood I sat down to write a novel. I meant it to be a comedy, but, having no control over the characters, I found that they insisted in making the story a farce. The result was *The Booming of Bunkie.* I thought it a very funny book, and I laughed at some of my own jokes and murmured, "Good!" I impatiently awaited the book's appearance, and when the day of publication came I sat down hopefully to await the press notices. The first one to come in was lukewarm.

"Why do papers send a funny book to an old fossil of a reviewer with no sense of humour?" I said, testily and waited for the next post. Well, it came; it brought three adverse notices and a letter.

"Dear Dominie, I admired your *Log,* but why, oh why, did you perpetrate such a monstrosity as *The Booming of Bunkie?*"

Then a friend wrote me a letter.

"Dear old chap,—You are suffering from the effects of the war. If the war has induced you to write *Bunkie,* I am all for hanging the Kaiser."

For weeks I clung to the belief that the crowd had no sense of humour . . . .then I re-read my novel. I still hold that it is funny in parts, but I see what is wrong. It is a specialised type of humour, or rather wit, the type that undergraduates might appreciate. In fact I was recently gratified to hear that the students of a Scots university were rhapsodising about it. The real fault of the book is that it is clever, and to be clever is to be at once suspect.

I naturally like to think that the circulation of a book is generally in inverse proportion to its intrinsic merit. J. D. Beresford's novels are, to me, much better than those of the late Charles Garvice, yet I make a guess that Garvice's circulation was many times greater than Beresford's. Still I cannot argue that the reverse is true—that because a book does not go into its second edition it is necessarily good. I find that the problem of circulations is a difficult one. I cannot, for instance, understand why *The Young Visiters* sold in thousands; I failed to raise a smile at it. Again, there is my friend although publisher, Herbert Jenkins. I didn't think *Bindle* funny, yet it has been translated into umpteen European languages. Jenkins himself does not think it funny, and that, possibly, is why he is my friend.

The most surprising success to me was Ian Hay's *The First Hundred Thousand.* I read Pat MacGill's *Red Horizon* about the same time, and thought Hay was stilted and superior with a public-school man's patronising Punch-like attitude to the working-class recruits. I thought that he didn't know what he was writing about, that he had not reached the souls of the men. MacGill, on the other hand, gave me the impression of a warm, passionate, intense knowledge of men; he wrote as one who lived with ordinary men and knew them through and through. Yet I fancy that *The Red Horizon*, popular as it was, did not have the sales of *The First Hundred Thousand*.

I was lunching with Professor John Adams one day in London. We got on to the subject of circulations, and he said that he had just been asking the biggest bookseller in London what novel sold best.

"Have a guess," said the Professor to me.

"*David Copperfield*," I said promptly.

He laughed.

"Not bad!" he said, "you've got the author right, but the book is *A Tale of Two Cities*."

He then asked me to guess what two authors sold best among the troops at the front during the war.

"Charles Garvice and Nat Gould," I said, and the Professor thought me a wonderful fellow, for I had guessed aright.

There is a whiskered Ford story which tells that Mr. Ford took a new car from his factory and invited a visitor to have a spin

They started off, and went seven miles out. Then the car stopped. Ford jumped out and lifted the bonnet.

"Good Lord!" he cried, "the engine hasn't been put in! The car must have run seven miles on its reputation!"

I think that books run many miles on reputation alone. Like a snowball the farther a circulation rolls the more it gathers to itself. But what is it that makes a book popular? The best press notices in the world will not send the circulation of a book up to a hundred thousand level. What sells a book is talk. Scores of people said to me: "Oh, *have* you read *The Young Visiters?*" I hasten to add, as a Scot, that I personally did not help to increase the circulation; I borrowed the book from an enthusiast. Talk sells a book, but we have to discover why people talk about *The Young Visiters* and not about—er—*The Booming of Bunkie.* The book that is to sell well must be able to touch a chord in the crowd heart, and *The Young Visiters* sold because it touched the infantile chord in the crowd heart; it brought back the happiest days of life, the schooldays: again, its naïve Malapropisms appealed to the crowd, because we are all glad to laugh at the social and grammatical errors we have made and conveniently forgotten about.

Bunkie did not reach the hundred thousand level because it was too clever; it was a purely intellectual essay in wit rather than humour. And the crowd distrusts wit, and that is why the witty plays of Oscar Wilde are seldom produced, while *Charley's Aunt* goes on for ever.

I am tempted to go on to a comparison of wit with humour, but I shall only remark that wit is an intellectual thing, whereas humour is emotional. Humour is elemental, but wit is cultural. Without a language you could have humour, but without language there could be no wit.

* * * * * *

I have just come across a small book entitled *Hints on School Discipline,* by Ernest F. Row, B.Sc.

"Boys will only respect a master whom they fear," he says. I have been preaching this doctrine for years . . . . that respect always has fear behind it . . . . and it pleases me to find that an exponent of the old methods should support my argument.

When I began to read the book I was amazed.

"Good Lord!" I cried, "this chap should have published his book in the year 1820. He advocates a system that modern psychology has shown to be fatal to the child. It is army discipline applied to schools."

I found it hard to finish the book, but I read every word of it and then I said to myself :· "The majority is on the side of Rov Eton, Harrow, many elementary teachers would agree with him. He is evidently an honest sort of fellow, and he must be reckoned with. I must try to see his point of view."

And I think I see it. He accepts current education with its set subjects, time-tables, order, morality, and he is trying to adapt the young teacher to what is established. Hence to maintain all these things, we must have stern discipline and swift punishment. But I wonder if Row has thought of the other side of the question ; I wonder if he has asked himself whether order and time-tables and obedience and respect are really necessary. I should like to meet him and have a chat ; I think I should like him, and further, I think that I could convert him to the other way . . . . if he is under forty.

Ah ! Horrid thought ! Is it possible that Row is pulling our legs ? No, he writes as an honest man. Perhaps he knows all about the modern movement ; perhaps he has studied Mont ssori, Freud, Jung, Homer Lane, Edmond Holmes, and found that they are all pathetically wrong. Mayhap he has proved that the child *is* a sinner.

"The young teacher should never address a boy by his Christian name or nickname," he says.

Oh, surely he *is* pulling our legs!

*   *   *   *   *   *

At intervals during the past few years I have been puzzled when people congratulated me on my village school in Lancashire. I had quite a number of misunderstandings on the subject. Then one day I discovered that there was a villag schoolmaster in Lancashire called E. F. O'Neill. I wrote him telling him that I was coming to see his school, and one July morning I alighted at one of the ugliest villages in the world, and I walked past slag-heaps and all the horrors of industrialism to a red building on the outskirts. Three or four boys were digging in the school garden. I walked into the school, and two seconds after entering I said to myself: "E. F. O'Neill, you are a great man!"

There were no desks, and I could see no teacher. Half-a-dozen children stood round a table weighing things and cutting things.

"What's this?" I asked.

"The shop," said a girl, and after a little time I grasped the idea. You have paste-board coins, and you come to the shop and buy a pound of butter (plasticene), two pounds of sugar (sand), and a bottle of Yorkshire Relish (a brown mixture unrecognisable to me). You pay your sovereign and the shop-keeper gives you the change, remarks on the likelihood of the weather's keeping up, and turns to the next customer.

I walked on and found a boy writing.

"Hullo, sonny, what are you on?"

"My novel," he said, and showed me the beginning of chapter XII.

A young man came forward, a slim youth with twinkling eyes.

"E. F. O'Neill?"

"A. S. Neill?"

We shook hands, and then he began to talk. I wanted to tell him that his school was a pure delight, but I couldn't get a word in edgeways. If anything, he was over-explanatory, but I pardoned him, for I realised that the poor man's life must be spent in explaining himself to unbelievers. I disliked his tacit classing of me with the infidel, and I indignantly took the side of the infidel and asked him questions. Then he gave me of his best.

He is a great man. I don't think he has any theoretical knowledge, and I believe that anyone could trip him up over Freud or Jung, Montessori or Froebel, Dewey or Homer Lane; but the man seems to know it all by instinct or intuition. To him creation is everything. I was half afraid that he might have the typical crank's belief in imposing his taste on the pupils, and I mentioned my doubt.

"No," he said, "we have a gramophone with fox-trots, ragtimes, Beethoven and Melba, and the children nearly always choose the best records."

Love of beauty is a real thing in this school. The playground is full of bonny corners with flowers and bushes. The school writing books are bound in artistic wallpaper by the children, and hand-made frames enclose reproductions of good pictures on the walls.

I saw no corporate teaching, and I should have asked O'Neill if he had any. If he hasn't I think he is wrong, for the other way—the learn-by-doing individual way—starves the group spirit. The class-teaching system has many faults, and O'Neill seems to have abolished spoon-feeding, but the class has one merit—it is a crowd. Each child measures himself against the others, not necessarily in competition. Perhaps it is the psychological effect of having an audience that I am trying to praise. Yes, that is it: the individual-work way is like a rehearsal of a play to empty seats; the class-way is like a performance before a crowded house. It is a projection of one's ego outward.

"This method," said O'Neill, "may be out-of-date in a month."

I think highly of him for these words alone. He has no fixed beliefs about methods of study; he himself learns by doing, and to-morrow will be cheerfully willing to scrap the method he is using to-day. If the ideal teacher is the man who is always learning, then O'Neill comes pretty near that ideal. I wish that every teacher in Britain could see his school.

The big problem for the heretical teacher is the problem of order, or rather of disorder. When a child is free from authority, he usually leaves his path untidy; he leaves his chisels on the bench or the ground; he strews the floor with papers; he throws his books all over the room. Now O'Neill's school was not untidy, and I marvelled.

"Oh, the kiddies look after that," he explained. "They have voluntary workers among themselves who do all that, and if a child does not do his job, the others naturally complain: 'Why did you take it on if you aren't going to do it properly?'"

But somehow I am not convinced; I want to know more about this business. To find so highly developed a social sense in small children runs dead against all my experience. I must write to O'Neill for further information.

* * * * * *

On re-reading the pages of this book I feel like throwing it on the fire. I find myself disagreeing with the statements I made a few weeks ago. When I began to write it I was a more or less complete Freudian, and in an airy fashion I explained away my actions. Why should pale blue be my favourite colour? I asked myself this when I painted my cycle blue, and I found a ready answer in a reminiscence . . . . my first sweetheart wore a blue tam-o'-shanter. This is called the "nothing but" psychology. Do I dream of a train? Quite simple! It is merely "nothing but" a sexual symbol!

Life is too complex for a "nothing but" psychology. Last night a girl told me a sexual dream she had had, but when she gave her associations we found that the deep meaning of the dream had nothing to do with sex. Freud says that about every dream is the mark of the beast, but then I think he believes in original sin.

I have been thinking a lot recently about the psychology of flogging. It is generally stated that the flogger is a sexual pervert, a Sadist, and undoubtedly there are pathological cases where men find sexual gratification in inflicting or in watching the infliction of pain. In the pathological case the gratification is conscious, but I believe that many respectable parents and teachers find an unconscious gratification. It is absurd to say to a man like Macdonald: "Your punishing is 'nothing but' Sadism." Yet I think that a little test might decide the matter. If the accused flogger is shocked or indignant at the idea I should be inclined to think that the accusation was a just one.

If I say to Simpson: "Excuse my mentioning it, old man, but I don't think you love your wife," he will laugh heartily, for he has been married for a month only, and is still very much in love. His laugh shows that his love is real; my rude remark touches no chord in his unconscious. But suppose I make a similar remark to Smith, who has been very much married for ten years! He will hit me in the eye, thereby betraying the fact that my remark touched what his unconscious knows to be true. His blow is physically directed to me, but psychically he is hitting to defend his conscious from his unconscious.

Hence if a flogger is angry when I accuse him of being a Sadist, I guess that he is a Sadist.

I tried the experiment on Macdonald. He shook his head sadly.

"Poor chap," he said feelingly, "you're daft!"

"Right!" I said, "you aren't a Sadist, anyway, Mac. You must flog because it is your method of self-assertion. As I've told you many times, you strap kids because wielding a strap is your childish way of showing your power."

Then Mac became angry, and when I hinted that my remarks must have hit the bull's-eye . . . . he laughed again. He is a baffling study in psychology.

"You don't know much about it, old chap," he said genially.

"Hardly anything at all," I said with true modesty, "only I know one thing about you, and that is that the fault always lies in yourself. When you flog Tom Murray, you are really chastising the Tom Murray in yourself . . . . that is, the part that your wife knows so well—the part of you that leaves the new graip out in the rain all night, that rebels against the authority of the School Board and the inspectorate. Tom is being crucified for your transgressions."

Barrie, wizard as he is, failed to understand the full significance of Shakespeare's line: "The fault, dear Brutus, lies not in our stars, but in ourselves."

* * * * * *

The opposite of the Sadist is the Masochist —the person who finds sexual gratification in being beaten or bullied. When 'Arriet proudly boasts about the black eye that 'Arry gave her on Saturday night, she is being masochistic, and the woman who likes to be bullied by the strong, silent man is likewise a masochist. I do not say "nothing but" a masochist, because she is also a Sadist, for Sadism and Masochism are complementary in the same person.

It is an understood fact that many people find joy in suffering, and I can recollect feeling something akin to joy when the dentist, before the days of the local anæsthetic, used to lay hold on my molars.

Hence I look back to the day when I whacked Peter Smith for cruelty to a calf, and I acknowledge that I was wrong. I recall explaining to him that I wanted him to realise what suffering meant, but I was completely mistaken. If Peter were a Sadist in his cruelty, my cruelty to him was giving unconscious gratification to the Masochistic part of him. If his cruelty to the calf was due to his self-assertion again I did the wrong thing, for the fear evoked by my strap merely inhibited his desire to assert himself in cudgelling calves. I think now that there was nothing to be done; his cruelty showed that his whole education had been wrong. Had he been allowed to create all the way up from one week old he would have applied his interest to making rabbit-hutches instead of to beating calves.

I remember a questioner at one of my lectures. I had been trying to elaborate the release theory, and had said that a boy should be encouraged to make a noise so that he will release all his interest in noise as power.

"If a boy liked torturing cats, would you encourage him on the theory that suppression by an adult would cause the child to retain his interest in torturing cats?"

"Certainly not," I said, and the lady crowed. I do dislike questioners at any time, but when they crow . . . . ! However, I tried to hide the murder in my heart by smiling.

"What would you do ?" she asked sweetly.

"I don't know, madam," I said, "but I can make a rapid guess . . . . I very probably would use the toe of my boot on him, thereby showing that my own interest in cruelty was still alive. But five minutes later I should try to discover what was at the back of the boy's mind."

Not long ago I studied a small boy whose chief pleasure was in pulling bees' wings off. I never mentioned bees to him, but I got him to talk about himself. He was suffering from a deep hatred of his teacher, and he had a bad inferiority complex. He feared to play games like football and hockey because of his sense of inferiority. All that was wrong with him was that he was regressing. Life was too difficult for him, and he took refuge in his infantile past; his pulling off wings was the destructiveness of the infant. But the important thing to remember is that destructiveness is simply constructiveness gone wrong. The child is born good, and all his instincts are to do good. Bad behaviour is the result of thwarted desire to do good. This is shown in the case of Tommy on page 331.

* * * * * *

At one time I was absolutely certain that the Great War was caused by economic factors; British and German capital were competing, and the losing party took up the sword. I am not so certain now. It may be that the cataclysm was a natural ebullition of human nature, and as a cause the economic rivalry may have been just as insignificant as the murder of the Archduke.

During the last few decades education has been almost wholly intellectual and material; intellectual education gave us the don, and material education gave us the cotton-spinner. The emotional and the spiritual in mankind had no outlet. In the unconscious of man there is a God and a Devil, and intellectual activities afford no means of expression to either. And when any godlike or devilish libido can find no outlet it regresses to infantile primitive forms; thus, while the brain of man was concerned with mathematics and logic, the heart of man was seeking primitive things—cruelty, hate, and blood.

It may be then that the war was the direct result of the world's bad system of education. No boy will destroy property if he is free to create property, and no nation will take to killing if it is free to be creative. Intellectual education allows no freedom for the creative impulse; it not only starves the creative impulse but it drives it into rebellion. An outlet is always a door to purification. The old men who sat at home hated the Hun because their libido was being bottled up, but the young men who were using up their libido in fighting talked cheerfully of "Old Fritz." The chained dog soon becomes savage, and the chained libido reverts to savagery also.

I have often said that the outrages of the German troops in Belgium became understandable to me when I studied a Scots school where suppressive discipline turned good boys into demons. The brutality of the German army was a natural result of the brutality of their discipline. So is it in the individual soul, and in the national soul. Intellectualism and materialism were the Prussian drill-sergeants who enslaved the emotional life of the citizen and of the nation. War was a means of releasing this pent-up emotion.

The ultimate cure for war is the releasing of the beast in the heart of mankind . . . . not the releasing after chaining him up, but the releasing of the beast from the beginning. Personally I do not believe that he is a wild beast until we make him one by chaining him ; he is primitive and animal and amoral, but I believe that by kind treatment we can make him our ally in living a goodly life. The Devil is merely a chained God.

The problem for man and for mankind is to reconcile the God and the Devil in himself. The saint represses the devil ; the sinner represses the god. The atheist cries : "There is no God!" because he has repressed the God in himself. Then, again, many people project their personal devil; the men who shouted "Hang the Kaiser!" were subjectively crying "Hang the Devil in me!"

Who and what is this devil we carry in our hearts? We cannot tame him unless we can know him. The Freudians would say that he is the primitive unconscious, the tree-dweller in us. But that explanation is not enough for me. The tiger has no devil in him, and why should our remote savage ancestors leave us a devil as legacy? Yet the tiger is a devil whenever man formulates a law against killing; the man-eater becomes bad because he is a danger to man, and because the tiger is bad it is assumed that man is good. The ox that is slaughtered for our dinners might well look upon man as its special objective devil.

I have often argued that it is Authority that makes the beast in children a wild beast. That is true, but it does not go down to first causes. Why do adults exercise authority? To keep down the devil in themselves, the beast that *their* parents and teachers made wild by authority. Truly a vicious circle! But the devil is the cause of authority in the beginning.

Since there is no devil in the tiger and the ox, the animalism of man cannot be his devil. But man made his animalism a devil when he began to have ideals. Then it was that he began to talk of crucifying the flesh; then it was that the spirit was willing but the flesh was weak. The devil in man is the negative of man's ego-ideal. The ethical self says that honesty is good, and dishonesty comes to be of the devil; it says that love is good, and hate then becomes devilish. No ego-ideal, no devil. The ox has no ego-ideal; therefore it has no devil. Man invented the devil to account for his failures.

This brings me to the question: why should man want to have an ego-ideal? Why should he praise self-sacrifice, love, charity, honesty, unselfishness, while he contemns hate, murder, cruelty, stealing, selfishness? It might be argued that he praises those attributes that make for the good of the herd, but I cannot take this argument as final. Rather am I inclined to look for the answer in what we vaguely call the divine. I think that there is a power . . . . call it God or intuition or the superconscious or what-not . . . . that draws man toward higher things. This spark of the divine raises man above the beast of the field, but yesterday he was the beast of the field, and like the *nouveau riche*, he scorns his humble origins.

I am forced to conclude that wars will not cease until man realises that his ego-ideal must be capable of being the working partner of his primitive animalism. When that time comes man will know that he is neither god nor devil, but . . . . mere man.

*   *   *   *   *   *

I am spending my days wandering round London suburbs looking for a school. Of an evening I sit and think about how I shall furnish it. There will be no desks; instead there will be tables for writing and drawing on, chairs of all descriptions—arm-chairs, deck-chairs, straight backed chairs, stools. The children will make the tables and stools, and we may make a combined effort to make and upholster an arm-chair.

Then we must have at least one typewriter, not for office use, but for the children's use. The children will use it to type their novels and poems, and I think they would be tempted to type out poems from Keats and Coleridge, binding their own anthologies in leather or coloured paper.

There will be no school readers and no school poetry books. I hope that with the aid of the typewriter each child will make his own selection of prose and poetry.

The wall decorations will be left to the children, and if they bring bad, sentimental prints from the Christmas numbers I shall say nothing when they hang them up. But as an active member of the community, I shall bring reproductions of the work of Rembrandt, Velasquez, Angelo, Augustus John

Cezanne, Nevinson ; I shall buy *Colour* every month.

So with music. I shall sing *Eliza Jane* with them if they want to sing *Eliza Jane,* but I shall bring to their notice *To Music* (Schumann), Blake's *Jerusalem,* and the bonny old English songs like *Golden Slumbers, Now is the Month of Maying, Polly Oliver.* Then a gramophone is a necessity, and all kinds of records will be necessary—Beethoven, Stravinsky, Rimski-Korsikoff, Harry Lauder, Fox Trots, Sousa. O'Neill told me that his Lancashire kiddies have tired of ragtime, and are now playing classical music only. Personally, I haven't reached that standard of taste yet ; I still have Fox Trot moods. I also want a player-piano—an Angelus, if possible.

Now for the library. I shall leave the choice of periodicals to the community, and I expect to find them select a list of this kind :—*Scout, Boy's Own Paper, Girl's Own Paper, Popular Mechanics, My Magazine, Punch, Chips, Comic Cuts, Tit-Bits, Answers, Strand, Sketch, Sphere.* It will be interesting to watch the career of *Chips* ; I will not be surprised if the community tires of *Chips* in a month.

Our book library will be stocked from the children's homes, I fancy. Each child will bring his or her favourite novel, and gladly hand it round. I shall certainly hand on my own fiction library :—Conan Doyle, Wells, Jack London, Rider Haggard, Cutcliffe Hyne,

Guy Boothby, Barrie, O. Henry, Leacock, Jacobs, Leonard Merrick, Seton Merriman, Stanley Weyman, and a host of others.

No, this won't do! How can I furnish before my self-governing school decides what furniture it will have? The children may demand desks and time-tables, but I do not think it likely. Anyhow, I am counting my chickens before they are hatched.

XIV.

I FINISH this book in the place where I began it, in Forfarshire, but not in Tarbonny Village. Hustling Herbert Jenkins sent me the galley proofs this morning with an urgent demand that I should return them at once. I do dislike publishers. At first I took them at their own valuation: I believed what they said.

"Machines waiting," Jenkins would wire. "Send MS. at once."

And I, simple I, would sit up late correcting proofs. I know better now. I know that Jenkins always divides time by 20. His "at once" means that twenty days hence he will say to his Secretary: "That new book of Neill's . . . . . has it gone to the printer yet?" And his Secretary will 'phone down to the office secretary and say: "You've got to send Neill's new book to the printer." Then this lady will order the office-boy to take the MS. to the printer . . . and I bet the little devil reads *Deadwood Dick on the Boomerang Prairie* as he crawls to the printer's office with my masterpiece under his arm.

Hence, understanding Jenkins, I tossed the

proofs into a corner this morning, and went out to continue the game of ring quoits that Nellie and I had to give up as darkness fell last night. Nellie is a Dundee lassie of thirteen and she is spending her holidays with her auntie here.

Nellie won, and we sat down on the bank and I began to ask her about her school-life.

" I dinna like the school, and I wish I was left," she said.

" Tell me why you dislike it, Nellie."

" If ye speak ye get the strap."

" What ! " I cried, " are you *never* allowed to speak ? "

" Only at playtime," she replied. " And ye never get less than six scuds."

And it was only the other day that a lady wrote me saying that when I preach against Prussianism in schools I am merely resuscitating a dead bogey for the purpose of knocking it down.

I get quite a lot of information of schools from children. I remember when I was in Lyme Regis last Easter I went out sketching one day. As I passed a village school a troupe of happy children came out. Joy lit up their faces.

" The ideal school ! " I cried, and stopped to speak to them.

" Tell me, children, tell me why you have laughter in your eyes," I said, " tell me of your happy school."

The oldest boy grinned.

"Master's gone off for the day to a funeral," he said.

I walked on deep in thought.

Nellie dislikes school. What a tragedy. She is a dear sweet child with kind eyes and a bonny smile. She spoke frankly to me at first but when I told her that I was a teacher she looked at me with fear and (I smiled at this) dropped her Dundee dialect and answered me in School English. I had to throw plantain heads at her for a full five minutes before the look of fear left her eyes and her dialect returned.

"I dinna believe ye *are* a teacher," she said to-night.

"Why not?"

"Ye're no like ane," she said hesitatingly. "Ye're ower—ower daft."

"But why shouldn't a teacher be daft?" I asked.

"They shud be respectable," she said, "or the children winna respect them."

I looked alarmed.

"What!" I cried, "don't you respect me?"

She laughed gaily.

"No!" she cried, then she added seriously: "But I'd like to be at your schule."

She returns to Dundee to-morrow, to a class of fifty, where silence reigns. Poor Nellie! What worries me is that when Nellie's teacher reads this book she will most probably agree with Nellie's remark that I'm "daft" But she won't mean what Nellie meant.

A telegraph girl approached.

" Machines are waiting.—Jenkins."

Nellie looked anxious.

" That's twa telegrams ye've got the day," she said. " Is onybody deid ? "

I looked at the words on the telegraph form.

" No, Nellie, unfortunately no ! " I said slowly, and I went in to read my galley proofs.

THE END.

A Dominie Dismissed

A.S. NEILL

TO THE

ORIGINAL

OF

MARGARET

A DOMINIE DISMISSED

I.

I HAVE packed all my belongings. My trunk and two big boxes of books stand in the middle of a floor littered with papers and straw. I had my typewriter carefully packed too, but I took it from out its wrappings, and I sit amidst the ruins of my room with my wee machine before me. It is one of those little folding ones weighing about six pounds.

The London train goes at seven, and it is half-past five now. It was just ten minutes ago that I suddenly resolved to keep a diary . . . only a dominie can keep a Log, and I am a dominie no longer.

I hear Janet Brown's voice outside. She is singing "Keep the Home Fires Burning" . . . and she was in tears this afternoon. The limmer ought to be at home weeping her dominie's departure.

Yet . . . what is Janet doing at my window? Her home is a good two miles along the road. I wonder if she has come to see me off. Yes, she has; I hear her cry to Ellen Smith: "He's packit, Ellen, and Aw hear him addressin' the labels on his typewriter." The besom!

Well, well, children have short memories. When Macdonald enters the room on Monday morning they will forget all about me.

I know Macdonald. He is a decent sort to meet in a house, but in school he is a stern one. His chief drawback is his lack of humour. I could swear that he will whack Jim Jackson for impudence before he is half an hour in the school.

I met Jim one night last week wheeling a box up from the station.

"I say, boy," I called with a pronounced Piccadilly Johnny accent, "heah, boy! Can you direct me to the—er—village post-office?"

He scratched his head and looked round him dubiously.

"Blowed if Aw ken," he said at last. "Aw'm a stranger here."

Yes, Macdonald will whack him.

I sent Jim out yesterday to measure the rainfall (there had been a fortnight's drought) and he went out to the playground. In ten minutes he returned looking puzzled. He came to my desk and lifted an Algebra book, then he went to his seat and seemed to sweat over some huge calculation. At length he came to me and announced that the rainfall was ·3578994 of an inch. I went out to the playground . . . he had watered it with the watering-can.

"There are no flies on you, my lad," I said.

"No, sir," he smiled, "the flies don't come out in the rain."

Yes, Macdonald is sure to whack him.

I shall miss Jim. I shall miss them all . . . but Jim most of all. What about Janet? And Gladys? And Ellen? And Jean? . . . Well, then, I'll miss Jim most of all the boys.

I tried to avoid being melodramatic to-day. It has been a queer day, an expectant day. They followed me with their eyes all day; if an inspector had arrived I swear that he would have put me down as a good disciplinarian. I never got so much attention from my bairns in my life.

I blew the "Fall in!" for the last time at the three o'clock interval. Janet and Ellen were late. When they arrived they carried a wee parcel each. They came forward to my desk and laid their parcels before me.

"A present from your scholars," said Janet awkwardly. I slowly took off the tissue paper and held up a bonny pipe and a crocodile tobacco-pouch. I didn't feel like speaking, so I took out my old pouch and emptied its contents into the new one; then I filled the new pipe and placed it between my teeth. A wee lassie giggled, but the others looked on in painful silence.

I cleared my throat to speak, but the words refused to come . . . so I lit the pipe.

"That's better," I said with forced cheerfulness, and I puffed away for a little.

"Well, bairns," I began, "I am——" Then Barbara Watson began to weep. I frowned at Barbara; then I blew my nose. Confound Barbara!

"Bairns," I began again, "I am going away now." Janet's eyes began to look dim, and I had to frown at her very hard; then I had to turn my frown on Jean . . . and

Janet, the besom, took advantage of my divided attention. I blew my nose again; then I coughed just to show that I really did have a cold.

"I don't suppose any of you understand why I am going away, but I'll try to tell you. I have been dismissed by your fathers and mothers. I haven't been a good teacher, they say; I have allowed you too much freedom. I have taken you out sketching and fishing and playing; I have let you read what you liked, let you do what you liked. I haven't taught you enough. How many of you know the capital of Bolivia? You see, not one of you knows."

"Please, sir, what is it?" asked Jim Jackson.

"I don't know myself, Jim."

My pipe had gone out and I lit it again.

"Bairns, I don't want to leave you all; you are mine, you know, and the school is ours. You and I made the gardens and rockeries; we dug the pond and we caught the trout and minnows and planted the water-plants. We built the pigeon-loft and the rabbit-hutch. We fed our pets together. We——"

I don't know what happened after that. I took out my handkerchief, but not to blow my nose.

"The bugle," I managed to say, and someone shoved it into my hand. Then I played "There's No Parade To-day," but I don't think I played it very well.

Only a few went outside; most of them sat and looked at me.

"I must get Jim to save the situation," I said to myself, and I shouted his name.

"P-please, sir," lisped Maggie Clark, "Jim's standin' oot in the porch."

"Tell him to come in," I commanded.

Maggie went out; then she returned slowly.

"P-please, sir, he's standin' greetin' and he winna come."

"Damnation!" I cried, and I bustled them from the room.

A quarter-past six! It's time Jim came for these boxes.

* * *

I am back in my old rooms in a small street off Hammersmith Broadway. My landlady, Mrs. Lewis, is a lady of delightful garrulity, and her comments on things to-day have served to cheer me up. She is intensely interested in the fact that I have come from Scotland, and anxious to give me all the news of events that have happened during my sojourn in the wilds.

"Did you 'ear much abaht the war in Scotland?" she said.

I looked my surprise.

"War! What war?"

Then she explained that Britain and France and Russia and the Allies were fighting against Germany.

"Now that I come to think of it," I said reflectively, "I *did* see a lot of khaki about to-day."

" Down't you get the pypers in Scotland ? " she asked.

" Thousands of them, Mrs. Lewis ; why, every Scot plays the pipes."

" I mean the pypers, not the pypers," she explained.

" Oh, I see ! We do get a few ; English travellers leave them in the trains, you know."

She thought for a little.

" It must be nice livin' in a plyce w'ere everyone knows everyone else. My sister Sally's married to a pynter in Dundee, Peter Macnab ; do you know 'im ? "

I explained that Peter and I were almost bosom friends. Then she asked me whether I knew what his wage was. I explained that I did not know. She then told me how much he gave Sally to keep house with, and I began to regret my temerity in claiming a close acquaintance with the erring Peter. Mrs. Lewis at once began to recount the family history of the Macnabs, and I blushed for the company I kept.

I decided to disown Peter.

" Perhaps he'll behave better now that he has gone to Glasgow," I remarked.

" But he ain't gone to Glasgow ! " she exclaimed.

I looked thoughtful.

" Ah ! " I cried, " I've been thinking of the other Peter Macnab, the painter in Lochee."

" Sally's 'usband lives in a plyce called Magdalen Green."

"Ah! I understand now, Mrs. Lewis. I've met that one too; you're quite right about his character."

If I ever write a book of aphorisms I shall certainly include this one: Never claim an acquaintance with a lady's relations by marriage.

I wandered along Fleet Street to-day, the most fascinating street in London . . . and the most disappointing. To understand Fleet Street you must walk along the Strand at mid-day. The Londoner is the most childish creature on earth. If a workman opens a drain cap the traffic is held up by the crowds who push forward to glimpse the pipes below. If a black man walks along the Strand half a hundred people will follow him on the off chance that he may be Jack Johnson. London is the most provincial place in Britain. I have eaten cookies in Princes Street in Edinburgh, and I have eaten buns in Piccadilly. The London audience was the greater. Audience! the word derives from the Latin *audio:* I hear. That won't do to describe my eating; spectators is the word.

I wandered about all day, and the interests of the streets kept my thoughts away from that little station in the north. Now it is evening, and my thoughts are free to wander.

A few of them would see Macdonald arrive to-day, and I think that in wondering at him they will have forgotten me. Children live for the hour; their griefs are as ephemeral as their joys, and the ephemeralism of their emotion is as wonderful as its intensity. A boy will bury his brother in the afternoon, and scream at Charlie Chaplin in the evening. He will forget Charlie again, though, when he lies alone in the big double bed at night.

Jim and Janet and Jean and the rest have loved me well, but I have no illusions about their love. Children are painfully docile. In two weeks they will accept Macdonald's iron rule without question, just as they accepted my absence of rule without question. Yet I wonder . . . ! Perhaps the love of freedom that I gave them will make them critical now. I know that they gradually developed a keen sense of justice. It was just a fortnight ago that Peter Shaw was reported to me as a slayer of young birds. I formed a jury with Jim Jackson as foreman, and they called for witnesses.

"Gentlemen of the jury, your verdict?" I said.

Jim stood up.

"Accused is acquitted . . . only one witness!"

I used to see them weigh my actions critically, and I had to be very particular not to show any sign of favouritism—a difficult task, for a dominie is bound to like some bairns better than others. Will they apply this method to Macdonald? I rather think he will beat it out of them. He is the type of dominie that stands for Authority with the capital A. His whole bearing shouts: "I am the Law. What I say is right and not to be questioned."

My poor bairns!

II.

I WENT to Richmond to-day, hired a skiff, and rowed up to Teddington. I tied the painter to a tuft of grass on the bank and lazed in the sunshine. For a time I watched the boats go by, and I smiled at the windmill rowing of a boatload of young Italians. Then a gilded youth went by feathering beautifully ....and I smiled again, for the Italians seemed to be getting ever so much more fun out of their rowing than this artist got.

By and by the passers-by wearied me, and I thought of my village up north. The kirk would be in. Macdonald would probably be there, and the bairns would be glancing at him sidelong, while I, the failure, lay in a boat among strangers. I began to indulge in the luxury of self-pity ; feeling oneself a martyr is not altogether an unpleasant sensation.

I turned my face to the bank and thought of what had taken place. The villagers accused me of wasting their children's time, but when I asked them what they would have me make their children do they were unable to answer clearly.

" Goad ! " said Peter Steel the roadman, " a laddie needs to ken hoo to read and write and add up a bit sum."

"Just so," I said. "When you go home to-night just try to help your Jim with his algebra, will you? I'll give you five pounds if you can beat him at arithmetic."

"Aw'm no sayin' that he doesna ken his work," he protested, "but Aw want to ken what's the use o' a' this waste o' time pluckin' flowers and drawin' hooses. You just let the bairns play themsells."

"That's what childhood is for," I explained, "for playing and playing again. In most schools the children work until they tire, and then they play. My system is the reverse; they play until they are tired of play and then they work....ask for work."

I know that the villagers will never understand what I was trying to do. My neighbour, Lawson of Rinsley School, had a glimmering of my ideal.

"I see your point," he said, "but the fault of the system is this: you are not preparing these children to meet the difficulties of life. In your school they choose their pet subjects, but in a factory or an office they've got to do work that they may hate. I say that your kids will fail."

"You aren't teaching them character," he added.

Lawson's criticism has made me think hard. I grant that I am not an efficient producer of wage-slaves. The first attribute of a slave is submission; he must never question. Macdonald is the true wage-slave producer.

He sets up authority to destroy criticism, and the children naturally accept their later slavery without question. Macdonald is the ideal teacher for the reactionists and the profiteers.

Will my bairns shirk the difficulties of life? There is Dan MacInch. He shirked algebra; he told me frankly that he didn't like it. I said nothing, and I allowed him to read while the others were working algebraical problems. In less than a week he came to me. " Please, sir, give me some algebra for home," he said, and in three weeks he was as good as any of them. I hold that freedom does not encourage the shirking of difficulties. I found that my bairns loved them. Some of them delighted in making them. Jim Jackson would invent the most formidable sums and spend hours trying to solve them.

Of course there were aversions. Jim hated singing and grammar. Why should I force him to take an interest in them? No one forces me to take an interest in card-playing....my pet aversion, or in horse-racing.

Freedom allows a child to develop its own personality. If Jim Jackson, after being with me for two years, goes into an office and shirks all unpleasant duties, I hold that Jim is naturally devoid of grit. I allowed him to develop his own personality and if he fails in life his personality is manifestly weak. If Macdonald can turn out a better worker than I can....and I deny that there is any evidence that he can.... I contend that he has done so at the expense of a boy's individuality. He has forced something from without on the boy. That's not education. The word derives from the Latin "to lead forth." Macdonald would have made Jim Jackson a warped youth; he would have Macdonaldised him. I took the other way. I said to myself: "This chap has something bright in him. What is it?" I offered him freedom and he showed me what he was—a good-natured clever laddie with a delightful sense of the comic. I think that his line is humour; more than once have I told him that he has the makings of a great comedian in him. I said this to Lawson and he scoffed.

"Good Lord!" he cried, "what a mission to have in life!"

"Better an excellent Little Tich," I replied, "than an average coal-heaver. To amuse humanity is a great mission, Lawson."

There was wee Doris Slater, the daughter of people who lived in a caravan. That child moved like a goddess. I think that if Pavlova saw Doris she would beg her mother to allow the child to become a dancer. Macdonald would try to make Doris a typist, I fancy, and pride himself on the fact that he had improved her social position. I would have Doris a dancer, for she looks like being fit to become a very great artist. Music moves her to unconscious ecstatic grace in movement.

I want education to guide a child into finding out what best it can do. At present our schools provide for the average child....and heaven only knows how many geniuses have been destroyed by stupid coercion. I want education to set out deliberately to catch genius in the bud. And what discovers genius cannot be bad for the children who have no genius.

I want education to produce the best that is in a child. That is the only way to improve the world. The naked truth is that we grown-ups have failed to make the world better than the gigantic slum it is, and when we pretend to know how a child should be brought up we are being merely fatuous. We must hand on what we have learned to the children, but we must do it without comment. We must not say: "This is right," because we don't know what is right: we must not say: "This is wrong," because we don't know what is wrong. The most we should do is to tell a child our experience. When I caught my boys smoking I did not say: "This is wrong"; I merely said: "Doctors say that cigarettes are bad for a boy's health. They are the specialists in health; you and I don't know anything about it."

When I tell a boy that a light should not be taken near to petrol I am handing on bitter experience of my own, but when I say that he must know the chief dates of history by Monday morning I am doing an absolutely defenceless thing, for no one can prove by experience that a knowledge of dates is a good thing. Macdonald would say: "Quite so, but could you prove that it is a bad thing?" I would reply that I could prove it is a senseless thing; moreover education should not aim at giving children things that do not do them harm. I don't suppose that it would do me any harm to learn up the proper names in the Bible beginning with Adam. The point is would it do me any good?

I once had a discussion with Macdonald on Socialism. He accused me of attempting to force humanity to be of a pattern.

"Socialism kills individualism," he said

I smile to think that the Conservative Macdonald is trying to mould children to a pattern, while I, a Socialist, insist on each child's being allowed to develop its own separate individuality.

The Socialist would appear to be the keenest individualist in the world, for it is from the heretical section of society that the demand for freedom in education is coming.

* * *

To-day I visited Watterson, an old college friend of mine. He is now in Harley Street, and is fast becoming famous as a specialist in nervous disorders.

"Your nerves are all to pot," he said; "what have you been doing with yourself?"

I told him my recent history.

"But, Good Lord!" he cried, "how did you manage to find any worry in a village?"

I tried to explain. Living in a village narrows one; the outside world is gradually forgotten, and the opinions of ignoramuses gradually come to matter. I found myself beginning to worry over the adverse criticisms of villagers who could not read nor write.

"You've got neurasthenia," said Watterson; "what you want to do is to settle down on a farm for six months; live in the open air and do nothing strenuous. Don't try to think, and for God's sake don't worry. Read *John Bull* and *The Pink 'Un*, and chuck all the weekly intellectual reviews. And....most important of all, fall in love with a rosy-cheeked daughter of the soil."

I have written to Frank Thomson, the farmer of Eagleshowe, asking if he still wants a cattleman. His last man was conscripted, and if the job is still vacant Frank will give it to me.

To-night I sit chuckling. The idea of a dismissed dominie's returning to a village to feed cattle is rich. The village will extract much amusement out of it. I imagine Peter Mitchell looking over the dyke and crying: "Weel, dominie, and how is the experiment in eddication gettin' on?"

* * *

I sit at a bright peat fire in Frank Thomson's bothy. I arrived at three o'clock and no bairn was about the station. I was glad, for I did not want to meet anyone. There was a queer feeling of shame in returning; I feared to meet anyone's glance. To return a few days after an affecting farewell is the last word in anticlimax; it is so horribly undramatic a thing to do. I wish that Lazarus had kept a diary after his resurrection ; I fancy that quite a few people resented his return.

I cannot write more to-night ; I am tired out. The most tiring thing in the world is to rise in one place and go to bed in another.

* * *

I was going out to fetch the cows this afternoon when I espied three girls in white pinafores at the top of the field. They waved their hands and ran down to meet me.

" We'll help you to take in the cows," cried Janet. They accepted my return without even the slightest curiosity, and I was glad.

" Righto ! " I said, " but wait a bit. I want to sketch the farm first."

I sat down on the bank and the three settled themselves round me.

" Please, sir," said Ellen, " Mr. Macdonald's a nice man."

I did not want to discuss Macdonald with my bairns, and I sketched in silence. I think they forgot all about my presence after that ; in the old days they used to talk to each other as if I weren't there. Once they discussed likely sweethearts in the village for me, and I am sure they forgot that I was there.

" He's nice to the lassies, Ellen," said Jean, " but not to the boys."

" What did he strap Jim Jackson for ? " asked Ellen.

" Aw dinna ken," said Janet, " but he was needin' the strap. Jim Jackson's a cheeky wee thing."

"Eh!" said Jean, "haven't we to sit awful quiet, Jan?"

"Weel," said Janet nodding her head sagely, "and so ye shud sit quiet in the schule. Ye'll no be learning yer lessons if ye speak."

I went on sketching.

Janet is already being Macdonaldised. She accepts his authority without question. Ellen and Jean are critical as yet, but in a week both will have adapted themselves to the machine.

They wandered off to pluck flowers. I finished my sketch and hailed them. Then they came to me and took my arms and we took the cows home.

In the evening I was mucking out the byre when Jim Jackson came for his milk.

"Good morrow, sir," I called from the byre door, "you didn't happen to see Mr. Thomson's elephant as you came up the road?"

He looked interested.

"Elephant?" he asked brightly.

"Yes. The white one; strayed away this afternoon from the chicken coop. Have you seen it?"

"No," he said, "not the white one, but the grey one and the tiger are sitting at the dyke-side down at the second gate. I gave the tiger a turnip when I passed it."

"Good!" I cried, "always be kind to animals."

"Yes, sir," he said, and he glanced down to the second gate. I think that he wouldn't have been very much surprised if he had seen a tiger there. Jim has the power of make-believe developed strongly. A few weeks ago he found a dead sparrow in the playground. He came to me and asked for a coffin. I gave him a match-box and he lined the class up in twos and led them with bared heads towards the grave he had dug. The four foremost boys carried the coffin shoulder high.

Jim laid ropes over the grave and the coffin was lowered reverently. A boy was just about to fill in the grave when Jim cried: "Hold on!" Then he took a handful of earth and sprinkled it over the coffin saying: "Dust to dust, and ashes to ashes."

I blew the Last Post over the grave afterwards. Jim was as serious as could be; for the moment he seemed to think that he was burying his brother.

When he had got his milk he came to the byre door and watched me work for a little.

"Please, sir," he asked, "do you like that better than teaching?"

I told him that I didn't.

"I wish Mester Macdonald wud be a cattle-man," he said fervently.

"Some folk might say that he is," I remarked.

"He gave me my licks the first mornin' he cam," he continued. "We got an essay 'How I spent my holidays,' and I said that I was in France and helped the Crown Prince to loot places. We quarrelled about how much we should get each and I shot him. The Mester gave me three scuds for tellin' lies."

"He would," I said grimly.

"But you used to tell me to tell lies!" he cried.

"I did, Jim. And you see the result....I muck out a byre."

When Jim went away I came to a sudden resolution: I would fight for Jim. I'll do all in my power to help the lad to preserve his own personality.....Frank Thomson is his uncle and I'll try to get Jim to see me often. Professional etiquette! Professional etiquette be damned! I'm not in the profession now anyhow, and all the professional etiquette in the world is as nothing to the saving of a soul.

* * *

I find that I enjoy my food now. Formerly I looked on a meal as an appetiser for a smoke; now I look on a meal as an event. I feel healthier than I ever did in my life before. The land dulls one, however. The old cry "Back to the Land" means "Back to Elemental Mental Stagnation." I spent this forenoon cutting turnips, and I know that I thought of nothing all the time. I have a theory that great thoughts are the product of disease. Possibly this is only another way of saying that genius is allied to madness. Shelley was a physical weakling; Ibsen and Nietzsche went mad. Yes, geniuses are diseased folk, but the converse does not hold.

Macdonald came up to see me to-night; he wanted to ask a few things about the school. We lay on a bank and lit our pipes.

"I can't find your 'Record of Work,'" he said.

"I never kept one."

"But....the Code demands one!"

"I know....but I didn't keep one. My record of work is my pupils in after life."

"Yes," he said drily, "I know all about that, but you are supposed to keep a record that will show an inspector what you are doing to produce this after life record."

"Macdonald," I said impatiently, "if you mean to tell me that any man can tell what I am doing to prepare children for after life by squinting at a crowd of entries of the Took-the - History - of - the - Great - Rebellion - this - week order....well, I don't understand your attitude to life in general."

"That's all very well," he protested, "but we aren't there to make the rules; we're paid servants who have to administer the laws of wiser men."

"How do you know that they are wiser?" I asked.

"They're wiser than I am anyway," he said with a smile.

"I'm not so sure of it, Macdonald; they are more unscrupulous than you are. They know what they want, definitely and finally; they want efficient wage-slaves."

"That's merely a Socialistic cry."

"It may be, but it's true. Who rule us? A definite governing class of trained aristocrats."

"H'm! I shouldn't call Lloyd George and that Labour man Hodge trained aristocrats."

"They aren't born aristocrats I admit, but they are aristocratised democrats. They've adapted themselves to the aristocratic tradition. They are on the side of aristocracy; you won't find them alienating the good opinion of the moneyed classes. We are governed from above; do you admit that?"

"In the main....yes," he said grudgingly.

"Very good! Well, then, our rulers believe in two kinds of education. They send their sons to the public schools where boys are trained to be governors, but they send the rest of the sons of the community to State schools where they are trained to be disciplined and content with their lot."

"That's nonsense."

"Possibly, ; but I suppose you know that the members of the House of Lords and the Cabinet don't send their sons to L.C.C. schools."

"You are simply preaching class war," he said.

"I am. There is a class war—there has been for generations—but it is a one-sided war."

"It is," said Macdonald grimly.

"The upper class took the offensive long ago, and it keeps it yet. Look at the squire down in the village. He won't ride in the same railway compartment with you or me; he won't sit beside us in the theatre....why, he won't lie beside us in the kirkyard: he's got that railed-off corner for his family. I don't blame him ; he has been educated up in his belief, just as you and I have been educated up in the belief that we are his inferiors. When I was down in the school I lectured the whole class one day because I saw a boy doff his cap to the squire and nod to his mother three seconds afterwards.

"Don't you see that this village is a little British Empire? Here there are only two classes—the big house and the village....the ruling class and the ruled. The school trains the ruled to be ruled, and the kirk takes up the training on the Seventh Day. The minister talks a lot of prosy platitudes about Faith and Love and Charity, but he never thinks of saying a thing that the squire might take umbrage at."

I broke off and refilled my pipe.

"How are you getting on?" I asked.

"Well enough. The bairns are nice."

"A little bit noisy," he added, "but, of course, I was prepared for that. I heard about your experiment months ago. By the way, what sort of a teacher is Miss Watson?"

"Excellent," I replied.

"How often did you examine her classes?"

"I never examined her classes, not formally, but her bairns spoke to me, and I judged her work from their conversation."

"I examined their work yesterday; her spelling is weak and her geography atrocious."

"Shouldn't wonder," I said carelessly. "I never bothered about those things; I judged her work by what her bairns were, not by what they knew. They're a bright lot when you ask them to think out things."

"No wonder they fired you out," he laughed; "you're impossible as a dominie, you know."

I smiled.

"How do you like Jim Jackson?" I asked suddenly.

"Cheeky devil!"

"He's clever," I said.

"You may call it cleverness, but I have another name for it. He is a fellow that requires to be sat on."

"And you'll sit on him?"

"I certainly shall....heavily too."

I tried to show Macdonald that he was making a criminal blunder, but he got impatient. "I can't stand cheek," he kept saying, and I had to give up all hope of convincing him that I was right. Macdonald is essentially a stupid man. I don't say that merely because he disagrees with me; I say it because he refuses to think out his own attitude. He cries that Jim is cheeky, but he won't go into the other question as to whether humour is impudence. Had he argued that humour is a drawback in life I should have pitied his taste, but I should have admired his ability to make out a good case.

III.

I HAVE spent a hard day forking hay along with Margaret Thomson. Margaret is twenty and bonny, but she is very, very shy. She attended my Evening class last winter, and she appears to be afraid to speak to me. I tried to get her to converse again and again to-day, but it was of no use. I think that she fears to make a mistake in grammar or to mispronounce a word.

I hear her voice outside at the horse-trough. She is bantering old Peter Wilson, and talking thirteen to the dozen. Her laugh is a most delightful thing. I wonder did Touchstone like Audrey's laugh!

The Thomsons are carrying out in farming the principles I set myself to carry out in education. They treat their beasts with the greatest kindness. There isn't a wild animal in the place. Spot the collie is a most lovable creature; the sheep are all tame, and the cows are quiet beasts; the bull has a bold eye, but he is as gentle as a lamb. The horses come to the kitchen door from the water-trough, and little Nancy Thomson feeds them with bread. Every member of the family comes into personal immediate contact with the animals, and the animals seem to love the family. There is no fear in this farmyard.

Mrs. Thomson is a kind-hearted soul. She

never goes down to the village unless to the kirk on Sunday. She works hard all day, but she is always cheerful. "I like to see them comin' in aboot," she says, and she seems to find the greatest pleasure in preparing the family's meals. On a Saturday bairns come up from the village, and she gives them "pieces" spread thick with fresh butter and strawberry jam. "I'm never happy unless there's a squad o' bairns roond me," she said to me to-day.

Frank Thomson is what the village would call a funny sort o' a billie. His eyes are always twinkling, and he tries to see the funny side of life. He hasn't much humour, but he has a strong sense of fun, and he loves to chaff the youngsters.

"Weel, Wullie," is his invariable greeting when his boy returns from school in the evening, "Weel, Wullie, and did ye get yer licks the day?"

On a Saturday Frank always has a troop of girls hanging on to his coat tails, and he is always playing practical jokes on them—locking them in the stable or covering them with straw.

"Goad!" he will cry, "ye're an awfu' pack o' tormentors; just wait er Aw tell the dominie aboot ye!" and they yell at him.

Mrs. Thomson tells me that he is inordinately proud of having me for a cattleman, and at the cattle mart he boasts about having an M.A. as feeder. I took two stots into the mart yesterday, and when they entered the ring a wag cried: "Are they weel up in the Greek, think ye, Frank?" and the farmers roared.

"Oh, aye," shouted Frank, "they're weel crammed up wi' a'thing that's guid!"

I think that the Scotch Education Department should insist on every teacher's going farming every three years. Inside the profession you lose perspective. The educational papers are full of articles about geography and history and drawing, but teachers seldom show that they are looking beyond the mere curriculum. The training colleges supply the young teacher with what they call Mental Philosophy or Psychology, but it is quite possible for an honours graduate in mental philosophy to have no philosophy at all.

The question for the teacher is: What am I aiming at? Macdonald is aiming at what he calls a bright show before the inspector. To be just to the man I admit that he is honestly trying to educate these bairns according to his lights. He wants to produce good scholars, but when I ask him what he considers the goal of humanity he is at sea.

He tells me that education should not be made to produce little Socialists as I seemed to try to do. But I deny that I ever tried to make my bairns Socialists. I told them the elemental truth that a parasite is an enemy of society; I told them that the world was out of joint. And I gave them freedom to develop their personalities in the hope that, freed from discipline and fear and lies, they might become a better generation than mine has been.

The Macdonalds of life have failed to produce thinking that is free ; I merely say : Let the children have a say now ; stop thrusting your stupid barbaric Authority down their little throats ; let the bairns be free to breathe. Give up all the snobbish nonsense about manners and respect and servility you ram into the child ; if he refuses to lift his hat to you, who the devil are you that you should coerce him into doing it ?

I think that some of the more important villagers were annoyed at the bairns' obvious lack of respect, or at least the semblance of respect. But they looked for faults. They told me of escapades after school hours, of complaints of bosses against boys who had been with me. I asked George Wilson, the mason, whether he would expand his criticism to include the minister. "Do you blame Mr. Gordon for every drunk and every theft in the village ? He has been here for thirty years, and, on your reasoning, he has been a failure."

"Aw dinna pay rates for keepin' up the kirk," he replied, "but I pay rates to keep up the schule, and Aw have a claim to creeticise the wye ye teach the bairns."

I see now that I never had a chance against the enemy. They could point to what they called faults.....Johnnie didn't know his History, Lizzie did too much sketching, Peter wasn't deferential. I could point to nothing. I had abolished fear, I had made the school a place of joy, I had encouraged each child's natural bent....and the village smiled scornfully and said : " We ken nae difference."

I found myself worrying over the opinions of small men who are of no importance in the world of ideas ; stupid fools led me into taking up an eternal position of defence. And I fumed inwardly, for I am not always a ready talker.

But now I am able to smile at the men who baited me a few weeks ago. They don't count. In the great world beyond the hills there are people who take the large broad view of education, and some day education will really be a " leading forth " not a " putting in."

* * *

I met Macdonald to-night, and I asked him how things were doing.

" I'm in the middle of prizes," he said wearily, " and if there's one thing I detest it's prizes."

I began to think that I had misjudged Macdonald.

" Excellent ! " I cried, " we agree for once ! What's your objection to prizes ? "

" They're such a confounded nuisance."

" Granted," I said.

" That's all I have against them. You never know how you are to distribute the things."

"Why do you object to them?" he asked.

I sat down on Wilkie's dyke and lit my pipe.

"I object to them on principle, Macdonald. They're tips, that's what they are."

"Tips?"

"Yes. I give a porter tuppence for seeing my bicycle into the van; I give Mary Ritchie a book for beating the others at reading. I tip both."

"I don't see it."

"The porter shouldn't get a tip; his job is to look after luggage. Mary's job is to read to improve her mind."

"But," said Macdonald, "life is full of rewards."

"I know." Here Peter Mitchell strolled up. "We're talking about prizes," I explained. "Life is full of rewards of all kinds, but the only reward that matters is the joy in doing a thing well. If I write a poem or paint a picture I'm not writing or painting with one eye on royalties or the auction room. I sell my poem or picture in order to live....in a decent civilisation I wouldn't require to sell it to live, but that's by the way. My point is that prizes are artificial rewards, just as strapping is an artificial punishment."

"Goad!" said Peter Mitchell, "do ye mean to tell me that Aw wasna thinkin' o' the reward when I selt my powney last Saturday?"

"Competition is a good thing," said Macdonald. "Look at running and sports and all that sort of thing."

"I admit it," I said, "you like to beat your partner at golf. But my contention is that the prize at the end is vulgar; the joy is in being the best sprinter in the country. After all you don't glory in the fact that Simpson took seven at the tenth hole; your glory lies in the thought that you did it in three.

"Prizes in school are not only vulgar: they are cruel. Take Ellen Smith. Ellen has always been a first-rate arithmetician; she has the talent. For the past four years she has carried off the first prize for arithmetic. Sarah Nelson is very good, but work as she likes she can't beat Ellen. Sarah becomes despondent every year at prize-giving time. Bairns aren't philosophical; they don't see that the vulgar little book they get isn't worth thinking about. The ignorant noodles who sit on School Boards (Peter Mitchell had moved on by this time) stand up at the school exhibition and talk much cant about prizes. 'Them that don't get them this year must just make a spurt and get them next year.' And the poor bairns imagine that a prize is the golden fruit of life."

I notice that the men who are keenest on school prizes are firm believers in school punishments. And they are generally religious. Their god is a petty tyrant who rewards the good and punishes the wicked. They try to act up to the attitude of their god....hence, I fancy the term "tin god."

* * *

I see that many eminent people are making

speeches about "Education After the War." I can detect but little difference between their attitude and that of the commercial men who keep shouting "Capture Germany's Trade!" "Let us have more technical instruction," cries the educationist, "more discipline; let us beat Germany at her own game!" The commercial man chuckles. "Excellent!" he cries, "first-rate....but of course we must have Protection also!"

And the educationist and the commercial man will have their way. Education will aim frankly at turning out highly efficient wage-slaves. The New Education has commenced; its first act was to abolish freedom. Free speech is dead; a free press is merely a name; the workers were wheedled into giving up their freedom to sell their commodity labour to the highest bidder, while the profiteer retains his right to sell his goods at the highest price he can get. Every restriction on liberty is alleged to be necessary to win the war.

The alarming feature of the present Prussianisation of Britain lies in the circumstance that the signing of peace will be but the beginning of a new war. If the plans of the Paris Economic Conference are carried out true education is interned for a century. Millions have lost their lives in the military war: millions will lose their souls in the trade war. Just as we have sullenly obeyed the dictates of the war government, we shall sullenly obey the dictates of the trade government. "We must win the trade war," our rulers will cry, and, if the profiteers say that men must work sixteen hours a day if we are to beat Germany, the Press and the Church and the School will persuade the public that the man who strikes for a fifteen hours day is a traitor to his country.

Will anyone try to save education ? The commercial men will use it to further their own plans ; the educationists will unconsciously play into the profiteers' hands ; the women....only the other day the suffrage band was marching through the streets of London displaying a huge banner bearing the words " We Want Hughes." Hughes is the Premier of Australia, a Labour man dear to the hearts of all the capitalist newspapers. His one text is " Trade after the War."

Who is there to save education ? The teaching profession could save it, but teachers are merely servants. They will continue to argue about Compulsory Greek and, no doubt, Compulsory Russian will come up for discussion in the educational papers soon. The commercially-minded gentlemen of Westminster will draw up the new scheme of education, and the teachers will humbly adapt themselves to the new method.

I don't think that anyone will save education.

IV.

I LAY on a bank this afternoon smoking. Janet and Jean and Annie came along the road, and they sat down beside me.

"I'm tired of the school," said Annie wearily; "Aw wish Aw was fourteen!"

"What's wrong now?" I asked.

"Oh, we never get any fun now, the new mester's always so strict, and we get an awful lot o' home lessons now."

"Annie got the strap on Friday," explained Jean. "Mester Macdonald's braces broke Aw think, at least something broke when he was bending doon and he took an awful red face ....and he had to keep his hands in his pouches till night time to keep his breeks up."

"Did Annie pull them down?" I asked.

Jean tittered.

"No, but she laughed and he gave her the strap."

"Aye," cried Annie in delight, "and they nearly cam doon when he was strappin' me!"

"Why do awkward incidents occur to dignity?" I said, more to myself than to the bairns, "my braces wouldn't break in fifty years of teaching." Then I laughed.

Margaret Thomson came down the road on her way to Evening Service, and she reddened as she passed.

"Eh!" laughed Janet, looking up into my

face, " did ye see yon ? Maggie blushed ! Aw wudna wonder if she has a notion o' the Mester ! "

" How could she help it, Jan ? ". I said. " Why, you'll be hopelessly in love with me yourself in a couple of years, you besom ! "

She stared before her vacantly for a little.

" Aw did have a notion o' you when ye cam first," she said slowly.

I put my arm round her neck.

" You dear kid ! " I said.

She smiled up in my face.

" Ye had that bonny striped tie on then, she said artlessly.

I pulled her hair.

" Ye shud marry Maggie Tamson," she said after a pause.

" Aye," added Jean, " and syne ye'll get the farm when her father dies. He's troubled wi' the rheumatics and he'll no live very long. And she wud be a gran worker too."

" Dinna haver, Jean," said Annie scornfully, " the Mester will want a gran lady for his wife, one that can play the piano and have ham and egg to her breakfast ilka morning."

" No extravagant wife like that for me ! " I protested.

" Aweel, an egg ilka day and ham and egg on Sundays onywye," compromised Annie.

" An egg every second morning, Annie," I said firmly, " and ham and egg every second Sunday."

" Ladies dinna mak good wives," said Janet. " Willie Macintosh along at Rinsley married a lassie that was a piano teacher, and she gets her breakfast in her bed and has a wumman to wash up. Aye, and she's ay dressed and oot after dinnertime. Aye, and she sends a' his collars to the laundry....and he only wears a clean dicky on Sawbath."

"Ah!" I said, "I'm glad you told me that, Janet; I won't risk marrying a lady. But tell me, Janet, how am I to know what sort of woman I am marrying?"

"It's quite easy," she said slowly, "you just have to tear a button off your waistcoat and if she doesna offer to mend it ye shouldna tak her."

"And speer at her what time she gets up in the mornin'," she added; "Maggie Tamson rises at five ilka mornin'."

"Why are you so anxious that it should be Margaret?" I asked with real curiosity.

Janet shook her head.

"Aw just think she's in love wi' ye," she said simply; "she blushed."

* * *

I went out with my bugle to-night, and I sounded all the old calls. I finished up with "Come for Orders," and I walked slowly down the brae to the farm. Jim Jackson and Dickie Gibson came running up to me.

"Ye played 'Come for Orders!'" panted Jim as he wiped his sweating face with his bonnet.

"We'll soon remedy matters," I laughed, and I played the "Dismiss."

Jim perched himself on a gate.

"We'll hae to fall oot, Dick," he said with mock resignation, "come on and we'll sit here till we get oor wind back." And Dick climbed up beside him.

"How are the lies getting on, Jim?" I asked.

He shook his head dolefully.

"We got an essay the day on The Discovery of America....and ye canna tell mony lies aboot that. Aw just said that Columbus discovered America, and wrote aboot his ships. The new Mester says we must stick to the truth."

"It is difficult to associate the truth with America," I said. "But there is a true side to this discovery business. To say that Columbus discovered America is a half-truth; the whole truth is that America isn't quite discovered yet. Andrew Carnegie was fairly successful, and Charlie Chaplin is another discoverer of note, but—"

Jim clearly did not understand; he thought that I was pulling his leg.

"How's the pond?" I asked, and was grieved to find that neither of the boys had any interest in it. "The Mester taks us oot and gies us object lessons on the minnows," said Dickie, and I groaned.

"And the pigeons?"

"Object lessons too," said Jim with evident disgust. "What family did he say doos belonged to, Dick?"

Dick had no idea.

"The word dove comes from the Latin *columba*," I said sententiously. "Hence the name Columbus who was named after the dove that was sent out of the Ark. When he learned this as a boy he resolved to live up to his name ....hence the American Eagle, which of course has transformed itself into a dove during Woodrow Wilson's reign."

Dick listened open-mouthed, but Jim's eyes twinkled.

"The Mester gives us derivations ilka day. He telt us the derivation of pond when he was giein' us the object lesson, but I canna mind what it was."

"A weight!" cried Dickie suddenly, and I complimented him on his industry.

"Aye," giggled Jim, "he *shud* mind it, for he had to write it oot a hunder times."

I made a cryptic remark about ponds and ponderosity, and then I told them of the boy who had to stay in and write the phrase "I have gone" many times in order that he might grasp the correct idiom. He filled five pages; then he wrote something at the bottom of the last page, a message to his teacher. The message read "Please, sir, I have went home." Dickie immediately asked whether the boy got a lamming next morning, and Jim looked at him scornfully. Dickie has not got an alert mind.

To-night I am doubting whether I was wise to return to the village. I seem to become sadder every day. My heart is down in the old ugly school, and I am jealous of Macdonald. I know that he is an inferior, but he has my bairns in his control I confess to a sneaking delight in the knowledge that he is not liked by the bairns. In this respect I think I am inferior to him ; I don't think he is jealous of my popularity but of course he may be after all.

Jim's answering my bugle call makes me want to cry. I can sit out the most pathetic drama unemotionally ; when the hero says farewell for ever to the heroine I sit up cheerfully. It is sweetness that affects me ; when the hero clasps his love in his arms I snivel. In the cinema when little Willie is dying to slow music and the mother is wringing her hands I smile, but if Willie recovers and sits up in bed to hug his teddy bear I blow my nose. I am unaffected when Peter Pan returns to find his mother's window shut against him, but when the fairies build a house over the sleeping lost girl I have to light my pipe and cough sternly.

I wish I hadn't gone out with my bugle to-night.

* * *

Macdonald is an ass. He came to me this afternoon. " Look here," he began, " I wonder if you've any objection to my making a few alterations in the school live stock ? "

" Want to introduce a cow ? " I asked. " You believe in utilitarianism in education I fancy."

"It's the pigeons and rabbits," he went on; "I was wondering if you would object to my getting rid of one or two."

"What's wrong?"

"It's the sex matter," he said hurriedly. "I don't like the thing; I don't so much mind the infants asking awkward questions, but why the deuce should they keep them till I am speaking to the infant mistress?"

"Refer them to the lady," I said with a chuckle.

He looked troubled.

"I must get rid of one sex," he said.

"Macdonald," I said severely, "I don't know that you can do that without the permission of the children. The rabbits and doos are their's; they bought them with their own money."

"That's no great difficulty," he said lightly.

"Possibly not....not for you, Macdonald. If you use authority the bairns will hardly question it. But I don't see that you have the right to be an autocrat in this affair."

"It is my duty to protect the children," he said with dignity.

"Protect yourself, you mean!" I cried; "you have just confessed that your one aim is to get rid of awkward questions."

"But what can I do?" he stammered.

"Do! Do nothing, just as I did. Let the creatures breed as much as they darned well please; that's what they are there for. You can't very well make sex an object lesson;

the logical thing to do is to give a lesson on pollination of plants and then go on to fertilisation of the bird's egg, but if you do that you'll get the sack at once. But there's quite enough of prudery in the world already without your turning a rabbit-hutch into a sultanless harem."

"There are things that children shouldn't know," he said with a touch of aggression.

"And there are things that grown-ups should know and don't," I said. "They ought to know that the sex conspiracy of silence is idiotic and criminal."

"Anyway," he said sullenly, "I'll tell them to-morrow that there are too many in the house and that I mean to get rid of a few."

"All right," I said resignedly, "you can lie to them if you want to." Then I added: "Although, mind you, Macdonald, I feel like telling the bairns the real reason for your action."

He looked startled.

"Don't be alarmed," I said with a smile, "I won't do it," and he looked relieved.

"Why not look in at the school some afternoon?" he said amiably when we parted, "but perhaps you feel that you've shaken off the dust from your feet down there?"

"I'll be delighted to come down," I said; "I didn't shake off the dust from my feet when I left....there was quite enough dust there already."

I think I'll go down to-morrow afternoon;

it was decent of Macdonald to ask me after all that I have said to him.

* * *

A man spends his life wishing he had done certain things and wishing that he had not done certain things. I half wish that I had not accepted Macdonald's invitation ; I feel lonely up here now : on the other hand I am glad that I went. I think now that Macdonald's real idea was to show me how he has improved the school.

From his point of view he has improved it. He showed me exercise books that were models of neatness and care ; he showed me classes swotting up subjects laboriously ; the rooms were as silent as the grave.

When I went in Macdonald shook hands with me formally, and I noticed that his school voice and manner were prim and professional. I turned to the bairns and said : " Hullo, kids ! " and they rose in a body and said : " Good afternoon, sir ! "

" Ah ! " I whispered to Macdonald, " I see I ought to have said : ' Good afternoon, children ! ' eh ? " and he smiled professionally.

The higher classes were drawing. The model was a vase. I walked round the class..and swore silently. I had spent two years persuading these bairns that there is no boundary line in nature ; a white vase appears to have lines as boundaries simply because it usually stands in front of a dark background. I made them work in the background to show up the model, although I never gave them vases or pails; my drawing was all outside sketching of trees and houses. He was making them "line in" the drawing.

"I am not much good at drawing," he explained apologetically, "as a matter of fact I know nothing about it."

"In that case," I said, "why not let them go on with the methods I gave them? I know something about the subject."

He asked what my methods were and I explained them in a few minutes. He expressed his gratitude and seemed honestly glad to learn something about the subject.

"I won't take them out drawing though," he said; "an inspector might come to the school in my absence."

"You conscientious devil!" I said, "let's heve a squint at their exercise books."

As he moved to the cupboard a boy whispered to his neighbour and Macdonald turned like a flash; the lad visibly quailed before his fixing eye. I fancied that the next inspector's report would commence with the words: "The discipline of this school is excellent."

The books were much neater than mine had been. I began to look for blots, but the search was hopeless.

"Oh! for God's sake, Macdonald, show me Peter Mackay's book; surely a good healthy blot will be found there!" But Peter's book was scrupulously clean.

"I had to deal with that boy with a stern

hand," said Macdonald grimly, and as I stood looking at the book I saddened.

"On the outside of this book you should write the words: 'Peter Mackay....a Tragedy, by William Macdonald,'" I said, but I don't think the man understood me.

The three o'clock interval came. "Stand!" commanded Macdonald, and the class rose as one child. "Front seat....quick march!" The boys saluted him as they passed out, and the girls curtsied. I tried not to laugh at the fatuous fellow's inculcation of "respect." Poor devil, I think they will hate him in after years; he is of the brand of dominie that is responsible for the post-schooldays habit of shying divots and opprobrious epithets at teachers passing along the road.

On the way out Janet touched my arm playfully, but the eagle-eyed disciplinarian saw the action and he glared at her.

"Had you any trouble with swearing?" he asked when the last boy had gone out.

"Not particularly. Have you?"

"I've put it down with a very firm hand."

"I never bothered about it," I said carelessly. "I very seldom heard it; if I did happen to hear a boy string together a few strong words I ridiculed him, told him they didn't mean anything. Once I was trying to unscrew a stiff nut from my motor-bike and I addressed it audibly. I heard a snigger and on looking round found that Jim Jackson had come up to watch my efforts."

Macdonald raised his eyebrows and whistled.

"Pretty awkward, eh?"

"Not in the least, Macdonald; I merely said: 'Jim, never waste good bad language; one day you may be a motor-cyclist and you'll need it all then.' Jim nodded approvingly."

"You would have persuaded Jim that he never heard your words," I added.

I find that I cannot dislike Macdonald. He is essentially a decent fellow with a kindly nature; sometimes I feel that I am quite fond of him. His equanimity is charming; he seldom shows the least trace of irritation when I talk to him. But his mental laziness riles me; he is so cock-sure about his methods of education, and I know that I never can induce him to think the matter out for himself. The tragedy is that there are a thousand Macdonalds in Scots schools to-day. Of course they are hopelessly wrong. I don't know whether I am right, but I know that they are wrong. They stick to a narrow code; they force youth to follow their silly behests regarding respect; they kill the individuality of each child. Why in all the earth does civilisation allow such asses to warp the children? Who is Macdonald that any human being should quail before his awful eye? Is he so righteous that he shall punish a boy for swearing? He spent a whole morning lately cross-examining the bairns to discover who wrote the words: "Mr. Macdonald is daft" on the pigeon-house door. At last one wee chap was intimidated into confessing, and Macdonald whacked him and then harangued the whole school. The bairns were convinced that the lad had committed the sin against the Holy Ghost.

What a mind the man has ! I discovered an obscene writing about myself three weeks after I had come to the school. The bairns held their breath while I read it. I sent for a cloth and erased the words.

"What's the use of scribbling silly rot like that ?" I said, and lit my pipe. There never was any more writing on the wall in my time.

How the devil are bairns to gain any perspective in life if a fool like Macdonald spends half a day investigating nothing ? Education should aim at giving a child a philosophy, and philosophy simply means the contemplation of the important things in life. If teachers emphasise the importance of things like silence and manners and dignity and respect, we cannot expect our children to rise higher in later years than the cheap gossipy lying press and the absurd system we call party politics.

The Macdonalds start out with the assumption that human nature is bad ; I start out with the realisation that human nature is good. That is the real distinction between the disciplinarian and the believer in freedom. When my boys stole turnips, wrote swear words on walls, talked and ate sweets as they sat in class I attached little or no importance to their actions ; all I tried to do was to bring out the best that was in a lad's nature....and I succeeded. Every child improved....no, I was forgetting one boy! He came from a city school, and his face was full of impudence. He looked round my free school and marvelled; he had come from a Macdonaldised school and he naturally concluded that I was a soft mark. One day I said to him very mildly: "My gentle youth, this school is Liberty Hall, not because I am weak but because I happen to be rather strong....I could whack you effectively if I started to you." But I never managed to fit that boy into my scheme of things. He left after a few months, and after he had gone he bounced to other boys that he had shoved many pens and ink-pots down a hole in the floor. I found that he was telling the truth.

What would have happened if the boy had remained at school I don't know, but I think that he would have gradually adapted himself to his environment. He had been reared in the schools where physical force reigned, and he understood no other system. Yes, I fancy I could have converted that youth. I think of Homer T. Lane and his Little Commonwealth in Dorset, where so called criminal children from the police courts are given self-government and become excellent citizens, and I know that the Macdonalds are wrong.

Not long ago Edinburgh School Board passed a motion asking the local magistrates to make their birch-rod sentences severe enough to be effective. Once upon a time people thought that lunatics were criminals and they lashed them with whips. A time came when people realised that a lunatic was a diseased person and they at once began to care for him tenderly. Nowadays the enlightened members of society realise that a criminal is a diseased person.... usually the victim of a diseased society....and they passionately advocate his being treated as a sick man is treated. And the School Board of the capital of Scotland recommend that extra stripes with the rod be given to poor laddies who steel a few pence.

I feel quite sure that no minister in the country mentioned the fact from his pulpit. I expect they were all too busy anathematising the "Hun" to consider what the attitude of Jesus Christ was to men and women taken in sin. I should like to preach to that School Board from the text "Suffer little children to come unto Me."

There are two ways in education : Macdonalds with Authority in the shape of School Boards and magistrates and prisons to support him ; and mine with the Christlike experiment of Homer Lane to encourage me.

I wonder why there are two sides to this question of education ? No one but a fool will contend that the birch rod is better than the Little Commonwealth. I think that ninety per cent. of the Macdonalds of Scotland would believe in the Little Commonwealth. Why then would they argue that their system of teaching is better than mine ? Obviously coercion and authority make a child less individual than he might be. Ah! it all turns on our respective attitudes to life. "Boys are innately bad," they say, "whack 'em!" "Boys are innately good," I say, "I'll light my pipe and ask them how their rabbits are getting on."

* * *

Macdonald came hurrying up to me to-night.

"I quite forgot to ask you when you came down what you used to do about your desk. The lock's broken; how long has it been like that?"

"Since my first week in school," I said.

"Good gracious! Mean to tell me your desk was open for two years?"

I nodded, and smiled at his consternation.

"I've sent down to the joiner. The situation is intolerable. Why, do you know what I found in it to-day?"

"A packet of sweets," I hazarded.... "chocolates if you were lucky."

"How did you guess?" he cried in amazement.

"My dear fellow, my desk was a sweety shop some days; they used to hide their packets in every corner of it, then they would come to me and say: 'Please, sir, my pockie is in the wee corner on the right; dinna let onybody touch it.' Who put them in?" I asked.

"Gladys Miller."

"You have all the luck," I said. "Gladys always buys liquorice rolls, you know them.... little yellow sweets with the sugarelly inside.

Man, I love yon sweets....and Gladys knew it, the besom!"

"Oh! It's all very well for you to make a joke of it," he said with annoyance, "but I tell you I don't like it, and after to-day I guess it'll be a long time till anybody opens my desk again. I talked to Gladys to some tune I can tell you."

I sighed wearily and filled my pipe.

"Two years!" said Macdonald musingly, "two years! What about all your private books? Anybody might have read your Log Book, or destroyed it even!" and the thought almost made him turn pale.

"And what about it? Nobody will ever read it anyway."

"Eh?" His mouth gaped at this latest heresy.

"What about it?" I continued, "what about the whole damned lot of registers and log books and Form 9 b's? I didn't care a rap who saw the inside of my desk or my log book. As a matter of fact no one saw what was in the log; never a child opened it. Why? Because there was no prohibition. You lock up all the blamed things and put the fear of God on any kid that dares touch your desk.... result! they look on all your belongings as forbidden fruit, and if they can handle your log book when you are safely out of the way you bet your boots that they'll do it. Can't you see that children are really decent kindly creatures with their own philosophy, that is, their own idea of the importance of things? What is important to them is a toy or a dog-fight or a quarrel or a love affair. They don't want to touch stodgy official books. But when you say to them: 'This desk is holy ground' why, every self-respecting kid has but one ambition in life....to poke his nose into your desk and hide your registers."

"Well," he said with a grim smile, "what about those tools in the woodwork room? If children are the saints you make them out to be, how did your boys come to spoil good tools?"

"I admit that I made a mistake," I said cheerfully. "I set out on the assumption that a boy can be trusted with tools. I dropped the belief. Wood was scarce and often I couldn't get enough to keep the boys working. Result!....they took to hammering nails into benches and walls. I see now that much of a boy is destructiveness. I might have known it, for as a boy I tore the inside out of everything to see how it worked. If I had a small class I could have kept them interested in making an article. Yet I remember seeing Tom Watson, the best worker in the school, make a good rabbit-trough; then when he had finished he deliberately chipped a chunk off a plane with a hammer."

"What did you do?"

"I simply chucked him out of woodwork; told him he wasn't beyond the infant-room stage, and gave him lessons with a class two grades below his own."

"Did you chuck him out forcibly?"

"I suppose I did."

"Ah!" Macdonald looked triumphant. "In other words you forgot your principles and punished?"

"Human nature is weak," I said sadly. "If I saw a boy sticking a pen-knife into the tyre of my bicycle I should kick him....kick him hard and then kick him again. There is such a thing as elemental rage in every man—even Christ used a whip in the temple. There are times when you cannot reason: you act impulsively. Principle can't touch this, but it comes in when rage is gone. If I am a magistrate and a boy comes before me charged with destroying a bicycle I personally have no rage against the boy, and if I punish him I'm merely serving out juridical vengeance. If I order him to be birched the jailor has no grudge against the boy. The main point is that the owner of the cycle acts before reasoning, while the magistrate acts after reasoning. And his reason cannot prompt him to behave any better than the injured owner did. The owner is primitive man for the time being: the magistrate stands for reasoning civilisation. In other words reasoning civilisation is no better than the barbarian. That's why I object to juridical punishment."

"Ha! Ha!" he laughed with a sneer, "when it touches yourself you let all your principles slide, just as the most extreme Socialist turns Tory if he happens to get money!"

" Macdonald," I said slowly, " I'm sorry you said that, for it means that you'll reject everything I bring forward. You'll grasp the idea that my views are useless because I tell you I can smite when I am angry, and you'll consequently reject everything I say. You're like the man who cries to a Socialist orator : ' Why don't you sell your watch and divide the proceeds among this crowd ? ' or like the man who tells a member of the no-hat brigade that he should go naked to be consistent. If I were to adopt your tactics I might ask why you don't get the School Boards to provide muzzles for the children on the plea that so much of your energy is taken up in keeping them silent. If you make them salute you I see no logical reason why you shouldn't carry respect to its extreme and force them to kneel down and kiss your boots. If you insist on perfect truthfulness why do you try to hide the truth about the sex of pigeons ? You pretend to be a believer in perfect obedience to authority, and yet I saw you ride a bicycle without a light the other night. I am quite willing to prove that every man is inconsistent. Bernard Shaw would no doubt find some difficulty in explaining how his humanitarian vegetarianism blends with his wearing of leather boots ; for I don't suppose that he has boots made from the hides of animals that died of old age. I gave up shooting and fishing because I saw that both were cruel, yet I will kill a wasp or a rat on occasion. If a tiger got loose down in the village I should at once borrow Frank Thomson's gun, but I should refuse to go tiger-hunting in Bengal. My dear chap, I am as full of inconsistencies as an egg's full of meat. So are you ; so is every man. The best of us are but poor weaklings, for we are each carrying the instincts of millions of our tree- and cave-dwelling ancestors on our backs. My point, however, is that in spite of our weaknesses and animalisms we are predominantly good. I am a caveman once in five years ; I am a reasoning humanitarian the rest of the time. You fasten on my elemental side and refuse to think that there can be any good in my humanitarian side.

"You see, I quite earnestly believe that your respect for law and authority is genuine, almost religious, and the fact that I saw you break the law by riding without a light doesn't make me doubt your respect for law."

"I had had a puncture," he explained.

"Exactly ! Extenuating circumstances. That's what I might plead when I kick the boy who deliberately punctures my machine ....but you would laugh. Why, I think I should start in to lecture *you* on your inconsistencies ! "

I find that the worst man to answer is the fundamental antagonist. I used to be stumped by the anti-socialist cry : Socialism will destroy enterprise !....until I discovered that the best answer to this was : If enterprise has made modern capitalism and industrialism, by all means let it be destroyed. Macdonald will crow over what he considers my failure to be consistent, but it will never once strike him that my frank self-analysis is a thing that he will never practise himself.

Confound Macdonald! He has led me into defending myself; he never defends himself when I attack him; he is far too cocksure to have any doubts about himself.

V.

I am losing Jim Jackson. The battle for his soul is unequal. Macdonald has him all the day, while I only see him at intervals. He came up to the farm to-night, and he was morose in manner. His face is gradually assuming a sneering expression, and his repartee is less spontaneous and more biting. I managed to bring back his better self to-night, but I fear that a day will soon come when he will sink his better self for ever. His father and mother are people after Macdonald's own heart. They are typical village folk, stupid and aggressive. Oh, I loathe the village; it reminds me of George Douglas's Barbie in *The House with the Green Shutters*; it is full of envy and malice and smallness. There are too many "friends" in the village. Mrs. Bell is Mrs. Webster's sister, and they have lived next door to each other for twenty-five years, during which time they have not exchanged a single word. They quarrelled over the division of their mother's goods. When the father dies they will meet and weep together over his coffin; they will be inseparable for a few days....then they will have a row over the old grandfather clock, and they won't speak to each other again.

Peter Jackson is a loud-mouthed fool, and his wife is a warrior. She has the jaw of a prize-fighter. Jim was dissecting the front wheel of his old bicycle the other night at the door, and I stopped to give him a hand with the balls. His mother came to the door.

"Jim!" she rasped, "come away to yer bed!"

"Wait till Aw get thae balls in, mother," he pleaded.

"Come away to yer bed this meenute!" she bawled, "or Aw'll gie ye the biggest thrashin' ye ever got in yer life!" And the poor boy had to leave his cycle and obey.

"What about this?" I said to the mother, and I pointed to the cycle.

"He'd no business takin' it to bits," she shouted and she slammed the door.

Poor lad! Between Macdonald and a mother like that he will live hardly. Each will break his will; each will insist on perfect obedience to arbitrary orders. I am honestly amazed at the small success I had with Jim. He was leaving my free school every night to go home to an atmosphere of anger and brutal stupidity. Now he is leaving his poor home every morning to go to the prison of Macdonald. No wonder the lad is lapsing. In a few years he will be a typical villager; he will stand at the brig of an evening and make caustic comments on the passers-by; he will sneer at everything and everybody. Macdonald is thinking about the answering Jim will do when the inspector comes; I was thinking of the Jim that would one day stand at the brig among his acquaintances. I didn't care a brass farthing what he learned or how much he attended; all I tried to do was to help him to be a fine man, a kindly man, a free man.

I recollect a young teacher who visited my school one morning.

"I should like to see you give a lesson," he said.

"With pleasure," I replied.

"What sort of lesson will it be?" he asked, "geography or history?"

"I don't know," I said, and I turned to my bairns.

"Why do rabbits have white tails?" I asked, and from that we wandered on through protective coloration and heredity to wolves and their fear of fire. We finished up with poetry, but I don't recollect how we got to it. When I had finished he pondered for a little.

"It's all wrong," he said. "That boy in the corner was half asleep; four of these girls weren't really attending to you, and two girls left the room."

"My fault," I said. "I took them to subjects they weren't interested in."

"No," he said decidedly, "it was only your fault in not forcing them to sit up and attend."

"But why should I?" I asked wearily. "Schooling is the beginning of the education we call life, and I want to make it as true to life as possible. In after life no one compels my attention or yours. We can sleep in church and we can sleep at a political meeting. We learn lots of things but we are interested in them. Tell me, what boy in this room answered best ? "

He pointed to a boy of twelve.

" I agree," I said, and I called the boy to my desk.

" Hugh," I said, " kindly tell this gentleman how long you have been at school."

" A week, sir," he replied.

" What school did you come from ? " asked the visitor.

" I never was at any school in my life," he said, " my father lives in a caravan and I never was long enough in a place to go to school."

I explained that Hugh had come voluntarily to me saying : " My father can't read or write, and I can't either, but I want to be able to read about the war and things like that."

" I don't know what to make of it," said my visitor.

" It is a great lesson on education," I said. " He feels that he wants to read....and he comes to school seeking knowledge. And that's what I want to supersede compulsion. If I had my way no boy would learn to read a word until he desired to read ; no boy would do anything unless he wanted to do it."

Then he brought forward the old argument that freedom like that was handicapping them for after life ; they would not face difficulties.

" Hugh was up against a greater difficulty than most boys ever come up against," I said, "and he faced it bravely and confidently. When you are free from authority you have a will of your own ; you know exactly what you want and you set your teeth and get it. You are on your own, you have acquired responsibility. Given a dictating teacher or parent a boy will do the minimum on his own responsibility. Good lord ! if I make all these youngsters sit up and attend strenuously to my speaking I am not training them to face difficulties ; I am simply bullying them, making them a subject race."

"You are training character."

"I would be training children to obey, and the first thing a child should learn is to be a rebel. If a man isn't a rebel by the time he is twenty-five, God help him ! Character simply means a man's nature, and I refuse to change a man's nature by force ; I leave the experiment to the judges and prison warders."

I want to ask every dominie who believes in coercion what he thinks of the results of many years' coercion. Obviously present-day civilisation with its criminal division of humanity into parasites and slaves is all wrong.

"But," a dominie might cry, "can you definitely blame elementary education for that ? "

I answer : "Yes, yes, yes ! "

The manhood of Britain to-day has passed through the schools ; they have been lulled to sleep ; they have never learned to face the awful truth about civilisation. And I blame the coercion of the teachers. Train a boy to obey his teacher and he will naturally obey every dirty politician who has the faculty of rhetoric; he will naturally believe the lies of every dirty newspaper proprietor that is playing his own dirty game.

* * *

I have been spending the week-end with a man I used to dig with in London. He is a great raconteur and we sat late swopping yarns.

"Did you ever hear a good yarn without a point?" he asked.

I said that I hadn't.

"Well, I'll tell you one," he said, and he trotted out the following.

In a small seaside town on the east coast an ancient mariner sits on the beach and yarns to visitors. When the Balkan War was going on my friend asked him if he had ever been to Turkey. My friend assured me that the man had never been farther than Newcastle in his life.

"Man," said the mariner reflectively, "Aw mind when an order cam from the Sultan o' Turkey to the sweetie works here for peppermints. The manager cam doon to me and he says to me, says he: 'Man, Jock, Aw wonder if ye would care to tak oot a cargo o' peppermints to the Sultan o' Turkey?'"

"Aweel, the 'Daisy' was lyin' in the harbour at the time, so Aw says that Aw wud tak them oot.

"Weel, we got them aboard, and awa we

sailed, and a damned rough passage we had too ; man, the Bay o' Biscay was as bad as Aw've ever seen it.

"Weel, we got to Constantinople, and here was the Sultan stannin' on the pier wi' his hands in his breek pooches. He cam aboard and said he wud like to hae a look o' the peppermints. He had a look o' them, and syne he comes up to me and he says : 'Look here, captain, Aw've been haein' a look o' yer crew, and....weel, to tell the truth, Aw dinna like the look o' them ; there's not wan that Aw wud like to trust up at the harem. So, captain, Aw was just thinkin' that Aw wud like ye to carry up thae peppermints yersel....ye're a married man, are ye no ?'

"Aw telt him that Aw was, and Aw started to carry up thae peppermints, and a damned hard job it was, man. They werena the ordinary pepperies, ye ken ; they were great muckle things like curlin' stanes. Weelaweel, Aw got them a' carried up, and Aw was standin' wipin' the sweat frae my face when the Sultan comes anower to me.

"'Aye, captain,' says he, 'that'll be dry wark ?'

"'Yes, sir,' says I, 'gey dry.'

"'Are ye a 'totaller ?' says he.

"'No,' says I, and he taks me by the arm and says : 'C'wa and hae a nip !'

"Weel, we gaed into a pub, and he ordered twa nips....aye, and damned guid whiskey it was too. We had another twa nips, and

Aw'm standin' wi' the Sultan at the door, just aboot to shak hands wi' him, ye ken, and he says to me, says he: 'Captain, wud ye like to see the harem?' and Aw said Aw wud verra much. So he taks haud o' my arm and we goes up the brae. We cam to a great muckle hoose, and he taks a gold key oot o' his pooch, and opens the door.

"Man, Aw never saw the likes o' yon! The floor was a' gold, and the window-blinds was gold. And the wemen! (The mariner conveyed his admiration by a long whistle.)

"Weel, Aw was standin' just inside the door wi' my bonnet in my hand, when a bonny bit lassie comes up to me and threw hersell at my feet and took haud o' my knees and sang: 'Far awa to bonny Scotland!'

"Man, the tears cam into my een as she was singin'.

"Syne the Sultan turns to me.

"'Aye, man,' he says, says he, 'speakin' aboot Scotland: Scotland's the finest country on earth; but there's wan thing Aw canna stand aboot Scotland, and that's yer dawmed green kail. There's no a continental stammick will haud it doon.'"

My friend informed me that he never met an Englishman who appreciated that yarn.

* * *

I begin to wonder whether I am falling in love. Ever since Margaret blushed when she passed me on the brae I have been extremely conscious of her existence. I find that I am beginning to look for her, and I go to the dairy on the flimsiest of pretences. I was there three times this afternoon.

"What do you want this time ?" she asked with a laugh at my third appearance.

"I hardly know," I said slowly, "but I think I wanted to see your bare arms again."

She hastily drew down her sleeves and reddened ; then to cover her confusion she made a show of putting me out forcibly. How I managed to refrain from kissing her tempting lips I don't know. I nearly fell....but it suddenly came to me that a kiss might mean so very much to her and so little to me and.... I resisted the temptation.

She is fast losing her shyness, and she talks to me with growing frankness. She has begun to read much lately, and she devours penny novelettes with avidity. She has a romantic mind, and my realism sometimes shocks her. I happened to meet her in town last Saturday, and I took her to the pictures. She was intensely moved by a romantic film story, and when I explained that the stuff was rank sentimentalism and rhetoric she seemed to be offended.

"You criticise everything," she cried angrily, "don't you believe that there is any good in the world ?"

"You will never be happy," she added seriously, "you criticise too much."

"Surely," I cried, "you don't imagine that I criticise you !"

"I do," she said bitterly. "You criticise yourself and me and everybody. I am always in terror that I make a slip in grammar before you."

"Margaret!" I cried with real sorrow, "I hate to think that I have given you that impression."

I was silent for a long time.

"Kid," I said, "you are quite right. I do criticise everything and everybody, but a better word is analyse; I analyse myself and then I try to analyse you."

"As a boy," I added, "my chief pastime was buying sixpenny watches and tearing their insides out to see how they worked.... but I never saw how they worked."

"Yes," she said, "and that's what you would do if you had a wife; you would tear her to bits just to see how she worked.... and you would never find out how she worked either."

"Perhaps I might," I said with a smile. "When I dissected watches I was inexperienced; nowadays I could take a watch to pieces and find out how it worked. Perhaps I might manage to put my wife together again, Margaret."

"There would be one or two wheels left over," she laughed.

"I should like her better without them," said I.

"Oh!" she cried impatiently, "why can't you be like other men? What's the use of looking into the inside of everything? Look at father; he never bothered about what mother was; he just thought her perfect and look how happy he is!"

"Ah!" I said teasingly, "I understand! You don't want a man to analyse you in case he discovers that you aren't perfect!"

She looked at me frankly.

"I wouldn't like to be thought perfect," she said slowly. "I sometimes think that mother would think far more of father if he saw some faults in her."

"I am quite puzzled," I said; "you grumble because I analyse people and now you grumble because your father doesn't. What do you mean, child?" But she shook her head helplessly.

"Oh, I don't know," she cried, and she sat for a long time in deep thought.

As I sat by her side in the picture-house tea-room I recollected a saying of her's one day last week. I was sitting at the bothy door reading *The New Age*, and at my feet lay *The Nation* and *The New Statesman*. She picked up *The Nation* and glanced at its pages.

"I don't know why you waste your money on papers like that," she said petulantly. "You spend eighteenpence a week on papers, and father only gets *John Bull* and *The People's Journal*."

It suddenly came to me that Margaret was not thinking of the money side of the question at all; what annoyed her was the thought that these papers were a symbol of a world that she did not know. And now I wonder whether woman is not always jealous of a man's work. It is a long time since I read *Antony and Cleopatra,* but I half fancy that Cleopatra was much more jealous of Antony's work than of his wife.

VI.

DICKIE GIBSON cut me dead to-night, and I think that Jim Jackson will one day look the other way when I pass. It is very sad, and I feel to-night that all my work was in vain. I cannot, however, blame Macdonald this time, for Dickie has left the school. I feel somewhat grieved at not being able to lay the fault at Macdonald's door. I should blame myself if I honestly could, but I cannot, for Dickie was a lad who loved the school.

I recollect the morning when we arrived to find a huge stone cast in the middle of the pond.

"It's been some of the big lads," said Dickie.

"But why?" I asked. "Why should they do a dirty trick like that? Would you do a thing like that, Dickie, after you had left the school?"

He thought for a minute.

"Aye," he said slowly, "if Aw was with bigger lads and they did it Aw wud do it too."

I suppose that if I had been a really great man I might have conquered the spirit of the village. I was only a poor pioneer striving to make these bairns happier and better. Dickie's cutting me proves that I was not good enough to lead him away from the atmosphere of the village. I used to forget about the homes; I used to forget that many a child had to listen to harsh criticisms of my methods. I marvel now that they were so nice at school. I wonder whether we could not form a Board to enquire into the upbringing of children. We might call it the Board of Parental Control. It would bring parents before it and examine them. Parents convicted of stupidity would be ordered to hand over their children to a Playyard School, and each child would be so taught that it could take in hand the education of its parents when it was seventeen.

My idea was to produce a generation that would be better than the present one, and I thought that I could successfully fight the environment of home. I failed....Dickie has cut me. The fight was unequal; the village won. After all I had Dickie for two short years, and the village has had him for fourteen. Poor boy, he has much good in him, much innate kindliness. But the village is stupid and spiteful. I am absolutely sure that Dickie cut me because he wanted to follow the public opinion of the village.

Am I magnifying a merely personal matter? Am I merely piqued because I was cut? No one likes to be cut; it isn't a compliment at any time. No, I am not piqued: I am intensely angry, not at poor Dickie, but at the dirty environment that makes him a cad. Lucky is the dominie who teaches bairns from good homes. Last summer when I spent half a day in the King Alfred School in Hampstead I envied John Russell his pupils They were all children of parents who were intellectual enough to seek a free education for their children in a land where the schools are barracks. "If I only had children like these!" I said to him, but a moment later I thought of my little school up north and I said: "No! Mine need freedom more than these."

The King Alfred School is a delightful place. There is co-education....a marvellous thing to an Englishman, but not noticeable by a Scot who has never known any other kind. There is no reward and no punishment, no marks, no competition. A child looks on each task as a work of art, and his one desire is to please himself rather than please his teacher. The tone of the school is excellent; the pupils are frankly critical and delightfully self-possessed. And since parents choose this school voluntarily I presume that the education we call home-life is ideal. How easy it must be for John Russell! If my Dickie had been going home each night to a father and mother who were as eager for truth and freedom as I was, I don't think that Dickie would have cut me to-night.

* * *

Dickie came up for his milk to-night, and I hailed him as he went down the brae.

"Here, Dickie!" I called, "why have you given up looking at me?"

He grew very red, and he stood kicking a stone with his heel.

"I don't want you to touch your cap,

Dickie, but you might at least say Hullo to me in the passing. Some of the big lads who left school before I came look at me impudently, and I know that their look means : 'Bah! I've left the school and I don't care a button for you or any other dominie !' But, Dickie, you know me well ; you never were afraid of me, and I know that you don't think me your enemy. Why in all the earth should you pretend that you do ? "

I held out my hand.

" Dickie," I said, " are you and I to be friends or not ? "

He hesitated for a moment, then he took my hand.

" Friends," he said weakly, and his eyes filled with tears. Then I knew that I had not been mistaken in thinking that there was much good in the boy.

Having made it up with Dickie I set off with a light heart to attend a meeting of the Gifts for Local Soldiers Committee. The chairman was absent and I was invited to take the chair. Bill Watson brought forward a motion that the Committee should get up a concert to provide funds.

" Mr. Watson's proposal is that we arrange a concert," I said. " Is there any seconder ? "

" Aweel," said Andrew Findlay, " Aw think that a concert wud be a verra guid thing. The nichts is beginnin' to draw in, and it wud be best to hae it as soon as possible. The tatties will be on in twa three days."

"The proposal is seconded. Any amendment, gentlemen ? "

"Man," said Peter MacMannish the cobbler, "man, Aw was just lookin' at Lappiedub's tatties the nicht. Man, yon's a dawmed guid crap."

"Them that's in the wast field is better," said Andrew.

"But the best crap o' wheat Aw seen the year," said Dauvid Peters, "was Torrydyke's."

"Any amendment, gentlemen ? "

"Torrydyke ay has graund wheat," said Peter. "D'ye mind yon year—ninety-sax.... or was it ninety-seeven ?—man, they tell me that he made a pile o' siller that year."

"Ninety-sax," growled William Mackenzie the farmer of Brigend, "it was ninety-sax, for Aw mind that my broon coo dee'd that summer."

"Aw mind o' her," nodded Andrew, "grass disease, wasn't it ? "

"Aye," said Mackenzie. "Aw sent to Lochars for the vet but he was awa frae hame. Syne Aw sent a telegram to the Wanners vet, and when he cam he says to me, says he—"

"Any amendment, gentlemen ? " I said.

"Goad, lads," said Andrew sitting up in his chair, "we'll hae to get on wi' the business."

"No amendment," I said. "Are we all agreed about this concert ? " and they grunted their assent.

"And now we'll settle the date," I said briskly.

Peter MacMannish looked over at Mackenzie. " When are ye thinkin' o' killin' that black swine o' yours, John ? " he asked.

Mackenzie growled and shook his head.

" She's no fattenin' up as Aw cud wish to see her, Peter," he replied. There followed an animated discussion of the merits and demerits of various feeding-stuffs. After a two hours' sitting the Committee unanimously appointed me secretary and organiser of the concert. I was given authority to fix a date and arrange a programme.

Attendance at many democratic meetings of this kind has led me to a complete understanding of Parliament.

* * *

It is Sunday to-day. I sat reading in the afternoon and a knock came at my bothy door.

" Come in ! " I shouted, and Annie walked in.

" Me and Janet and Ellen are going for a walk over the hill, and we thocht you might like to come too."

" Certainly ! " I cried, and I threw Shaw's latest volume of plays into the bed.

" Margaret's wi' us too," said Annie as if it were an afterthought.

There was a fight for my arms.

" Annie was first," I said, " and we'll toss up for the other arm."

" Let Margaret get it," said Janet mischievously, and Margaret's nose went almost imperceptibly higher in the air.

"Excellent!" I said, and I took her arm and placed it through mine. Janet and Ellen walked behind, and they sniggered a good deal.

"Just fancy the mester noo!" said Janet, "linkit wi' Maggie! He'll hae to marry her noo, Ellen!" And poor Margaret became very red and began to talk at a great rate.

"G'wa, Jan," I heard Ellen say, "he's far ower auld. Maggie's only twenty next month, and he's—he could be her faither."

"He's no very auld, Ellen; he hasna a mootache yet!"

"Aw wudna like a man wi' a mootache, Jan; Liz Macqueen says that she gave up Jock Wilson cos his mootache was ower kittly."

"Weel, she was tellin' a big lee," sad Janet firmly. "If she loved him she wud ha' telt him to shave it off."

We lay down in the wood at the top of the hill. Annie was in a reminiscent mood.

"D'ye mind the letters we used to write to one another?" she asked.

I pretended that I had forgotten them.

"Do ye no mind? One day when I wasna attendin' to the lesson ye wrote 'Annie Miller is sacked' on a bit paper and gave it to me?"

"Ah, yes, I remember, Annie, now that you come to mention it. But I can't remember your reply."

"Aw took another bit o' paper, and Aw wrote: 'Mr. Neill is sacked for not making me attend.'"

"Yes, you besom, I remember now. I'll

sack you ! " and I rolled her over in the grass.

" There was another letter, Annie," I said, " do you remember it ? " and she said " No ! " so quickly that I knew she did remember it.

I turned to Margaret.

" Annie came to school one day with her hair most beautifully done in ringlets," I explained, " and of course I fell in love with her at once. I wrote her a letter..... 'My Dear Annie, do you think yourself bonny to-day ? ' and the wee besom replied : 'No, I don't ! ' Then I wrote her again..... 'Do you ever tell lies ? ' and to this she answered : 'No, never ! " Then I calmly handed her the *Life of George Washington.*"

" But Aw never read it ! " she cried with a gay laugh.

" I know....and that's why you have never reformed, my dear kid," I said.

" Ellen," said Janet, " d'ye mind that day when you and me got up and walked oot o' the room ? "

" What day was that ? " I asked ; " you two went out of the room so often that I gave up trying to see you."

" It was the day when a man cam to the schule and stood in the room when ye was teachin' us. There was a new boy, the caravan boy that had never been to schule in his life, and ye said that he was better than any o' us."

" So Jan and me took the tig," said Ellen, " and we went oot and sat on the dike."

Janet hee-heed.

"D'ye mind what we said, Ellen? We said we werena to go back to the schule; we were to go up to Rinsley schule to Mester Lawson."

"Aye," said Ellen, "and we said we wudna gie ye another sweetie....no, never!"

"And I suppose you gave me sweeties next day?" I suggested.

"We gave ye a whole ha'penny worth o' chocolate caramels," said Janet. Her head rested on my knee and she smiled up in my face. "Ye were far ower easy wi' us," she said seriously, "we never did half the lessons ye gave us to do."

"I know, Jan, but I didn't particularly want you to do lessons; all I wanted was that you should be Janet Brown and no one else. I wanted you to be a good kind lassie....and of course, as you know, I failed." And she pulled my nose at this.

"I didn't like the school when I was there," said Margaret; "I never was so glad in my life as when I was fourteen."

"Poor Margaret," I said, "your schooling should be the pleasantest memory of your life. What you learned from books doesn't matter at all; what matters is what you were. And it seems that memory will bring to you a picture of an unhappy Margaret longing to leave school. What a tragedy!"

"Is being happy the best thing in life?" asked Margaret.

"Not the best," I answered; "the best

thing in life is making other people happy.... and that's what the books mean by 'service.'"

* * *

Margaret came over to my bothy to-night to ask if I would help Nancy with her home lessons.

"She's crying like anything," said Margaret.

I went over to the farmhouse. Nancy sat at the kitchen table with her books spread out before her. She was wiping her eyes and looked like beginning to weep again.

"It's her pottery," explained Frank, "she canna get it up at all."

Macdonald had ordered the class to learn the first six verses of Gray's *Elegy*, and threatened dire penalties if each scholar wasn't word perfect.

"I'm afraid I can't help you much, Nancy," I said. "You'll just have to set your teeth and get it up. Don't repeat it line by line; read the six verses over, then read them again, then again. Read them twenty times, then shut the book and imagine the page is before you, and see how much of the stuff you can say." I used to find this method very effectual when I got up long recitations in my younger days.

Macdonald gives his higher classes long poems. They have learned up pages of *Marmion* and pages of *The Lady of the Lake*; and now he is giving them the long and difficult *Elegy*. I must ask him some day what his idea is. I made learning poetry optional when I was in the school. I eschewed all long poems, and I never asked a child to stand up and "say" a piece. My view was that school poetry should be school folk-song; I used to write short pieces on the board and the classes recited them in unison. I gave no hint of expression, for expression should always be a natural thing. have been timid of expression ever since the day I heard, or rather saw, a youth recite *The Dream of Eugene Aram.* When he came to the climax . . . . "And lo! the faithless stream was dry!" I suddenly discovered that I was dry too, and I did not wait until Eugene was led away with "gyves upon his wrists." I once saw Sir Henry Irving in *The Bells.* I was a schoolboy at the time and I straightway spent all my pocket money on books dealing with elocution; *I* also would tear my hair before the footlights! Looking back now I wonder why Irving bothered with stuff of that sort; why his sense of humour allowed him to grope about the stage for the axe to kill the Polish Jew I don't understand. All that melodramatic romantic business is simply theatrical gush. It appeals to the classes that devour the *Police News.*

Expression when taught is gush. When I gave my bairns a bit of *The Ancient Mariner* the whole crowd brightened up and shouted when they came to the verse:—

I bit my arm, I sucked the blood
And cried: "A sail! A sail!"

They understood that part, but they put no special expression into the stanza :—

All in a hot and copper sky,
The bloody sun at noon
Right up above the mast did stand,
No bigger than the moon.

The boys used to emphasise the adjective in the second line, but that was perhaps natural in a community where strong language is the prerogative of grown-ups. I suppose that a teacher of expression would have pointed out that the right arm must be raised gracefully at the third line, and the voice lowered awfully to show the marvellous significance of the fact that the crudoric sun was no bigger than the moon.

All I tried to give my bairns was an appreciation of rhythm. They loved the trochaic rhythm of a poem, *Marsh Marigolds,* by G. F. Bradby, that I discovered in a school anthology :—

Slaty skies and a whistling wind and a grim grey land,
April here with a sullen mind and a frozen hand,
Hardly a bird with the heart to sing, or a bud that dares to pry,
Only the plovers hovering,
On the lonely marsh, with a heavy wing
And a sad slow cry.

And it used to make me joyful to hear them gallop through Stevenson's delightful *My Ship and I* :—

Oh ! it's I that am the captain of a tidy little ship,
Of a ship that goes a-sailing on the pond,
And my ship it keeps a-turning all around and all about,
But when I'm a little older I shall find the secret out
How to send my vessel sailing on beyond !

I never gave them a poem that needed any explanation. I picture Macdonald painfully explaining the *Elegy*. . . . . " Yes, children, the phrase ' incense-breathing morn ' means. . . . ." I'm gravelled ; I haven't the faintest notion of what the phrase means. Gray annoys me ; he is far too perfect for me. I fancy that he rewrote each line about a score of times in his mania for the correct word. Gray is Milton with a dictionary.

I once read that Stevenson studied the dictionary often, used to spend a rainy day reading the thing, and his prose does give me the impression that he cared more for how he said a thing than for the thing itself. I think George Douglas a greater writer ; indeed I should call him the greatest novelist Scotland has produced. His style is inevitable ; his whole attention seems to be riveted on the matter of his story, and his arresting phrases seem to come from him naturally and thoughtlessly. When you read of Gourlay's agony in Barbie market on the day that his son's disgrace is known to everyone, you see the great hulk of a man, you hear his great breaths. . . . you are one of the villagers who peep at him fearfully. Every word is inevitable ; the picture is perfect. I should be surprised if anyone told me that Douglas altered a single word after he had written it.

When I want to feel humble I take up *The House with the Green Shutters.* I have read it a score of times, and I hope to read it a score of times again.

VII.

MARGARET looked up from the novelette she was reading.

"Are the aristocracy really like what they are in this story?" she asked.

"I don't know," I replied; "I'm not acquainted with the aristocracy, but I should say that they aren't like the aristocracy in that yarn. You see, Margaret, I happen to know some of the men who write these novelettes. Murray is a don at them; he'll turn one out between breakfast and dinner. To the best of my knowledge Murray has never dined in any restaurant more expensive than an A.B.C. shop . . . . and his characters always dine at the Ritz."

"But have you never met anybody with a title?"

"I once collided with a man at the British Museum door," I said. "He was a Scot. . . . . I know that because neither of us apologised; we merely jerked out 'Oh!' I am almost sure that the man was Sir J. M. Barrie. And I shook hands with two dukes and three lords at a university dinner, but they possibly have for gotten the incident."

No. I don't know the aristocracy well.

I met a titled lady last summer. I was staying at a country house near London, and this lady had the neighbouring house. She came over on the Sunday afternoon. My host informed me that she had lost two sons in the war. After she had gone I was asked what I thought of the English aristocracy, and I gave my opinion in these words :—" To the English aristocracy property alone is sacred. That woman has given the lives of her two sons willingly for her country, but if she were asked to give half an acre of her estate to help pay for the war she would go mad with rage and disgust."

When I heard that lady grumble about the wickedness of the munition-workers. . . . . " And, my dear, women in shawls are buying pianos and seal-skin jackets ! " . . . . I realised how hopeless was the cry of *The New Age* for the Conscription of Wealth. The powerful classes will resist Conscription of Wealth as strenuously as they resist the Germans. Yet the Conscription of Men was in very many cases a Conscription of Wealth. One had only to read the Tribunal cases to discover that thousands of men had to deliver up all their wealth when they joined the army. There was Wrangler the actor ; his property was his talent to portray character, and from that he drew his income. His property was conscripted along with him. It was fitting that he should give up all when the State required him to give it up. But the State requires all the wealth of the moneyed classes, and because economic power controls political power the State will not conscript the wealth of its real governors.

I see now that our education is founded on the unpleasant fact that property is more sacred than life. Teachers are encouraged to make their pupils patriotic ; every boy must be brought up in the belief that it is great and glorious to die for one's country. A real patriotism would lead a boy to realise that it is a great and glorious thing to live for one's country ; the true patriot would teach his lads to make their country a great and glorious country to die for. Somehow our schools for the most part ignore this branch of patriotism ; it does not seem so important as the flag-waving and standing to attention that passes for patriotism.

Macdonald is decorating the walls of the school with coloured prints of our warships. " To make them realise how much the navy means to them," he explained to me as I looked at them.

" Excellent ! " I said. " The navy deserves all the respect we can give it. But, Macdonald, in your position I should give a further lesson on patriotism ; I should point out to these bairns that while the glorious navy is defending our shores from a foreign enemy the enemy within is plundering the nation. I should tell them that under the protection of the navy the profiteers are raising the prices of necessaries hand over fist All the patriotic flag-waving in the world won't help these bairns to understand that the patriotism of the masses is being exploited by the self-seeking of the dirty few."

Patriotism! We have popular weeklies that endeavour to make the people patriotic They lash themselves into a fury over momentous questions: The Ich Dien on the crest of the Prince of Wales Must Go; The Duke of So-and-So must have his Garter taken from him; Who was the Spy who sent Kitchener to his doom?

The only way to encourage children to be patriotic is to tell them the sober truth about the important things of life. The invention of the word "shirker" managed to effect that the most timid of men should fight for his country; public opinion will always look after the patriotism necessary for war. But my complaint is that public opinion will not look after the patriotism necessary for peace. If we were all true patriots there would be no slums, no exploitation, no profiteering. And the "patriotic" lesson in school should deal with economics instead of jingo ballads of victories won.

* * *

I cycled twelve miles to-night, and I raised a comfortable thirst. When I came to the village I dropped into the Glamis Arms and had a bottle of lager. As I came out I ran into Macdonald.

"Lucky fellow!" he laughed, "you have no position to maintain now and you can afford to quench a thirst!"

"Position be blowed!" I said, "I drink when I'm dry, and I always did. When I was dominie here I dropped in here more than once in the hot weather."

"And they sacked you!"

"Not because of that," I said, "but in spite of it. Believe me it was the one thing that made one or two villagers more amiable to me."

The Scot's attitude to the public-house is entertaining. If you have any position to keep up you must not enter a public-house.... you must get it in by the dozen. When I first went to London and entered a saloon bar in the Strand I was amazed to find women sitting with their husbands; I was also amazed to find no drunks about. In a Scots bar the most apparent phenomenon is wrangling. I never heard an argument in a London bar, and I have been in many: I never saw a drunk man in London, and I was there for two years.

The public-house in Scotland is not respectable: in England it is. Why this should be I can only guess. The Scot may be a bigger hypocrite than the Englishman; what is more probable is that he may be a harder drinker. In Scotland entering a public-house is synonomous with getting drunk. Yet there are what you might call alcoholic gradations. A respectable farmer may enter a bar without comment, but a teacher must not enter it. He is the guide of the young, and he must be an example. Teachers seldom enter village bars....and yet Scotland is notorious for drinking. If the teachers determined to become regular bar customers I conclude that Scotland would drink herself off the face of the map.

I have a theory that the Calvinistic attitude to the public-house is the chief cause of Scots drunkenness. When a Scot enters a bar he knows that he won't have the courage to be seen coming out again....and he very naturally says to himself: "Ach, to hell! Aw'll hae another just to fortify mysel' for gaein' oot!" The public-house isn't a public-house at all; it is the most private of houses. Peter Soutar the leading elder in the kirk here always carries a bundle of church magazines in his hand when he enters the Glamis Arms; when the date is past magazine time he enters by the back door. Jeemes Walker the leading Free Kirk elder goes in to read the gospel to old Mrs. Melville the invalid mother of the landlord, and the village is uncharitable enough to remark in his hearing that he really goes to interview his brother "Johnny." I think that it was the doctor who originated that joke.

A public-house is no place for a public man in Scotland.

* * *

The opening of the coal mines has brought to the neighbourhood a new type of person. He is usually an engineer who has spent a good few years abroad, and he is usually married....very much married. His wife is always a grade above the wife of the engineer next door, and the men appear to spend most of their leisure time in mending quarrels that their wives began. Most of the men are amiable fellows with the minimum of ideas and the maximum of knowledge of fishing and card-playing. They have a certain dignity, and they instantly freeze if you casually ask where such-and-such a light railway is to run.

The wives seem to have no interest other than in servants and their manifold wickedness and cussedness. They hold their noses high when they pass through the village, and they bully the local shopkeepers.

When I was a dominie these women patronised me delightfully, but now that I am a cattleman they are quite frank with me. I puzzled over this for some time, and the solution came to me suddenly. They are all English women, and in the English village the dominie is on very much the same social level as the vicar's gardener.

Mrs. Martinlake likes to chat to me now. She is a middle-aged lady who loves to reminisce about duchesses she has known. She once complained to me because the boys did not touch their caps to her, and on my suggesting that they hadn't been introduced she became very indignant. She called to me this morning as she passed the field I was working in.

"Ah! Good morning! I've been looking for you for a long time. I wanted to tell you how much the children have improved; every village boy touches his cap to me now!" and she laughed gaily.

"Good!" I cried. "If this sort of thing

goes on they will be touching their caps to their mothers next."

"And why not?" she demanded with a slight touch of aggression.

I shrugged my shoulders.

"As you say—why not? I think that you ought to persuade your little boy to touch his cap to all the mothers in the village. I notice that he doesn't do it. You take my tip and send him down to Macdonald's school; he'll soon pick it up."

She went off without a word, and I realised that I had been distinctly rude to her. Somehow I felt glad that I had been rude to her.

I told Margaret about the incident afterwards.

"I hate manners, Margaret," I said.

"But," she said wonderingly, "you are very mannerly."

"To you I believe I am, Margaret," I laughed. "But that is because you don't look for manners. Mrs. Martinlake is eternally looking for manners. and to her manners mean respect, deference, boot-licking. She doesn't want the boys to doff their caps to her because she is a woman; no, she wants them to recognise the fact that she is Mrs. Martinlake, self-alleged friend of duchesses. She doesn't care a tupenny damn for the boys and their lives; she is thinking of Mrs. Martinlake all the time. She once talked to me of the respect due to motherhood....and you know that she sacked Liz Smith when she discovered that Liz had had an illegitimate child.

"Women of that type get my back up," I went on. "They are stupid, low-minded, arrogant. They are poor imitations of the Parisian ladies who curled their lips contemptuously at the plebeian rabble that led them to the guillotine. The Parisian ladies had a fine pride of race to redeem their arrogance, but these women have nothing but pride of class. Margaret, if a teacher failed to teach a boy anything except the truth that deference is one of the Seven Deadly Virtues, I should say that that teacher was a successful teacher."

* * *

The concert was a success to-night. The singing was good, but the speech of the chairman, Peter MacMannish, was great.

"Ladies and Gentlemen,

"We're a' verra weel pleased to see sik a big turn-oot the nicht. Aw need hardly say onything aboot the object o' this concert, but it's to get a puckle bawbees to send oot a clean pair o' socks and maybe a clean sark to oor local sojers oot in France.—(Cheers).

"Weel, ladies and gentlemen, Aw've made mony a speech on this platform in the days when Aw fought for the Conservative Candidate, Mester Fletcher (cheers, and a voice: 'Gie it a drink, cobbler!')"

The light of battle leapt to Peter's eyes.

"Aw ken that wheezin' Radical's voice!" he cried, "and Aw wud just like to tell that voice that there's no room for Radicals in this war. What was the attitude o' that man's party to Protection? When Mester Chamberlain stood up in Glesga Toon Hall what did he say?" I gently touched Peter on the arm and reminded him of the concert and its object.

"Ladies and Gentlemen, we'll no touch on thae topics here, for ye cam here for another object than to listen to me (several voices: 'Hear, hear!') Afore we begin to the programme Aw wud just like to say that we have to thank oor late dominie for gettin' up this concert. Some o' us had no love for him as a dominie, but Aw say let bygones be bygones. We a' ken that he's no a teacher (laughter), but he's a clever fellow for a' that, and we'll maybe see him in Parliament yet. That hoose has muckle need o' new blood. When Aw think o' Lloyd George and that man Churchhill; when Aw see the condeetion they've brocht the country till; when Aw think o' the slack wye they've let the Trade Unions rob the country; when Aw see—" I coughed here, and Peter drew up.

"Weel, Ladies and Gentlemen, this is no a poleetical meetin', and Aw've muckle pleasure in callin' upon Miss Jean Black for a sang," he peered at his programme, "a sang enteeled: A Moonlight Sonnita." Miss Jean Black forthwith sat down at the piano.

During the interval Peter digged me in the ribs.

"What d'ye think o' my suggestion, dominie, eh?"

"What suggestion?"

"Aboot standin' for Parliament. It's a payin' game noo-a-days....fower hunner a year and yer tea when the hoose is sittin'. Goad, dominie, think o' sittin' takkin' yer tea wi' Airthur Balfoor!" and he sighed wistfully as a child sighs when it dreams of fairyland and wakes to reality.

"Aye," he said after a long pause, "Aw wance shook hands wi' Joe Chamberlain. His lawware says to him: 'This is Mester MacMannish, wan o' yer chief supporters in the county,' and Aw just taks my hand oot o' my breek pooch. 'Verra pleased to meet ye,' says Aw....'and hoo is yer missis and the bairns?' Man, he lauched at that. Goad he lauched!"

Peter forgot the crowded hall; he stared at the ceiling unseeingly, and he lived over again the greatest day of his life. It was fitting that a Scot should have originated the title "Heroes and Hero-Worship."

VIII.

MACDONALD came up to-night. I hadn't seen him for weeks.

"I am making out a scheme of work for the Evening School," he said. "What line did you take?"

"My scheme was simple," I replied, "and luckily I had an inspector who appreciated what I was trying to do. I made the history lessons lessons in elementary political economy. Arithmetic and Algebra were the usual thing."

"What about Reading and Grammar?" he asked.

"We read David Copperfield, and I meant to read a play of Shakespeare and Ibsen's *An Enemy of the People,* but I never found time for them. The class became a sort of debating society. I gave out subjects. We discussed Votes for Women, Should Women Smoke? Is Money the Reward of Ability? I told them about the theory of evolution; I began to trace the history of mankind, or rather tried to make out a likely history, but at the end of the session we hadn't arrived at the dawn of written history."

"Did you find any pupil improving?"

"Macdonald, you are a demon for tangible results. The only tangible result of my heresies I can think of is the fact that Margaret Thomson smokes my cigarettes now."

" Have a look at this scheme," he said, and he handed me a lengthy manuscript. The arithmetic was a detailed list of utilitarian sums....how to measure ricks of hay and fields, how to calculate the price of papering walls and so on. My own attitude to utilitarian sums is this: if you know the principles of pure mathematics all these things come easily to you, hence teach pure mathematics and let the utilitarian part take care of itself.

His English part dealt minutely with grammar; he was to give much parsing and analysis; compound sentences were to be broken up into their component parts.

In History he was to do the Stuart Period, and Geography was to cover the whole world " special attention being paid to the agricultural produce of the British Colonies."

" It is a ' correct ' scheme," I said.

" Give me your candid opinion of it."

" Well, Macdonald, your ways are not my ways, and candidly I wouldn't teach quite a lot of the stuff you mean to teach. Grammar for instance. What's the use of knowing the parts of a sentence? I don't suppose that Shakespeare knew them. If education is meant to make people think, your Evening School would be much better employed reading books. If you read a lot your grammar takes care of itself.

" The Stuart Period is all right if you don't emphasise the importance of battles and plots. I haven't the faintest notion whether Cromwell won the battle of Marston Moor or lost it, but I have a fair idea of what the constitutional battle meant to England. The political war was over before the first shot was fired ; the Civil War was a religious war. If I were you I should take the broad principles of the whole thing and skip all the battles and plots and executions.

"As for the British Colonies and their agriculture you can turn emigration officer if you fancy the job. The idea is good enough. My own personal predilection in geography is the problem of race. I used to tell my pupils about the different 'niggers' I met at the university, and of the detestable attitude of the colonials to these men."

Macdonald shook his head.

"No, no," he said, "a black man isn't as good as a white man."

So we went off at a tangent. I told him that personally I had not enough knowledge of black men to lay down the law about them, but I handed him a very suggestive article in this week's *New Age* on the subject. The writer's theory is that in India black men are ostracised merely because they are a subject race, and he points out that in Germany and France the coloured man is treated as an equal. When I was told by a friend that the natives of India despised Keir Hardie because he carried his own bag off the vessel when he arrived in India I realised that the colour question was too complicated for me to settle

I have a sneaking suspicion that the coloured man is maligned ; the average Anglo-Indian is so stupid in his attitude to most things that I can scarcely suspect him of being wise in his attitude to the native. I regret very much that I had not the moral courage to chum up with the coloured man at the university: prejudices leave one after one has left the university.

I wish I knew what Modern Geography means. A few years ago the geography lesson was placed in the hands of the science teacher in our higher grade schools, and the educational papers commenced to talk of isotherms. I have never discovered what an isotherm is; I came very near to discovering once ; I asked Dickson, a man of science, what they were, but a girl smiled to me before he got well into the subject (we were in a café), and I never discovered what an isotherm was.

The old-fashioned geography wasn't a bad thing in its way. You got to know where places were, and your newspaper became intelligible. It is true that you wasted many an hour memorising stuff that was of no great importance. I recollect learning that Hexham was noted for hats and gloves. I stopped there once when I was motor-cycling. I asked an aged inhabitant what his town was noted for.

"When I coom to think of it," he said as he scratched his head, "the North Eastern Railway passes through it."

But the old geography familiarised you with

the look of the map. Where it failed was in the appeal to the imagination. You learned a lot of facts but you never asked why. I should imagine that the new geography may deal with reasons why; it may enquire into racial differences; it may ask why London is situated where it is, why New York grew so big.

For weeks before I left my school my geography lesson consisted of readings from Foster Fraser's *The Real Siberia.* I began to feel at home in Siberia, and what had been a large ugly chunk of pink on the map of Asia became a real place. There is a scarcity of books of this kind. Every school should have a book on every country written in Fraser's manner. I don't say that Fraser sees very deeply into the life of the Russian. I am quite content with his delightful stories of wayside stations and dirty peasants. He paints the place as it is; if I want to know what the philosophy of the Russian is I can take up Tolstoy or Dostoeivsky or Maxim Gorki.

To return to isotherms....well, no, I think I'll get to bed instead.

* * *

I was down in the village this morning. A motor-car came up, and two ladies and a gentleman alighted.

"Where is the village school?" asked the gentleman, and I pointed to the ugly pile.

"We are Americans," he drawled in unrequired explanation, "and we've come all the way from Leeds to see the great experiment."

"Yes," said one of the ladies—the pretty one—"we are dying to see the paradise of *A Dominie's Log*. Is it so very wonderful?"

"Marvellous!" I cried. "But the Dominie is a funny sort of chap, sensitive and very shy. You mustn't give him a hint that you know anything about his book; simply say that you want to see a Scots school at work."

They thanked me, and set off for the school. I loafed about until they returned.

"Well?" I said, "what do you think of it?"

"The fellow is an impostor!" said the man indignantly. "I expected to see them all out of doors chewing gum and sweets, and—"

"There wasn't a chin moving in the whole crowd!" cried the young lady.

"The book was a parcel of lies," said the other lady, "and when I next want a dollar's worth of fiction I reckon I'll plump for Hall Caine or Robert Chambers. The man wouldn't speak."

"I mentioned Dewey's *Schools of To-Day*," said the man, "and he stared at me as if I were talking Greek."

I directed them to the village inn for lunch, and I walked up the brae chuckling.

I had had my dinner, and was having a smoke in the bothy when I heard the American's voice: "We want to see the dominie!" Margaret came to the door, and I walked out into the yard. The trio gasped when they saw me;

then the man placed his arms akimbo and looked at me.

"Well I'm damned!" he said with vehemence.

"Not so bad as that," I said with a grin, "*had* is a better word." Then they all began to talk at once.

He explained that he was a lawyer from Baltimore: I told him that his concern about the absence of chewing-gum had led me to conjecture that he manufactured that substance. This seemed to tickle him and he made a note of it.

"Be careful!" smiled the pretty lady—his daughter—, "he'll hand over his notes to the newspaper man when he goes back home."

The lawyer knew something about education, and he told me many things about the new education of America; he was one of the directors of a modern school in his own county.

"Come over to the States," he said with eagerness; "we want men of your ideas over there. I reckon that you and the new schools there don't differ at all."

I gave him my impressions of the American schools described by Dewey in his book.

"It seems to me," I said, "that these schools over-emphasise the 'learn by doing' business. Almost every modern reformer in education talks of 'child processes'; the kindergarten idea is carried all the way. Children are encouraged to shape things with their hands."

"Sure," he said, "but that's only a preliminary to shaping things with their heads."

"I'm not so sure that the one naturally leads to the other," I went on. "Learning by doing is a fine thing, but when little Willie asks why rabbits have white tails the learning by doing business breaks down. In America you have workshops where boys mould metal; you have school farms. But I hold that a child can have all that for years and yet be badly educated."

He looked amazed.

"But I thought that was your line," he said with puzzled expression, "Montessori, and all that kind of thing!"

"I don't know what Montessorianism is," I said; "I have forgotten everything I ever read about Froebel and Pestalozzi. All I know is that reformers want the child to follow its own processes—whatever that phrase may mean. I heartily agree with them when they say that the child should choose its own line, and should discover knowledge for itself. But my point is that a boy may act every incident in history, for instance, and never realise what history means. I can't see the educational value of children acting the incident of Alfred and the burnt cakes."

"Ah! but isn't self-expression a great thing?"

"It is," I answered, "but the actor doesn't

express himself. Irving expressed himself.... and the result was that Shakespeare was Irvingised. A school pageant of the accession of Henry IV. may be a fine spectacle, but it is emphasising all the stuff that doesn't matter a damn in history."

"But," he protested, "it is the stuff that matters to children. You forget that a child isn't a little adult."

"This brings us to the vexed question of the coming in of the adult," I said. "You and I agree that the adult should interfere as little as possible; but the adult will come in in spite of us. Leave children to themselves and they express their personalities the live-long day. Every game is an expression of individuality. The adult steps in and says 'We must guide these children,' and he takes their attention from playing houses to playing scenes from history. And I want to know the educational value of it all."

"It is like travel," he said. "When you travel places become real to you, and when you travel back into mediæval times the whole thing becomes real to you."

"I see your point," I said, "and in a manner I agree with you. But why select pageants? You will agree with me when I say that the condition of the people in feudal times is of far greater importance than the display of a Henry."

"Certainly, I do."

"And the things of real importance in history

are incapable of being dramatised. You can make a modern school act the Signing of Magna Charta, but the children won't understand the meaning of Magna Charta any the better. You can't dramatise the Enclosure of the Public Lands in Tudor Times; you can't dramatise the John Ball insurrection; all the acting in the world won't help you to understand the Puritan Revolution."

"You are thinking of children as little adults," he said.

"But they *are* little adults! Every game is an imitation of adult processes; the ring games down at the school there nearly all deal with love and matrimony; the girls make houses and take in lodgers. And if you persuade them to act the part of King Alfred you are encouraging them to be little adults. They are children when they cry and run and jump; whenever they reason they reason as adults. They are very often in the company of adults ....and that's one of the reasons why you cannot trust what are called child processes. Child processes naturally induce a child to make a row....and daddy won't put up with a row. The child cannot escape being a little adult. It's all very well for a Rousseau to deal abstractly with child psychology. I am not Rousseau, and I tackle the lesser problem of adult psychology. The problem before me is —or rather was—painfully concrete. I set out to counteract the adult influence of the home. I saw Peter MacMannish shy divots at the Radical candidate because Peter's father was a Tory; I saw Lizzie Peters put out her tongue at the local Christabel Pankhurst because Lizzie's mother had said forcibly that woman's place is the home."

"I see," said the American thoughtfully, "you used your adult personality on the ground that it was the lesser of two evils? But don't you think that that was a mistake? Was the freedom of behaviour and criticism you allowed them not the best antidote to home prejudices?"

"If the children had not been going to homes at night I should have trusted to freedom alone. As it was the poor bairns were between two fires. I gave them freedom....and their parents cursed me. One woman sent a verbal message to me to the effect that I was an idiot; one bright little lassie came to me one day with the words of the woman next door, 'It's just waste o' time attendin' that schule.' Do you imagine that all the child processes in the world could save a child from an environment like that?"

When the American departed he held out his hand.

"I came to see a reformer of child education," he said with a smile, "and I discover that you aren't a reformer of child education at all; your job in life is to run a school for parents."

IX.

THE school is closed for the Autumn Holiday....commonly called the Tattie Holiday here. Macdonald has gone off to Glasgow. The bigger boys and girls are gathering potatoes in the fields here, and I am driving the tattie digger. At dinnertime they come to the bothy and eat their bread; Mrs. Thomson gives them soup and coffee in the kitchen, but they bring their bowls over to my bothy. Much of the fun has gone out of them; the constant bending makes them very tired, and they drop off to sleep very easily. Janet and Ellen lay in my bed all dinnertime yesterday and slept. Occasionally a boy will sing a song that always crops up at tattie time:—

O! I'm blyde I'm at the tatties,
I'm blyde I'm at the tatties,
I'm blyde I'm at the tatties,
Wi' auchteenpence a day!

Blyde means glad, but there is but little gladness in the band that trudges up the rigs in the morning twilight.

Jim Jackson is sometimes in good form. He has taken on the swaying gait of the young ploughman; he hasn't got the pockets that are situated in the front of the trousers, but he shoves his hands down the inside instead, and he says: "Ma Goad, you lads, hurry up afore the Boss comes roond wi' the digger again!" They call me the Boss now; Macdonald is the Mester. They seldom mention the school at all; if they do it is to recall some incident that happened in my time. But already the memory of our happy days is becoming hazy; life is too interesting for children to recall memories.

To-day Jim sat and gazed absently at my bothy fire.

"Now, bairns," I said, "Jim's got an idea. Cough it up, Jim."

"Aw was thinkin' o' the tattie-digger," he said slowly; "it seems an awfu' roondaboot wye o' liftin' tatties. Could we no invent a digger that wud hoal the tatties and gaither them at the same time?"

"Laziness is the mother of invention," I remarked.

"But....cud a machine no be invented?" he asked.

"You could have a sort o' basket," he went on, "that ceppit a' the tatties as they were thrown oot."

"Dinna haver!" interjected Janet, "it wud cep a' the stanes at the same time."

"If spuds were made o' steel," said Jim, "ye cud draw them oot wi' a magnet."

"And if the sky fell you would catch larks," said I.

"If the sea dried up!" said Ellen, and Jim instantly forgot his patent tattie-digger.

"Crivens! What a fine essay that wud

mak! Why did ye no gie us that for an essay?"

"Take it on now," I suggested, but he ignored the suggestion.

"The Mester gae me a book to read in the holidays," he said irrelevantly, "and it's called *Self Help*; it's a' aboot laddies that got on weel."

I ceased to listen to their talk. I thought of Samuel Smiles and his Victorian ideals. The book is iniquitous nowadays; it is the Bible of the individualist. Get on! I'm afraid that Smiles' idea of getting on is still popular in Scotland; the country might well adapt the popular song "Get Out and Get Under," changing it to "Get On or Get Under" and making it the national anthem of Scotland.

I once compared *Self Help* with Lorimer's *Letters of a Self-made Merchant to his Son*, and was struck by the similarity of the ideals. Lorimer's book is an Americanised *Self-help*. Smiles is slightly better. With him getting on means more than the amassing of wealth; it means gaining position, which being interpreted means returning to your native village with prosperous rotundity and a gold chain.

Lorimer has no special interest in gold chains and symbols of wealth; he doesn't care a button for position. He preaches efficiency and power; to him the greatest achievement in life appears to be the packing of the maximum of pig into the minimum of tin in the minimum of time. A business friend of mine tells me that it is the greatest book America has produced. Evidently it didn't require the Lusitania incident to prove that America is a long-suffering nation.

Jim was back to the subject of inventions again.

"Aw read in a paper that there's a fortune waitin' for the man that can invent something to haud breeks up instead o' gallis's."

"Ye cud hae buttons on the foot o' yer sark," suggested Janet.

"Aye," said Jim scornfully, "and if a button cam off what wud haud up yer breeks?"

"Public opinion....in this righteous village," I murmured; "it's almost strong enough to hold up any pair of breeks, Jim," but no one understood me.

"Ye cud hae sticks up the side," said Ellen, "and yer breeks wud stand up like fisherman's boots."

"And if ye wanted to bend?" demanded Jim.

Ellen shoved out her tongue at him.

"Ye never said onything aboot bendin', and ye dinna need to bend onywye."

"What aboot when ye're gaitherin' tatties?" crowed Jim.

Ellen tossed her head.

"Aw wasna thinkin' o' the sort o' man that gaithers tatties; Aw was thinkin' o' gentlemen's breeks....the kind o' breeks ye'll never hae, Jim Jackson."

Jim sighed and gave me a look which I took to mean: "Women are impossible when it comes to arguing." He thought for a time; then he looked up with twinkling eyes.

"Aw've got it!"

"Well?"

"Do away wi' breeks a'-the-gether, and wear kilts."

"And what will ye do wi' yer hands?" put in Fred Findlay; "there's nae pooches in a kilt."

"Goad, Fred," said Jim, "Aw never thocht o' that; we'll just hae to wrastle on wi' oor breeks and oor gallis's."

"Ye cud wear a belt," suggested Janet.

"And gie mysel' pewmonia! No likely!"

"It's no pewmonia that ye get wearin' a belt," said Janet, "it's a pendicitis."

"G'wa, lassie, what do you ken aboot breeks onywye?"

"Aw ken mair than you do, Jim Jackson. For wan thing Aw ken that it's no a subject ye shud speak aboot afore lassies. Come on, Ellen, we'll go ootside; the conversation's no proper."

Jim glanced at me doubtfully.

"It was her that said that breeks cud be buttoned to yer sark!" he exclaimed. He jumped up and hastened to the door.

"Janet Broon," I heard him cry, "dinna you speak aboot sarks to me again; sarks is no a proper subject o' conversation for young laddies."

I think it was Fletcher of Saltoun who said that he didn't care who made a nation's laws if he made its ballads. To-night I feel that I don't care if Macdonald hears the bairns' opinion of Charles I. so long as I hear their opinion of sarks and breeks.

* * *

A Trade Union official delivered a lecture on Labour Aspirations in the village hall to-night. I was sadly disappointed. The man tried to make out that the interests of Capital and Labour are similar.

"We are not out to abolish the capitalist," he said; "all we want is a say in the workshop management. We have nothing to do with the way the employer conducts his business; we want to mind our own business. We want to see men paid a living wage; we want to see....." I ceased to be interested in what the man wanted to see. I fancy that he requires to see a devil of a lot before he is capable of guiding the Trade Unions.

Why are these so-called leaders so poor in intellect? Why are they so fearful of alienating the good opinion of the capitalist? If the Trade Union has any goal at all it surely is the abolition of the capitalist. The leaders crawl to the feet of capital and cry: "For the Lord's sake listen to us! We won't ask much; we won't offend you in the least. We merely want to ask very deferentially that you will see that there is no unemployment after the war. We beseech you to let our stewards have a little say....a very little say....in the management of the shops. Take your

Rent and Interest and Profit as usual; as usual we'll be quite content with what is left over."

If a bull had intelligence he would not allow himself to be led to the shambles. If the Trade Unions had intelligence they would not allow their paid leaders to lead them to the altar.

The lecturer had evidently been told that I was the only Socialist in the village, and he called upon me to say a few words. I have no doubt that later he regretted calling upon me.

"The speaker is modest in his demands," I said. "He has told you what Labour is asking for, and now I'll tell you what I think Labour *should* ask for. Labour's chief aim should be to make the Trade Unions blackleg proof. When they have roped in all the workers they will be able to command anything they like. They should then go to the State and say: 'We want to join forces with the State. Capitalism is un-Christlike, and wasteful, and we must destroy it. We propose to take over the whole concern ourselves; we propose to abolish Rent, Interest, and Profit ....and Wagery. At present we are selling our labour to the highest bidder, and in the process we are selling our souls along with our bodies. Each industry will conduct its own business, not for profit but for social service; no shareholders will live on our labour; we shall give our members pay instead of wages.'

"Gentlemen, I call an organisation of this kind a Guild, but you can call it what you like. It is the only organisation that will abolish wagery, that is, will prohibit labour from being a commodity obeying the Laws of Supply and Demand."

"What about nationalisation of land and mines and railways ?" said the official. "These are on our programme, and they will revolutionise industry."

"Hand over the mines and the railways to the State," I said, "and you have State capitalism. You won't abolish wages; you'll buy the mines and railways, and you'll draw your wages from what is left over after the interest due to the late shareholders is paid."

"Ah !" he interrupted, "you want to confiscate ?"

"If necessary, certainly. We have conscripted life because the State required men to give their lives; why not conscript wealth in the same way? The State requires the wealth of the rich, not only for the purpose of paying for the war; it requires it to pay for the peace to come."

"Control of industry by producers has always failed," he said. "*The New Statesman* Supplement on the Control of Industry proved this conclusively."

"Of course it has always failed," I said. "Flying always failed, but the aeroplane experimenters did not sit down and wail: 'It's absolutely no good; men have always failed to fly.' If the Railway Trade Union got the offer of the whole railway system to-morrow to run as it pleased it would make a bonny hash of it. Why? Because management is a skilled business. But if the salaried railway officials had the vision to see that their interests lay with the men instead of with the masters, then you would find a difference. The Trade Unions without the salaried officials are useless.

"I read the Supplement you mention. One of the causes of failure given was that the producers had an interest in the plant and they were always unwilling to scrap machinery in order to introduce better machines."

"That's quite true," he nodded.

"Is it? Why does Bruce the linen manufacturer in the neighbouring town here scrap comparatively new machinery when better inventions come out? He has an interest in the plant, hasn't he? Why then does he not stick to the old methods?"

"He knows that he will gain in the end."

"Exactly. And a society of workers running their own business would not have the gumption to see that the new methods would be a gain in the end?"

"The fact remains that they have tried and failed," he said.

"That merely proves that the workers without their managers are hopeless," I said. "What can you expect from a section of the community that has never been educated? You can't make a man slave ten hours a day for a living wage and then expect him to have the organising ability of Martin the cigar merchant, or the vision of Gamage the universal provider. A rich merchant in London said to me when I asked him point blank if he always thought of his profits: 'Profits be blowed! The great thing is the game of business.' I don't see any reason in the world why the manager of say The Enfield Cycle Company should not be as energetic and as capable if he were managing a factory for the Cycle Guild."

"The workers would interfere with him," said the official; "every workman who had a grudge against him would try to get him put off the managership."

"Lord!" I cried, "for a representative of Labour you seem to have a poor opinion of the democracy you speak for! If that is your attitude to your fellow-workmen I quite understand your modest demands for Labour. If the rank and file of the Trade Unions can't rise higher than squabbling about whether a manager should be sacked or not, the Trade Unions had better content themselves with the programme their leaders have arranged for them. They had better concentrate their attention on trifles like a Minimum Wage or an Old Age Pension."

A disturbing thought comes to me to-night. Democracy means rule by the majority.... and the majority is always wrong. The only comfort I can find lies in the thought that the majority of to-day represents the opinions of the minority of yesterday. Democracy will always be twenty years behind its time.

* * *

To-day has been a very wet Sunday. I did not get up till one o'clock. Margaret came over about tea-time and invited me to sample some drop scones she had been making. She was in a skittish mood, and she began to turn my bothy upside down on the allegation that it was time for autumn cleaning. I ordered her to the door, and she sat down on my bed and laughed at me. I said that I would throw a drop scone at her head if it were not for the danger of shying weights about indiscriminately, and she threw my pillow at me. I rose from my chair and went to her.

"Out you come, you besom!" I cried and I seized her by the shoulders. We struggled ....and I suddenly realised that as we paused for breath her face was very near mine. I threw my arms around her and kissed her straight on the lips. Then slowly we parted and we stood looking at each other. Her face had become very serious.

"You—you shouldn't have done that!" she gasped.

"Why not?" I asked lamely.

She gazed at me wildly for a long moment; then she rushed from the room.

It happened....and I don't believe in crying over spilt milk. If I had been a strong man it wouldn't have happened; if Margaret had not been in that skittish mood it wouldn't have happened. Carlyle says somewhere: "Mighty events turn on a straw; the crossing of a brook decides the conquest of the world." Mighty events! Is this a mighty event? I have kissed many a girl. To me, no; but to Margaret I fear that it is. It was most likely her first kiss since she became a woman. I feel very like Alec D'Urberville, the seducer of Tess, to-night....only I don't think I'll take religion as he did and try to lead Margaret to salvation as he did Tess. It suddenly strikes me that I am more like Angel Clare. He was an educated man learning farming; I am an educated man tending cattle. He fell in love with the dairymaid Tess; I..... But have I fallen in love with anyone? In general I should say that when a man asks himself whether he is in love or not he is not in love. Love over-rules the head; every marriage means a victory of heart over head. Presumably the men who have no heads make the best lovers. Hamlet could not love Ophelia because he had a head; Romeo loved Juliet because he hadn't a head. The whole problem of H. G. Wells' later novels lies in the fact that his men have heads. They are all analytical....and the man who analyses himself always appears before the public as a selfish brute. The analytical man cannot make a martyr of himself; he is a weakling; he has his fun....and he pays for it, but he makes a woman pay for it also.

I suppose that in ancient times love was a simple thing. You desired a woman, and you hit her father on the head with a stone axe and carried her off to your cave. In the majority of cases it is a simple business yet; you don't knock your prospective father-in-law on the head with a hatchet; you take a filial interest in your prospective mother-in-law's rheumatics instead. When Smith the shopwalker falls in love with Nancy of the hat department his chief concern is to know how he is going to keep house on his salary. He never sits down of an evening saying to himself: "Now, is Nancy my soul-mate? Is her sense of humour something like my own? May we not be absolutely incompatible in temperament?" Smith hasn't the faintest idea what sort of man he is himself, and if you aren't disturbed by doubts about yourself you won't be disturbed with doubts about your future wife. I should guess that Mr. and Mrs. Smith will live happily together.... if she is a passable cook.

I fear greatly that the introspective man is doomed to connubial misery. Margaret likes to read penny novelettes, and she will probably take a fancy to Charles Garvice some day soon. She knows nothing about music or painting or literature. Unless we are ragging each other we have not a single topic of common interest; we should certainly bore each other during the first-class honeymoon journey south.

Then why in the name of thunder did I

kiss her? I suppose that I kissed her because kissing is more elemental than thinking. When she had rushed out I was joyous in the realisation that her lips were sweet, that her neck was gloriously graceful, that her eyes were deep and wonderful. But now her physical charms have gone with her, and doubts crowd in upon me.

I wonder what she is thinking of! I know that she has no doubts about herself, but I fancy that she has her doubts about me. Poor lassie....and well she might!

* * *

She was milking to-night. I went over and stood beside her. She looked up, and her eyes shone with a new brightness. She could not meet my gaze, and she flushed and looked the other way.

"Margaret," I said softly, "I love you!"

She held up her lips to me....and then I walked out of the byre.

And, you know, I intended to say something very different. I intended to say: "Margaret, I was a fool last night. Try to forget all about it."

I kissed her instead. I'm afraid I was a fool last night, and a fool to-night, and a fool all the time. However, I am a happy fool to-night.

X.

MACDONALD has returned. He has brought a man Macduff with him, a college friend of his, and now the headmaster of a big school in Perthshire. He has mentioned Macduff to me more than once. Macduff is his ideal schoolmaster, a stern disciplinarian and a great producer of "results." When they came up to see me to-night Macdonald's face glowed with anticipation; it was evident that he had come to my funeral. Macduff was to slay me, bury me, and write my epitaph. I thought of agreeing with Macduff as much as possible, so as to rob Macdonald of his triumph, but I found it impossible to find more than a few points of agreement. I managed, however, to carry the war into the enemy's camp, and Macduff found himself acting on the defensive more than once.

"I read your *Log*," he said agreeably, "and I must congratulate you on it. I laughed at many of the yarns you have in it."

"The worst of being called a humorist," said I, "is that everybody seizes on your light bits, and ignores your serious bits."

"I didn't ignore your serious bits," he said, "I read them carefully....and, to be frank, thought them damned nonsense. You don't mind my saying so, do you?"

"Certainly not, my dear fellow! When you've read the evening paper critics' opinion of yourself you can stand anything. I am all for a free criticism; it lets you know where you stand at once."

We both became very amiable after that, and I offered him a fill of Macdonald's baccy. Then I brought out a bottle of whiskey, and we sat round the bothy fire like brothers.

"And now," I said, "tell me all about the damned nonsensical parts."

"Well," he laughed, "it seems a dirty trick to drink a chap's whiskey and slate his ideas at the same time, doesn't it?"

"It might be worse," I said with a smile; "you might slate his whiskey and drink in his ideas at the same time; and I've never met a man who could stand being accused of keeping bad whiskey, although I know dozens of men who will sit with a grin on their faces while you tear their philosophy of life to pieces."

"They grin at your ignorance, eh?"

"Exactly!"

Macdonald held up his glass to the light and eyed it thoughtfully.

"Macduff's theory is that if you spare the rod you spoil the child," he said.

"Yes," said Macduff, "I agree with old Solomon. You know, it's all very well to be a heretic, but you are up against the wisdom of the ages. All the way from Solomon downwards parents have agreed that youngsters must be trained strictly. You can't smash up the wisdom of the ages as you try to do."

"The wisdom of the ages!" I mused..... "When I come to think of it the wisdom of the ages taught men that the earth was flat, that the sun went round the earth, that the touch of a king cured King's Evil. Do you mean to say that because a thing has a tradition behind it it must be believed for ever? Because Solomon said a thing is it eternally true? The wisdom of the ages must be made to give place to the wisdom of the age."

"Then you would have each generation ignore all that had been said by men of previous generations?"

"I don't mean that. By all means find out what wise men of old have said, but don't worship them; be ready all the time to reject their wisdom if you feel you can't agree with it. This using the rod business is a tradition because men found it the easiest method for themselves. A child was weak and he was noisy; the easiest thing to do was to whack the little chap. Do you allow conversation in your school?"

"I do not!" he said grimly.

"And why?"

"They can't work if they are talking."

"And that's your sole reason?"

"Yes."

"If an inspector stood at your desk chatting to you about the war, would you have a silent room?"

"Certainly."

"But why?"

"Oh," he said impatiently, "for various reasons. They aren't there to talk; and they've got to be disciplined, to understand that they are not free to do as they like whenever they like."

"Also," I suggested, "the inspector might be annoyed?"

"There's that in it," he confessed with a little confusion.

"The wisdom of the ages agrees with you," I said, "and I think that in this case the wisdom of the ages is wrong. In the first place I want to know what you're trying to produce."

"Educated citizens," he replied.

"And since the Solomon tradition has been in vogue for quite a long time, do you consider that it has produced educated citizens as yet?"

"More or less," he answered.

"I can't see it," I said. "When nine-tenths of the population of these isles live on the border line of starvation you can't surely argue that they are educated citizens. They are bullied citizens....and the first step in the bullying of them was the refusal of authority in the shape of the parent and the pedagogue to spare the rod."

"But look here," he interrupted, "come back to the school. Do you think it wrong for a teacher to compel a boy to attend to a lesson?"

"I do. If he has to be compelled the lesson clearly fails to interest him. I would have childhood a garden in which one could wander wherever one pleased; I would abolish fear and punishment."

"And do you mean to tell me," he demanded, "that a boy will offer to learn his history and geography and arithmetic and grammar of his own free will?"

"It depends on the boy. Here, again, we come up against the wisdom of the ages. The wisdom of the ages has decreed that these subjects are the chief things in education. But are they? I should imagine that it is more important for a boy to know something about feminine psychology than about Henry the Eighth. He will one day be called on to choose a wife, but he'll never be called on to choose a king. Again why should geography be of more importance than anatomy? A man never wants to know where Timbuctoo is, but he very often wants to know whether the pain in his tummy is appendicitis or heart-burn."

"Go on!" he laughed, "find a substitute for arithmetic now!"

"Arithmetic," I said, "is the trump card of the man who wants a utilitarian education. I can do lots of sums—Simple Interest, Profit and Loss, Ratio and Proportion, Train Sums, Stream Sums.....I could almost do a Cube Root. So far as I can remember I have never had occasion to use arithmetic for any purpose other than adding up money or multiplying a few figures by a few figures. Your utilitarianism somehow leads in the wrong direction most of the time. I was brought up under the wisdom of the ages curriculum, and I'll just give you an idea of some of the things I don't know. I don't know the difference between a mushroom and a toadstool ; I haven't the faintest idea of how they make glass or soap or paint or wine or whiskey or beer or paper or candles or matches ; I know nothing about the process of law ; I don't know what steps one takes to get married or divorced or cremated or naturalised ; I don't know the starboard side of a ship ; I don't know how a vacuum brake works. I could fill a book with a list of the things I don't know....a book as big as the Encyclopædia Britannica.

"What I want to know is this : How are we to determine what things are important to know ? From a utilitarian point of view it is more important to know how to get married than how to find the latitude and longitude of Naples. As an exercise of thinking it is quite as important to inquire into the working of a Westinghouse brake as to inquire into the working of a Profit and Loss sum."

"Then what curriculum would you have ?"

"I wouldn't have any curriculum. I would allow a boy to learn what he wanted to learn. If he prefers kite-making to sentence-making I want him to choose kite-making. If he wants to catch minnows instead of reading about

Napoleon, I say let him do it; he is learning what he wants to learn, and that's exactly what we all do when we leave the compulsion of the schoolroom."

"It won't do!" cried Macduff.

"Look at it in this way," I said. "Suppose I am three stone heavier than you. And suppose that I think it would benefit you if you knew all about—let us say Evolution. I come to you, take you by the back of the neck and say: 'Macduff, you get up the Darwinian Theory word perfect by Monday morning. If you don't I'll bash your head for you.' I reckon that you would call in the police.... and they would naturally call in the local prison doctor to inquire into my sanity. That is exactly what you are doing in your school ....only, unfortunately, the police and the prison doctor are on your side. Personally I could make out a strong case for your being certified as a dangerous lunatic with homicidal tendencies."

"Ah!" he said, "but the two cases are different. Your arbitrary insistence on my learning all about Darwin has no right on its side; it's merely your opinion that I should know all about Evolution. But when I make a boy learn his history and grammar I am not acting on my own opinion. Personally I confess that I teach lots of things and don't see the use of them."

"You obey the -er- the wisdom of the ages?"

"I suppose I do."

"Education," I said, "should lead a boy to think for himself, but if teachers refuse to think for themselves in case they disagree with the wisdom of the ages I don't see that they are the men to lead children to think for themselves."

Later we discussed motor-cycles, and I learned many tips from Macduff. He is a mine of information on the subject.

When they had gone I thought out the problem of the curriculum. To abolish the curriculum involves abolishing large classes. I would have classes of not more than a dozen pupils. In the free school I picture, classes would not in fact exist; if there were a hundred and twenty scholars there would be ten teachers. They would act as guides to be consulted when necessary. Each teacher would learn with his or her pupils. A teacher is not an encyclopædia of facts; he is an enquirer.

When we tarred the pigeon-house I did not say: "Now, boys, listen to me, and learn how to put on tar." The boys brought chunks of pitch in their pockets (pretty certainly sneaked from the heaps used for tar-spraying the roads). We got an old pail and melted the solid stuff then we tried to put it on. The trial was a complete failure; the tar would not run. We sat down to consider the matter.

"Tell you what, boys," said Cheery Smith, "we'll thin it wi' some paraffin."

We thinned it with some paraffin and the stuff ran quite easily.

When I told Macdonald of the incident he cried: "Yes, but think of the time you wasted!"

What's wrong with Macdonald and Macduff is that they know too much to be good teachers. They have nothing to learn. They know all the facts about curriculum subjects; they know exactly what is right and what is wrong; they know that their authority is infallible; they know that swearing is bad, that cap-lifting is good; they know that obedience is a great virtue, that disobedience to their authority is an unforgiveable sin. They are the Supermen of education; their attitude to the school is exactly the attitude of Charles I. to his Parliament. They believe in the Divine Right of Dominies. The dominie can do no wrong. Macdonald's bairns consider him something beyond a human being; he knows everything; he is above temptation. He has no weaknesses; his pipe goes into his pocket when he meets a child; he wouldn't allow a child to see him kiss his wife for all the gold in the Bank of England.

But there are expectations down at the schoolhouse. And I would almost sell my soul to be in the classroom on the morning when Macdonald enters it with the word paternity writ large on his prim face. I bet my boots that, without saying a single word, he will manage to give the bairns the impression that he had nothing to do with the affair at all.

* * *

A friend of mine, a Londoner, came to stay

the week-end with me. To-day we rambled over the hills, and a pair of new boots began to make my friend's feet take on a separate existence. We were about three miles from home, and the prospect of walking that distance painfully was rather disheartening to him. Luckily Moss-side milk cart came along, and the boy asked us if we wanted a lift to the village; he was taking the day's milk to the station.

When we left the cart my friend turned to me in amazement.

"Here," he cried, "didn't you give him something?"

"Good Lord, no!" I laughed.

"Oh, you blooming Scotchman!" he said with fervour. "If I had known I'd have given the chap a tip myself."

"I never thought of tipping him," I said, "and if I had I wouldn't have tipped him all the same. You blessed Englishmen can never rise above your stupid feudal idea of rewarding the lower classes. In your south country a countryman is a Lickspittle; he touches his cap to anything with a collar on. We don't breed that kind of specimen in Scotland. That young lad is a stranger to me, but he and you and I were equals; there was no servility about him; he chatted to us as an equal. He expected nothing, and if you had offered him a shilling you would have patronised him, posed as his superior."

"But, damn it all, the chap earned a bob!'

"He didn't; all he earned was your gratitude. The boy was doing a decent kindly thing for its own sake, and you want to shove a vulgar tip into his hand. If I had come along in a Rolls-Royce car and given you a lift, would you have offered to reward me? What's wrong with you southerners is that you always think in classes; your tipping isn't kindness; you tip to save your self-respect; you are afraid that any man of the lower orders should think you mean. The Scot is not as a rule hampered by class distinctions, and he often refuses to tip because he hates to insult a man. You Londoners put it down to meanness, but I would have felt myself the meanest of low cads if I had tipped that ploughboy. Scotland is comparatively free from the rotten tipping habit. A few gamekeepers get tips from English sporting gentlemen, and a few porters get tips from English travellers."

"You have spoilt that boy for the next unfortunate pedestrian," he said; "the next time he sees a man limping along the road he will say to himself: 'Never again!'" I knew then that he had not been listening to my argument.

If tipping is degrading to the man who tips and the man who holds out his palm, I cannot see that school prize-giving is any better. The kindly School Board members who are anxious to encourage the bairns to work for prizes have essentially the same outlook as my friend from town. I fancy that the modern interpretation of Christianity has something to do with this national desire for reward and punishment. To me the whole attitude is distasteful. Obviously I am what I am; I was born with a certain nature, and I was brought up in a certain environment. The making of my ego was a thing outside my direction altogether. To reward me in an after life for being a religious man is as unfair as to punish me for being a thief. We don't award a gold medal to an actress for being beautiful; we don't offer Shaw a peerage because he is Christlike enough to hate killing animals for sport. Shaw can no more help being humanitarian than Gladys Cooper can help being bonny. Down in the school there Ellen Smith can no more help being the best arithmetician than Dave Ramsay can help being the biggest coward.

Speaking of Dave....when Macdonald was worrying over the allocation of prizes the other week, he asked me if Dave was good at anything.

"Well," I said, "he holds the record for spitting farther than any boy in the school; I think he deserves a prize for that. Believe me, Macdonald, every boy in the class would rather hold that record than carry off the prize for arithmetic....and I don't blame them either."

The subject of Scots and tipping puts me in mind of what is probably the best "Scot in London" yarn.

A DOMINIE DISMISSED

A Scot, followed by his five children, entered the Ritz Hotel, and sat down in the lounge.

" Waiter ! A bottle o' leemonade and sax tumblers ! " he cried.

The waiter was too dumbfounded to do anything but bring the liquor. He stood in open-mouthed amazement as the Scot divided the bottle among the six glasses, but, when the Scot took a bag of buns from his pocket and proceeded to distribute them, the waiter set off blindly to find the manager.

The manager approached. He tapped the Scot on the shoulder, and in a stern voice he said : " Excuse me, but I'm the manager of this establishment."

The Scot looked up at him sharply.

" O, ye're the manager, are ye ? Weel, why the hell's the band's no playin' ? "

XI.

MACDONALD had a sort of cookie shine to-night, and I was invited. The other guests were Mitchell, the assistant-manager of the railway construction department, and Willis, the head of the water department. We played Bridge, and I spent four hours of misery. I hate cards ; I can't concentrate at all, and I never have the faintest idea what the man on my left has discarded. Willis and I won.

I always look upon cards as a veiled insult to guests. I want to know what a man is thinking when I meet him ; on the few occasions on which I have brought out a pack of cards to entertain guests I have done so on the frank realisation that their conversation wasn't worth listening to.

Later when we sat round the fire to chat I grudged the time lost over the game. Mitchell had been for many years in India, and his stories of life there were of great interest to me. He did not theorise about India ; he accepted without thought the attitude of the average Anglo-Indian....the nigger is a beast that has to be knocked into shape ; the Anglo-Indian mode of government was tip-top, couldn't be beat ; asses like Keir Hardie ought never to be allowed to put their foot in India ; what's wrong with India is what's wrong with the working classes here—we give 'em too much education, make 'em discontented.

Willis was of a more intelligent type. He had been all over the world, and, although a Conservative to the backbone, he had made some study of modern problems. He had studied Socialism, thought it a fine thing, but...." You've got to change human nature first," he said.

* * *

If I were writing a novel I should now head a chapter thus :—Chapter XXIV., in Which Macdonald and I become Brothers in Affliction.

He came up to see me to-night.

" You've put your foot in it this time," he began.

" What is it ? " I cried in alarm.

" Old Brown—Violet's father—wants to slay you. His wife heard from Mrs. Wylie that you said to Wylie that he, Brown, had the intellect of a boiled rabbit."

" That's bad," I said in dismay. " The old fool was talking puerile rubbish about the wickedness of the working-classes. Wylie was there, and after Brown had gone I did make the impatient remark that he had the intellect of a boiled rabbit. But, Good Lord ! I didn't want the thing to go back to his ears. How I can ever look the man in the face again I don't know."

" You should have thought of that before you spoke," said Macdonald with a smile.

" Oh," I replied, " I don't regret saying it

in the least; at the time I felt it was the only thing to say. What I regret is the meanness of Wylie or his wife. Brown is a decent old chap, and I'm rather fond of him. Why the devil are people so dirty in mind, Macdonald? We all say things that we don't want carried to the person we are speaking about. I say things about you that I would hate you to hear, and I guess that you are in a similar position with regard to me. But the unpardonable social crime is to tell one man what another has said about him. It's the lowest down trick I know."

"What'll you do about it?"

"I'll go straight down to Brown and apologise for Wylie's bad taste."

"And your own!"

"Not at all. I'll tell him I've said worse things than that about him, but I'll implore him not to let them make any difference in our friendship."

"I've got a nasty little problem myself," said Macdonald. "You know that confounded committee of villagers that has charge of the Soup Kitchen Fund?"

"I do," I cried fervently.

"Well, I called a meeting for last night.... and I forgot to post Mrs. Wylie's invitation."

"Call that a nasty problem?" I cried; "my dear chap, you've raised a whirlwind and tempest combined....and there won't be any still small voice at the end of 'em either. You've committed the Unforgiveable Sin this time."

"She's in an awful wax," he continued; "says that she never was insulted like this before. She came up to-night and gave me beans....told me that you were a perfect gentleman!"

"I took care never to omit her when I called the committee," I said modestly.

"She'll never forgive me," said Macdonald dolefully.

"Oh, yes she will....if you play your cards well. Your game is to send a notice of the meeting to the local paper. Then commence a new paragraph thus:—The Convener, Mr. Macdonald, intimated that Mrs. Wylie's invitation to the meeting had been unintentionally overlooked, and he expressed his very earnest regret that his mistake had deprived the meeting of the always helpful advice of the injured lady.

"Publicity salves all wounds in the village, Macdonald. Do as I suggest and Mrs. W. will support you for all eternity."

"They are so small-minded," he said.

"They are hyper-sensitive," said I. "Mrs. Wylie is quite sure that you made a mistake. She can forgive you for that, but the thing that she will find it hard to forgive is the fact that you did not pay special attention to her letter, send it by registered post as it were. No one who knows me would accuse me of self-depreciation, but I tell you, Macdonald, every villager down there has more self-appreciation in his little finger than I have in my whole body. Old Jake Baffers never had a bath in his life, and he would be secretly proud of his record if an urchin were to shout at him: 'G'wa and tak a wash!' Yet if the secretary forgot to send him a notice of the Parish Council Meeting Jake would hate the man for all eternity."

"What does it all mean?" asked Macdonald.

"The innate love of publicity lies at the root of all the village hate and narrowness. They spend their little lives looking for trouble, and the trouble they look for specially is a personal slight. The village is always full of this kind of trouble. They like to have a finger in every pie. You don't want them to run your Soup Kitchen; you could do it fifty times better yourself."

"Perhaps they think I'd sneak the cash, eh?"

"No! No, to give them their due, they don't think that. You may rob the Committee of all their cash if you like (think of the fine talk they would have over it!); what you mustn't do is to rob them of their publicity. Some of them will always hate you because you wear a linen collar and don't talk dialect. Also, you are an incomer. I once attended a public meeting in a Fife village. A man stood up to give his opinion about a public matter, and they shouted him down with the cry: 'Sit doon! Ye're an incomer!' The man had been resident in that village for twenty-three years, but he had come from Forfarshire originally."

"And this is democracy!" exclaimed Macdonald.

"This is education," said I. "All the history and geography and grammar in the world won't produce a better generation in this village. What is really wrong is narrow vision due to lack of wide interest. Obviously the village thinks of small things, things that don't count to us. The villager left school at fourteen and he never had any training in thinking."

"Well, and what's the remedy?"

"Remedy be blowed!" I cried. "Come on, I'm going down with you and I'll have it out with old Brown."

* * *

Brown was in no mood to be friendly. Indeed he was quite nasty. He told me frankly that our friendship was at an end, and I felt pained about the matter. Suddenly a brilliant inspiration came to me. As I stood at the door I turned to him sharply.

"You've had your say, Mr. Brown," I said sternly, "and now it's my innings. I didn't mean to mention it, but you've forced me to do it."

I paused to note his sudden look of alarm.

"Yes," I went on, "I want to know what the devil you meant by saying that I suffered from swelled head?"

"When did I say that?" he stammered.

I shrugged my shoulders.

"I refuse to give away the man who told me," I said stiffly.

He was now in great excitement. He wiped his brow with his hand.

"Graham is a liar!" he cried passionately, "it was *him* that said it to *me*!"

"But you agreed with him?" I insinuated.

Brown drew himself up stiffly.

"Well, damn you, I did!"

"Quits!" I cried, and I held out my hand.

Later as we sat together over a hot whiskey I tried hard to persuade him that Graham had never said a word to me; I told him again and again that I had made a lucky guess, and at last I managed to persuade him to believe me. Yet somehow I feel that he'll look askance at poor Graham the next time he meets him.

* * *

We were threshing to-day. During the dinner interval Margaret and I chanced to meet in the barn. I threw my arms round her and kissed her. A chuckle came from the straw. I looked up to find the eyes of Jim Jackson upon us.

"Aw'll no tell!" he cried, and Margaret fled blushing from the barn.

"Right, Jim! We'll trust you with the secret. Margaret and I are in love with each other."

"When is it to be?" he asked eagerly.

"You are thinking of the wedding feast I presume, my lad, what?"

He did not answer ; he seemed to be thinking.

" Bob Scott has a' the luck," he said dolefully ; " when he was ten his mither was married, when he was eleven his sister Bets dee'd, and syne when he was twel his father was married. Aw've only had a marriage and a daith. Aw like marriages better gyn daiths ; ye get mair to eat, and ye dinna hae to look solemn. A christenin' doesna coont ; ye jest get a wee bit o' cake, and the minister prays."

" Jim," I said suddenly, " will you be my best man ? "

He gaped.

" Will Aw be yer—? " He was too much surprised to complete the sentence.

" Yes, and carry the ring," I said.

His eyes danced.

" And kiss the bridesmaids," I continued.

His face fell.

" No," he said slowly, " Aw'm ower young to be a best man." He considered for a while. " But Geordie Tamson wud kiss them for a hank o' candy," he said half aloud.

" No," I said, " you can't delegate your powers to another in a case of this sort. But of course if you think Geordie would be the better man to sit on the dickey of the carriage, and lead the bride to the wedding feast, and throw out the sweeties and pennies to the children, and—"

" Aw'll be yer best man ! " he roared.

XII.

TO-NIGHT I made up my mind to speak to Frank Thomson and his wife. I knew that Jim would be miserable as long as he carried so weighty a secret on him ; I knew that he was itching to rush through the village shouting : " The Mester's gaein' to be married to Maggie Tamson....and Aw'm to be his best man ! "

I went over about eight o'clock. The children were in bed, and Margaret sat in the kitchen with her father and mother.

" I want to marry Margaret," I said when I entered.

Frank was reading *The People's Journal*. The paper fluttered slightly, and that was the only sign of surprise that came from him.

" Yea, Mester ? " he said slowly. " Man, d'ye tell me that na ? Aw see that the Roosians are makin' some progress again." He buried his head in his paper after throwing a look to his wife. The look clearly meant : " This is a matter for you to tak up, Lizzie."

Mrs. Thomson laid down her knitting carefully ; then she rubbed her glasses with her apron. She glanced at Margaret, and Margaret rose and left the room quietly. I knew that she left the door half-closed so that she might hear from the stair-foot.

Her mother looked at me over her glasses.

" She's gey young," she said.

" A year older than you were when you married," I said with a smile.

She sat in deep thought for a long time. Then she turned to her husband.

" Frank," she said in a matter-of-fact voice, " ye'll better bring oot the whiskey."

That was all. Neither of them asked a question about my financial position, or my hopes. Mrs. Thomson went to the door and called Margaret's name, and when she entered the kitchen her mother simply said : " Maggie, ye micht bring a few coals like a lassie."

A stranger from a foreign land looking on would have wondered at the unconcern of the whole thing. The family talked about everything but the subject of the moment, but I knew by the way in which they made conversation that they were striving to hide their real feelings.

When I rose to leave I turned to Frank.

" I don't know what plans I have," I said, " but the chances are that I'll go to live in London some day soon."

Frank waved a protesting hand.

" Never mind that ee'noo," he cried. " Maggie !. . . . ye'll better see the Mester to the door, lassie ! "

" They're awfu' pleased ! " whispered Margaret at the door.

" Are they, Margaret ? " I said tenderly.

" Yes ! But it isn't because you are so clever, you know ! "

" Rather because I am so handsome ? "

" No. They're pleased because you are an M.A."

Then she laughed at my look of chagrin.

* * *

This morning I met Jim.

" Jim," I said, " you are free to speak now."

He made no reply ; he sprang over a gate and flew towards the village.

The girls came up in a body at four o'clock.

" Is't true ? " cried Janet as she ran up breathlessly.

" What ? Is what true ? "

" That you and Maggie are to be married ? "

" The answer is in the affirmative," I said pompously.

Janet's face fell.

" Eh, if Aw had that Jim Jackson ! He telt us that he was to be yer best man ! "

" He was aye a big leer ! " cried Ellen, then she saw that I was smiling.

" It's true after a' ! " she cried.

" Yes," I said, " it's true, bairns," but to my surprise they rushed off and left me. I understood their action when I turned to look ; they had seen Margaret emerge from the kitchen door. Poor Margaret ! The whole crowd of them insisted on pinching her arms for luck. They seemed to have forgotten my existence ; then suddenly they all came running towards me.

" Let me tell 'im, Jan ! " I heard Annie cry,

but Jan tore herself from restraining arms and was first to come up.

"The Mester's gotten a little baby!" cried Janet.

"Janet's wrang!" cried Annie; "it's no the Mester: it's his wife!"

I tried to look my surprise.

"And did you congratulate him, Jan?" I asked.

Janet tittered.

"He took an awfu' reid face when he cam in this mornin', did'n he, Jean?"

"Aye, and he was grumpy a' day. He was ay frownin' at a' body. We cudna help his wife haein' a bairn!"

"He looked as if he was angry at his wife haein' the bairn," said Barbara.

I recalled my conjecture that he would try to give the bairns the impression that he had nothing whatever to do with the affair, and I laughed uproariously.

I suddenly realised that Gladys was asking me a question.

"Eh? What's that, Gladys?"

"I was speerin' if you and Maggie are to hae a bairn?"

Janet gasped and cried: "Oh, Gladys!" and Jean cried: "Look at Maggie blushin'!"

"Certainly!" I said with a laugh, "a dozen of them, won't we, Margaret?"

"Bairns is just a scunner," said Sarah. "Ye'll hae to stop yer typewriter or ye'll waken them."

"That's awkward, Sarah," I said, "for if I stop my typewriter I'll starve them."

"The Mester'll hae a big hoose," said Jean, "and he'll type his letters in the parlour and Maggie'll rock the cradle in the kitchen, winna ye, Maggie?"

"Perhaps," I suggested, "Jim Jackson will be able to invent a patent that will enable me to rock the cradle as I strike the keys."

"Aye," said Janet with scorn, "and kill the bairn! Aw wudna trust Jim Jackson wi' ony bairn o' mine....him and his inventions!"

"Ye'll mak a nice father," said Gladys, and she put her arm round my neck.

"Ye'll spoil yer bairns," said Ellen. She turned to Margaret. "Maggie, dinna let him tak chairge o' them, or he'll mak them catch minnows a' day instead o' learnin' their lessons."

"G'wa, Ellen," cried Sarah, "they're no married yet! And ye dinna get bairns till ye're married a gey lang time."

"Some fowk has them afore they get married," said Barbara thoughtfully, and I chuckled when I saw how the others looked at her. Disapproval was writ large on their faces.

"Ye shudna mention sic things afore Maggie!" said Janet in a stage whisper, and I had to hold my sides. Margaret could not keep her gravity either, and she laughed immoderately.

Later they pleaded with me to tell them when the wedding was to take place. I told them that I did not know, but that it would be soon, and I promised to invite them all.

" But no Mester Macdonald ! " said Jean. " Aw wudna feel so free wi' him there."

I told them of the widower whose friends tried to persuade him to take his mother-in-law with him in the front funeral coach. After some persuasion he said resignedly : " Verra weel, then ; but it'll spoil my day." Then I sent them home.

* * *

The story I told the girls set me thinking of funeral stories. I have heard dozens of them, but the only other one I can remember is the one about the farmer whose wife was to be buried. As the men carried the coffin along the passage they stumbled, and the coffin came into violent contact with the corner. The lid flew off, and the wife sat up and rubbed her eyes. She had been in a trance.

Twenty years later the wife died again. The men were carrying the coffin through the passage when the farmer rushed forward.

" Canny, lads ! " he cried, " canny wi' that corner ! "

* * *

" Look here," said Macdonald to me to-night, " the School Board election is coming off soon ; why don't you stand ? "

" I thought that I would be the last man on earth you would want on the School Board," I replied.

"Not at all," he said with a smile. "You and I differ about education, but our difference isn't so great as the difference between me and men like Peter Mitchell."

I thought to myself that the difference between his idea and mine was infinitely greater than the difference between his idea and Peter Mitchell's, but I said: "It's very decent of you to suggest it, old chap, but I'm not standing."

"But why not?"

"Possibly for the same reason that H. G. Wells and A. R. Orage and Bernard Shaw and G. K. Chesterton don't stand for Parliament."

"You place yourself in good company!" he laughed.

"I'm not claiming kindred, Madconald; what I mean to suggest is that I stand to Peter Mitchell and Co. very much in the same relationship as Shaw and Orage stand to Lloyd George and Co. Roughly there are two types of mind, the thinkers and the doers. Orage has better ideas than Lloyd George, but I fancy that Lloyd George is the better man to run a Ministry of Munitions. I've got better ideas than Peter Mitchell (I think you'll grant that), yet Peter is probably the better man to arrange for the gravelling of the playground."

I smoked for a while in silence.

"The best men don't enter public life," I continued. "No man with a real passion for ideas could tolerate the jobbery and gabble of the House of Commons. Public life is for the most part concerned with small things. The Cabinet settles mighty things like war and peace, but if you read Hansard you'll find that ninety-nine per cent. of the members' speeches deal with little things like Old Age Pensions or the working of the Insurance Act. So in the School Board you have to deal with the incidental things. The Scotch Education Department settles the broad lines of education, and the local School Boards simply administer the Education Act of 1908. What could I do on the Board anyway ?....arrange for the closing of the school at the tattie holidays, discuss your application for a rise in screw, grant a certain amount of money for prizes. I couldn't persuade the Board to convert your school into a Neo-Montessorian Play-Garden ; if I did persuade them the Department would very likely step in and protest. Besides I haven't the type of mind. I hate all the formalism of public meetings ; I had enough of it at the 'varsity to last me a life time ; the debating societies spent most of their time reading minutes and moving 'the previous question.' I'm not a practical man, Macdonald. In art I like pure black and white work, and I think in black and white ; I see the broad effect without noting the detail. Detail gives me a headache, and the public man must have something like a passion for detail. Look at the Scotch Education Department ; it is full of splendid officials who will spend a week nosing out an error of ten attendances in an unfortunate dominie's registers. That's what should be; the official should have the mind of a ready-reckoner.... rather, he must have, else he would drown himself after a day in Whitehall."

Macdonald has a passion for detail, and I smiled to note a growing look of aggression on his face.

"Somebody's got to do the detail work," he growled.

"Most of it could very well be left undone," I suggested. "You have to calculate laboriously all the attendances for the year, how many have left school, how many are of such and such an age, and so on. What for? Simply to allow the busy officials of Whitehall to settle what grant should be paid."

"How could they settle it otherwise?" he asked.

"In fifty ways. The obvious way is to find out how much the school requires to run it each year. I would go the length of abolishing the daily register. You don't call the roll in a cinema house or a kirk or a political meeting. Why, man, in the big schools in the cities the headmaster is a junior clerk; his whole time is spent in making up statistical returns for the Department."

"You couldn't get on without the returns," said Macdonald.

"Possibly not at present," I said, "seeing that the system of grants obtains, but if an

Education Guild of Teachers controlled the education of Scotland most of the returns could be scrapped. All the returns needed for your school would be a list of expenditure on salaries, books, etc.; main headquarters would control the broad policy and pay the bills."

"And attendance wouldn't count?"

"Not if I had any say in the matter. To have an average attendance of 96 per cent. is about the lowest ideal a dominie can aim at. The teachers and the school boards aim at a high average because of the higher grant; the Department, with an eye on Blue Book statistics, encourages them to aim at a high average because a high average means a country with the minimum of illiteracy."

"Would you abolish compulsory attendance?"

"Certainly—so far as the children are concerned. Make their schools playgrounds instead of prisons, and you'll have no truancy. But I would have compulsion for parents. The State should have the power to say to parents: 'You are only the guardians of these children, and we can't allow you to keep them from education to do your work for you.'"

"You aren't consistent," he said, "here you are advocating Authority!"

"Macdonald," I said wearily, "you must have authority and law of a kind. You must have a law that you take the left side of the road when you are cycling for instance. You must give the community power to overpower a man like that lunatic who assaulted Mary Ramsay the other day, and if the community feels that it must protect children from assaults on their bodies, surely to goodness it must step in and protect little children when parents try to commit assaults on their souls. Compulsion should step in to destroy compulsion."

"Now, what in all the earth do you mean by that?"

"A man compels his son to stay from school; the compulsion of the State overrules the compulsion of the father. So with compulsion of men for military purposes; in theory at least the Military Service Act compels men to fight in order that they may overrule the compulsion that Germany is trying to force on Europe. The Fatherland and the father are interfering with human souls, but if a boy does not want to go to school he is a free agent choosing as he wills, and interfering with the soul of no one."

"What about his children coming after him?"

"A good point," I cried; "in other words you mean that no man liveth unto himself and no man dieth unto himself, eh? Yes, that's quite true, but we don't know what the boy is to turn out. Given a home of comfort and food....as every boy would have in a well-ordered community....I think that the lad who could resist the attraction of a play-garden school with its charms of social intercourse with other children would be either a lunatic or a genius. Besides we have given up the idea in other departments. I expect that the community is of opinion that the teachings of Christianity are good for a man to hand on to his children, yet I don't think that the community would pass a law that every parent must send his family to a Sunday School. The whole trend of society is to recognise and provide for the conscientious objector, and society should certainly recognise the conscientious objector to school-going."

"A boy doesn't know his own mind."

"Neither do I," I sighed. "I can't make up my mind about anything; rather, I make up my mind to-day and change it to-morrow. And I don't want it to be otherwise; when my opinions become definite and fixed I shall be dead spiritually. The boy doesn't know his own mind! Well, how the deuce can I claim to help him to make it up when I can't make up my own? It's his mind, not mine. I don't mind telling him what I think of a subject, but I wouldn't compel him to do a blamed thing."

"You have a queer idea of education," he said with a dry laugh.

"Macdonald," I said, with real modesty, "I don't know that I have any idea of education. I am simply groping. I don't exactly know what I want, but I have a pretty definite notion of what I don't want....and that is finality. I begin to think that what I want education to do is to train men not to make up their minds about anything."

Macdonald rose to go.

"Matrimony does that, old chap," he said with a chuckle, "and you'll soon discover that you won't get the chance of making up your mind ever."

XIII.

I FEARED that I was losing Jim and Janet and the others, but I have not lost them.

They conform to Macdonald's reign of authority when they are in school, but they do it with their tongues in their cheeks. But only the select few have followed my banner. Jim is the only boy, and the only girls are Janet, Jean, Ellen, Annie, and Gladys. Barbara is of divided allegiance. The others are Macdonaldised. I find it a very difficult thing to define Macdonaldisation. Possibly its most distinguishing characteristic is what I might call a dour pertness. The bairns have lost their standard of values; they don't know limits. I pinched Mary's cheek when I met her this morning on her way to school, and she tossed her head in the air and looked at me with a cheeky expression which meant: " What do you think you're doing ? " If I rag Eva she answers with brazen impudence. I have given up speaking facetiously to the boys, for they also were impudent. They were not like that when I had them ; I could play with them, joke with them, rag them and they took it all with the best good humour ; they teased me and played jokes on me, but they did it in the right spirit.

I have seen it again and again. Strict discipline destroys a child's values of good taste and bad taste. Naturally when freedom is denied them they do not know what freedom means. The atrocities committed by the super-disciplined German army are quite understandable to me; like Macdonaldised bairns they did not understand the freedom they suddenly found themselves enjoying, and they converted it into licence. I can tell the character of a village dominie when I stop to ask a group of boys the way to the next village when I am cycling.

Jimmy Young slouches past me now with a stare of hostility, and it isn't six months ago since he came running to me on the road one night for protection from the policeman who was after him for stealing a turnip from Peter Mitchell's field. The policeman came up and in a loud voice accused the laddie, while at the same time he threw in a hint or two that my lax discipline had something to do with the case.

"If they got a little mair o' the leather, things wud be different," he growled.

I do not like policemen; their little brief authority somehow manages to get my back up.

"What's the row?" I asked mildly.

"This young devil has been stealin' neeps," he roared, "and Mitchell's gaein' to mak a pollis court case o't."

I said nothing; I took Jimmy by the arm and walked towards the gate of Mitchell's field. I vaulted it and deliberately pulled up a turnip and peeled it and ate it, while the constable stood writing down notes voluminously.

"Understand," I said to him, "that I am not primarily encouraging Jimmy to steal turnips; my one aim is to appear in the police court with him if he is charged. I would rather a thousand times be with him in the dock than with you and your farmer in the witness-box."

Peter Mitchell did not prosecute.

In these days Jimmy realised that he and I were friends; we understood each other. Now he does not think of trying to understand me; I am an ex-dominie, and that's enough for him. Macdonald is the real dominie; Jimmy must be circumspect when he is about else there will be ructions. I don't count: I have no authority. I should like to hear Macdonald's remarks to Jimmy if the constable came to the school to tell of one of the laddie's escapades.

I have lost Jimmy and a hundred others, but I thank heaven for the bairns left to me. They come up nearly every night, and they spend Saturdays and Sundays with me.

Last Saturday Macdonald came into the field where we were playing. Janet and the other girls froze at once; all the fun went out of them, and they looked at him timidly. He tried to show that he also could be playful and he tried to romp with them for a while. The romp wasn't a success; they were acting all the time, and when a girl "tigged" him she did so with a woefully apologetic air as if she would say: "Excuse my touching you, sir, but it's only a game, you know. I'll take care not to presume when we meet on Monday morning."

Luckily he did not stay long, and the girls resumed their attempt to tie my legs together with grass ropes, their motive being to stuff my mouth with brambles. I invited them down to the bothy for tea, and they rushed off to lay the table.

"And we'll look into a' yer drawers and places," cried Jean, "and read a' yer love-letters."

"If you could read I believe you *would* read them," I shouted after her.

"Eh! What an insult!" she cried. "Aw'll just go straucht doon to Maggie and tell her no to hae ye!"

After tea Gladys suddenly said: "Come on, we'll play at schules, eh?" The idea was hailed with delight, and Annie requisitioned the services of my new braces for a strap, and ranged us round the fire.

"Now," she said, "this is playtime and you are all outside, and when I blow the whistle you'll all come in."

"Blaw yer bugle," said Jean, "just to mak it like it was when ye were at the schule." So I played the "Fall In" and went out to play. I came in late.

"Why are you late"? demanded Annie.

I looked round the room vacantly.

"Yes!" I said with a nod of enlightenment.

The girls giggled, and Annie had to bite her lip to keep from laughing.

"Where have you been, sir?"

"Oh, no!" I cried, "at least I don't think so!"

Annie had to sit down and laugh.

"That's no fair," she said, "there shud be nae funnin' in the schule."

I sat down on the fender and pulled a face that Alfred Lester might have envied. Annie went into fits of laughter.

"Tell ye what, Annie," said Ellen, "we'll put the Mester oot, and we'll play oorsells," and I was dismissed the school. After deliberation they agreed to allow me to be an inspector provided I did not say anything.

When bairns play school they always put on the fine English. The teacher's main duty is to call erring pupils out and punish them.

"Now, Ellen Smith, what is two and two?"

"Four."

"Very good. Now we'll have an object lesson. What animal do we get milk from, Janet?"

"The cow."

"Very good. Now we'll have some geograpy. Where is the town of —?"

"Give us spellin' instead," cried Gladys.

"Come out, girl!" and Gladys was punished severely. Then Jean was punished for laughing.

"It's my chance o' bein' teacher noo," cried Ellen and Janet at the same time, and a treble scuffle for the strap followed. Janet got it.

"Now," she began, "I'll be Mister Macdonald. Put yer hands behind yer backs, and the first one that moves will hear about it!" They sat up like statues.

"Now, Jean Broon, you stand up and recite the *Elegy Written in a Country Churchyard!*" And Jean stood up and recited the first verse dramatically.

"That'll do. Sit down. Ellen Smith, I want you to say the first verse of Wordsworth's *Ode to the Imitations of Immorality.*"

"P-Please, sir," tittered Gladys, "the inspector's laughin' like onything!"

I laughed immoderately, but it wasn't at Janet's malapropism that I laughed so much. I thought of Mrs. Wilks, the charwoman, who looked after the flat another man and I shared in Croydon. One morning she did not arrive to make the breakfast, and I went out to look for her. I found the old woman—she was sixty-three—standing at the foot of the stairs weeping.

"Great Scot!" I cried, "what's the matter?"

"My 'usband aint goin' to allow me to char for you young gentlemen again."

"What for?" I asked in amazement.

"He. . . .he accuses me of 'avin' immortal relations wiv you," she sobbed.

I hasten to add that her relations with us were not immortal: we sacked her a week later for pinching the cream.

"Sorry, Janet," I said at length, "proceed

with your Imitations of Immorality, although personally I don't see the need for them ; the real thing's good enough for me."

"Now," she said, "I'll be Mister Neill now."

Annie at once began to sing "Tipperary" ; Ellen began to pull Gladys's hair ; Jean pretended that she was biting a huge apple.... and the teacher Janet took a cigarette from the box on the table and lit it.

"You gross libellers !" I cried, and I chased them out of the bothy.

* * *

To-night I had a long walk with Margaret. I tried to make her talk, for I want so much to know her views on things.

"You talk," she said ; "I like to listen."

"But," I protested, "I'm always talking to you, and you listen all the time. I want to know what is in that wee head of yours.... although I suppose that I ought to be satisfied with its exterior."

"You see," she said slowly and somewhat sadly, "I am not clever ; I am only an ordinary farmer's daughter working in the dairy and the fields. If I told you what I was thinking you would not be interested."

We walked many yards in silence.

"It is all a mistake !" she suddenly burst out passionately. "I am not good enough for you, and when my bonny face is gone you will hate me. We have nothing in common, and if you met me in London you wouldn't be interested in me at all. You will bring clever women to the house and I—I will sit in a corner and say nothing, for I won't understand the things that you talk about. I am afraid to go to London with you."

"We'll stay here then," I said quietly.

"No!" she cried, "not that! I will stay here, but you must go to your work and your clever friends. O! it's all been a mistake!" She sat down on a fallen tree and wept silently. I sat down beside her and placed my arm round her shoulders.

"Margaret," I said softly, "we'll have a soul to soul talk about it. I'll tell you very very frankly what I think about the whole matter, and I'll try to deceive neither you nor myself.

"Intellectually you are not a soul-mate to me. That can't be possible seeing that you have never had the chance to develop your intellect. I know girls whose intellect is brilliant and whose sense of humour is delicious ....but I don't love them. I like them; I love a witty conversation with them, but.... I don't want to touch them. The touch of your hand sends a thrill through me, and there is no other hand in the world that can do that. I want to caress you, to hug you, to kiss your lips, to kiss your lovely neck. Margaret, I want you....and you are not my soul-mate. Margaret, I must have you.

"You see, dear, love is a thing that cannot be reasoned with. I once wrote down on paper a list of the qualities I wanted in the woman who should be my wife. She was to have blue eyes, a Grecian nose, auburn hair; she was to be tall and imperious; she was to be a fine pianist. Dear, your eyes are grey; your nose isn't Grecian; you aren't tall, and your limit as a pianist is *I'm a Little Pilgrim* played with one finger. You're hopeless, madam, but, dash it all!....I'll buy an auto-piano!

"According to all the rules I oughtn't to find any interest in you at all. Do you know that popular song *You Made Me Love You*? That's the only popular song I ever struck that has any philosophy in it. It has more real pathos in it than *The Rosary* and Tosti's *Goodbye* rolled into one.

"'You made me love you; I didn't want to do it,'....Margaret, that's the true story of love. Love is blind they say, but the truth is that love is mad. I didn't want to love you; my mind kept telling me that you were not the right woman....and here I sit in paradise because your head is on my shoulder. The whole thing's absurd and irrational. I almost believe that there is a real Cupid who fires his arrows broadcast; of course the little fellow is blind and he hits the wrong people."

I turned her face towards mine.

"Margaret, do you love me?"

"I love you," she whispered and she nestled more closely into my shoulder.

"And I love you," I replied, and kissed her brow. "It may be all a mistake, darling, but you and I are going to be man and wife."

"Anyway," I added, "we have no illusions about it. We've looked at the thing frankly and openly. We are blind, but we are going into it with our eyes open."

"You are getting silly again," laughed Margaret, and we forgot all our doubts and fears, and became two children playing with the toy we call love.

* * *

Margaret came to me to-night.

"Mr. Macdonald's evening school opens to-night. Do you think I should join it?"

"Why should you?" I asked.

"Oh, I have no education, and I want to learn things."

"Well," I said consideringly, "you'll learn things all right down there. You'll learn how to measure a field, and how to analyse a sentence; you'll learn a few things about the Stuart kings, and a few things about the British colonies. But, my dear, do you specially want to learn things like that?"

"I don't know what things I want to learn," she said sadly. "I think I want to know about the things you used to speak about at your evening school. Things that I don't agree with when you say them."

She laughed shortly.

"You know," she continued, "you used to make me angry sometimes. When you said that you didn't object to girls smoking I was wild with you. And I remember how shocked I was when you said that swearing navvies were no worse than we were. When you said that the text 'Children, obey your parents' gave bad advice I nearly got up and left the room."

"I expect that I *was* a sort of bombshell," I laughed.

"You made me think about things that I had never thought about before."

"That was what I was paid for, Margaret; I was educating you."

"What is education?" she asked.

"Education is thinking, Margaret. Most people take things for granted; they won't face truth. You don't like your sister Edith; she is catty and jealous. But you won't confess to yourself that you dislike Edith. All your training tells you that brotherly love is the accepted thing, and if you confessed to yourself that you are fonder of Jean Mackay than you are of Edith, you would think yourself a sinner of the worst type. If you want to be educated you must be ready to question everything; you must doubt everything. You must be very chary of making up your mind. Do you believe in ghosts?" I asked suddenly.

"Of course not!" she said with a smile. "Do you?"

"I don't know," I answered. "Lots of people claim to have seen them, and for that reason I leave the question open. There may not be ghosts, but I don't know enough about the subject to deny that they exist. I am quite ready to believe you if you tell me that you saw a ghost in the granary. I asked the question just to use it as an illustration. Popular opinion laughs at the idea of a ghost, but the thinking person won't accept the conventional view. Keep an open mind, Margaret, and believe when you are convinced.

"Education never stops; we are being educated every day of our lives. Why, only yesterday, I was up in the top field, and I heard a great squealing. I hurried to the place and was just in time to rescue a tiny rabbit from a weasel. I had seen a weasel kill a rabbit many a time before that, and I had never thought anything about it. But yesterday a sudden thought came to me. I remembered the words 'God is good,' and I began to think about them. Then I suddenly said to myself that the words were not true. The world is full of pain and terror; the great law of nature is: Eat or be eaten. I realised for the first time that every hedgerow is a horrid den of suffering and fear. Cruelty is Nature's name, Margaret."

"But," she cried in perplexity, "isn't there much good in the world too?"

"Yes, dear, there is much good in the world, but cruelty is much more powerful. You and I are cruel unthinkingly. We kill wasps before they sting us; we aren't good enough to give the poor brutes the benefit of the doubt. Your father is a very kind-hearted man, yet he never once thinks of the cruelty he perpetrates when he rears sheep and cattle and lambs for the butcher's knife. You and I dined on roast lamb often this summer, and we never thought of the poor wee creature's agony when the butcher cut its throat. Your mother is kind, yet she will kill a mouse without a thought, and the mouse is to me the bonniest creature that lives. Its great big glorious eyes fascinate me. Think of the kindly people who chase a poor half-starved fox with hounds and horses ; sport is the cruellest thing in the world. Shooting, fishing, hunting....men are as cruel and as devilish as the tiger or the hawk, Margaret."

"Animals maybe don't feel the same as we do," she said.

"Don't you lay that flattering unction to your soul," I cried. "I used to believe that comforting tale of the scientist that the lower animals do not feel. I ceased to believe it when I tried to put a worm on a fish-hook. When I saw it wriggle about I said to myself : 'This is pain, or rather it is agony.' Think of the pain that your mares and cows suffer when they are having their young. You and I heard the screams of Polly when that dead foal was born this year.

"When you think of it, Margaret, man's chief end is not to glorify God as the Catechism says ; his chief end is to eliminate pain.... human pain. You have heard of vivisection ? Performing operations on animals, often without chloroform. What's it all for ? Not cruelty, as Bernard Shaw suggests; it's all done with the kindly purpose of finding out new ways to abolish human pain. Rabbits and guinea-pigs are dosed with all sorts of microbes so that scientists might discover how to protect human beings from the pain of disease. The doctors sometimes do manage to discover a new way to abolish a certain pain, and the pathetic thing is that while they torture animals to find a way to abolish pain a thousand scientists are busily engaged inventing weapons that will bring more pain into the world. It is an alarming thought that our doctors and nurses spend their lives trying to keep the unfit alive, while our armament makers spend their lives planning means to send the fit to their death. Lots of people have said that this war shows the failure of Christianity; what it really shows is the failure of Medicine. Medicine's primary aim is to keep people alive as long as possible; War's primary aim is to kill as many people as possible. War is really a battle between two branches of science, between shells and senna. The shell scientist won....and the medicine man buckled on a Sam Browne belt and went out to help his rival's victims. If the doctors of the world had realised that war was a defeat of their principles they would have gone on strike, and would no doubt have stopped the war by doing so. Every doctor should be a pacifist, but as a matter of fact very few doctors are pacifists."

" What is a pacifist ? " asked Margaret.

" A pacifist is a man who loves peace so much that people look up almanacs to see whether his name was Schmidt a generation back, Margaret. He is usually a nervous man with the physical courage of a hen, but he has more moral courage than three army corps. He is usually a Conscientious Objector, and it takes the moral courage of a god to be that."

" They are just a lot of cowards ! " cried Margaret with indignation.

" No," I said, " I can't agree with you. No coward will face the scorn of women and the contempt of men as these men do. Think of the life that lies in front of a Conscientious Objector. Nobody will ever understand him ; he will be an outcast for ever. Dear, it takes stupendous courage to put yourself in that position, and I can't think that any man could do it unless he were following principles that were dearer to him than the judgment of his fellow men. You see, Margaret, ordinary courage and moral courage are totally different things. I know a man who won the V.C. for a very brave deed, and that chap wouldn't wear a made-up tie for all the decorations in the world ; he wouldn't have the moral courage to be seen walking down the street with a Bengali. The more imagination you have the higher is your moral courage. but imagination is fatal to physical courage. Moral courage belongs to the thinker ; physical courage to the doer. And I can't help thinking that moral courage goes with unhealthiness. I am quite sure that physical courage is primarily dependent on physical health. If my liver is out of order I tremble to open a letter ; I can't walk ten yards in the dark ; and the arrival of a telegram would give me a fainting fit. Nerves are always unhealthy, and as thinkers are always highly strung people I conclude that thinking is unhealthy. Thinkers are mad, Margaret, mad as hatters."

"Mad!"

"Yes. The lunatic is merely the man whose brain is different from the brain of the average man. The average man does not imagine himself to be Jesus Christ, and when a man does imagine himself to be Christ we say that he is mad, and we shut him up. He may be a Christ for all we know. I don't know why the community didn't shut up Shaw when he first preached that obedience was one of the Seven Deadly Virtues. The average man didn't agree with him, and we can say that Shaw is therefore mad. You see, dear, man is firstly an animal ; Joe Smith the butcher down in the village is an animal, a fine healthy animal. He is primitive man, and thinking is the last thing he could attempt. Thinking is an acquired characteristic ; it isn't a natural thing, and anything unnatural is diseased. A thinker is as much a freak as a man born with two heads. And that's why I say that thinkers are unhealthy. Blake the great poet was mad ; Ibsen the great Norwegian dramatist died in the mad-house ; Shelley was diseased ; Milton was blind, Keats a consumptive ; nearly every great composer of music who ever lived was mad."

"But," laughed Margaret, "you said that education was thinking, and now you say that thinkers are all mad."

"Yes, but madness is what the world needs. All these villagers down there are absolutely sane, but the world won't be a scrap the better for their existence. I prefer a world of Shelleys and Ibsens to a world of Jack Johnsons and Sandows....and Joe Smiths. A great German philosopher called Nietzsche preached the gospel of Superman. He wanted a fine race of powerful men who would rule the world. Some people say that Napoleon and Cæsar and Cromwell were Supermen, but the real Supermen were men like Christ and Ibsen and Darwin and Shelley ; a fighter is a nobody, but a man with a message is a Superman."

"I don't understand," said Margaret dully ; "what do you mean by having a message ?"

"A messenger is a man who forces people to consider things that they wouldn't consider without being prompted. Christ's message was love ; He encouraged men to act according to the good that was in them ; the kindliness, the charity, the love. And the fact that shooting and hunting and lamb eating still persist shows that we pay but little attention to Christ's message. Shelley's message was freedom, freedom to think and to live one's own life. You'll find that there are only the two kinds of message ....love and freedom."

"The evangelists who were holding meetings in the school last winter used to speak about their 'message,'" said Margaret. "Would you say that they were Supermen?"

"They were Superwomen," I said hastily. "They depended on emotionalism. They said nothing new, and they would refuse to consider anything new if you asked them to. They had no power to think; they quoted all the time. Consequently their message evaporated; when the magnetism of their appeal went away the converts lapsed into their old sinful ways. They didn't understand the message they tried to deliver; they had never really thought out Christ's philosophy. They had got hold of a catch phrase or two, and they kept shouting: 'Though your sins be as scarlet they shall be made whiter than snow.' But I am quite sure that they did not know what they meant by sin. Christ's chief message was: 'Love one another,' but they made it out to be: 'Love yourself so well that you may cry for salvation from the wrath to come.'

Margaret looked at the clock on my mantelpiece.

"O!" she cried, "it's eight o'clock....and the class began at seven! I can't go now."

At the door she paused for a moment; then she came back slowly.

"I won't attend his class," she said thoughtfully; "I think I'll just come over to see you every night, and you'll talk to me and educate me."

"Well," I smiled, "I will give you a wider education than Macdonald can give you. For example....this!"

"I could get any amount of teaching in kissing," she tittered.

"Possibly, darling....but there is no teacher hereabouts with my knowledge and experience of the art."

"You horrid pig!" she laughed, and she pulled my hair.

XIV.

JANET and Annie came up to me to-night.
"Hullo!" I cried, "what's become of Ellen and Gladys and Jean?"

"We're no speakin' to them," said Annie loftily.

"Cheeky things!" said Janet with scorn.

I became interested at once.

"Rivals in a love affair?" I asked.

They sniffed, and ignored the query.

"It was Jean," said Annie bitterly. "She went and telt the Mester that Aw spoke when he was oot o' the room."

"Aye," said Janet, "she put doon my name tae. Wait er I get her at hame the nicht!"

I understood. Macdonald evidently favours the obnoxious practice of setting a bairn to spy on the others....a silly thing to do.

"Aye," went on Annie, "and she called us navvies' lasses!"

"And you replied?"

"Aw telt her to g'wa hame and darn the hole in her stockin'. 'Aye,' Aw said, 'and ye can wash yer neck at the same time, Jean Broon!'"

"But," I said, "Jean never has a dirty neck, Annie."

"Weel, what did she say that Aw was a navvy's lass for then?" she demanded indignantly.

" I'm afraid that she has seen you speaking to navvies, Annie."

Annie became excited. She clutched Janet by the sleeve.

" Eh ! What an insult ! " she cried. " Janet Broon, div Aw speak to navvies ? "

" Never in a' yer life," said Janet firmly, " never wance....unless yon day that the twa o' them speered at ye the wye to the huts."

" But Aw didna answer," said Annie quickly ; " Aw just pointed."

" Are you sure ? " I asked.

" Sure as daith," she declared solemnly, and she cut her breath. " Aw maybe wud ha' spoken," she admitted, " but Aw had a muckle lump o' jaw-stickin' toffee in my mooth, and Aw cudna speak supposin' Aw had wanted to."

" Pointing was as bad as speaking," I said.

" If it was," said Annie tensely, " Jean never washes her neck. So there ! "

They departed, and in half-an-hour the enemy came up. They sat in the bothy in silence for a time.

' Well," I said cheerily, " what's the news to-night ? "

" We're fechtin'," said Gladys, " fechtin' wi' Annie and Janet."

" What's it all about, eh ? "

" The Mester gar me write doon the names o' them that was speakin'," blurted out Jean, " and Aw put doon their names."

"Yes," chimed in Ellen, "and syne they ca'ed Jean a tramp, and said that the Mester gae her the job o' writin' doon the names cos she was sic a bad writer and needed practice."

"Aye," said Gladys, "and they telt me my mither got my pink frock dyed black when my faither deed."

"And it wasna her pink frock," cried Ellen; "it was her green ane."

"This is alarming," I said with concern. "But tell me, Jean, did you say anything to them?"

"Aw never said a word!"

"Not one word?"

"They cried to us that we was navvies' dochters, and Aw just said: 'Aw wud rather be a navvy's dochter than the dochter o' Annie Miller's faither onywye.'"

"They telt Jean to wash her neck," said Gladys.

Jean smiled grimly.

"Aye, but they got mair than they bargained for! I just says to them, Aw says: 'Annie Miller, gang hame and tell yer faither to redd up his farm-yaird. Aye, and tell yer mither to wash yer heid ilka week instead o' twice a year!'"

"But," I protested, "Annie gets her hair washed every Saturday night!"

"And Aw get my neck washen ilka mornin'!"

"All right, Jean, but you haven't told me what you said to Janet."

"Jan! I soon settled her! I just says to

her says Aw: 'Wha stailt the plums that mither brocht hame on Saturday nicht?'"

"And did Jan steal the plums?" I asked.

"She did that!"

"And you never touched them?"

"No the plums," she said frankly; "Aw wasna sic a thief as that. Aw only took a wee corner o' the fig toffee."

I scratched my head thoughtfully.

"This is a bonny racket, girls. I don't know what to make of it. I think you'll better make it up."

"Never!" cried Jean stoutly. "Ellen and Gladys and me's never to speak to them again; are'n we no, Ellen?"

"Never!" cried Ellen.

"No if they were to gang doon on their bended knees!" declared Gladys.

"That's awkward for you, Jean," I said. "Do you mean to tell me that you won't speak to Jan when you are sleeping together?"

"Aw'll just gie her a dig in the ribs wi' my elbow to mak her lie ower, but Aw'll no open my mooth."

"And what if your mother says to you: 'Jean, tell Janet to feed the hens?'"

"Aw'll just hand her the corn-dish and point to the henhoose."

"And put oot my tongue at her," she added.

"Jean," I said suddenly, "I'll bet you a shilling that you are speaking to Jan and Annie by to-morrow night at four."

" Aw dinna hae a shillin'," she said ruefully, " but Aw bet ye a hapenny Aw'm no ! "

* * *

To-night Jean came running up to me when school was dismissed.

" Gie's my hapenny ! " she cried ; " Aw didna speak to Annie and Janet a' day ! "

" Honest ? "

" It's true," said Ellen, " isn't it Gladys ? "

" Then I'll pay up my debt of honour," I said, and I held out a ha'penny.

Jean took it, and then she set off round the steading in great haste. She returned with her arms round Janet and Annie.

" Aw got Bets Burnett to tell them aboot the ha'penny," she confessed, " and to speer them no to speak to me a' day and Aw wud gie them a bit o' sugarelly."

" You scheming besom ! " I cried and I laid her on my bothy table and sat on her.

" Eh ! Jean ! " said Gladys, " if only ye had said ye wud bet a shillin' ! "

" Dear me," I said hastily, " when I come to think of it I did bet a shilling. Jean bet a hapenny, but I distinctly remember saying that I was betting a shilling. Here you are, Jean ! " but Jean refused it with indignation. Not one of them would touch it.

" Right ! " I cried. " I'm going down to get cigarettes. Who's coming ? "

I spent a shilling on sweets and chocolate. No one would accept a single sweetie.

"I'll give myself toothache if I eat them," I said. They paid no heed.

"I won't invite one of you to my marriage if you don't take them." They wavered, but did not give way.

"All right," I said with an air of great determination, "here goes!" and I tossed the bag into the field. They made no sign of interest, and we walked up the brae. Jim Jackson was coming down with his milk.

"Jim," I began, "if you go down to that first gate, and look over the hedge you'll find—"

I got no farther.

"Come on!" cried Janet, "Aw dinna want them, but Jim Jackson's no to get them onywye!"

I was glad to note that they gave Jim a handful as he passed.

* * *

To-day was fair day, and the bairns all went to town. I cycled in in the afternoon, and took the girls on the hobby-horses. I also stood Jim Jackson and Dickie Gibson into the stirring drama entitled: "The Moaning Spirit of the Moat....a Drama of the Supernatural." I had a few shies at the hairy-dolls, and won two cocoanuts and a gold tie-pin. Then I stood fascinated by the style of the gentleman who kept the ring stall. Several articles were hung from hooks, and you tried to throw a ring on to a hook. His invariable comment on a ploughman's attempt was: "Hard luck for the alarum-clock! Give the gentleman a collar-stud."

About five o'clock Jim came up to me.

"How now, duke," I said breezily, "how much money have you left?"

I was astonished to hear that he had half-a-crown.

"Why!" I cried, "you told me at three o'clock that you had only ninepence left!"

He smiled enigmatically.

"Aw've been speculatin'," he said proudly. "Have ye seen the mannie that's sellin' watches and things at the Cross? Aw was standin' there wi' Geordie Steel this mornin', and the mannie speered if onybody wud gie him a penny for a shillin', and naebody wud dae it at first. Syne a ploughman gae him a penny and he got the shillin'. Syne the mannie speers again, and Geordie got a shillin' for a ha'penny. Syne he began to sell watches, and the first man that bocht a watch got his money back. Syne he held up a gold chain, and the man that bocht that he got his money back. Syne he held up anither gold chain and said he wud sell it for half-a-crown. So Geordie ups and hauds oot his half-croon, and it was a' the money he had. Weel, he gets the chain, but no his money back. 'Don't go away,' says the mannie; 'each and every man as buys an article of jewellery will have his reward.'

"Weel, Aw waited for half-an-hoor, but Geordie hadna got onything by that time, so Aw goes and sees the boxin' show. After that

Aw had a shot o' the shoagin' boats, and syne Aw went back to the Cross. Geordie was ay waitin' for his reward. So Aw says to him: 'He's likely forgot a' aboot it, Geordie; tell him!' So Geordie hauds up his gold chain and says: 'Hi, mannie, ye said Aw was to get a reward!' 'O, yes,' says the mannie, 'and so you shall! I want you to keep these eighteen carat gold sleeve-links as a memento of this occasion,' and he shoved a pair o' links into Geordie's hands. After that he shut his box and said he wud hae anither sale at four punctual.

"Weel, Aw began to think aboot the thing, and when he began again he did the same thing. 'Will anyone oblige me by giving me a penny for half-a-crown?' he says, and Aw was just puttin' up my hand when a man held up his penny. 'Hi!' I cried, 'Aw'll gie ye tuppence if ye like!' and the mannie that was selling the things he lauched and handed me the half-croon. 'You're the kind of lad I'm looking for for an apprentice,' he says, but whenever Aw got the money Aw turned and ran awa, and he cries after me: 'Yes, you are the lad I want, but I see you are too clever for me.'"

I asked Jim to show me the half-crown, and I examined it. It was quite genuine, but I said to Jim: "Men like that usually give away bad money." He was off like a flash, and when he came back he carried twenty-five pennies and ten hapennies.

"If he starts to sell again," he announced, "Aw'll get Geordie to hand up the penny, but Aw'll no stand aside him."

The girls each brought my "market" to me to-night....a packet of rock. I asked about their spendings. Janet had bought three lucky-bags and nine lucky eggs. She had had no luck, and was somewhat grieved at the fact that Jean had bought only one lucky-egg and had got a new hapenny in it. Janet would have bought another egg with the hapenny, but I was not surprised to hear that Jean had bought sugarelly. Ellen had bought a tupenny note-book and a copying-ink pencil, a rubber and a card of assorted pen-nibs. Gladys had spent her all on lemon-kailie, the heavenly powder you get in oval boxes, with two wee tin spoons to sup it with.

Jim came up later. His pockets contained three trumps, or Jewish harps as they are called in catalogues, three copying-ink pencils, a pencil that wrote red at one end and blue at the other, two mouth-organs, a wire puzzle, and....Geordie's gold chain. The latter he had bought for tuppence and a double-stringed trump.

"Aw spent three and fowerpence," he said, "but dinna tell the Mester!"

"Why not, Jim?"

"Cos he'll be angry. He told us yesterday no to spend oor money at the market, but to bring it and put it in the Savin's Bank."

I wonder what becomes of the money that

children put into the Savings Bank. I think that their parents usually collar it at some time or another. I half suspect that quite a number of cottage pianos owe their appearance to the children's bank-books. I stopped the saving business when I was down in the school. Bairns seldom get money, and sugarelly is like Robinson Crusoe: you must tackle it when you are young, or you never enjoy it thoroughly. I think it cruel to make a bairn bank the penny it gets for running a message. Spending is always a pleasant thing, but a bairn gets more delirious joy out of buying a hapenny lucky-bag than an adult gets out of buying a thousand guinea Rolls Royce motor.

Some parents are foolish enough to give their bairns too much to spend. Little Mary Wallace has a penny every day of the year. I think that foolish of her mother. Spending must be a very rare thing if it is to yield the highest pleasure.

I would advise bairns to save when they have a definite object in view. To lay up treasure in the Post Office Savings Bank is, for a bairn, about as tempting as laying up treasure in heaven. Bairns can't entertain remote possibilities. You can tell a boy that a sum in the bank will help him to buy clothes or a bicycle when he is a man, and the prospect does not thrill him. You can't persuade a boy to cast his eyes on the years to come when his eyes are rivetted on a cake of chewing-gum in the village shop window. If he saves it should be for a direct tangible object. He takes up a Gamage catalogue (the most delightful of books to a boy), and he sees an illustration of a water-pistol costing a shilling. If he is a boy of spirit he will deny himself sweeties for a month in order to get that pistol. The self-discipline necessary to enable a village boy to buy a water-pistol will do him infinitely more good than all the discipline of all the Macdonalds in Scotland. I would have all children poor in money, but I would give them the opportunity of earning enough money to buy their toys. A little poverty is good for anybody ; I would recommend a young man to live on twelve shillings a week for a year or two ; he would begin to see things in proportion.

A friend of mine bases his antipathy to Socialism on this view of poverty. He argues that poverty brings out self-reliance, pluck, grit. When I ask him why he doesn't support Socialism as a means of bringing all these advantages to the poor wealthy folk, he is at a loss. In a manner I agree with him ; poverty will often give a race splendid characteristics. But Socialism recognises that the wealth of the world is divided most unequally. At one end you have luxury that makes men degenerate ; at the other end you have poverty that makes men swine. If Shaw's idea of equal incomes could be carried out each person would be in the position of a member of the present lower middle class ; he would be rich enough to be well-fed and happy, and he would be poor enough to discipline himself to make sacrifices to attain an object. I don't think that any man should satisfy more than one desire at a time. If Andrew Carnegie wants a motor-car and a four manual organ he has simply to tell his secretary to write out two cheques. But if I want a motor-cycle and an Angelus player-piano I've got to give up one desire. I know that I'll tire of either, and all I have to do is to sit down and wonder which novelty will last the longer. I want both very much. A $2\frac{3}{4}$-h.p. Douglas would be delightful, and an Angelus with lots of rolls would charm the long nights away. But.... there is Margaret. I begin to think of blankets and sheets and pots and pans. I don't want any of these plebeian articles, but I want Margaret very much, and I know that along with her I must take the whole bunch of kitchen utensils.

I begin to feel sorry for millionaires. One of the finer pleasures of life is the desiring of a thing you can't buy. The sorriest man in story is the millionaire who arrived at a big hotel very late, so late that he couldn't be served with supper. He straightway sent for the proprietor and asked the price of the hotel. He wrote out a cheque on the spot....and called for his sausage and mashed—or whatever the dish was. No wonder that millionaires complain of indigestion.

That story contains a fine moral. I don't exactly know what the moral is, but I hazard the opinion that the moral is this :—Never buy a hotel in order to get a plate of sausage and mashed. Millionaires might be defined as men who buy hotels in order to get sausage and mashed....and they can't digest the sausage when they have got it. When a Carnegie builds a great organ in a great hall he is really buying the whole hotel. He is taking an unfair advantage of his fellow music-lovers. A plate of sausage and mashed would be of far greater moment to G. K. Chesterton than to the millionaire, but G. K. couldn't buy the whole hotel ; he would merely swear volubly and tighten the belt of his waistcoat....if that were possible. The millionaire should not have this advantage over Chesterton. So a millionaire should not have any advantage over a music-lover. Collinson, the Edinburgh University organist, has no doubt a greater appreciation of organ music than a Carnegie, but he has to go down to his church organ on a winter night if he wants to play a Bach fugue. Money is power, they say, but money is worse than power ; it is tyranny. A successful pork-merchant whose one talent is his ability to tell at a glance how much pig it takes to fill a thousand tins of lamb cutlet, may buy up half the treasures of the world if he likes. Priceless pictures and violins lie in millionaires' halls, while students of genius study prints and practise on two guinea fiddles. At first sight this seems a problem that Horatio Bottomley would handle eagerly and popularly, but the problem is really a deep one. When humanity abolishes the power to amass millions who is to have the priceless treasures? In the case of art the community of course. (I see in to-day's paper that Rodin has bequeathed all his works to France.) But what of the Stradivarius violins? I would have them lent to the geniuses. Who is to decide who the geniuses are? That is a question of fundamentals, and if I had left the question to Mr. Bottomley I think he would have recommended his readers to "write to John Bull about it."

I begin to feel that I am talking through my hat as the vulgar phrase has it. My baccy's finished, and I can't concentrate my attention on any subject. What I meant to do was to show that a millionaire is a man to be pitied. To buy a Titian painting when your tastes lie in the direction of Heath Robinson's *Frightful War Pictures* is as pathetic a thing to do as to sit out a classical concert when your tastes lead you to a passionate love for ragtime. And buying a Titian is a simple case of buying the hotel in order to get the sausage and mashed that you can't eat.

Millionaires....no, it's no good; I'll have to fold up my typewriter till I get some more baccy.

XV.

MARGARET was reading a few pages of my diary to-night.

"Why," she said, "it's all about yourself!"

"Not all," I said hastily, "some of it is about you....but I won't let you read that part until you are my wife. If you knew the terrible things I have written about you you would go off straightway and marry Joe Smith."

"You think quite a lot of yourself," she said with a laugh.

"Everybody thinks a lot of himself, Margaret. If I died to-night you would probably have forgotten the shape of my nose by the time you were sixty, but you'll never forget that I told you your neck was the loveliest neck in the county. My old grandmother used to tell me again and again of the man who stopped her on the road when she was seven and told her that her eyes were like blue stars. His name was Donald Gunn....but she could never recollect the names of the girls she played with.

"The people who don't think much of themselves are people who have no personality to be proud of....personally I haven't yet met any of the brand. We all have something that we're conceited about, dear. You are conceited about your eyes and your neck and your hair. Jean Hardie is about the plainest girl in the village, but I could bet that she thinks her hair the most glorious in the place.... and it is too.

"Very often we are conceited about the things that we can do worst. I can draw pretty well, but I'm not conceited about it. I can't sing for nuts....and if anyone left the room when I was warbling I should hate him to all eternity. I like a man to be an egotist....if he has got an ego of any value. Peter MacMannish is a type of egotist that should be put into a lethal chamber. He has no ego to talk about, but he imagines that his stomach is his ego, and he will talk to you for an hour about the 'yirkin'' of the organ in question."

"What is an ego?" asked Margaret. "I never heard the word before."

"It is the Latin word for 'I,' and a person who uses the pronoun 'I' very often is called an egotist. The other word egoist has a different meaning; it means a person who thinks of himself all the time, a selfish person. You can be an egotist without being an egoist, and vice versa. Peter Mitchell never talks about himself; while you talk about yourself he is thinking out a method of selling you something at double its value.

"There are two kinds of egotist....the man who talks about what he does, and the man who talks about what he thinks. When I get letters from my friends they are full of "I's." Dorothy Westbrook, a college friend of mine, a medallist in half-a-dozen classes, fills eight pages with small talk.....' I went to see Tree in the Darling of the Gods last night,' and so on. I generally skip the eight pages and look at the post-script. May Baxter, another college friend, a girl who wouldn't recognise a medal if you showed her one, writes ten pages, and she usually commences with something like this :—' I was re-reading *The New Machiavelli* last night, and I think that I begin to despise Wells now." I read her letter a dozen times. When she does take a fancy for the other kind of egotism she is delightful : she doesn't tell me what she does ; she tells me what she is.

" I have half a mind to leave you for a year, Margaret, just to give you a chance of writing about yourself. I won't be able to write to you in the same strain : I wrote myself out when I fell in love at twenty-two. You can only be a good letter-writer once, and that is when you are discovering yourself for the first time, and ramming it down on paper as fast as you can. I used to write letters of twenty foolscap pages, but now I never write a letter if I can help it. Life has lost most of its glamour when you realise that you have discovered yourself. It's a sad business discovering yourself, dear. You set out to persuade yourself that you are a genius or a saint, and, after a long examination of yourself you discover that you are a sorry creature. You set out with Faith and Hope at your elbow, and at the end you find that they have long since left you, but you find that Charity has taken their place. Charity begins at home says the proverb, and I take this to mean that Charity comes to you when you find yourself at home, when you discover yourself. I used to be the most uncharitable of mortals, but now I seldom judge a man or woman. Peter MacMannish gets drunk; I do not condemn him, for I have looked on the wine when it was red. Mary MacWinnie has had two illegitimate children; I am a theoretical Don Juan. Shepherd, the rabbit-catcher, has an atrocious temper; I do not judge him, because, although my own temper is pretty equable, I can realise that the man can no more help his temper than I can the size of my feet. Charity comes to you when you have discovered how weak you are, and that's what kept me from being a good code teacher. I was such a poor weak devil that I couldn't bring myself to make the boys salute me or fear me."

"You say that, but you don't believe it."

"I believe it, Margaret. My whole theory of education is built on my abject humility. My chief objection to Macdonald is that he ignores his own weaknesses. He has never analysed himself to see what manner of man he is. If he could look into his heart and discover all the little meanesses and follies and hypocrisies he would not have the courage to make a boy salute him; he would not have the impudence to strap a boy for swearing. One of the worst things about Macdonald and a thousand other dominies is that they have forgotten their childhood. A dominie should never grow up. I would take away from all students their text-books on School Management and Psychology, and put into their hands Barrie's *Peter Pan* and Stevenson's *A Child's Garden of Verses*.

"Margaret, why can't people see that the Macdonald system is all wrong? What in all the world is the use of dominies and ministers and parents posing before children? What is respect but a pose? What is Macdonald's sternness but a pose? He is a kindly decent fellow outside his school. The bairns meet with pose the first thing in the morning when they enter the school. They stand up and repeat the Lord's Prayer monotonously, and without the faintest realisation of what they are saying. The dominie closes his eyes and clasps his hands in front of him, and I don't believe there is a single dominie in Scotland who really prays each morning. For that matter I don't believe that there are half-a-dozen ministers who repeat the prayer on Sundays with any thought of its meaning. The morning prayer is a gigantic sham. When I said to Macdonald that I would have it abolished in schools he almost had a fit. The bigger the sham is the louder is the screaming in its defence if you attack it.

"Think of all the shams that parents practise. They pretend that babies come in the doctor's pocket; they pretend that a lie is as much an abomination to them as it is to the Lord;

they imply by their actions that they never stole apples in their lives; they hint that they don't know what bad language means. They live a life that is one continuous lie."

"I don't understand that," said Margaret with a puzzled look.

"A mother lies to her child when she tells it that it is wicked when it makes a noise; a father lies to his son when he tells him that he will come to a bad end if he smokes any more cigarettes. Worse than that they lie by negation. The father changes his 'Hell!' into 'Hades!' when he hits his thumb with a hammer; the mother says 'Tut Tut!' when she means 'Damnation!' Both go to church as an example to their offspring....and going to church is in most cases a lie. Nearly every father of a family says grace before meat, and he generally delays the practice until his first-born is old enough to take notice. Then there is the lie about relationship. A child never discovers that its father has about as much love for its mother's aunt as he has for the King of Siam.

"Convention is one huge lie, Margaret. You lift your hat when a coffin goes by; you beg my pardon when I ask you to pass the marmalade; you stand bare-headed when a band plays the National Anthem. It's all a lie, dear, a pretty lie perhaps, but a lie all the same. But after all, the manners business is a minor affair; you can't abolish it, and if you try you will only make yourself ridiculous.

But the other lies, the hypocritical lies that are told to children....these are dangerous. An ardent republican will doff his hat when the band plays *God Save the King*, and be none the worse; the unpleasantness that might follow his keeping his hat on his head wouldn't be worth it. But if I pretend to a child that I am above human frailty I am doing a hellish thing that may have devilish consequences."

"Your language is awful!" cried Margaret in feigned protest.

"I was quoting *The Ancient Mariner*, dear; you read it at my evening class, and you have evidently forgotten it. Since the beginning of humanity children have been warped by the attitudinising of their elders. A child is imitative always; he hasn't the power to think out biggish things for himself. He is tremendously docile; he will believe almost anything you tell him, and he will accept an older person's pose without question. If one of the village boys were to see Macdonald stotting home drunk he would be like the countryman who, when he saw a giraffe for the first time, cried: 'Hell!.....I don't believe it!' And the sad thing is that they never are able to distinguish between pose and truth. The villagers who used to tell my bairns that I was daft don't realise what pose is; they have never found the right values. When they criticise the minister or the dominie they invariably fasten on the wrong things. They are beginning to criticise Macdonald because he insists on a bairn's bringing a written excuse when he has been absent, but they believe in all his poses —his love for respect, his authority, his whackings, his hiding of his pipe when a child is near, his passion for sex morality, his dignity, his....his frayed frock coat that he wears in school."

"The poor man's only wearing out his old Sunday coat!" protested Margaret.

"I never thought of that, Margaret; I'll cut out the coat. But he shouldn't have a frock coat anyway. When we get married I shall insist on dressing in an old golfing jacket, flannel bags, and a soft collar. The only danger is that men of my stamp are apt to make unconvention conventional. It's a very difficult thing to keep from posing when you are protesting against pose."

"Oh! I don't understand the half of what you say," said Margaret wearily.

"That means that you think my lips might be better employed, you schemer!" and I.... well, I don't think I need write everything down after all.

* * *

"There was a venter locust at the schule the day," remarked Annie. I was brushing my boots at the bothy door, and the girls sat on the step and watched me.

"A what?" I asked.

"A venter locust. Ye paid a penny to get in, and Jim Jackson gaithered the pennies in the mannie's hat and got in for nothing, for he didna put his ain penny in."

"What sort of show was it, Annie?"

"He had a muckle doll wi' an awfu' ugly face, and he asked it questions."

"Did it answer them?"

"Aye. It opened its great big mooth."

"There maybe was a gramaphone inside," suggested Gladys.

"Jim Jackson said that it was the mannie that was speakin' a' the time," said Janet.

"Jim Jackson was bletherin'," said Annie with scorn. "Aw watched 'im, and his mooth never moved a' the time."

"Perhaps he was talking through his hat, Annie," I said.

"He wasna," she cried, "for his hat was on the Mester's desk fu' o' pennies!"

"Well," I ventured, "the proverb says that money talks, you know."

"Weel," tittered Annie, "there wasna much money to talk, for the pennies was nearly a' hapennies!"

"Aw dinna understand how that doll managed to speak," said Ellen, and I proceeded to explain the mysteries of ventriloquism to them. Then I told them my one ventriloquist yarn.

A broken-down ventriloquist stopped at a village inn one hot day, and stared longingly through the bar door. He hadn't a cent in his pocket. He sat down on the bench and gazed wearily at a stray mongrel dog that had followed him for days. Suddenly inspiration came to him. He rose and walked into the bar.

"A pint of beer, mister!" he cried, and pretended to fumble for his money, when the landlord placed the tankard on the bar counter.

The dog looked up into his face.

"Here, mister," said the dog, "ain't I going to get one?"

The landlord started.

"That's a remarkable animal," he said with staring eyes.

"Pretty smart," said the ventriloquist indifferently.

"I'll—I'll buy that dog," said the landlord eagerly; "I'll give you five pounds for him."

The ventriloquist considered for a while.

"All right," he said at length, "I hate to part with an old friend like him, but I must live, and I have no money."

The landlord counted out the five sovereigns, and the ventriloquist drank up his beer and made for the door.

"Better come round and take hold of the dog," he said, "or he'll follow me."

The landlord lifted the bar-flap and took hold of the dog by the collar.

At the door the ventriloquist looked back. The dog gazed at him.

"You brute," it cried, "you've sold me for vulgar gold. I swear that I'll never speak again."

I paused.

"And, you know, girls, he never did."

"Eh," cried Janet, "what a shame! The public-hoose mannie wud leather the puir beast to mak' it speak."

"That's the real point of the story, Jan. A story is no good unless it leaves something to the imagination."

"The Mester gae us a story to write for composition the day," said Annie. "It was aboot a boy that was after a job and a' the boys were lined up and they had to go in to see the man, and he had a Bible lyin' on the floor, and a' the lads steppit over it, but this laddie he pickit it up and got the job."

"That's what you call a story with a moral, Annie. It is meant to teach you a lesson. The best stories have no morals....neither have the people who listen to them."

"We had to write the story," said Ellen, "and syne we had to tell why the boy got the job. Aw said it was becos he was a guid boy and went to the Sunday Schule."

"Aw said it was becos he was a pernikity sort o' laddie that liked things to be tidy," said Gladys.

Annie laughed.

"Aw said the man was maybe a fat man that cudna bend doon to pick it up. What did you say, Jan?"

"Aw dinna mind," said Janet ruefully, "but when the Mester cried me oot for speakin', Aw picked up a geography book on the floor, just to mak the Mester think that Aw had learned a lesson frae his story, but he gae me a slap on the lug for wastin' time comin' oot."

"Jim Jackson got three scuds wi' the strap for his story," said Annie.

"Ah!" I cried, "what did he write?"

"He said that the laddie maybe hadna a hankie, and his nose was needin' dichted and he didna like to let the man see him dichtin' it wi' the sleeve o' his jaicket, so he bent doon to pick up the Bible and dicht his nose on the sly at the same time."

"Yes," I said sadly, "that's Jim Jacksonese, pure and simple. Poor lad!"

"The Mester said he was a vulgar fellow," said Janet.

"A low-minded something or other, he ca'ed him," said Gladys.

"But he didna greet when he got the strap," said Annie, "he just sniffed thro' his nose and —and dichted it wi' his sleeve."

I knew then that all the Macdonalds in creation couldn't conquer my Jim.

XVI.

MACDONALD and I were comparing notes to-night.

"I found that Monday was always a noisy day in school," I said; "the bairns were always unsettled."

"I don't find that," he said; "Friday is their worst day. I don't understand that."

"Friday was my free day," I said.

"What do you mean by free day?"

"Every bairn did what it liked."

"Good Lord!" exclaimed Macdonald.

"That's nothing," I laughed, "why, I gave them a free week once."

"What was your idea. Laziness?"

"Laziness! My dear boy, I never put in such a hard week in my life. A boy would come out and ask for a certain kind of sum, then a girl would bring out a writing book and ask for a setting; by the time I had attended to these, a dozen were waiting."

"Did they all work?"

"They were all active. Dickie Gibson spent the week in sketching; Geordie Steel read five penny dreadfuls; Janet Brown played at anagrams; Annie Miller read *The Weekly Welcome;* Ellen Smith worked arithmetic all week and Jock Miller wrote a novel. Jock spent half his dinner-hour writing."

"That's what a school should be," I added.

"Ah! So you think that reading penny dreadfuls is education?"

"Everything you do is education."

"So you say, but I want to know the exact educational value of penny dreadfuls. My idea is that they do boys harm."

"That's what the magistrates say, Macdonald. They trace all juvenile crime to penny dreadfuls and the cinema. The British have a passion for scapegoats. We have war with Germany. 'Who did this?' demand the public indignantly. 'Who's going to be whopped for this?' They look round and Haldane's rotund figure catches their eye. Haldane becomes the scapegoat. So with poor Birrell when the Sinn Fein rebellion occurred. So the magistrates fasten on the poor penny dreadful and the picture-film. Obviously they do so because they are too stupid to think out the problem of crime. Picture-houses have about as much to do with crime as Birrell had to do with the dissatisfaction in Ireland."

"Come, come," said Macdonald impatiently, "keep to the point: what educational value has the penny dreadful?"

"The educational value that any reading matter has. It doesn't give you many ideas, but you can say the same thing about Barrie's novels or Kipling's. It gives a boy a vocabulary and it exercises his imagination."

"Wouldn't he be better reading good literature? Dickens for instance?"

"I don't see it," I said; "he isn't ripe enough

to understand Dickens's humour, and for a boy I should say Dickens is bad. His style is grandiose and stilted his periphrasis is the most delightful in the world to an educated person, but it is bad for a child. About half of *David Copperfield* is circumlocution, but a boy should learn to speak and write boldly. The penny dreadful goes straight to the point. 'Harold looked straight into the blue barrel of a Colt automatic.' Translate that into Dickensese (an ugly word to coin, I admit) and you have something like this :— 'Harold contemplated with extreme apprehension the circular muzzle of a Cerulean blue automatic pistol of the kind specifically manufactured by the celebrated world-famous American firm of Colt.' "

" Poor Dickens," laughed Macdonald.

" But you see my point ? " I persisted. " Circumlocution is a Victorian nuisance. Any man who has anything to say says it simply and without trappings. And, mind you, Macdonald, people who use circumlocution in style use it in thought. The average man loves flowery literature, and he loves flowery thoughts. The contest between the plain style and the aureate style is really the old contest between realism and romance. The romantic way to look at crime is to fix your attention on drink and penny dreadfuls and cinema shows ; the realistic way is to look bravely at the economic division of wealth that causes poverty and disease, the father and mother of crime."

" You're away from the point again," said Macdonald with a smile. " How do you defend Janet Brown's week of anagrams ? "

" It doesn't need any defence ; it was Janet's fancy to play herself and I fail to see that she was wasting time. You really never waste time unless you are under coercion."

" Another rotten paradox," he laughed, " go on ! "

" When I allow convention to force me to play cards I feel that I am wasting time, for I hate the blamed things. But if I spend a day pottering with the wheels of an old clock I am not wasting time : I am extremely interested all the time."

" No, no ! It won't do ! Janet was wasting time, and you know it, in spite of your arguing ! "

" I'll tell you what's wrong with you and all your fellow educationists, Macdonald," I said. " You've got utilitarian commercial minds. You worship work and duty, and you have your eyes on monetary success all the time. You look upon bairns as a foreman mechanic looks upon workmen, and your idea of wasted time is the same as his. If I were Bruce, the linen merchant, I should certainly accuse a girl of wasting time if I caught her reading a novelette during working hours. Bruce has one definite aim—production of linen. He knows exactly what he wants to produce. You don't, and I don't. We don't know what effect puzzling out anagrams will have on

Janet's mentality. We have no right to accuse her of wasting time."

"Don't tell me," he cried; "there is a difference between work and play. Janet has no more right to play during school hours than a mill-girl has to read novelettes during working hours."

"The mill-girl is a wage-slave, and I don't think that dominies should apply the ethics of wage-slavery to education. Her master, Bruce, goes golfing and fishing on working days, only, he is economically free, and he can do what he likes. And I don't suppose you will contend that tending a loom is the goal of humanity. If you want to make Janet an efficient mill-girl by all means coerce her to work in school. But, Macdonald, I have argued a score of times that education should not aim at turning out wage-slaves. If Janet is to be a mill-girl all your history and grammar won't make her tend a loom any better; so far as the loom is concerned the composing of anagrams will help her quite as much as grammar will."

When Macdonald had gone I made up my mind that I wouldn't argue about education with him again. I'll bring out my pack of cards when he next visits me.

* * *

I have had a sharp attack of influenza, and have been in bed for a week. When my temperature fell I commenced to read a book on political philosophy, but I had to give it up. I asked Margaret to borrow a few novels from Macdonald's school library, and I found content. I read *The Forest Lovers*, *King Solomon's Mines*, and one of Guy Boothby's Dr. Nikola stories, and was entranced.

When you are ill you become primitive; the emotional part of you is uppermost, and you weep over mawkish drivel that you would laugh at when you are well. Any snivelling parson could have persuaded me to believe that I was a sinner, had he come to my bed-side three days ago.

Luckily no snivelling parson came, but the girls came every night.

"Aw hope ye dinna dee," said Annie.

"Ye wud need an awfu' lang coffin," said Janet as she measured me with her eye.

"You've got a cheerful sort of bed-side manner, Jan," I said.

"Wud ye hae an oak coffin?" she asked.

"Couldn't afford it, Jan. You see I'm saving up for my marriage."

"But if ye need a coffin ye'll no need a wife."

"The wedding-cake will do for the funeral feast," I said hopefully. "I've ordered it."

Janet laughed.

"Eh! It wud be awfu' funny to eat weddin' cake at a burial!" she cried. "Wud'n it?"

"I don't think I would be in a position to appreciate the fun of the thing, Janet."

"Maggie wudna see muckle fun in it either," said Gladys.

"Wud Jim Jackson be yer chief mourner?" asked Ellen.

"Possibly," I said, "but don't mention the fact to him. He'll become unsettled. He's an ambitious youth, Jim, and his position as best man at my marriage will merely make him long for other worlds to conquer."

"Ye wud hae a big funeral," said Janet thoughtfully.

"We wud get a holiday that day," she added brightly.

"Ah!" I said, "that settles it, Jan. Leave me to die in peace. Let me see—this is Tuesday; if I die now that will mean Saturday for the funeral. That's no good. What do you say to my putting off the evil day till Friday? That will mean a holiday on Tuesday."

"But ye canna dee when ye want to!" she laughed.

"I can easily borrow some of Mrs. Thomson's rat poison."

"Syne ye wud be committin' sooicide," cried Annie, "and they wud bury ye at nicht, and we wudna get oor holiday."

"Ah! Annie! You've raised a difficulty. I hear Jim whistling outside. Bring him in and we'll see if he can solve the problem."

They brought Jim to my bedside. I explained the difficulty, and Jim scratched his head.

"If ye was murdered they wudna bury ye at nicht," he said after some deliberation.

" A brilliant idea, Jim, but who is to murder me ? "

" Joe Simpson wud dae it...quick," he answered. " He has a notion o' Maggie."

" Aw wud get another holiday," he added, " when Joe was tried. Aw wud be a witness."

" So wud Aw," said Annie.

" And me too," said Janet.

" Ye wudna," said Jim with scorn, " lassies canna swear, and ye have to put yer hand on the Bible and swear when ye are a witness."

" We'll have to give up the murder idea," I said firmly : " it's unfair ; I can't have Jim getting two holidays while the girls get only one."

" We micht get another holiday when Joe was buried," suggested Ellen.

" No," said Jim, " they bury a hanged man in the jile."

" Ye'll just need to get better again," said Janet.

" You'll lose your holiday in that case, Jan."

She put her arm round my neck.

" Aw was just funnin'," she said kindly, Aw dinna want ye to dee. Aw wud greet."

" You would forget me in a week, Jan."

" Na Aw wudna," she protested. " Aw wud put flowers on yer grave ilka Sabbath, and Aw wud cut oot the verse o' pottery in the paper. Aw cut oot the verse aboot my auntie Liz."

" What was it ? "

"Aw dinna mind, but it was something like this :—

> "We think, when we look at yer vacant chair,
> Of yer dear old face and yer grey hair,
> But ye are away to the land of above
> Where ye'll never more have care."

"Very nice, Jan. Now you'll better set about composing a verse for me."

"A' richt," she laughed, "we'll mak a line each, and here's the first one :—

> "'He was goin' to be marrit, but he dee'd afore his time

"You mak the next line, Annie."

> "'And Jim Jackson ate so muckle at the funeral that he got a sair wime.'"

"Nane o' yer lip," growled Jim.

"Come on, Gladys," I said, "third line."

> "'He dee'd o' effielinza, and he'll no hae ony mair pain."

"Last line, Ellen!"

> "'But in the Better Land we'll maybe meet him again.'"

"There shud be something aboot 'gone but not forgotten,'" said Jim. "When auld Rab Smith dee'd his wife had 'gone but not forgotten' in the papers....and the corp wasna oot o' the hoose."

"Aw've got a new frock," said Janet, and the conversation took a cheerier direction.

On the following evening Margaret came in when they were with me.

"Come on!" cried Janet, "we'll mak Maggie kiss him!" and they seized her.

"No," I said, "influenza is catching, and I don't want Margaret to be ill."

"Eh!" cried Annie, "d'ye think we believe

that? Aw believe she's kissed ye a hunder times since ye was badly."

"Not a hundred, Annie," I said; "the truth is that she kissed me once; I had just taken my dose of Gregory's Mixture, and she vowed that she would never kiss me again."

"Aw wud chuck him up if Aw was you, Maggie," said Jean, "he tells far ower many lees."

"Should I?" laughed Margaret.

"Aye," cried Jean with delight, "gie him back his ring!"

Margaret drew off her ring and handed it to me, and the girls clapped their hands gleefully.

"Very good," I said resignedly, "you girls will better cancel the orders for wedding frocks. And, Jean, just look in and tell Jim Jackson not to buy a new dickie, will you?"

The girls looked at each other doubtfully.

"Ye're just funnin'," said Jean with a forced laugh.

"Funning? My dear Jean, when a girl hands back the engagement ring, do you mean to tell me she is funning?"

Children live in two lands—the land of reality and the land of make-believe. A serious look will make them jump from the one to the other. They looked at my serious face and believed that Margaret had really given me up. Then they glanced at Margaret; she laughed, and their clouded faces cleared. I knew that they would try to make me believe that they still considered I was in earnest.

"Aw'll cry in and tell Jim aboot the dickie," said Jean.

"It's a pity ye ordered the weddin' cake," said Annie.

"Ye can gie it to the Mester to christen his bairn," suggested Janet.

"It'll be ower big," said Gladys.

"Aweel," retorted Janet, "he can gie the half o't to the Mester, and maybe the other half will do for Peter Mitchell's funeral."

"What!" I cried, "is Peter dead?"

"No exactly," said Janet hopefully, "but he's badly wi' the chronic, and he'll maybe dee."

"That settles the question of the cake," I said, "but you have still to settle the question of Margaret."

"She can marry Joe Simpson," suggested Ellen.

"Aye," said Jean, "and she'll hae to work oot, and feed the three black swine. She wud be better to tak Dave Young, for he has only twa swine to feed."

"Be an auld maid, Maggie," said Janet, "and keep a cat. A man's just a fair scutter onywve....especially a delicate man that taks effielinza and lies in his bed. Ye'll be far better as an auld maid, Maggie. Ye'll no hae ony bairns, but bairns is just a nuisance."

"I'll be an old maid then," said Margaret.

"Now you've disposed of the cake and

the lady," I said, "what is to become of me ? "

" You ! " said Janet. " You can be an auld bachelor and live next door to Maggie, and she'll send a laddie ower wi' a bowl o' soup when she has soup to her dinner."

" Aye," said Gladys, " and she'll wash yer sarks and mend yer socks for you."

" Sounds as if I am to have all the joys of matrimony without its sorrows," I said. " I'm afraid, Margaret, that we'll have to get married after all. The other way is too expensive : we should require to pay the rent of two houses "

" But," cried Annie, " if ye get married ye'll hae bairns to keep, and they'll cost mair than the rent o' two hooses ! "

" Then in Heaven's name what am I to do ? " I cried in feigned perplexity.

Janet took Margaret's hand and placed it in mine.

" Just tak Maggie," she said sweetly ; " and by the time ye hae bairns Aw'll maybe be marrit mysell, and Aw'll mak my man send ye a ham when he kills the swine."

So I placed the ring on Margaret's finger and kissed her. Then I drew Janet's head down and kissed her too.

" Eh ! " cried Annie, " that's no fair ! "

" What do you mean ? " I asked.

" Ye've kissed Jan," she laughed, " and she'll maybe tak effielinza and—and get a holiday."

Then I kissed Annie and the others three times, and they all went out laughing. The tears came into my eyes....but then I was weak and ill.

XVII.

I OBJECT to the type of man who practises practical jokes. Young Mackenzie and Jim Brown have just played a nasty one on Willie Baffers, the village lunatic. Poor Willie invented a new aeroplane ; he took an old solid-tyred boneshaker bicycle and fixed feathers to the spokes. Mackenzie and Brown inspected the invention, and told Willie that his fortune was as good as made.

Next morning the post brought a letter to Willie from the Munitions Ministry, offering him four million pounds and threepence hapenny for the patent rights, and asking Willie to meet a representative at the Royal Hotel in the town. Willie rode the old bike into town, and feathered it in the hotel yard. Mackenzie with a false beard on, handed him a cheque for the four millions, and Willie ran nearly all the eight miles home to tell of his good fortune.

Macdonald told me the yarn to-night as a rich joke, but I failed to find any humour in it. It was a low-down trick.

"Good Lord!" I cried, "neither of them is much more intelligent than Willie. Any man of average ability could take them in as easily as they took in poor Baffers."

"All the same," tittered Macdonald, "the joke is funny."

"There always is something funny in idiotic things, Macdonald. If I had seen Willie's invention I should probably have roared; but the glimpse would have satisfied me. I roar at Charlie Chaplin's idiotic actions, but I wouldn't be so ready to roar at them if Charlie were really an idiot. Any fool could spend a lifetime playing jokes on village lunatics. I could write Willie a letter offering him the command on the Western front, and signing it 'Lloyd George,' but that sort of fun doesn't appeal to me."

"I'm different," said Macdonald. "I would think that a good joke. You think Jim Jackson funny, on the other hand, and I think there's nothing funny about him."

"What has he been doing now?"

"I gave them an essay on their favourite pets yesterday, and he wrote one about his pet bee and elephant."

"What did he say about them?"

"Oh, the thing was just a piece of nonsense. He said the bee's name was Polly, and—I have the thing in my desk," he said, "you can read it for yourself."

I copied the essay out to-night. Here it is:—

POLLY AND PETER.

Polly is the name of my pet bee, and Peter is my elephant. They are very friendly, Polly often sits on Peter's ear but Peter never sits on Polly's. They eat out of the same dish. Peter ate Polly by mistake one day, but she stung him on the tongue and when he opened his mouth to roar she flew out. Polly used to sleep in Peter's trunk. One night he sneezed and Polly was lying a mile away next morning.

In the summer time Polly lives in a wood house in the garden and it is called a hive and that is where she keeps the honey. I take it away when she is not looking and she thinks it is Peter that does it, at least she kicks him for it. I have told her to watch for Zeps. She sits on the roof all night watching, she is to sting the Kaiser on the nose if he comes. She is an old maid. She had a lad called Archibald, but father sat on him one night and then he swore when he tried to sit down for weeks after. Archibald died.

Peter is a nice animal and he has a thousand teeth, but Polly only has twenty. Peter looks like he has two tails he wags them both but the front one is a trunk for eating. He is an awful big eater. He says his prayers every night and I hope he will go to heaven when he dies. He had pewmonia and Polly had pendisitis, and the doctor made an operation and put in nineteen stitches. Peter works all day, the road-roller man is at the war and Peter has to roll about on the road to bruise the metal. He fills his trunk with water and wets the road first. Polly tells him when the moters are coming.

"I don't see anything funny in that," said Macdonald.

"Possibly not," I said, "but Jim's idea of fun isn't the same as yours or mine. A bairn laughs at ludicrous things: I'm sure Jim laughed when he imagined the scene where his father sat on Archibald. The essay is full of promise."

Macdonald handed me Alec Henry's book.

"That's a better essay," he said.

I read the essay.

"It's English is better," I said, "the sentences are correctly formed, but there isn't an idea in the whole essay. Anybody can describe a pet rabbit."

"That's so, but composition is meant to teach a boy to write good English."

"What's the good of writing good English if you haven't any ideas to write about?" I cried. "Every member of Parliament can write good English, but there aren't half-a-dozen men of ideas in the House. Personally, I don't care a damn how a boy writes if he shows he is not an average boy. Jim Jackson has talent: Alec Henry is a mere unimaginative cram. You encourage Henry and you sit on Jim.....I wish he had Archibald's power to sting you!"

"But what is his nonsense to lead to?" he said.

"We don't know. As dominies our job is to encourage Jim in his natural bent. It is enough for us that he is different from the scholarly Henry. We have a good idea of what Alec will come to; we know nothing about Jim. You have tried to fit Jim into the Alec mould, and you have failed."

"Jim knew that you were on his side," growled Macdonald.

"I suppose he did, Macdonald. But you have got all the others; surely you don't grudge me Jim and the five girls?"

"That's all right," he said with a short laugh, "I've given up wooing them. I allow Jim to choose his own line now....but I'll never like the laddie."

* * *

I have always disliked all the pomp and circumstance of weddings. Margaret wanted a quiet wedding before a registrar but her father was eager to make a fete of the occasion, and we allowed him to have his way. Besides Jim and the girls were expecting a great day.

I can't say that I enjoyed my wedding. The bairns seemed to have lost their identity when they donned their wedding garments. Jim sat on the dickey beside the driver; there was pride in his face but his smile was gone. The occasion was too great for him. The girls stood about the dining-room in awkward attitudes, and I noted the fine English of their speech.

And Jim failed at the wedding-feast. Part of his duty was to propose the health of the bridesmaids, and when the minister called upon him for his speech he fled from the room.

Peter MacMannish proposed the toast instead.

Margaret and I set off in a hired motor in the afternoon. We were going to London. When we reached the station Margaret suddenly said: "If only we could have stayed for the dance to-night!"

"Yes," I said, "the bairns will be in form to-night."

"We should really be there," continued Margaret sadly, "it's our dance you know."

"And here we are going off to a hotel among strangers, Margaret!"

Margaret clutched my arm.

"Let's go back," she said eagerly, "we'll spend the first bit of our honeymoon in the dear old bothy!"

I beckoned to a taxi-driver.

As we drove up the brae to the farm Margaret laughed.

"Do you know what I am laughing at?" she said. "I was thinking about you coming back. It's a sort of habit of yours coming back, isn't it? You don't care for me one bit; you are in love with Janet and Annie."

"Who proposed coming back, madam?"

"I did," she cried in great glee: "I noticed that you didn't seem keen on buying the tickets, and I knew you didn't want to go."

When we walked into the dining-room there was consternation. Margaret's mother went very white.

"What's wrong?" she stammered.

"Goad! They've quarrelled already!" exclaimed Peter MacMannish in a hoarse whisper.

"Did ye miss the train?" asked Janet.

"No, Jan, we missed the supper, and we made up our minds that it was too good to miss. We're going to do an original thing; we're going to dance at our own wedding."

The blacksmith struck up a waltz, and my wife and I waltzed round the room. I don't think that a wedding party was ever so jolly as ours.

The bairns escorted us to our bothy at two in the morning, and Margaret insisted on giving them a cup of tea before they went home.

Janet looked round the wee room.

"Eh, Maggie, what an awfu' place to spend yer honeymoon in!"

"Yes," said Margaret, "that's what comes of marrying a mean man. It's disgraceful, isn't it, Jan?"

"What do ye ca' it when ye stop bein' married?" asked Annie.

"A divorce," I said.

"And is there a feed at a divorce?" asked Jim with an interested expression.

"No, Jim; you are fed up before the divorce proceedings."

"Aw wud divorce him, Maggie," said Annie.

"It's difficult," laughed Margaret.

"Ye cud say he wudna gie ye a proper honeymoon," put in Gladys.

Annie sat down on my knee.

"Why did ye come back?" she asked.

"I came back to find out how you performed your duties, Annie. I'll begin with the best man. Jim Jackson, give an account of your stewardship."

"Aw had three helpin's o' the plum-duff, twa o' the apple-pie, three o' the —"

"I'm not taking an inventory of your interior furnishings," I said severely; "what I want to know is whether you performed your duties. Did you kiss the bridesmaids?"

"Eh!" gasped Janet, "he'd better try!"

"Do you mean to tell me he didn't?" I demanded.

"Aw had a broken-oot lip," said Jim apologetically, "and Aw didna want to smit onybody."

"And the bairn next door to oor hoose has the measles," he added hastily.

"And Aw lookit at a book aboot etikquette and it didna say onything aboot kissin' the bridesmaids."

"The bridesmaids didna want to kiss yer dirty moo, onywye, Jim Jackson," said Janet.

"Aw've got a better moo than Tam Rigg, onywye," said Jim cheerfully.

Janet gazed at his mouth curiously.

"Your's is bigger, onywye."

"Now, now," I said, "don't you set a newly married couple a bad example by quarrelling."

I turned to Jean.

"What did you think of the wedding, Jean?"

"Jean grat," said Gladys, "and so did Jan. What was ye greetin' aboot?"

"Aw dinna ken," said Jean simply. "Aw saw Maggie's mother greetin' so Aw just began to greet too. What was yer mother greetin' for, Maggie?"

"I don't know, Jean."

"Aw think she had the teethache," said Jim, "cos Aw heard the minister say to her to try a drap o' whiskey."

"It wasna the teethache," said Annie scornfully, "but Aw ken why she grat."

"To mak fowk think she was so fond o' Maggie that she didna want her to ging awa," suggested Gladys.

"Na it wasna," said Annie, "she maybe was thinkin' o' Maggie's auldest sister Jean that dee'd when she was saxteen."

"G'wa," cried Jim, "it's the fashion to greet at a marriage and a burial, but ye dinna greet at a christenin'."

"Why no?" asked Jean.

"Cos ye wudna be heard: the bairn greets a' the time."

Janet glanced at Margaret.

"That'll be the next party," she said brightly. "the christenin'. Did ye keep the top storey o' the cake, Maggie?"

Margaret blushed at this.

Janet seized her by the shoulders.

"Ye needna tak a reid face, for Aw ken fine that ye did keep a bit o' the cake for the christenin.' Ye'll no need to keep it long or it'll get hard!"

"Jan," cried Jean, reprovingly "ye shud na say sic things!"

"Why no? The minister said something aboot a family when he was marryin' them."

"Aye," said Jean, "but a minister's no like other fowk. If Mester Gordon says 'Hell' or 'damnation' in the pulpit it's religion, but if you say it it's just a swear."

"Aw was at the manse when the minister fell over my barrow," said Jim, "and he said 'Hell!' Was that religion or a swear?"

"Aw wud ca' it a lee," said Jean with a sniff; "only ministers and married fowk shud speak aboot bairns, and ye shud ken better, Jan."

Janet looked at me timidly.

"Did Aw do any wrong?"

"Of course you didn't, you dear silly! Jean is a wee prude. Why shouldn't you talk about bairns if you want to? The subject of bairns is the only important subject in the world, Jan, and if you find anyone who thinks the subject improper you can bet your boots that they've got a dirty mind. Jean is simply trying to follow the conventions of all the stupid grown-ups in the village."

These bairns are all innocent. When I looked at Jim's composition book the other day I read an essay with the title "The Church." Jim did not describe the church: he described an event in the church—his own marriage. He was an officer on short leave from the Front. He described the ceremony, then he went on:—"I spent my honeymoon in Edinburgh and a wire came telling me to go back to the trenches. Three weeks later I was wounded and sent home and found that my wife had had a baby."

I wrote at the end of the essay "The speeding-up methods of America are bad enough when applied to industry, but...."

They are innocent souls, and already Jean is affected by the damnable conspiracy of silence. And the amusing thing is that there is nothing to be silent about.

* * *

The Educational Institute has sent a deputation to London to confer with the Secretary for Scotland on educational reform. The deputies dwelt on larger areas, the raising of the school age, and the raising of the salaries of the profession. Mr. Tennant answered them at length in guarded language. Part of *The Scotsman* report runs thus:—

"Asked by Mr. MacGillivray for his views on the suggestion that the school age should be raised to fifteen, the Secretary for Scotland said that, however desirable that might be in the interests of the child, it was a highly controversial proposal, upon which employers and in many cases parents, and even the State, would have a great deal to say. The expenditure involved would, he was afraid, make such a proposal prohibitive at present."

It is significant to note that he places the employers first, just as in his previous remarks on education he places trade first...."People realised that if we were going to compete in the great markets of the world, in ideas, in the progress of invention, and in the general progress of mankind and civilisation, we must improve our machinery for the training and equipment of the human being."

The Educational Institute of Scotland, like the Trade Unions, is very humble in its demands. Why, in the name of heaven, ask for larger areas ? Mr. Tennant rightly replied that it was news to him that the County Council is a more progressive body than the small School Board. Introduce larger areas and your village pig-dealer and shoemaker give place to your county colonel and manufacturer....the men who are interested in the maintenance of discipline and of wage-slavery. What the Institute should really do is to give up thinking and talking of education for this generation. The leading members come from our large city schools, and if they haven't yet realised that their damned schools are factories for turning out slaves they ought to be jolly well ashamed of themselves.

I visited a large city school a few days ago. It had nine hundred pupils, and it was four stories high. The playground was a small concrete corner ; the discipline was like prison discipline ; the rooms were dingy soul-destroying cages. How dare the teachers of Scotland ask that the school age be raised to fifteen when our city schools are barracks like that ? I would have the age lowered to six if these prisons are to continue.

One of the delegates, Mr. Cowan, showed that he was looking at education in a broad light. "Education," he said, "if it is to be real, is bound up with the questions of housing, public health, medical treatment, and the like;.... hence education should be in the hands of some body that wouid view the matter as a whole....viz., the County Council."

He might have added that education is primarily bound up with profiteering. Our city schools are necessarily adjuncts to our factories and our slums; the dominie is clearly the servant of the capitalist....and the poor devil doesn't know it. It's absolutely useless to talk of larger areas and larger salaries and larger children; the fundamental fact is that capital calls the tune, and larger areas will do as much for education as tinkering with the saddle spring of a motor-bike will do for a seized engine bearing.

Larger salaries will attract better men and women to the profession, says the Institute representative, and I ask wearily: "What difference will that make? You'll merely get honours graduates to do the profiteer's dirty work more effectively. You can't reform the schools from within. The prisons are built, and you will merely tempt your highly specialised teacher into a soul-destroying hell. The slums and the sweating will go on as usual next door; your city children will be starved and ragged and diseased as of yore."

I think it a pity that this deputation ever

went to the Scots Secretary at all. Why should the teaching profession go begging favours from the State? The wise business men who rule us will smile grimly and say:—"The blighters gave themselves away when they asked for larger salaries." They won't appreciate the fact that the deputies were honest men with a real desire for a better education.

I should like to suggest to the Institute that it might have written a nice letter to Mr. Tennant. Why, bless me, I'll have a shot at composing one myself! Here goes!

"Dear Mr. Tennant,

"We aren't asking any favours this time; we are simply writing you a friendly letter telling you what we are going to do.

"Firstly, we are now beginning to make a determined attempt to take over the control of Scots Education....and we'll succeed even if we have to go on strike for our rights. Our Educational Institute will become the Scots Guild of Teachers....a sort of polite Trade Union, you know, just like the Medicine Union and the Law Union—only more so. Is that quite clear?

"Well, our Guild, when it is strong enough, will come up to town one fine morning to see the Cabinet. Our words will be something like these: 'We are the Teachers' Guild of Scotland, old dears, and we've come to tell you that we're going to run the show now.'

"Of course the Cabinet will get a shock at

first. Then they will laugh and say: 'We wish you luck! By the way how do you propose to get the money?' And when we answer that we expect to get it from the State they will roar with mirth. We shall wait politely till the laugh is over, and then we shall calmly tell them our proposal....rather, our demand. We shall demand money from the State to carry on the whole thing. Education isn't a profiteering affair, and we must draw every penny from the people....just as the State does now.

"Then a member (Lloyd George in all probability) will remark: 'Yes, yes, gentlemen, but don't you see that all your demand amounts to is a change of management? You want to abolish the Education Department and substitute your President for my friend Sir John Struthers.'

"We shall shout 'No!' very very viciously at this....you've heard them shout 'No' when they sing 'For he's a jolly good fellow?' Well, then, we'll shout it just like that, and then we'll explain thus:—

"'We aren't going in for a change of management: we are going to build a new house. We are done with grants and Form 9 B's and inspectors and Supplementary Classes for ever. We are going to spend....Oh! snch a lot of money. You'll be surprised when you know what we are going to do. You know Dundee? Mr. Churchill there made it famous....well, Dundee, is one of the dirtiest slums in creation.

At present it has lots of big grey schools. We are going to knock 'em down. After that we are going to build bonny wee schools out in the country; schools that won't hold more than a hundred pupils. There will be lovely gardens and ponds and rabbit-houses; there will be food and —.' At this stage the Cabinet will telephone for the lunacy experts.

"Do we make ourselves clear, Mr. Tennant? As you know well the State will be terribly unwilling to give us more money. If we make our schools decent places the poor profiteers will be in the soup, won't they? Our present schools do no harm; the discipline of the class-room prepares a bright lad for the discipline of the wagery shop, and, of course, a girl accustomed to the atmosphere of a city school won't object to the ventilation obtaining in the factory. When we insist on taking the kiddies to bonny wee schools the profiteer will realise with dismay that his factory and his slum-hovels will have to adapt themselves to the new attitude of the kids.

"Mind you, we quite admit that we're going to have a hell of a fight. We even go the length of saying that we may be beaten at first; for we have no economic power, and the men with the economic power will crush us if they can. Our only weapon will be the strike, but even the strike will, in a manner, be playing into the profiteers' hands; 'Geewhiz!' they'll cry, 'the teachers are on strike....now for cheap child labour!' Our only hope is that the citizens will realise the importance of a dominies' rebellion.

"Now, we don't want you to take this letter as a personal insult, or even as a vote of censure. You may be of opinion that Scots education is quite safe in the hands of the Secretary for Scotland, and you may imagine that we've got profiteering on the brain. We have. But we can't agree with you that education is safe in the hands of the Secretary for Scotland. Why, you might get another post tomorrow, and your colleague Runciman might step into your job. And it was only the other day that he was defending war-profits on the ground that they were forming a fund to compete with neutral trade after the war. The worst of you political fellows is that you've all got profiteering on the brain, just like us....only, it's a natural healthy growth in your case, while in our case it is a malignant tumour. We've got profiteering thrust upon us, so to speak; you fellows were born with it.

"Well, well, isn't this rotten weather, what?

"Best wishes to Mrs. Tennant.

"Yours sincerely,

"The Educational Institute of Scotland."

* * *

Jim came to the bothy last night, and his face was troubled.

"What's the matter?" I asked.

"Aw—Aw didna gie ye a marriage present," he stammered, "Aw didna hae ony money."

"The present Margaret and I want from you

doesn't cost money," I said; 'we want you to write a description of the wedding."

He brightened at once.

"Can Aw tell lees?" he asked eagerly.

"Please yourself," I said, and he went away cheerful.

This morning the description came by post. I think I shall make it the last entry in my diary.

* * *

THE MARRIAGE OF MR. NEILL AND MAGGIE THOMSON.

By JAMES JACKSON, Esq., B.M. (Best Man).

They were married on Friday and I was the best man. Janet and Annie and Jean and Gladys and Ellen were the bridesmaids, but they were too many to kiss. They got a present each, a ring with diamonds in it, but I don't think the diamonds were real ones. I got a knife with four blades and a corkscrew and a file and a thing for taking things out of horses' feet, and I had a fight with Geordie Brown for saying it didn't have a pair of scissors in it and I licked him, but there was no scissors in it.

Their was a lot of people their and some of the women was crying and we got apple-pie and plum-duff for our dinner.

Maggie had a white dress on and Mr. Neill had a black soot on with tails on the coat and a big wide waistcoat but you couldn't see the end of his dickey for I looked. He had cuffs on too. I liked the plum-duff, but I liked the wedding cake best but you only got a little bit of it. The girls kept there bit to sleep on and have nice dreams but I ate mine and had dreams too but they were not nice dreams. I dreamt that an elephant was sitting on my head.

I had a ride on the dickey to fetch the people and there was a white ribbon on the whip and the horses was gray. I had to scatter the pennies and sweeties and Tommy Sword threw a bit of earth at me and I would have fought him but I didn't want to clorty my clean dickey.

The marriage seramany was not very interesting and I had to carry the ring and it was in my waistcoat pooch but I pretended to look first in my breek pooches and had to empty them on the table. I just wanted them to see my new knife.

I made a speech about the bridesmaids and I said they were all very nice girls but they are not for Janet is always fighting with me, she will make an awful wife when she is married.

The happy cupel went away in a moter for there honeymoon but they came back again at night and Geordie Brown says that it was a tinker's marriage because he did not have enough money to go in the train. Martha Findlay said that they came back because he was ashamed to take Maggie to London because she is just a farmer's daughter and I told her she was wrong because they came back because he gets a sixpenny paper sent by the post every Saturday morning and he would have had to buy one to read in the train, but I don't think she believed me, she is a jelus cat and she is just wild because Maggie has got a man.

There was a party at night and I drank seven bottles of lemonade and Frank Thomson sang a song and Peter MacMannish tried to sing a song at the same time and Mrs. Thomson told me to put the bottle at the other end of the table, they were not very good singers, Peter sang five songs after one another so Mrs. Thomson told me to put the bottle beside him again and he stopped singing. He did not sing again but he went round telling everybody that he was not drunk though nobody said he was. I always thought that he was a very stern man but I liked him at the dance.

Mr. Macdonald was there but he did not sing and he did not get a drink out of the bottle but Mrs. Thomson took him into the parlour and then she came back for the bottle. After that he was a nice man not like he is in the school, he was laughing and dancing like anything. He was in the parlour four times.

Then we sang Auld Lang Syne and Peter McMannish said he would sing it by himself just to show us that he was not drunk but he fell asleep before he got started to the first verse.

After it was finished the happy cupel went over to the bothy to there honeymoon and

Martha Findlay said it made the marriage common and that anybody could have a bothy for a honeymoon, so I just said to her "Oh, aye, Martha, ye'll likely spend your own honeymoon in a bothy but you won't get an M.A. with a dickey that you canna see the end of for a man, but Margaret deserved him for she is so bonny." Martha was awful wild at me.

Geordie Brown says that the best man at the marriage has to hold the baby at the christnin but it does not say anything in the etikquette book, and I telt him he was a liar. He said it would maybe be twins and I got a black eye but he lost three teeth. I hop it will not be twins because I said I would give Geordie my knife if it was twins.

P.S.—Please do not have the twins.

THE END.